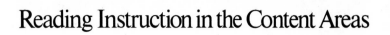

Reading Instruction in the Content Areas

Walter J. Lamberg
University of Texas at Austin

Charles E. Lamb
University of Texas at Austin

Rand McNally College Publishing Company/Chicago

Rand McNally Education Series
B. Othanel Smith, Advisory Editor

Sponsoring Editor: Louise Waller
Project Editor: Mary M. LaMont
Designer: Gene Rosner

80 81 82 10 9 8 7 6 5 4 3 2 1

For Alan and Jennie Lynne

Contents

ASSESSING CONTENT-AREA READING Part 2

Contents

APPENDICES   Part 5

Preface

The idea of reading instruction in high school strikes some students and teachers as both a new and troubling notion. Isn't reading, after all, a basic skill that is taught—and learned—in the elementary grades? If a middle, junior, or secondary school has a reading program, doesn't that mean there are large numbers of students who are "remedial"? And what can English or science or mathematics teachers do about reading, anyway?

Actually, the idea that attention should be paid to secondary-school reading is as old as this century. There has also been a long-standing belief that reading is not a single, basic skill. Reading is a complex intellectual and linguistic process, which should be developed throughout life. While some students have not made desirable progress in reading and need special instruction, all secondary-school students need assistance if they are to become able and sophisticated readers.

This book is addressed to middle- and secondary-school teachers of school subjects, which we call the content areas. By this we mean academic subjects—like English, mathematics, the social and natural sciences, and foreign languages—as well as other subjects such as music and art appreciation, health and physical education, business and vocational education, and home economics.

Readers of this book may be teachers of many years' experience or prospective teachers who are completing requirements for certification.

Content-area teachers need not neglect their special fields of study to provide lessons in reading. As this text will show, an effective teacher of content includes reading as a part of the subject matter of the course. Such a teacher recognizes that proficient reading is the key to success and independence in learning and provides varied opportunities for reading in the content area. Such teachers also give students the opportunity to demonstrate and develop their understanding of content and assist students in meeting and overcoming difficulties encountered in their textbooks. In addition, teachers are aware of and provide for differences in their students' reading abilities, comprehension, and interests.

In Parts 1, 2, and 4 of this book, material applicable to all content areas is discussed. The two introductory chapters of Part 1 present key ideas about proficient reading and reading problems. The next three chapters identify and illustrate skills in vocabulary, comprehension, and methods for developing those skills. The last chapter of Part 1 discusses strategies for planning and conducting instruction that are applicable to any reading skill and any content area.

Part 2 discusses instruments and procedures for measuring or assessing students' reading abilities. One chapter in this section deals with the measurement of materials to determine the level of difficulty and potential problems.

Part 3 contains separate chapters on each of the content areas. Readers may study the general sections and then go directly to the chapters related to their teaching interests before reading related chapters. For example, those interested in natural science are encouraged to study the chapter on mathematics.

Part 4 moves beyond the daily reading lesson and presents strategies for designing instructional units, promoting positive attitudes toward reading, assisting students with special needs, and working with other faculty to develop a schoolwide reading program.

You should take advantage of particular features of this book. Each chapter begins with an overview of the main topics and a list of key ideas to be addressed. Illustrations and figures present examples of passages from actual secondary textbooks and of teaching and testing procedures written for those textbooks, along with sample student responses. Each chapter also has suggested activities, which are open-ended to allow for use with different content areas. A variety of responses from informal discussion to formal papers can be used to complete these activities. Each chapter concludes with a list of recommended readings.

The authors wish to acknowledge the following persons for their help with this text. We appreciate the support and patience of our wives, Susan and Cathy, and are indebted to our students in education courses and to those public-school teachers with whom we have worked. They have helped us to identify key questions and concerns about reading instruction. We also thank Alice D. Lamb for her help in preparing the manuscript. We have profited from the specific suggestions for improving the manuscript made by Phyllis Coston of West Virginia Wesleyan College, Nicholas DiObilda of Glassboro State College, Kenneth Dulin of the University of Wisconsin, J. Howard Johnston of the University of Cincinnati, and Betty J. Moore of Southwest Texas State University. Finally, at Rand McNally and Company, we wish to thank Charles Heinle, Executive Editor, Louise Waller, Sponsoring Editor, and Mary LaMont, Project Editor, for their assistance and guidance.

W.J.L.
C.E.L.

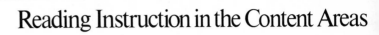

Understanding the Demands
of Secondary Reading

Teachers in the content areas can be more effective when they have an understanding (1) of the many and varied demands of reading faced by their students and (2) of basic instructional strategies for assisting students in meeting those demands. Chapter 1 introduces key ideas about the reading process and the need for reading instruction in secondary schools. Chapter 2 serves as a further introduction to this text by identifying common reading problems and ways secondary schools attempt to meet these problems. Chapters 3, 4, and 5 present a thorough analysis of vocabulary, comprehension, and study skills, respectively. Chapter 6 discusses effective strategies for planning and conducting instruction that will relate reading and content-area learning.

1

The Reading Process and Learning to Read

Human beings have been reading for thousands of years, but attempts to describe the reading process are only fairly recent in history. Theorists and researchers from different fields of studies have speculated about both the reading process and the learning-to-read process. Different conceptions of these processes have resulted in differences in the way reading is taught at the elementary level.

This chapter will provide background to the secondary teacher as an aid to understanding both the reading process and the learning-to-read process.

OVERVIEW

Proficient reading requires the recognition of words and meaningful word patterns.

The three kinds of skills a reader must master are: word recognition, comprehension, and study skills.

Reading courses and content-area courses have different goals.

Reading should be taught in secondary content areas.

Key Ideas

THE READING PROCESS
What is Reading?

If the word *reading* were used in a very broad sense, the following could be considered examples of the act of reading:

- A two-year-old looks intently at a picture book. He stops at each page and tells his mother about the pictures.
- A first-grade student reads a page aloud. While her pronunciation of the words is perfect, she cannot tell what the page was about.
- As another first-grade student reads a page, he "misreads" a few words but gives an accurate, complete summary of the page.
- A group of fourth-grade students are able to answer the teacher's questions about places and directions when looking at a map.
- A sixth-grade student carefully reads the back of a cereal box during breakfast. However, five minutes later, she cannot remember a single word she read.
- A ninth-grader carefully and slowly follows a series of numbers in a math class and solves a problem.
- A tenth-grader speed-reads a column in a magazine in five seconds. If asked, he can give a detailed account of the content.
- During a football game, the defensive team correctly reads the offensive team and stops them from scoring a touchdown.
- The marching band strikes up a tune; they are reading the music printed on small cards.
- A blind student smiles as she runs her finger along a line of braille.

Are these students all actually reading? The answer to the question depends upon how one defines *reading*. If we limit our definition to "responses to written or printed words," some of the examples would not be appropriate because they involve symbols that are not letters. These symbols could be numbers or other kinds of meaningful patterns, such as the arrangement of an offensive football team. If our definition focuses on *meaning*—finding, receiving, or using meaning—the child who was able to say the words correctly but could not tell what they meant would not be reading.

What Is Proficient Reading?

John Carroll has attempted a fairly simple description of what appears to be involved in the proficient reading of text.[1]

He states that the eyes move swiftly and with coordination during the act of reading. However, at different points in the text, the eyes stop moving; these stops are called *fixations*.

During a fixation, the reader receives "an impression of a certain

---

[1]John B. Carroll, "The Nature of the Reading Process," in Harry Singer and Robert B. Ruddell, eds., *Theoretical Models and Processes of Reading,* 2nd ed. (Newark: International Reading Association, 1976), pp. 8–18.

amount of printed material."[2] This impression results from "instantaneous" recognition of words. Carroll notes that there is debate on exactly how words are recognized.

While this recognition of words is occurring, there is also some sort of recognition of meaningful word patterns. The result is *comprehension* or "an impression of a meaningful message."[3] Carroll notes that while there is disagreement on what comprehension is, there is widespread agreement that comprehension is an active process and that we do not simply passively receive the meaning of the text. Carroll's description is in harmony with the idea of reading as information processing.

A SIMULATION OF LEARNING TO READ

It is necessary to consider different ways of reading, particularly those important to the different content areas of English, science, mathematics, and other fields. These will be discussed further throughout this text. Differences must be considered between the proficient reading process and the learning-to-read process; that is, the difference between what is done by an individual who has mastered reading and what is done by another individual who is only learning to read.

One way to present those differences is to provide a task which simulates the experience of the beginning reader. Before going further in this chapter, try to read the text presented in Figure 1.1. The figure shows a series of pictures, each with a caption written in a code which you do not know. As you try to read the captions, you will be forced to learn some of the code. You, of course, have an important advantage over the true beginning reader in that you are already familiar with at least one written code, English.

Follow these steps. First, look at the pictures and try to guess what the caption might say—what is shown in the picture? Next, look at some of the words and try to guess at them. Then look at some of the "letters" in the words you have figured out and see if you can figure out other words. If you get stuck, go to Figure 1.2, which has additional exercises to help you learn some of the "letters." Finally, Figure 1.3 has the entire "alphabet." When you have finished the exercise, resume reading the text.

This exercise is modeled after one developed by Paul McKee.[4] The purpose of such exercises is to remind adults of what it was like to be a beginning reader. How did you feel? A bit frustrated perhaps by the difficulty? What did you do? Rely on the pictures to guess? Focus on particular words and try to memorize them? Try to relate the strange

---

[2]Carroll, "The Nature of the Reading Process," p. 8.
[3]Carroll, "The Nature of the Reading Process," p. 10.
[4]Paul McKee, *Reading: A Program of Instruction for the Elementary School* (Boston: Houghton Mifflin, 1966), pp. 3–21.

Figure 1.1 A Simulation of Learning to Read

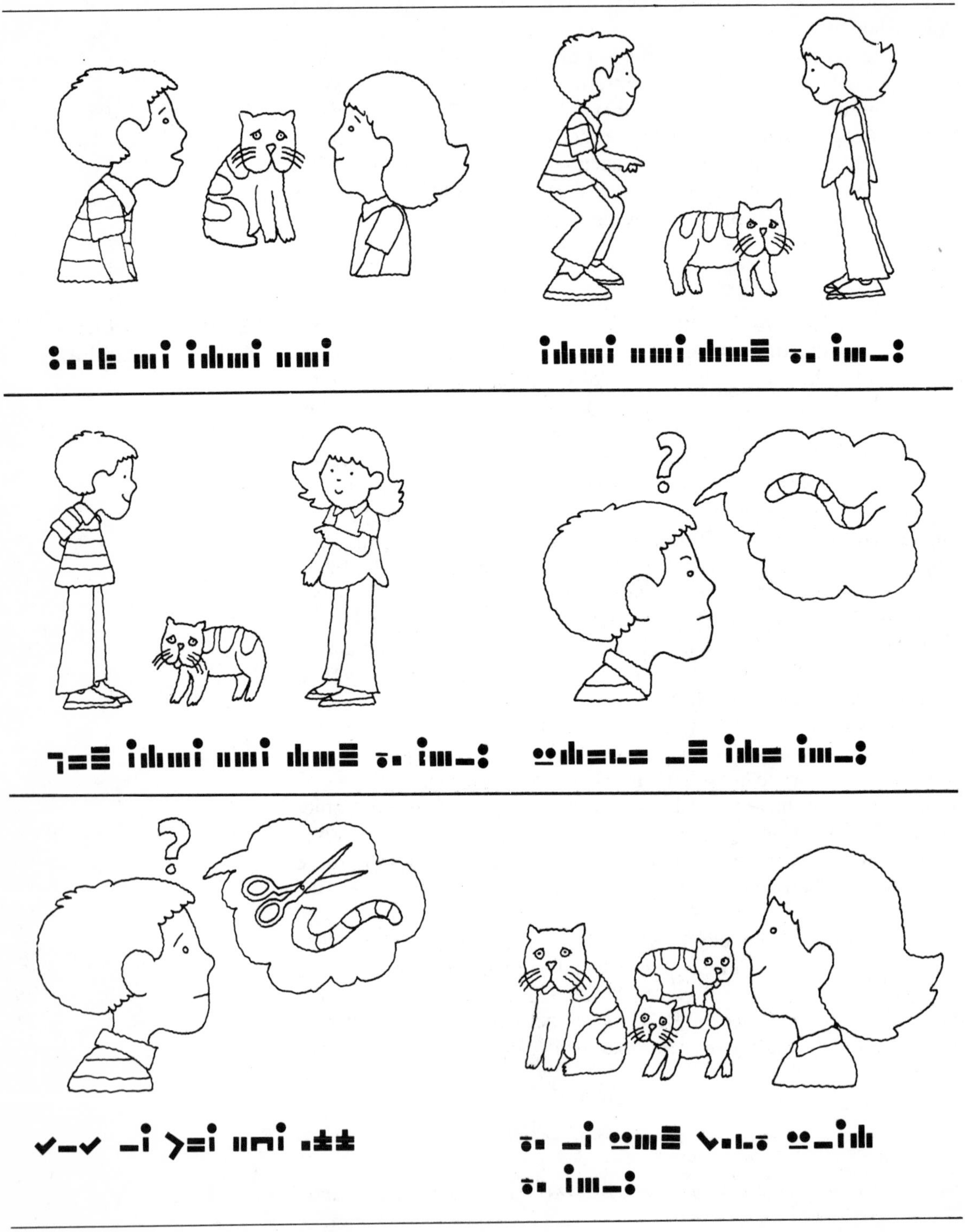

code to English letters? Skip back and forth from one picture to another? Or did you give up and look at the second exercise?

WHAT A READER LEARNS

Carroll has identified what the skilled reader must learn. While he believes there is general agreement on these "items," he feels there is also widespread disagreement as to how precisely the skills and under-standings are employed in reading and the most desirable sequence for learning them. The student must learn 1) to understand and speak the spoken language, 2) to recognize printed words, 3) to associate the printed words with spoken words and their meanings, 4) to analyze unfamiliar words, 5) to discriminate the letters of the alphabet, 6) to process information, generally, in a left-to-right movement, 7) to expect patterns of letters and words, and 8) to think about what he or she is reading.[5]

One basic scheme for organizing the beginning reading program is in widespread use. In this scheme, reading is divided into what Ruth Strang, Constance McCullough, and Arthur Traxler call "the main competencies, or skills, or goals" of reading.[6] The three skill areas are word recognition, comprehension, and fluency or speed.

Word recognition involves responses required for what is sometimes called recognizing, identifying, discriminating, or decoding words. Three aspects of a word are recognized: its form *(hat,* not *that),* its pronunciation *("hat"),* and its meaning. Most words become familiar and are recognized instantly on sight through *sight-word recognition.* Unfamiliar words must be figured out through four types of word-attack or word-analysis skills. (These will be discussed in more detail in chapter 3 on vocabulary.)

Word Recognition

Phonic analysis involves breaking down a word into its letters and letter combinations, matching those parts with their corresponding sounds, and blending the sounds together. For example: *that th-a-t* "th-a-t" "that."

Structural analysis involves breaking down words into their larger, more meaningful parts, such as prefixes, roots, and suffixes. For exam-ple: *construction con-struc-tion* "con-struc-shun" "construction."

Context analysis involves analyzing the context in which the un-familiar word appears—that is, the surrounding words—to identify the meaning and function of the unknown word. In *Jane lost her hizic wrench,* the context suggests the unknown word is an adjective, iden-tifying a type of wrench.

---

[5]Carroll, "The Nature of the Reading Process," p. 10
[6]Ruth Strang, Constance McCullough, and Arthur E. Traxler, *The Improvement of Reading* (New York: McGraw-Hill, 1967), p. 11.

Figure 1.2
Simulated Exercises
for Learning Letters

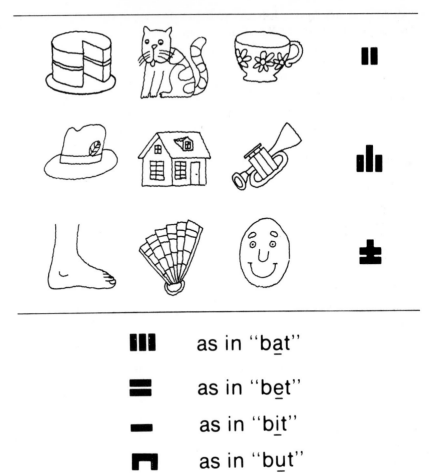

Figure 1.3
A Simulated Alphabet

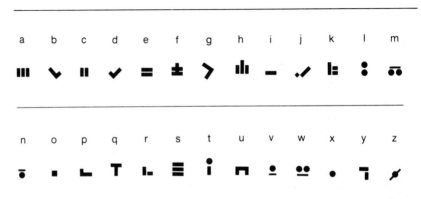

Dictionary analysis is employed, usually, when the other types of analysis are not effective. The reader relies on the pronunciation key and lists of meanings found in the dictionary.

Comprehension involves deriving or gaining meaning from the recognized words. Many educators believe there are different levels of comprehension or understanding. Strang, McCullough, and Traxler propose three levels. With *literal comprehension,* the reader derives explicit meaning or that which is found in the word patterns. With *interpretive reading,* the reader "reads between the lines," deriving implicit meanings, implied ideas, moods, and purposes. The highest level of comprehension is "reading beyond the lines," going beyond the words, often beyond the entire text, to arrive at implications and judgments. (Comprehension will be discussed more thoroughly in Chapter 4.)

Comprehension

Fluency refers to the speed and ease of reading and, in oral reading, to expressiveness and appropriate intonation. For the reader to focus on the meaning, most words must be processed quickly and easily. When unfamiliar words are encountered, the reader must also analyze them fairly quickly and easily. The nonfluent reader, who laboriously and slowly tries to analyze words, often looses the train of thought and quite often is also unsuccessful in figuring out the words; he or she becomes bogged down with the letters and their discrete sounds. (Fluency will be discussed more thoroughly in Chapter 5 on study skills and flexibility.)

Fluency

Educators often make a distinction between skills courses and content-area courses. Skills courses include reading, as in the beginning reading program in elementary schools, and remedial and developmental programs at the secondary level. Other skills courses would be band, orchestra, chorus, driver education, and physical education. Content-area courses include the academic subjects—English, mathematics, social studies, science, and foreign language—and such subjects as art appreciation or health and safety.

READING COURSES VS. CONTENT-AREA COURSES

Differences between skills and content-area courses may not be noticeable when observing particular learning experiences. For example, one might observe a seventh-grade reading course for a week and see students taking a vocabulary and spelling test, reading short stories, and answering comprehension questions on the stories. One might also go next door to a seventh-grade English class and find students doing similar activities. The reading teacher's main concern may have been the development of reading comprehension; he or she selected materials with an interesting content and form as a means to that end. The English teacher's main concern may be to develop an understanding of the short story as a literary form; he or she realizes that such understanding demands successful comprehension of particular selections.

The differences between reading courses and content-area courses lie in different conceptions of the curriculum and different emphases, goals, and responsibilities of the teachers. Harold Herber presents one view of these differences:

> The reading teacher's curriculum is a set of reading skills. Certainly he hopes to develop students' interests in the use of these skills to enlarge their interests, appreciations, and understandings of life around them, but his primary responsibility is to teach the skills. He arranges the skills in a logical sequence, following a pattern prescribed by a manual or one he has established through study and experience. He analyzes the needs of students in his classes, and this analysis determines where he enters the sequence for a given student, as well as the level of sophistication at which he teaches the skill (or skills). . . . The content teacher has a set of ideas as his curriculum. These ideas have order; definite relationships exist among them. He establishes a sequence for the ideas based on logic, study, and experience. Either the basic text for the course or the curriculum guide may determine the sequence.[7]

Simply put, the content-area teacher is primarily concerned with the content area and the knowledge, concepts, principles, language, and modes of inquiry by which scholars seek to understand reality. The effective content-area teacher is aware that knowledge and understanding of the content area require acquisition and development of reading skills.

The reading teacher is primarily concerned with the acquisition and development of basic reading skills and the development of positive attitudes toward reading. The effective reading teacher is aware that skills are developed in a meaningful context. Therefore, the reading teacher considers the content of the materials students read. (Reading and content-area programs will be discussed further in Chapter 2.)

WHY TEACH SECONDARY READING?

Although the idea of reading in secondary schools is new to many prospective and beginning teachers, it has been discussed and encouraged throughout the century. As early as 1902 Allan Abbot called for high-school teachers to help students develop their reading tastes.[8] Arthur Jordan reemphasized this recommendation in 1926.[9] Along with a concern for reading tastes and interests, there has also been a long-standing concern for providing instruction in reading skills beyond the elementary school. Ruth Strang's research in 1938 provided the founda-

---

[7]Harold L. Herber, *Teaching Reading in Content-Areas* (Englewood Cliffs, N.J.: Prentice Hall, 1970), pp. 9–10.
[8]Allan Abbot, "Reading Tastes of High School Pupils: A Statistical Study," *School Review* 10 (October 1902): 586.
[9]Arthur M. Jordan, *Children's Interests in Reading* (Chapel Hill: University of North Carolina, 1926).

tion and impetus for that instruction.[10] By 1957 Margaret Early was reporting that secondary reading programs did exist in many states, but mainly as a part of English courses.[11] Finally, William Martin has reported an increase in secondary reading programs during the 1960s.[12]

In the 1970s concern over what appears to be a nationwide decline in literacy has caused a heightened interest in secondary reading. Educators and others cite declining standardized test scores, including those on college entrance examinations, and the increase in the number of universities establishing remedial reading and writing courses. Educators also cite the standardized reading test results reported by school districts which suggest that large numbers of students are not making desirable progress in reading. Carroll notes that on one commonly used test from 10 to 15 percent of students in grades seven through nine had scores three years below their grade levels.[13] John Goodlad argues that secondary teachers can expect approximately one-third of their students to read below their grade level.[14]

In the school years 1970–71 and 1974–75, the Office of Education of the Department of Health, Education, and Welfare funded the National Assessment of Educational Progress.[15] This assessment project tested ability in reading and other skills and knowledge of school subjects, such as literature and science. Although many aspects of this project have been highly criticized, the reading tests do provide useful information about reading in content areas. The skills tested are those believed important to reading in all school subjects:

1. understanding words and word relationships
2. reading and interpreting graphic materials
3. understanding and following written directions
4. knowing and using reference materials
5. reading for significant facts
6. reading for main ideas and organization
7. drawing inferences
8. reading critically

Comparing the results from the two assessments, Diane Lapp and Robert Tierney note that the reading abilities of 13- and 17-year-old students have shown little change, but that 9-year-old students appear to

[10]Ruth Strang, *Problems in the Improvement of Reading in High School and College* (Ephrata, Penn. Science Press, 1938).
[11]Margaret J. Early, "About Successful Reading Programs," *The English Journal* 46 (1957): 395–405.
[12]William R. Martin, "A New Look at Secondary School Reading Programs in the Upper Midwest," *Journal of Reading* 12 (1969): 467–70, 512–13.
[13]John B. Carroll and Jeanne S. Chall, eds., *Toward a Literate Society: A Report from the National Academy of Education* (New York: McGraw-Hill, 1975), p. 11.
[14]John I. Goodlad, *School, Curriculum, and the Individual* (New York: Xerox Corporation, 1966).
[15]*National Assessment of Educational Progress, Reading in America: A Perspective on Two Assessments*, Report No. 06-R-01 (Washington, D.C.: U.S. Government Printing Office, 1976). Reports on test results for different reading skills were published separately by the Education Commission of the States, Denver, Colo. and are also available from the U.S. Government Printing Office.

be reading better.[16] Richard Venezky questions even the positive results and notes that the increases shown by 9-year-olds are very small even though they are statistically significant.[17] He argues that one cannot determine the educational significance of the results until schools decide what constitutes desirable performance levels. The average scores for students of most age groups fall within a range of 60 to 70 percent of items answered correctly. One state recently set 90 percent as the level indicating mastery.[18]

Results of the national assessments and other assessments conducted by states, school districts, and colleges and universities strongly indicate that many students are not making desirable overall progress in reading and that many more have not achieved mastery in skills believed important to reading and study in content-area courses. As a result, all secondary teachers, not just those designated as reading teachers, are being called upon to provide more and more effective attention to reading-skill development.

SUMMARY   The reading process, in its complexity, has resisted simple brief definitions. Educators in different disciplines have attempted to develop theoretical models of the reading process and the learning-to-read process. Although there are differences in the models, there are some points of agreement which have implications for teachers of content areas. Development in reading involves the whole person: visual response, linguistic competence, cognitive processes, attitudinal, emotional, and social development. The learning-to-read process is an open-ended learning experience. Students do not learn everything involved in reading in the first four years of elementary school but continue developing their reading ability as long as they are exposed to different content areas, new concepts, new materials, and new methods of inquiring into experience.

Suggested Activities
1. Discuss one of the Key Ideas listed in the Overview at the beginning of this chapter.
2. Read a discussion of one or more theoretical models (as noted in the Recommended Readings). Discuss the implications for instruction.
3. Select and read a piece of content-area material. Describe the process you went through in reading and understanding the material.
4. Examine a commercially published beginning-reading program. Discuss its features in terms of sequence of instruction, format of instruction, word recognition skill(s) emphasized, and provision for individualization.
5. Reflect upon your experience in secondary content-area courses. What reading skills were important to success in these courses?

[16]Diane Lapp and Robert J. Tierney, "Reading Scores of American Nine-Year-Olds: NAEP's Tests," *The Reading Teacher* 30:7 (April 1977): 756–60.
[17]Richard L. Venezky, "NAEP-Should We Kill the Messenger Who Brings Bad News?" *The Reading Teacher* 30:7 (April 1977): 750–55.
[18]*Starting Tomorrow*, the newsletter of the Education Service Center, Region XIII, Austin, Texas, 1979.

Aukerman, Robert. *Approaches to Beginning Reading.* New York: Wiley, 1971.

Burns, Paul C., and Roe, Betty D. *Teaching Reading in Today's Elementary Schools.* Chicago: Rand McNally, 1971.

Burton, Dwight L. et al. *Teaching English Today.* Boston: Houghton Mifflin, 1975, chap. 6.

Carroll, John B., and Chall, Jeanne S., eds. *Toward a Literate Society: A Report of the National Academy of Education.* New York: McGraw-Hill, 1975.

Chall, Jeanne B. *Learning to Read: The Great Debate.* New York: McGraw-Hill, 1967.

Farr, Roger J. Tuinman, and Rowls, M. *Reading Achievement in the United States: Then and Now.* Report for Educational Testing Service. Washington, D.C.: U.S. Government Printing Office, 1974.

Goodman, Kenneth S., and Niles, Olive S., eds. *Reading: Process and Program,* Urbana, Il.: National Council of Teachers of English, 1970.

Guszak, Frank J. *Diagnostic Reading Instruction in the Elementary School.* New York: Harper & Row, 1972.

Herber, Harold L. *Teaching Reading in Content-Areas.* Englewood Cliffs, N.J.: Prentice-Hall, 1970.

Huey, Edmund B. *The Psychology and Pedagogy of Reading.* 1908. Reprint. Cambridge, Mass.: M.I.T. Press, 1968.

Lapp, Diane, and Tierney, Robert J. "Reading Scores of American Nine-Year-Olds: NAEP's Tests," *The Reading Teacher,* 30:7 (April 1977): 756–60.

Macklin, Michael D. "Content-Area Reading is a Process for Finding Personal Meaning," *The Journal of Reading* 22:3 (December 1978): 212–15.

National Assessment of Educational Progress, Reading in America: A Perspective on Two Assessments. Report No. 06-R-01. Washington, D.C.: U.S. Government Printing Office, 1976.

Palmer, William S. "Toward a Realistic Rationale for Teaching Reading in Secondary Schools," *The Journal of Reading* 22:3 (December 1978): 236–39.

Samuels, S. Jay, ed. *What Research Has to Say About Reading Instruction.* Newark, Dela.: International Reading Association, 1978.

Singer, Harry, and Ruddell, Robert R., ed. *Theoretical Models and Processes of Reading,* 2nd ed. Newark: International Reading Association, 1976.

Smith, Frank. *Understanding Reading.* New York: Holt, Rinehart, & Winston, 1971.

Smith, Donald E. P., eds. *A Technology of Reading and Writing.* New York: Academic Press, 1976, 1977.

Strang, Ruth; McCullough, Constance; and Traxler, Arthur E. *The Improvement of Reading.* New York: McGraw-Hill, 1967.

Venezky, Richard L. "NAEP—Should We Kill the Messenger Who Brings Bad News?" *The Reading Teacher* 30:7 (April 1977): 750–55.

Williams, Joanna P. "Learning to Read: A Review of Theories and Models," *Reading Research Quarterly* 8:2 (Winter 1973): 121–46.

Recommended Readings

2

Reading Programs and the Secondary Curriculum

This chapter serves as an overview for the rest of the book. It will introduce a number of concepts about secondary reading which will receive more attention in subsequent chapters. While Chapter 1 focused on the reading process and the learning-to-read-process, in general, this chapter will focus on secondary reading—problems students have and programs schools have developed to meet these problems. For organizational purposes, the discussion is divided into four categories: content-area reading, developmental reading, remedial reading, and recreational reading. In actual practice, however, these categories tend to overlap.

OVERVIEW

Key Ideas

Students of all ability levels face difficulties in content-area reading.

Students show a lack of general development of reading skills in different ways.

Remedial reading can treat a variety of problems.

Recreational-reading programs can address problems in interest and motivation.

Secondary schools need comprehensive reading programs.

CONTENT-AREA READING

No one would imagine that Linda and Ted, two 12th-graders, have reading problems. Both tested out above grade level; both have been honor-roll students throughout high school, and yet both have problems related to reading that are serious enough to cause them great anxiety in school. Linda, a straight-A student, has never had any difficulty with reading or her other work. This semester, though, she is taking an advanced world-history course and has a 30-page paper to write. The largest paper she has ever written was five pages long. Halfway through the course, Linda realized she was not accomplishing anything on the project. She decided to complete it the next weekend. On Saturday, she went to the university library, selected armfuls of books, and spent hours taking copious notes. On Sunday, she read over her notes and panicked. She could think of no way to organize them, so she put them aside and tried to write the paper anyway. For the next two weeks she tried to compose the paper in her head. By this time she was falling behind in her other courses.

Ted had never had any problems in his academic work, but he did not like mathematics. Fortunately, in the 10th and 11th grades, his teacher, Mr. Henna, made the course "fun and interesting" in Ted's words. To accomplish this Mr. Henna provided a variety of concrete examples to help students understand key concepts. In the 12th grade, however, Ted had Mr. Stout for calculus. Mr. Stout assumed that students would have no trouble reading the text. Therefore, he neither supplemented it nor directly checked the students' understanding. His method of teaching was to ask students to work the problems on their own and then present the solutions to the class for discussion. Ted, who had been dependent on teachers for motivation and help, could not handle this new independence.

Both Ted and Linda are having difficulty not with reading per se, but with the products of their reading—writing a paper and solving problems. Both lack knowledge of study techniques by which they could break up large assignments into small, manageable tasks. Linda should have identified her topic, done a little reading, written an informal outline, and finally begun taking relevant notes. Ted should have scheduled short periods of time throughout the week to work on his math. He should have tackled one type of problem at a time and read his text selectively for understanding of the key vocabulary and of the concepts involved in working that type of problem.

Reading Problems

These examples are not meant to suggest that only above-average students have problems related to content-area reading. In fact, students who have weaknesses in reading have a double problem: first, with the reading assignments themselves and, second, with the reading "products." The demands students encounter in all content areas can be placed within the following five categories: technical vocabulary, types of writing, special skills, textbook reading, and study skills.

Technical Vocabulary. As students read textbooks, they will encounter words and usages of words which are unfamiliar to them. Roughly speaking, these words can be categorized as either general or technical. Words in the general or common vocabulary are in widespread use and are not restricted to particular content areas or fields of study.

Technical vocabulary, as Martha Dillner and Joanne Olson define it, consists of words and usages of words peculiar to content areas.[1] Three subcategories of technical vocabulary are technical words, special words, and symbols and abbreviations.

Technical words are those which are associated with particular fields of study, such as *noun phrase,* used in linguistics, English grammar study, and, sometimes, foreign-language study. *Special words* are those which have common meanings in general use but also have special meanings in content areas, such as the words *root* and *square* in mathematics. There are also symbols and abbreviations peculiar to content areas, such as 4^2 in mathematics and *DNA* in science.

The categories are not static or fixed and, therefore, cannot always be easily applied to a particular text. Words in the general vocabulary may take on special meanings after new developments in a particular field of study. When these developments affect the secondary curriculum, these new usages will appear in secondary textbooks. One example is the word *transform,* which acquired a special meaning in transformational grammar. Simply put, the word designates types of structures possible in the sentences of a language; it also designates the process by which sentence structures are generated out of more simple structures. For example,

The cat was hit when it ran across the street.

is a transform of

The cat ran across the street. The cat was hit.

Common words may acquire special limited meanings, and technical words may gain in familiarity. The use of technical words may extend beyond a particular field of study or profession. For example, the terminology of the metric system is becoming more common, whereas, at one time in this country, it appeared only in mathematics and science. The space program popularized terminology of engineering and astronomy, and, during the Watergate affair, the public was exposed to, and sometimes instructed in, the language of constitutional law.

---

[1]Martha H. Dillner and Joanne P. Olson, *Personalizing Reading Instruction in Middle, Junior, and Senior High Schools* (New York: Macmillan, 1977), pp. 19–20.

Figure 2.1

A Page from a History Textbook

any other convention we can obtain may be able to make a better constitution. For, when you assemble a number of men to have the advantage of their joint wisdom, you . . . assemble with those men all their prejudices, their passions, their errors of opinion, their local interests, and their selfish views. From such an assembly can a perfect production be expected? It therefore astonishes me, . . . to find this system approaching so near to perfection as it does; and I think it will astonish our enemies, who are waiting with confidence to hear that our councils are confounded, . . . and that our states are on the point of separation, only to meet hereafter for the purpose of cutting one another's throats. Thus I consent, sir, to this Constitution, because I expect no better, and because I am not sure that it is not the best.

Probably no delegate was satisfied with every part of the Constitution, but most shared Franklin's feeling that they had written the best Constitution possible. Of the 42 men present that day, 39 were willing to sign the document. Their work completed, the delegates said goodbye to each other on September 17, 1787, and left Philadelphia for their homes.

The Constitution Is Adopted

Now that a new plan of government had been developed, it was sent to the states for their approval. In each state the voters elected representatives to a special state convention whose task it was to approve or reject the new Constitution. Meanwhile, throughout the country—in homes, in taverns, and in the streets—the Constitution was the chief topic for discussion. Many Americans strongly favored the new government; others were firmly opposed to it.

Some Americans are opposed to the strong government outlined in the Constitution. Those Americans who opposed the

232

Constitution thought that too strong a central government might prove dangerous. They had fought a long war to protect liberties threatened by the mother country's strong central government. Now they learned that the government outlined in the Constitution would be able to tax the people, regulate commerce, make laws, and compel the people to obey them. Those who opposed the Constitution questioned that this new strong government could be trusted to respect their rights.

Jefferson calls for a Bill of Rights. These fears were well expressed by Thomas Jefferson, the author of the Declaration of Independence. Jefferson had not attended the Constitutional Convention because he was then the representative of the United States in France. When he received a copy of the Constitution, he found much in it to approve. But in a letter to James Madison, he also noted important weaknesses:

I like the organization of the government into legislative, judicial and executive [branches]. I like the power given the [Congress] to levy taxes, and . . . I approve of the greater House being chosen by the people directly. . . . I will now tell you what I do not like. First, [there is no] bill of rights, providing clearly . . . for freedom of religion, freedom of the press, protection against standing armies, . . . and trials by jury in all matters [that may be tried] by the laws of the land. . . . Let me add that a bill of rights is what the people are entitled to against every government on earth. . . .

Those favoring the Constitution campaign for its adoption. In answer to Jefferson's objections, friends of the Constitution maintained that the rights of the people would be perfectly safe. They pointed out that no laws could be passed by Congress without the consent of the people's representatives in the House. And they called attention to the many

Source: Raymond J. Wilson and George Spiero, *Liberty and Union* (Boston: Houghton Mifflin, 1972), p. 232. Used with permission

Figure 2.1 presents a passage from a history text which contains some technical language. Many teachers might not consider this language technical because it is so familiar to them, but there are a number of technical and special terms which are important to history and political science including *constitution, state convention, central government, legislative, judicial,* and *executive.* This passage illustrates the need for students to learn precise meanings of words in different contexts. Notice that the word *representatives* has three uses on this one page: (1) as the *representatives* to a constitutional convention, (2) as ambassadors (Jefferson was our *representative* in France), and (3) as elected officials in Congress.

Types of Writing. Students may encounter new words and meanings in unfamiliar types of writing. Students will need to become familiar and comfortable with these different types of writing and may benefit from direct instruction in the characteristics peculiar to certain types of writing.

Students must realize that textbooks do not simply present information to them; rather, they present information in different ways for different purposes. Functions or purposes are implicit in a textbook's organizational patterns; the ability to analyze these organizational patterns is a reading comprehension skill. For example, a history text will usually present events in chronological order; therefore, students must attend to both the specific events and their time sequence. If the author uses a comparison/contrast pattern, students must attend to the similarities and differences between events.

Dillner and Olson recommend instructing students in four common patterns of organization: chronological, cause/effect, enumerative, and comparison/contrast.[2] These four patterns may be found in individual paragraphs or multiparagraph units. Often, passages will have more than one pattern, but one will be dominant. For example, in history textbooks, while the dominant pattern is frequently chronological, there is some comparison/contrast, cause/effect, and enumerative writing (see Figure 2.1).

Educators have also examined the functions and patterns in larger, multiparagraph sections of textbooks. Jane Catterson finds two basic patterns in mathematics textbooks: *explanation* and *problem.*[3] Since the function of an explanation pattern is to present a specific concept, the pattern may consist of several paragraphs and may include sample problems to help students develop the concept. The problem pattern will usually appear after two or more explanation sections and will present new problems to test the students' ability to apply the concepts.

---

[2]Dillner and Olson, *Personalizing Reading Instruction,* pp. 76–78. The same patterns are discussed in Harold L. Herber, *Teaching Reading in Content-Areas* (Englewood Cliffs, N.J.: Prentice-Hall, 1970), pp. 104–06; and Ruth Strang, Constance M. McCullough, and Arthur E. Traxler, *The Improvement of Reading,* 4th ed. (New York: McGraw-Hill, 1967), pp. 253–54.
[3]Jane H. Catterson, "Techniques for Improving Comprehension in Mathematics," in Gerald G. Duffy, ed., *Reading in the Middle School* (Newark: International Reading Association, 1975), pp. 153–65.

The Metric System of Measurement

The International System of units of measurement (also called
the metric system) works like our decimal system of numeration.
The units are related to a basic unit just as the place values are
related in our numeration system. The table shows how metric
units of length are related to the basic unit, called the meter.

kilometer	(symbol, km)	$1000 \times$ basic unit	1000	meters
hectometer	(symbol, hm)	$100 \times$ basic unit	100	meters
dekameter	(symbol, dam)	$10 \times$ basic unit	10	meters
meter	(symbol, m)	$1 \times$ basic unit	1	meter
decimeter	(symbol, dm)	$\frac{1}{10} \times$ basic unit	0.1	meter
centimeter	(symbol, cm)	$\frac{1}{100} \times$ basic unit	0.01	meter
millimeter	(symbol, mm)	$\frac{1}{1000} \times$ basic unit	0.001	meter

Write *tenth, thousand, thousandth,* or *hundredth* to
complete the pair.

1. (kilo-, _?_)   **3.** (centi-, _?_)
2. (milli-, _?_)   **4.** (deci-, _?_)

Complete.

5. 1000 m are _?_ km   **9.** 100 cm are _?_ m   **13.** 1000 mm are _?_ m
6. 100 m are _?_ km   **10.** 10 cm are _?_ m   **14.** 10 mm are _?_ cm
7. 4×100 m are _?_ km **11.** 1 cm is _?_ m   **15.** 10 mm are _?_ m
8. 10 m are _?_ km   **12.** 6×10 cm are _?_ m   **16.** 100 mm are _?_ cm

Source: Ernest R. Duncan et al, *School Mathematics: Concepts and Skills.* Teacher's Edition (Boston:
Houghton Mifflin, 1976), p. 82. Used with permission.

Complete.

34. 5 m 67 cm are _?_ m   **39.** 19.3 cm are _?_ cm _?_ mm
35. 4.63 m are _?_ m _?_ cm   **40.** 404 mm are _?_ cm _?_ mm
36. 9 m 83 cm are _?_ m   **41.** 7.872 km are _?_ km _?_ m
37. 6.82 m are _?_ mm   **42.** 8165 m are _?_ km _?_ m
38. 1035 mm are _?_ m   **43.** 2.075 km are _?_ km _?_ m

Source: Ernest R. Duncan et al, *School Mathematics: Concepts and Skills.* Teacher's Edition (Boston:
Houghton Mifflin, 1976), p. 83. Used with permission.

Figure 2.2 presents part of an explanation section from a mathematics textbook. Figure 2.3 shows the problem section, which has more difficult exercises. In this math text, the authors rely heavily on exercises to develop the students' understanding. An easier text would have more explanation of the concepts and of the procedures for working the problems. A similar type of organization will appear in textbooks for other content areas that demand student application, such as grammar, composition, chemistry, foreign language, industrial arts, and home economics.

Specific Skills. Each content area needs and uses reading skills that are either peculiar to the area or of special importance to the area. For example, math and science courses require the special recognition and comprehension skills demanded by mathematical language. Social studies, as well as mathematics and science, demands the ability to read tables and charts as in Figure 2.2 The study of grammar uses symbolic systems for analyzing sentences.

Some reading skills may not be exclusive to a particular content area but may be especially important to successful reading in that area. For example, figurative language (usually comparative expressions, such as metaphors) is a natural part of language. Individuals often use figurative expressions, such as "It was raining cats and dogs." But literature demands especially close attention to figurative language. Similarly, unfamiliar proper names, which many readers sometimes skip over in recreational reading, have critical importance in the study of history.

Textbook Reading. Although there seems to be greater use of supplementary reading and of multimedia approaches, the textbook, in many situations, remains the primary source of content.[4] Students may need help in recognizing and understanding the different organizational patterns and functions of texts and other materials. They also need to be aware of and to practice using *textbook aids*. These are features intended to make textbooks more readable; that is, more interesting and less difficult. They include 1) features to help students see the overall organization of the book and to locate particular information within the book, such as the table of contents and the index, 2) features to help students see the chapter organization, such as chapter introductions, summaries, and subheads, and 3) features to help students with new terms and concepts, such as italicized words, pronunciation keys, glossaries, definitions within the text, application exercises, and visual aids (pictures, graphs, charts, tables, and maps).

A major problem is that many students are unaware that these features are intended to help them. As Harold Herber notes, many students view these features as filler.[5] They do not look over the sub-

---

[4]Robert C. Aukerman, *Reading in the Secondary School Classroom* (New York: McGraw-Hill, 1972), p. 2.
[5]Herber, *Teaching Reading in Content Areas*, p. 104.

AUTOMOBILE SALES

The Pictograph   **311**

1. You have seen that the way data are to be used may often determine how the data should be organized. After the data are organized, they may then be presented in various ways to tell a story, to make an idea clear or more interesting, or to emphasize a particular feature.

2. Is a table a method of presenting data? *Yes* Another way to present data is shown at the top of the page. It is called a **pictograph.** A small picture, or symbol, is used to represent a certain number of items of data. The pictograph above presents data on the sales of new automobiles in five towns in a recent year. Look at the "key" in the lower right-hand corner of the pictograph. How many automobiles does each symbol represent? How many cars were sold in Essex? *10; 60*

How many cars are represented by the half symbol at the end of the line picturing sales in Sharon? *5*

3. Make a list of the number of cars you think were sold in each town. *List at bottom of page*
Which city's sales represent the mode? *Sharon* the median? *Lyons*

4. The table at the right shows the actual automobile sales in ranked form. Does the pictograph present data as accurately as does the table? In which *No* presentation, the table or the pictograph, is it easier to compare the data?

Town	Number of Cars
Sharon	75
Essex	61
Lyons	59
Wooster	51
Chelsey	41

heads to first gain an idea of the chapter organization. When presented with a new term, they do not refer to the illustration which would help them visualize the concept. In doing research, they fail to use the table of contents or index to locate the source of needed information within a text. (Procedures for testing students' knowledge and ability to use these textbook aids and for teaching their use will be presented in later chapters.)

In fairness to the student, it should be noted that all features are not always, or equally, helpful. Subheads sometimes mislead by not reflecting the actual organization of the text. Sometimes there are so many illustrations they are distracting, and key terms are often introduced without thorough explanations.

The passage in Figure 2.4 presents a special type of graph, the pictograph, along with a helpful explanation of it. Quite often, however, graphs are presented without explanation, and the teacher must help students to interpret them.

Study Skills. Generally speaking, students read for the purpose of acquisition and comprehension of the content. Practically speaking, students read to prepare for other academic performances: participation in discussions, problem solving, test taking, paper writing, and note taking from lectures, films, and other media.[6] It is through these performances that students apply what they have read and gain even greater understanding of the content. It is also through these performances that students are evaluated.

These performances require proficiency in study skills (or learning skills). Many students who have no difficulties reading or understanding content fall down because they lack a conscious technique for preparing for tests or relating notes taken from reading and lectures. Learning study techniques can help students who have difficulties either in understanding content or in reading. Students with and without reading problems may also have difficulty in the practical day-to-day matters of managing their study, such as scheduling their work. Self-management or work-study strategies can be taught as study or learning skills.

The Reading Program

Many educators have said that in a school with an effective content-area reading program, every teacher is a reading teacher. That does not mean that the content-area teacher must or should teach separate lessons in reading. Rather, it is both possible and desirable to design instruction to simultaneously facilitate the learning of content and the acquisition of reading skills. Close cooperation among teachers is an important characteristic of a successful program because it provides students with instruction not only in skills peculiar to content areas but also in study skills and textbook reading.

---

[6]This analysis of study skills is indebted to Ruth Cohen et al., *Quest: Academic Skills Program* (New York: Harcourt Brace Jovanovich, 1973), pp. 1–2.

**DEVELOPMENTAL
READING**

Jerry and Greg, both solid C students, are having difficulty with reading short novels in ninth-grade English. Jerry tested out one year above grade level; Greg, one year below. The comprehension and vocabulary tests did not reveal that Jerry and Greg read well below an average rate for secondary students (below 250 words per minute). As a result, both students have trouble completing assignments on time, and both become bogged down in the small units of reading, such as sentences and paragraphs, and cannot follow the larger meanings developed from one chapter to another. Greg's weakness in vocabulary compounds his difficulties.

Both students are having difficulties with the reading in their content-area courses. An informal test of rate and comprehension on a chapter of one of the novels might help the teacher become aware of the nature of their problems.

Reading Problems

The student who successfully meets the varied demands of content-area reading should show overall improvement in the three skill areas of reading: comprehension, vocabulary, and flexibility. Most educators agree that the learning-to-read process is open ended, rather than a process to be completed at the end of the elementary or even secondary years. Strang, McCullough, and Traxler published an extensive list of skills and distinguished between those a student should master at certain

Table 2.1

	Preschool & Kindergarten	Primary Grades	Intermediate Grades	Junior High School	Senior High School	College	Adults
Work-Study Skills							
Sits still long enough to attend to reading	O	OB	X	M			
Skims skillfully for different purposes • to find a certain fact • to get a general impression • to get main ideas • to find out what questions the passage will answer • to get clues to organization or plot			BX	X	X	X	X
Learns to read maps, graphs, charts, diagrams, formulas			O	BX	X	X	
Learns to read out-of-school material—road maps, menus, signs, and time-tables	O	O	BX	M			
Learns to locate and select pertinent information on a topic and to use it in a report			B	X	X	X	X

Key:
O—Introduced incidentally   B—Special instructional and practice
X—reinforced, practiced, and applied   M—Thoroughly learned
Source: Ruth Strang, Constance M. McCullough, and Arthur E. Traxler, *The Improvement of Reading,*
4th ed. (New York: McGraw-Hill, 1967), p. 139. Used with permission.

levels or grades and those a student should develop throughout and beyond formal schooling.[7] Table 2.1 presents part of their list.

The Reading Program

A developmental reading program would have two goals: 1) to insure that students who are making desirable progress continue developing as readers, and 2) to help students overcome weaknesses and come up to grade level. Attempts to meet these goals vary from one school system to another.

Some school districts provide developmental reading courses that are not related to content in both junior and senior high schools. In one school system, for example, all students take a year-long seventh-grade reading course as well as a seventh-grade English course. In the ninth and tenth grades, students can choose from a variety of 12-week courses which cover such areas as speed-reading, study skills, and vocabulary development. Other schools provide direct attention to reading as part of language-arts courses. Still others rely on content-area courses to provide for development in reading.

REMEDIAL READING

Melinda, Sidney, and Amir are sixth-, seventh- and eighth-graders, respectively, who have been assigned to a remedial-reading program. Three times a week, they are excused from English to work with a reading teacher on a third-grade phonics program simply because the students tested at the third-grade level. Unfortunately, they have very different problems. Because Melinda is weak in word-analysis skills, she benefits somewhat from the program. Sidney had intensive phonics instruction in elementary school but no direct attention to comprehension. Since his weakness is in comprehension, a review of phonics will be of no aid to him. The phonics program is also no help to Amir, who has difficulty with English vocabulary. He is, however, a successful reader in his native language, Persian.

Reading Problems

These examples illustrate the point that students with severe reading difficulties do not share a single problem. They may have only one problem or a combination of problems in the areas of comprehension, word recognition, vocabulary, language generally, fluency, and, in some cases, speech, hearing, or vision.[8] The variety of problems calls for variety of instruction.

Low reading-test scores have demonstrated that many students apparently are not making desirable reading progress. In many schools, students are designated remedial if their scores are two or more years below their grade level. Of those students, many test out at the elemen-

[7]Strang, McCullough, and Traxler, *The Improvement of Reading*, p. 139.
[8]Robert M. Wilson, *Diagnostic and Remedial Reading for Classroom and Clinic*, 2nd ed. (Columbus, Ohio: Charles E. Merrill, 1972), pp. 1-14.

tary levels; that is, their test performance is equivalent to that of average elementary students. Very low test scores, first grade (or below) to third, suggest a lack of mastery of basic skills, or those skills taught in beginning or primary reading.

These elementary-level readers differ greatly from one another. Some are nonreaders in the sense that they cannot successfully do basic tasks, such as: 1) reading complete sentences or multisentence text (connected reading); 2) analyzing unfamiliar words; 3) recognizing common sight words, such as *from, was, that,* and *what;* 4) discriminating between similar letters, *b, d,* or *p;* or 4) discriminating between similar sounds, "fl," "fr," "str," or "st."

Other students can do connected reading at the first-grade level or higher. Some may have an overall weakness in one skill area, such as comprehension or word recognition, and others may have specific strengths but also specific weaknesses in a given skill area. For example, a student may be able to sound out words with single initial consonants (*b* in *but* or *f* in *foot*) but not be able to sound out words with initial consonant blends (*bl* in *blight* or *fl* in *flight*). In some cases, students may not have learned to make a particular response (sounding initial consonant *bl*). In other cases, students may be able to make the response but without sufficient speed and ease for the response to sound automatic.

The Reading Program An effective remedial program should provide instruction in all areas in which students may lack mastery including word recognition, vocabulary, comprehension, fluency, flexibility, and study skills. This instruction should be selectively addressed to the particular skill needs of the particular students.

School systems provide remedial instruction in a variety of ways. Some have special programs which are outside the regular curriculum. Students are released from English or other courses two or more times a week to work under the supervision of a reading teacher or reading specialist. They may be tutored, work in small groups, or do largely independent work. More commonly, remedial instruction is provided as part of the regular curriculum through special sections of either reading or language-arts courses. Bertha Means and her associates have developed the following list of skills, which are used in a special senior-high-school remedial-reading course taught in the Austin, Texas Independent School District:

Comprehension Skills:
Identifying the main idea
Arranging a list of events in a sequence
Perceiving cause and effect relationships
Evaluating and making judgments
Distinguishing between fact and nonfact
Making inferences and drawing logical conclusions
Arriving at a generalization

Following written directions
Using parts of books to locate information
Using graphic sources to get information

Vocabulary Skills:
Structural analysis
Dictionary analysis
Word relationships (synonyms, antonyms)
Context analysis

Other:
Reading rate
Recreational reading
Study skills[9]

RECREATIONAL READING

Linda, the 12th-grader mentioned at the start of the chapter, has heavy demands made on her in her four advanced academic courses. Until her recent difficulty with the history paper, she not only completed all reading assignments but found time to do a variety of reading for leisure. Ted also reads for pleasure, but his interests are strictly limited to articles and books on history. Jerry, the solid-C student, will read only when his parents and teachers stay on his back. Greg, the other C student, says reading does not mean anything to him, but at home he devours sports magazines. Melinda, the remedial student, says she likes to read but does no reading outside of her remedial course. Sidney says he hates to read, but on his way to and from school he pours over paperback fiction.

Reading Problems

The examples above illustrate two points about motivation and reading interests. First, secondary students will differ in interests and motivation as greatly as they differ in skills. Second, some students will be indifferent to—or even hostile to—school reading.

Educators divide learning into three areas or domains: cognitive, skill, and affective. Throughout the century, some educators have expressed concern that the emphasis on the cognitive and skills areas has resulted in a neglect of the affective domain. Several educators in the field of adolescent reading, including Louise Rosenblatt, Dwight Burton, Margaret Early, Daniel Fader and Elton McNeil, share this concern.[10]

Major problems seem to result from a lack of attention to affective

---

[9]Bertha Means et al., *Reading Tutorial: A Teaching Guide* (Austin, Tex.: Austin Independent School District, 1978), pp. 50–51.
[10]Louise M. Rosenblatt, *Literature as Exploration* (New York: Noble & Noble, 1938); Dwight Burton, *Literature Study in High Schools,* 3rd ed. (New York: Holt, Rinehart, & Winston, 1970); Margaret Early, "Stages of Growth in Literary Appreciation," *English Journal* 49 (March 1960): 161–67; and Daniel Fader and Elton B. McNeil, *Hooked on Books: Program and Proof* (New York: Berkley, 1968).

aspects of reading: 1) Many students do not pursue reading as a leisure or recreational activity. 2) Many students who do find some reading pleasureable have very limited interests in their school subjects and related reading. 3) Many students read only when external rewards or punishments exist; for example, students will do assigned reading only when it is covered on tests. 4) Many do not willingly select high quality, adult literary works in spite of the emphasis on these works in English classes. 5) Many lack confidence in their ability to interpret and evaluate reading on their own. 6) Many have hostile attitudes toward reading either because of years of frustration with too-difficult materials and tasks or because school reading does not satisfy their immediate interests and concerns.

The Reading Program   Two approaches have been recommended to solve these problems: *extensive reading* and *self-selected reading.* These approaches have been employed more often in reading and English courses than in other content-area courses.

Extensive reading. In English courses, students typically read relatively few works, but they are expected to read them with great thoroughness. For example, in a course or unit on the novel, students may read only one novel, but will be asked to consider all key aspects: plot, characterization, setting, theme, and style. The alternative to this intensive reading is extensive reading where students read a great quantity and variety of materials. Some works may be treated rather thoroughly, but for most reading, students will be expected to make only a selective, informal response—for example, a short entry in a journal. In some cases, students simply read the work, and do not need to make any oral or written response. An assumption behind this approach is that students need the opportunity for a quantity of reading before quality in selection and response can be expected.

Self-selected reading. Self-selection can encourage students to read extensively. Students choose what they wish to read from a variety of offerings in the classroom, school, or public library. Two assumptions here are that 1) students should have the opportunity to read materials that satisfy their immediate interests, and 2) students are better able to select materials that interest them than their teacher is. Teachers can provide self-selected reading on a regular and frequent basis—for example, a full class period every Friday or the first 10 minutes of each class. As Marvin Oliver notes, self-selected reading has a variety of names, all of which identify important characteristics of this approach: high-intensity practice (HIP), uninterrupted, sustained, silent reading (USSR), read-in, free reading, and recreational reading.[11] A teacher in a junior-high

---

[11] Discussions of programs providing extensive self-selected reading area are found in Fader and McNeil, *Hooked on Books;* and Marvin E. Oliver, *Making Readers of Everyone* (Dubuque, Iowa: Kendall/Hunt, 1976).

reading course in Austin, Texas developed the following form for out-of-class recreational reading:[12]

Name: _____

Week Ending: _____

Reading Practice Record

How many minutes did you read? _____

What did you read? _____

Parent's Signature _____

SUMMARY

Reading problems fall within four major categories: content-area, developmental, remedial, and recreational or interest reading. Some schools have developed one or more of the types of programs discussed in this chapter, and others have moved in the direction of a *comprehensive* reading program, one that addresses all four problem areas.[13] Such programs attempt to meet the needs of all ability levels, either through individualized instruction within courses or through several course offerings. These programs are characterized by their variety in assessment, materials, and learning experiences. Because teachers recognize that a single method will not be suitable for all students, no single method is used. Such programs assume that students' difficulties in reading correlate with their previous instructional experiences, which may not have been appropriate for them.

Suggested Activities

1. Discuss one of the Key Ideas listed in the Overview at the beginning of this chapter.
2. Select and read a book on one of the following types of reading programs: content-area, developmental, remedial, recreational.
3. Write a description of your experiences as a reader in secondary school. What help was and was not provided to you in reading?
4. Systematically observe and report on one secondary reading program. Identify some of the problems students might be having and discuss some of the ways these problems are addressed.
5. Tutor a student in a reading program in a secondary school. Keep a journal or daily log which includes the student's difficulties, areas of reading treated, types of activities, types of materials, and the student's responses to the activities.

---

[12]Laura Woolsey, "Record of Recreational Reading" (Austin, Tex.: Austin Independent School District, 1977). Used with permission.

[13]Duane A. Whitson and Robert L. Fishback, *A Comprehensive Reading Program for the Secondary School* CS 001 388. (Urbana: ERIC Clearinghouse on Reading and Communication Skills, 1974).

Recommended Readings

Aukerman, Robert C. *Reading in the Secondary School Classroom.* New York: McGraw-Hill, 1972.

Burmeister, Lou F. in *Reading Strategies for Secondary School Teachers.* Reading, Mass.: Addison-Wesley, 1974, Chapter 12.

Dillner, Martha H., and Olson, Joanne P. in *Personalizing Reading Instruction in Middle, Junior, and Senior High Schools.* New York: Macmillan, 1977, Chapter 12.

Duffy, Gerald G., ed. *Reading in the Middle School.* Newark, Del.: International Reading Association, 1975.

Effective Reading Programs: Summaries of 222 Selected Programs. Urbana, Ill.: National Council of Teachers of English, 1975.

Fader, Daniel, and McNeil, Elton B. *Hooked on Books: Program and Proof.* New York: Berkley, 1968.

Hafner, Lawrence E. *Developmental Reading in Middle and Secondary Schools: Foundations, Strategies, and Skills for Teaching.* New York: Macmillan, 1977.

Halpern, Honey. "Contemporary, Realistic Young Adult Fiction: An Annotated Bibliography," *Journal of Reading* 21:4 (January 1978): 351–56.

Hansell, T. Stevenson. "Increasing Understanding in Content Reading," *Journal of Reading* 19:4 (January 1976): 307–10.

Harris, Albert J. "Ten Years of Progress in Remedial Reading," *Journal of Reading* 21:1 (October 1977): 29–35.

Konenke, Karl. "ERIC/RCS: Remedial Reading in the High School," *Journal of Reading* 21:7 (April 1978): 646–49.

Marcetti, Alvin J. "Individualized Reading: Current Programs in the Secondary Schools," *Journal of Reading* 22:1 (October 1978): 50–54.

Reis, Ron. "A Curriculum for Real Life Reading Skills," *Journal of Reading* 21:3 (December 1977): 646–49.

Robinson, Frances P. *Effective Study.* rev. ed. New York: Harper & Row, 1961.

Robinson, H. Alan. *Teaching Reading and Study Strategies: The Content-Areas.* Boston: Allyn & Bacon, 1975.

Rosenblatt, Louise M. *Literature as Exploration.* New York: Noble & Noble, 1938.

Smith, Richard J., and Barrett, Thomas C. *Teaching Reading in the Middle Grades.* 2nd ed. Reading, Mass.: Addison-Wesley, 1979.

Spache, George D. *Diagnosing and Correcting Reading Disabilities.* Boston: Allyn & Bacon, 1976.

Strang, Ruth, and Linguist, Donald M. *The Administrator and the Improvement of Reading.* New York: Appleton-Century-Crofts, 1960.

Whitson, Duane A., and Fishback, Robert L. *A Comprehensive Reading Program for the Secondary School* CS 001 388. (Urbana: ERIC Clearinghouse on Reading and Communication Skills, 1974.)

Wilson, Robert W. *Diagnostic and Remedial Reading for Classroom and Clinic.* 3rd ed. Columbus, Ohio: Charles E. Merrill, 1972.

3

Vocabulary

OVERVIEW

Some educators view vocabulary as a crucial factor related to reading ability. Others categorize vocabulary as a skill area of reading, encompassing word-recognition skills. But overall, there is widespread agreement that vocabulary development is closely associated with growth in reading ability.

Traditionally, content-area teachers give some attention to vocabulary. Because many teachers regard vocabulary as an important component of content-area learning, they provide regular, systematic instruction in selected terms and symbols, which designate key concepts in their content area. The procedures they use are just as helpful in developing reading skills as they are in teaching content. Many other teachers, however, provide only sporadic attention to vocabulary; they assume, incorrectly, that all students should be able to learn the new words and concepts without assistance.

This chapter will present a thorough discussion of vocabulary development and will address the following topics: 1) vocabulary difficulties encountered in content areas, 2) necessary vocabulary skills, 3) instructional procedures, and 4) components of an effective program for vocabulary development. The discussion of procedures is indebted to the work of David Shepherd, Harold Herber, and, in particular, Edgar Dale and Joseph O'Rourke.[1]

Appendix A will supplement this chapter by presenting vocabulary games. These games and aids can serve as an important instructional tool for the teacher as he or she attempts to encourage vocabulary development.

---

[1]David L. Shepherd, *Comprehensive High School Reading Methods* (Columbus, Ohio: Charles E. Merrill, 1973); Harold L. Herber, *Teaching Reading in Content-Areas* (Englewood Cliffs, N.J.: Prentice-Hall, 1970); and Edgar Dale and Joseph O'Rourke, *Techniques of Teaching Vocabulary* (Palo Alto, Calif.: Field Educational Publications, 1971).

Key Ideas Vocabulary difficulties include problems with technical words and words with multiple meanings.

Mastery of vocabulary skills is necessary for both reading and content-area study.

Learning technical language is necessary for concept development.

Understanding the relationships between words is necessary to develop a good vocabulary.

Ms. Gordon has been teaching the 10th-grade literature course at Valley High School for over 10 years. Her knowledge of literature, as well as her recognition of student difficulties in the field, gives her a head start on planning for instruction. Often, she will make in advance a list of key terms and concepts for students to learn in her course. Terms identified by Ms. Gordon include those related to literary forms and techniques, such as *short story, dramatic scene, metaphor,* and *symbol.* As a means of teaching these new terms, Ms. Gordon's literature instruction has four characteristics: 1) Examples of the concept are provided in the context of complete literary works or passages from the works, not in isolated words or phrases. 2) Rather than relying on a single text, Ms. Gordon provides a variety of collections of literary works, including student-written ''magazines'' and good literature written specifically for adolescents. 3) As a major part of their study, students write their own literary works, thereby producing their own examples of key terms. 4) Students are expected to use dictionaries in their study.

Ms. Gordon tested students on dictionary use at the beginning of the course and provided systematic instruction to those students who demonstrated the need for it.

VOCABULARY DIFFICULTIES Vocabulary difficulties in content-area reading include problems with technical words and words with multiple meanings. As discussed in Chapter 2, technical words are those terms peculiar to a particular area of study, such as *cosine* in mathematics. An example of a word with multiple meanings would be *point* which is used in mathematics as well as in ordinary language.

Technical Words and Symbols When one reads a textbook in a particular content area, two basic types of words must be dealt with: general and technical. General or common words are those used similarly in all subject areas and include such words as *a, the, on, off, of,* and *and.* Technical words are those words that are peculiar in meaning and usage to a specific content area. They fall into three categories: 1) words which are used only in that content area; 2) words in common usage which have special emphases or meanings in the specific content area; and 3) specialized symbols and abbreviations.[2]

There are specific words in any content area which are peculiar to that particular field of study. This type of word might present any one of three problems to the reader. First, the word might be entirely new. In this case, the student might be unsuccessful at pronunciation or the employment of word-analysis skills. Second, the concept represented by the word may be unfamiliar to the reader. Third, the word may not have a simple concrete referent (for example, the word *polynomial* in mathematics which means, simply, a sum of two or more algebraic expressions). The following list provides some examples for several different content areas:

- English: *noun phase, determiner, transitional paragraph, personification*
- Social Studies: *socioeconomic status, ex post facto, cloture, theocracy*
- Mathematics: *sine, cosine, polynomial, polygon, chord*
- Science: *valence, electron, Avogadros' number, chemical reaction, fusion*
- Foreign Language: *declension, conjugation, cognate, nominative case, strong nouns*
- Fine Arts and Music: *fugue, allegro, mural, mobile, scroll painting*
- Industrial Arts and Home Economics: *ohmmeter, braising, micron, differential, pinking*

Frequently words take on a new meaning or special emphasis in particular content areas. Examples of such words include the following:

- English: *short story, dramatic, symbol, style, development*
- Social Studies: *Iron Curtain, state, colony, assembly, bill*
- Mathematics; *root, point, slope, square, rational numbers, series, sequence*
- Science: *bond, mixture, element, compound, solution*
- Foreign Language: *case, possession, tense, irregular, polite form*
- Fine Arts and Music: *chord, relief, perspective, texture, scale*
- Industrial Arts and Home Economics: *drafting, wrench, dart, braid, circuit*

All content areas have specialized symbols, abbreviations, and acronyms. Some of these are familiar because they are used in everyday expression, and others are very specific to their content area. The

---

[2]Martha H. Dillner and Joanne P. Olson, *Personalizing Reading Instruction in Middle, Junior, and Senior High Schools* (New York: Macmillan, 1977).

following list presents some of the more common types of symbols and abbreviations that are used in many content areas:

1. Maps and symbols for map legends
2. Symbols in graphs, tables, and charts
3. Symbols and abbreviations of quantities, qualities, and operations in mathematics
4. Symbols and abbreviations for grammatic units and relationships
5. Editing symbols and abbreviations
6. Diagrams of structures and devices
7. Abbreviations for periods of time, countries, and organizations

Multiple Usages and Meanings   In listening and reading, students need to understand the precise usage, meaning, and effect of a word in a given context and be able to use the word with precision in both speaking and writing. As an example, *European colonies, insect colonies,* and *space colonies* all have ideas in common but also, obviously, important differences. In a study of colonial American history, students will need to make a distinction between French, Dutch, and British colonists and also between British colonists in the northern and southern colonies.

A study of denotative and connotative meanings is another aspect of vocabulary which confronts students with the need for precision in choice and definition of word.

Denotations are generally the common meanings of words and are often the literal meanings listed in the dictionary. A word's connotation, according to Dale and O'Rourke, "is the circle of ideas and feelings surrounding that word and the emotions that word evokes."[3] For example, these synonyms have the same basic meaning but different connotations: *servicemen, soldiers, EM(enlisted men), GI,* and *grunt.*

Attention to connotative meaning is particularly important (and a potential source of difficulty) in four situations: 1) literary writing; 2) persuasive writing, such as propaganda and advertisements; 3) discussions of controversial issues; and 4) the student's own writing. Even textbooks, which students and teachers might assume to be neutral in tone and attitude, might exhibit positive or negative bias in word choice. Consider the effect of the adjectives used in describing Bach's music in the following passage:

> The continuing vitality of his music is not, of course, due to its historical significance as a summation of the late Baroque, but to the qualities of the music itself: the concentrated and individual themes, the copious musical invention, the balance between harmonic and contrapuntal forces, the strength of rhythm, the clarity of form, the grandeur of proportion. . . .[4]

---

[3]Dale and O'Rourke, *Techniques of Teaching Vocabulary,* p. 53.
[4]Donald J. Grout, *A History of Western Music* (New York: Norton, 1960), p. 400. Used with permission.

As discussed in Chapter 2, vocabulary development is, in part, a quantitative matter. Students need to increase the number of words which are familiar in their *receptive* vocabularies (listening and reading) and in their *expressive* vocabularies (speaking and writing). Vocabulary development is also qualitative. Perhaps the key quality is precision.

Necessary vocabulary skills can also be termed word-recognition skills. The area of word-recognition skills can be divided into 1) sight recognition, and 2) word-analysis or word-attack skills.

NECESSARY VOCABULARY SKILLS

With sight-word recognition, readers recognize those words which are familiar to them. Readers have seen these words a sufficient number of times to recognize them instantly on sight; they are part of the reader's sight-word vocabulary. Success in learning to read is facilitated by having words which occur with great frequency in that vocabulary. Lists of frequently occurring or common words include common nouns, verbs, pronouns, adjectives, and function words, such as prepositions, auxiliary verbs, and connectives. Proficient readers, of course, go far beyond these lists by steadily increasing their sight vocabulary.

Sight Recognition

When a word is unfamiliar, the reader must analyze it. The four types of word-analysis skills are 1) phonic, 2) structural, 3) context, and 4) dictionary analysis. Most educators believe that a proficient reader has mastered all these types of analysis.

Word-Analysis Skills

Phonic Analysis. In phonic analysis, the reader matches the *graphemes* (written symbols) with their corresponding *phonemes* (distinct sounds). To do this, the reader has to visually analyze the word to identify letters and letter combinations, match them with the sounds, and then blend the sounds together. For example, the word *strike* might be broken down into *str-ike,* or less efficiently, into *st-r-i-k-e.* The reader then tries to sound out the elements ("sssta—rrra—i—") until he or she produces a sound (or series of sounds) which can be matched with a familiar spoken word. With strike, the reader might do something like: "Sssta-rrra-i. Oh, strike."

Some educators feel that phonics is the least efficient and effective means of analysis. First, the reader has to concentrate on the visual and oral information rather than on semantic or syntactic information.

Second, there are more sounds in the English language than letters (more than 40 sounds versus 26 letters). As a result, there is no simple one-to-one correspondence between letters and sounds. Rather, some sounds are represented by more than one letter ("ee" = *-e, ea,* and *ae*); one letter can have more than one sound (*e* = long-*e*, short-*e*, and "uh"). Letters have different sounds in different combinations and positions within words (th*e*ir vs. th*e* and *b*at vs. clim*b*).

To master phonics the reader must learn all consonant sounds: those in the initial position (the first letter of the word), those in the final position, and those in combinations. In *consonant blends,* the reader must blend the sound of two or more consonants (*bl* = "ba-la" = "bla"). In *consonant digraphs,* the combination has a sound different from that of the two consonants that compose it (*th* = "th" not "ta-ha"). The following list gives some of the responses involving consonants:

Single   Consonants

Initial	*Final*
b	b
hard c	hard c
soft c	soft c
d	d
f	f ("f")
	f ("v")
hard g	hard g
soft g	soft g
h	
j	
k	k
l	l
m	m
n	n
p	p
q	
r	r
s	s ("s")
	s ("z")
t	t
v	v
w	w
x	x
y	
z	z

Silent Consonants

b in final position
b before t
g before n
k before n
p before n

Combinations

Blends	*Digraphs*
bl	ch
br	nd
cl	ng
cr	ph
dr	sh
fl	th
fr	wh
gl	
gr	
pl	
pr	
sc	
scr	
sl	
sm	
sn	
sp	
sr	
tw	
tr	

With vowels, the reader must learn single vowel sounds, vowel combinations, and the sounds of consonant-vowel combinations or *phonograms* like those in the following list:

Single

Short	*Long*
a in pat	*a* in a
e in pet	*e* in we
i in hit	*i* in hi
o in lot	*o* in oh
u in rut	*u* in usage

With silent-e

a in gate
e in here
i in bite
o in note
u in use

Schwa-Sound *(UH)*

a in a
e in lighten
i in pencil
o in ton
u in under

In Combination:

Digraphs	*Dipthongs*
ai in bait	*oi* in boil
ay in bay	*ou* in louse
au in fraud	*ow* in how
ea in bear	*oy* in boy
ea in beat	
ee in beet	
ei in sleigh	
ie in lie	
oa in boat	
oo in look	
ou in bout	

In Combination with Consonants (Phonograms): *ack, ad, ard, ate, aze, ear, eam, eck, ense, elve, ick, ied, ignt, ing, inger, ock, old, ond, ound, ough, uck, un, uch, ung, ust*

Structural Analysis. In structural analysis, as in phonic analysis, the reader must break down the unfamiliar word into its component parts. The key difference is that with structural analysis the reader tries for larger, more meaningful word structures. These larger, more meaningful structures are prefixes, roots, and suffixes. For example, in the word *reinvestigation,* the student might cue on the prefix *re* meaning "back," the root in *investigate* meaning "to track," or the suffix *tion* meaning "state of being." Combining these, the reader would obtain the idea of back tracking; that is, something would be in the state of being reexamined or looked at again. Notice that a unit may have a different sound than those of its individual letters (for example: tion—"shun"). This may cause difficulties for some students attempting to analyze a new word.

In addition to suffixes, prefixes, and roots, two other kinds of word structures are *inflectional endings* and *compound words.* Examples of inflectional endings are the verb endings *ed, d, ing,* and *s,* as well as endings which indicate plurals and possession. Compound words are new words which are formed by joining two or more words. Table 3.1 illustrates the parts of a word's structure that can be analyzed.

Context Analysis. In context analysis, rather than analyzing the particular word in isolation, the reader analyzes the context (that is, the surrounding words) for clues to the meaning and grammatical function of the unknown word. With sufficient clues, the reader can make a good, educated guess at the unknown word. (The many different kinds of context clues will be discussed later in this chapter.)

As readers grow more proficient, they can use more clues and a larger context (with surrounding words in the sentences, paragraph, or multiparagraph section). Many educators consider context analysis

Prefixes	Suffixes	Inflectional Endings	Compound Words
*a*fire	consider*able*	jump*ed*	sidewalk
*ad*vent	post*age*	less*en*	anyone
*anti*freeze	post*al*	less*er*	everything
before	appear*ance*	church*es*	livingroom
*con*struct	necess*ary*	happi*est*	tabletop
*dis*appear	independ*ence*	jump*ing*	
*en*trance	independ*ent*	happi*ly*	
exit	fruit*ful*	jump *s*	
into	anti*septic*	(singular verb)	
*post*box	politic*al*	jump *s*	
*pro*ceed	rest*less*	(plural noun)	
*non*sense	happi*ness*		
*re*view	constru*ction*		
*syn*onym	pic*ture*		
*tele*vision			
*un*happy			

Table 3.1
Word Structure

more efficient than either phonic or structural analysis because it involves immediate attention to meaning. Context analysis is often employed in conjunction with other word-analysis skills.

Dictionary Analysis. None of the three types of analysis will always work. In some cases, readers will not be able to figure out a word, or they will lack confidence in their "guess." Therefore, if recognition of the unknown word is important to comprehending the materials, the reader must rely on dictionary analysis. The reader, in a sense, must rely upon someone else's analysis when he or she looks up the word in the dictionary and makes use of the pronunciation key and the list of possible meanings. Effective dictionary use requires the reader to test out each of the dictionary meanings against the context in making his or her selection.

LEARNING TECHNICAL LANGUAGE

In their study of content areas, students will meet new terms and symbols. Some, but not all, secondary textbooks are potentially very helpful to students in presenting these new terms. Technical language is defined thoroughly within the text, and there are other aids, such as italicized key words, subheads, illustrations, glossaries, and pronunciation keys. Teachers should insure that students can and do take advantage of these aids. And if such help is not available in the textbook, teachers will need to compensate. Regardless, teachers will always need to help students progress beyond a simple knowledge of the technical language to the development of the more advanced concepts designated by the terms and symbols.

Concept Development

The essence of both vocabulary development and learning in content areas is the development of concepts. *Concepts* result from individuals' attempts to understand their experiences. They observe, compare and contrast, and then categorize particular experiences. They arrive at generalizations which allow them 1) to group specific experiences together, or categorize them, on the basis of common characteristics, and 2) to distinguish these experiences from others. As individuals learn and encounter more and more experiences, the categories are continually revised and expanded. A child's early experience with eating illustrates this process.

Shortly after infants learn to take food and liquid out of a dish and cup, they begin to react strongly when they see those objects. They have apparently learned to associate the feelings of hunger and its satisfaction with the objects. One day an interesting event occurs. Children see their parents with their own dishes and cups, and they react by waving their arms and making the same noises they do when they see their own dish and cup. Apparently, the children have discovered the common characteristics of these different utensils and have grouped them together.

Later, children will begin distinguishing among these objects. They will learn that certain utensils are their own and that other utensils belong to their parents. They will also learn that utensils with particular shapes and sizes have specialized purposes. Still later, they will learn to associate words with the objects: *dish, cup, my dish.* Eventually, they will learn more precise terms (and subcategories): *dish, plate, saucer, juice glass,* and *water glass.*

When a child enters school, the sequence in learning concepts is often reversed. The typical learning experience begins with the introduction of the term by the teacher or the textbook: "Today, we will study the *simple sentence.*" At this point, the terminology may be meaningless. Next comes a definition, commonly a statement of the concept: "A *simple sentence* is a grammatically complete utterance with one subject and one predicate." Notice that the statement has additional terminology which may also be meaningless to the student.

The concept is further defined by example: "*Tom hit the ball* is a simple sentence." Sometimes nonexamples are presented to provide students with a comparison/contrast by which they can discover distinctive features: "*Tom, the ball* is not a simple sentence just as *Tom hit the ball, and Anne caught it* is not a simple sentence."

The concept has been introduced but not yet learned. Students must now have the opportunity to develop and demonstrate their understanding. If students do nothing more than memorize the definition, they may only have learned to associate a group of meaningless words. Possible active responses for concept development include:

1. *Selecting Examples:* Which of the following are complete simple sentences?
   a. He felt very lonely.
   b. Felt very lonely.
   c. Very lonely.
   d. The dog bit her.
   e. Bit her.
   f. The dog bit.

2. *Transforming Nonexamples into Examples:* Rewrite the following as complete simple sentences.
   a. Looked around
   b. He saw
   c. She running away
   d. the house was

3. *Explaining Examples:* Why are the following complete simple sentences?
   a. She was tired.
   b. He fought with his brother.

4. *Identifying Examples in Different Forms:* I will say some utterances. Tell me when I say a complete simple sentence.
   a. "Looking for you"
   b. "He is looking for you"

5. *Identifying Examples in Larger Contexts:* Read this paragraph. Underline each complete simple sentence.

6. *Creating Examples:* Write five complete simple sentences.

7. *Establishing Subcategories:* Here are three patterns of simple sentences.

Tom hit the boy	N	V	N
Tom was sad	N	V	Adj
Tom was at home	N	V	Adv

   Label the following sentences and explain which pattern they fit.
   Cindy enjoyed the movie
   It was humorous

Illustrating Concepts. The learning of new technical terminology is a difficult task. Meaningful learning requires the development of concepts, which are the referents of the technical terms and symbols. The most powerful learning experience relates abstract concepts to concrete experience—the experience of the five senses. Teachers can provide concrete examples (or representations of examples, such as pictures) or they can give students opportunities to find or create their own examples. For example, a highly abstract concept in mathematics, such as zero, can be exemplified in many different ways:

1. 0
2. { }
3. $3 - 3 =$ _____ .
4. The number used to describe a set with no members.
5. 3073
     0 hundreds
6. Tommy had three dollars. He bought a toy that cost $3.00. How many dollars does he have left? ___0___

Defining Terms and Concepts. Some teachers try to rely on short, general definitions of concepts; for example, *A sentence is a complete thought.* However, the definitions themselves may be very abstract and require understanding of related concepts. There are many ways of defining terms, and given the difficulty in developing concepts, the more ways a teacher can employ the better. At the same time, students must learn to use different approaches to finding a definition if they are to become independent learners. Dale and O'Rourke present seven types of definitions.[5]

1. Words can be defined with a formal, general definition. Such a definition identifies the term as a member of a class of similar items, and identifies the features of that item which distinguish it from other items in the same class.
2. Words can be defined by examples. Often a formal definition includes one or more examples. The generalization is related to particulars.
3. Words can be defined by a description of the object, process, or other phenomenon which is the referent of the word.
4. Words can be defined by comparison/contrast; that is, by noting similarities and/or differences between the words.
5. The definition can use one or more *synonyms* (words with the same or similar meanings) or *antonyms* (words with different or opposite meanings).
6. A word can be defined by apposition. Apposition is a grammatical term designating a noun or phrase "placed next to another noun or phrase to identify it."[6] The item may be a synonym, an antonym, or a classification.
7. A word can be defined by its origin. Definition by origin clarifies the meaning of a word by attention to earlier meanings or usages and/or by identification of how the word derived from a word in

---

[5]Dale and O'Rourke, *Techniques of Teaching Vocabulary*, pp. 28–32.
[6]Dale and O'Rourke, *Techniques of Teaching Vocabulary*, p. 31.

another language. It is not uncommon for an abstract word to have as its origin a word denoting a concrete object or experience. For example, the abstract word *interval* is derived from the Latin word for the spaces between ramparts on fortifications.

An additional way of defining words, not noted by Dale and O'Rourke, is in terms of functions or effects. Often, the meaning of an abstract term is not fully understood until functions or effects are noted and observed. For example, the concept of a paragraph is often inadequately defined by description: "A paragraph has more than one sentence. The first sentence in a paragraph is indented." Full understanding of the concept of a paragraph requires examination of the different functions of paragraph types within a whole composition.

A paragraph may introduce or suggest the central idea and/or arouse the reader's interest. A paragraph may develop a point important to the central idea by illustrating that point with one or more examples, presenting reasons for the point, or noting similarities and differences. A paragraph may also serve to provide a transition in a composition. Such a paragraph often summarizes, or quickly notes, previous points and announces to the reader the points to be addressed in the following discussion. Finally, a paragraph may conclude a composition in a number of ways, by restating the central idea, by summarizing the development of the idea, by raising a new but related point or question, or by presenting and developing the most convincing point in the discussion.

The following definitions of the word *atom* illustrate the eight kinds of definition.

1. By formal definition. *An indivisible particle of which material is composed.*
2. By example. Given by showing a scale model.
3. By description. *The smallest part of an element which can exist alone or in combination.*
4. By comparison/contrast. *An atom is similar to a compound in that both can be parts of a larger entity. They are different in that the compound can be broken down easily into constituent parts, whereas the atom cannot.*
5. By Synonym. *Bit; tiny part of*
6. By Apposition. *Atoms, particles of matter, have different numbers of electrons.*
7. By origin. *From the Greek, meaning indivisible.*
8. By Function. *Serves as the building block for study of molecular structures.*

Higher Level Abstractions. Teachers should consider the level of abstraction in the concepts they want students to develop.[7] A teacher

---

[7]The idea of abstraction level in concepts is discussed in Dillner and Olson, *Personalizing Reading Instruction*, pp. 123–28.

can measure the level of abstraction by ease or difficulty of illustrating the concept. Stated another way, the farther away the concept is from concrete experience, the higher the level of abstraction.

To illustrate the difference in levels of abstraction, consider the science teacher presenting lessons on the concept of "natural cycles," which are necessary to sustain life. *Natural cycles* is a very high-level abstraction. It can neither be experienced nor explained directly or simply. Instead, the teacher will need to discuss particular natural cycles. Likewise, *the water cycle* is a high-level abstraction, but it is less abstract than natural cycle. However, it cannot be fully illustrated, unless the teacher has an elaborate model available which has an artificial atmosphere and entities representing bodies of water and areas of land. However, various aspects of the cycle can be readily illustrated. For example, the idea of water falling from the atmosphere *(precipitation)* will be readily understood since students have experienced it. The idea of water running off the land and collecting in bodies of water can be demonstrated easily with a model or with pictures. The idea of bodies of water which eventually empty into the sea can also be illustrated with pictures of lakes and rivers or with maps. Finally, the concept of evaporation, or water returning to the atmosphere, can be demonstrated with a homemade science experiment or shown with pictures. All of these components of the water cycle are actually related concepts which are at a lower level of abstraction than water cycle or natural cycle.

The higher the abstraction level of a particular concept, the greater the number of related concepts there are to be understood. Consider the difference in the demands on understanding and knowledge between:

- In science, the concepts of *water* and *water cycle*.
- In geography, the concepts of *desert region* and *uninhabitable region*.
- In mathematics, the concepts of *one* and *more than one* and the concepts of *positive* and *negative numbers* $((-1) + (-1) + (+2) = 0)$.
- In English, the concepts of *singular* and *plural nouns* and the concepts of *agreement in number* between nouns and pronouns and between nouns (or pronouns) and verbs. (There *are* many *friends* here tonight. Does *everyone* have *his* contribution?)

WORD RELATIONSHIPS   When students learn to define terms in different ways, they derive three benefits. 1) They will develop thorough rather than superficial meanings of new terms; 2) they will learn different ways to approach new terms; and 3) they will learn to study word relationships.

Understanding the different relationships between words is regarded as an important part of vocabulary development. Generally, there are three key relationships: Synonyms are words that are the same or similar in meaning; antonyms are words which are different, sometimes oppositie in meaning; and analogies are words that are conceptually related.

Simple learning activities for synonyms and antonyms require that the student be aware only that words can be related because they are similar or different. The activities do not require the student to make fine distinctions between meanings of similar or different words.

Many simple exercises require a matching response. The same types of exercises can be developed for both synonyms and antonyms; the difference will be in the directions for the exercise: "Match the words that are the same (synonyms) . . . ," or, "Match the words that are different. . . ."

Several examples of matching exercises follow. First, students can match pairs of words:

Match the words (that are similar or different):
1. when   a. *por que*
2. where   b. *cuando*
3. why   c. *donde*

Second, students can match two or more words that are similar or different. This type of activity requires a student to see the possibility of multiple meanings of words:

Underline the words (that are similar to or different from) the first word:
1. nation   village   state   race   continent
2. citizen   native   foreigner   subject   alien

Third, the student can match a word with a synonymous phrase or identify a phrase which does not give a good definition.

Match the word with the phrase which defines it:
1. metaphor   a. nonhuman thing given human
2. simile   characteristics
3. personification   b. implied comparison
                     c. explicit comparison

More difficult and interesting exercises require that the student find (and write down) the words. Students might use either the dictionary or textbooks to find the words:

Find one synonym (or antonym) for each word:
1. romanticism
2. classicism
3. realism

Find two or more synonyms (antonyms) for each word or symbol:
1. x-coordinate
2. y-coordinate
3. R^2

For each word, write a synonymous phrase:
1. chemical compound
2. mixture
3. chemical reaction

Higher Level Learning Activities   Vocabulary development is both a quantitative and qualitative process. Students need to increase the number of words they can relate to as synonyms or antonyms. They must also learn to make qualitative judgments about word relationships. To use Dale and O'Rourke's terms, students must see "fine distinctions" and make "discriminating choices."[8]

In the following tasks, students must make discriminating choices:

Match the word which is closest in meaning:
1. allegro   fast   briskly   racing
2. allegretto   quickly   fast   briskly
3. moderato   fast   flowing   quickly

Match the word that is opposite, not just different, in meaning:
1. positive   zero   nonnegative   negative nonzero
2. negative   zero   nonpositive   nonzero positive
3. addition   multiplication subtraction   division
               extrapolation

Select the most precise word for completing the sentence:
1. If the particle were almost microscopic; it would be small/little/ minute.
2. If the effect of its radioactivity were ephemeral; it would last a brief time/momentarily/a short time.
3. If it disintegrated instantly, it would disappear soon/in a while/ immediately.

Some tasks require students to be aware of word connotations. For example, students must sometimes distinquish among words which have similar denotative meanings but different connotative meanings:

Which of the synonyms in each set has the most positive connotation?
1. thin   skinny   slender
2. peace officer   policeman   cop
3. statesman   politician   official

In the following example, students must find synonyms that differ in connotation:

---

[8]Dale and O'Rourke, *Techniques of Teaching Vocabulary*, p. 53.

List three synonyms for each word and label them as positive or negative in connotation.

1. self-assured
2. moral
3. intelligent

The following exercises go beyond consideration of synonymous words to the discovery of the relationships of the concepts represented by the words. As discussed earlier, the development of a concept involves the discovery and understanding of ways to categorize experiences. The following exercises require students to see words (and other symbols) as designating categories, subcategories, and particulars of experience.

1. Place the following terms under the relevant branch of government:

   legislative   executive   judicial
   congress   attorney general   legislate
   senate   speaker of house   enforce
   cabinet   president   appeal
   justice

2. Arrange the following terms in a chart to show their relationships:

   sentence   noun phrase   verb phrase
   determiner   adjective   adverb
   noun   verb

3. For each of the following problems, circle the numbers that are hundreds and box in the numbers that are tens.

4 4 4	55	725	125
+ 3 6 6	+33	+ 36	+ 5

4. Select the appropriate word to complete the following analogy:
   1. Short story is to novel
      as ballad is to _____ .
   2. Theme is to short story as
      thesis is to _____ .
   3. Plot is to subplot as
      main character is to _____ .

As discussed earlier in this chapter, context analysis is one type of word-recognition skill or one strategy for attempting to figure out unfamiliar words. When students meet new technical terms and symbols in their texts, they can employ context analysis by analyzing the surrounding words and attempting to narrow down the possibilities for what the new term or symbol may be. Context analysis can be taught through a study of context clues and through the use of cloze exercises.

Developing Skill in Context Analysis

Context Clues. When employing context analysis, readers recognize different clues in the text which signal or at least suggest the meaning of

unfamiliar words. Educators have attempted to list different types of
context clues. The most recent and extensive listing is found in the work
of Douglas Tomas, who was primarily concerned with research.[9]
Shorter lists have been offered to teachers to help them structure a study
of context clues.

Earlier this chapter presented eight ways of defining words. That
same list identifies the ways words are defined in text, or, more accurately, types of textual context clues which readers can use to define
new words.

Ruth Strang, Constance McCullough, and Arthur Traxler offer a
somewhat different list of six clues: (1) direct explanation; (2) experience of the reader (including familiar expressions or language experience); (3) comparison/contrast; (4) synonym or restatement; (5) summary; and (6) reflection of mood.[10] Their list has been employed in the
Austin Independent School District's curriculum guide for secondary
reading. The following list and examples are taken from that curriculum
guide.[11]

1. *Direct explanation or definition:* A *phoneme* is one of a group of
   distinct sounds that make up the words of a language.
2. *Description:* A *tangerine* is a round, orange, easily peeled citrus
   fruit.
3. *Comparison and contrast:* Ed was *loquacious,* but Bill talked
   very little.
4. *Synonyms and antonyms:* Jack Spratt was quite thin while his
   wife was *obese.*
5. *Familiar expression or language experience:* The drowning man
   was carried to the beach where he was given artificial *respiration.*
6. *Appositive or restatement:* Snake venom, or poison, has two
   main effects on an animal that receives it.
7. *Summary:* The carping critic didn't like the play and said so. He
   found fault with the actors' performances. He was severely
   critical.
8. *Reflection of mood:* The night was dark and still with no moon
   and no breeze. In the distance a howling sound began. Goose
   bumps formed on my neck. When I heard a footstep outside the
   bedroom window, I became utterly *stupefied.*

[9]Douglas A. Tomas, "A Comparative Study of the Contextual Clues Found in Prose and Prose Forms of Literary Discourse." (Ph.D diss., The University of Texas at Austin, 1977), pp. 67–91.
[10]Ruth Strang, Constance M. McCullough, and Arthur E. Traxler, *The Improvement of Reading,* 4th ed. (New York: McGraw-Hill, 1967), pp. 230–31.
[11]*The First R Expands: A Resource Manual for Secondary Reading* (Austin, Tex.: Austin Independent School District, 1977), pp. 57–58. Used with permission.

Systematic and Incidental Learning. Context clues can be taught both systematically and incidentally. With systematic instruction, teachers will need to find or create exercises which provide repeated practice in particular clues. The following exercise focuses on recognition and use of synonyms as context clues. The exercise has two additional benefits: it is another exercise in word associations; and it is a means of introducing students to key terms in a mathematics unit.

Choose the correct term (synonym):
1. The x-coordinate (abcissa, ordinate) was 4.
2. The y-coordinate (abcissa, ordinate) was 3.
3. Two lines which intersect at 90° (right, straight, left) angles are said to be perpendicular.
4. The set of negative (nonpositive, nonnegative, positive, nonzero) numbers is used commonly in mathematical literature.
5. The base-two (binary, 2nd base, decimal) numeration system has important applications in the computer industry.

With incidental learning, the teacher uses context clues in the textbook as aids in teaching new terms. When the teacher conducts a discussion and oral reading of selected portions of the text, students can make four different group responses. Students can attempt 1) to identify a new key term, 2) to guess at its meaning based on the context, 3) to identify words in the text which helped them make their guess, and 4) to generalize about the type of clue.

The *cloze task,* simply put, presents a student with a sentence or passage *The Cloze Task* from which a word was deleted and asks the student to supply the missing word. In some tasks, the student must supply the exact word deleted, and in others, a good synonym is allowed; that is, a word with a close meaning and the same grammatical function and form. A number of good synonyms could be supplied for *Maria was _____ down the block.* For example, *running, walking, racing,* and *jogging* are all appropriate. Inappropriate responses would be *run, ran, thinking,* or *drawing.* The cloze task forces students to use, or learn to use, context analysis, since phonics, structural analysis, or dictionary analysis are not possible.

The word *cloze* is originally from the German language and has a similar meaning to the English verb *close.* As Strang, McCullough, and Traxler note, the cloze procedure or task "is based on the gestalt idea of closure—the impulse to complete a structural whole by supplying a missing element."[12] The Gestalt school of psychology developed the

---

[12]Strang, McCullough, and Traxler, *The Improvement of Reading,* p. 249.

idea of closure, which originated in Germany. Members of the Gestalt school were interested in how humans and other animals could learn in sophisticated ways without direct instruction and, apparently, without trial and error. They theorized that, when confronted with a new experience, the learner could not initially see the meaningful structure (or whole) in that experience, but that through insight the learner could discover how to relate the parts of the experience.

Sentences or passages with deleted words are incomplete patterns. With their knowledge of the language (that is, of the meaningful syntactic and semantic patterns in language), readers cannot resist attempting to complete the pattern by supplying the missing word.

The cloze procedure was originally developed in 1953 by Wilson Taylor as a tool for assessing *readability* or the relative ease or difficulty of text.[13] Since that time, a great deal of research has been conducted, by John Bormuth in particular, on the use of cloze in assessing both readability and comprehension.[14] (The value of cloze in assessment will be discussed in Part 2 of this text.)

The cloze procedure has also been used as an instructional task for both vocabulary and comprehension development. Richard Robinson compiled an extensive annotated bibliography of research.[15] (Chapter 4 on comprehension will discuss the use of cloze as a procedure for developing comprehension.)

Cloze for Context Analysis. Students can practice context analysis by responding to materials with deleted words. The teacher can help develop understanding of context analysis by asking students to explain why they chose a particular word and to compare their choices and decide which words are appropriate and which, if any, are better or best for a particular context.

Teachers can provide systematic development in context clues in four ways. They can start students with a relatively easy task, such as a sentence or short passage with only one deletion. Students can then practice tasks with increasingly more words deleted and with increasingly less context to take advantage of. The conventional procedure is to delete every fifth word; therefore, a 250-word passage would have 50 deletions. In the following example, each deletion has a blank 10 spaces long so that students cannot use the length of the word as a clue.

---

[13]Wilson S. Taylor, "Cloze Procedure: A New Test for Measuring Readability," *Journalism Quarterly* 30 (Fall 1953): 415–33; and "Recent Developments in the Use of the Cloze Procedure", *Journalism Quarterly* 33 (Winter 1956): 42–48, 99.

[14]John R. Bormuth, "Literacy in the Classroom" in William D. Page (ed.) *Help for the Reading Teacher: New Directions in Research* (Urbana: ERIC Clearinghouse in Reading and Communication Skills, 1975) pp. 60–90.

[15]Richard D. Robinson, *An Introduction to the Cloze Procedure: An Annotated Bibliography* (Newark, Dela.: International Reading Association, 1972).

Bach, as an organist _____ a devout Lutheran, was _____ concerned with the chorale. _____ the approximately 170 chorale _____ which he made for _____ , all types known to _____ Baroque are represented; moreover, _____ with other forms of _____ , Bach brought the organ_____ to a summit of _____ perfection.[16]

Some teachers provide systematic practice by designing exercises in which particular parts of the sentence are deleted; for example, first main verbs are deleted, then subjects, and finally adjectives modifying the subject. This approach is also used in English courses for grammar study. For example, in a lesson on verb forms, students have to supply both the missing verb and its correct form. They may be given a choice, as in *The car went* _____ *out of control* (race/racing).

A third approach is to design exercises which provide repetition in the use of particular context clues. For example, sentences can include an explicit or formal definition and omit the word defined.

A fourth approach is to provide two or more choices and ask the student to pick the most precise rather than just any synonym or antonym (see the exercise on page 46). Such exercises also help students study multiple meanings of words and subtle differences in related words.

Robert Emans as well as Richard Smith and Thomas Barrett recommend a cloze task that reduces the number of possible choices for the missing word.[17] With one procedure the teacher includes one or more letters from the missing word in the blank: "The central government is also called the f d____government." The more letters supplied, the easier the task should be. A second procedure is to use dashes to indicate the number of letters, rather than one unbroken line of standard length: "A decrease in buying power results from _ _ _ _ _ _ _ _ _."

One activity which provides systematic instruction is the compilation of a *personal dictionary*. Such an activity is described in the Austin Independent School District's curriculum guide and is used as a weekly activity in some senior- and junior-high reading courses.[18]

In a separate notebook, students build their own dictionary for words they are learning. Each week, students learn from five to ten new

THE PERSONAL DICTIONARY

[16]Donald J. Grout, *A History of Western Music* (New York: Norton, 1960), p. 386. Used with permission.
[17]Robert Emans, "Use of Context Clues," in *Teaching Word Recognition Skills* (Newark, Dela.: International Reading Association, 1971), pp. 181–87; and Richard J. Smith and Thomas C. Barrett, *Teaching Reading in the Middle Grades,* 2nd ed. (Reading, Mass.: Addison-Wesley, 1979), p. 39.
[18]Bertha Means et al. *Reading Tutorial: A Teaching Guide* (Austin: Austin Independent School District, 1978), pp. 24–25.

words. These words can be selected because they are key terms in the content-area textbook or simply because they are words students have seen or heard in other situations and would like to learn. For each word, students compose an entry in their dictionary which includes five responses: 1) the word correctly spelled, with syllables indicated (and perhaps a clue for pronunciation); 2) a guess at the meaning of the word, based on the context in which it was encountered; 3) a dictionary definition which fits, or is close to, the meaning of the word in that original context; 4) an additional synonym; and 5) an original sentence using that word.

With such an activity, students have the opportunity to focus their efforts on groups of words which they need to learn. In making the responses, they are receiving practice in the four forms of word analysis (phonic, structural, context, and dictionary). A point system can be used with the activity to measure progress and evaluate work. For example, each response can be assigned 2 points; a completed entry is worth 10 points; and a completed weekly activity (ten words and entries) is worth 100 points.

Systematic Study Students can use the personal dictionary as a basic activity for systematic study of vocabulary. Each Monday, students can pair up, exchange dictionaries, and test each other on 10 words. The student giving the test is exposed to new words as he or she pronounces the test words. The student taking the test would have to supply 1) the meaning, 2) a synonym, and 3) a sentence using the word. If students respond correctly to all the words, they have completed their word study for the week. If all the words are not correct, students should study the words further, perhaps as homework and then retake the test one or more times during the week during class periods set aside for independent work.

Varying Activities Teachers can vary this student activity to provide a more thorough study of some of the aspects of vocabulary discussed in this chapter. Each variation could receive one or more weeks of attention.

For work on synonyms and antonyms, students could provide additional synonyms or additional antonyms in their dictionary entries in place of the sentence using the word. For work on formal definitions, students could write a complete definition in place of a synonym or phrase. In place of the sentence using the word, students could write sentences describing the term, comparing and contrasting it with other terms, and identifying its functions or effects.

For each word in a week's dictionary, students can find words that are more general and words that are more specific and list them in a sequence of increasing specificity or in categories. For example, the categories could be animals, then two- and four-legged animals, and then species for each subcategory. For a different activity, students could find words with similar denotative but different connotative meanings and label them as positive and negative in connotation.

For work on structural analysis, students can find different words with the same root, prefix, or suffix of the words in their dictionaries, or they can find and list different forms of the same words (the same root but different affixes). For context analysis, students can write cloze exercises for their classmates to respond to by first writing the sentences and then deleting words.

SUMMARY

The development of vocabulary is just as important to learning in the content area as it is to the growth of reading ability. Basic vocabulary skills include: sight-recognition skills and word-analysis skills, including phonic, structural, context, and dictionary analysis.

Major aspects of vocabulary study include concept development, methods of definition, word relationships, and understanding words in context. In the content area, a student's vocabulary development is not something to be assumed. It is a complex phenomenon to be dealt with through a broad variety of instructional techniques.

Suggested Activities

1. Select one of the Key Ideas listed in the Overview at the beginning of this chapter. Discuss the point as it relates to your content area.
2. Select a chapter or other selection from a content-area text and identify the key terms and concepts. Evaluate the material according to the amount and variety of help provided the reader in understanding the terms; that is, context clues, illustrations, glossaries, and other aids.
3. Select one key term and present a thorough discussion of its meaning, employing the different kinds of definitions discussed in this chapter.
4. Plan a learning experience for a key concept. Your plans might include a variety of illustrations to introduce the concept (perhaps a display on a bulletin board) and/or a set of student activities.
5. Outline a plan for testing and teaching dictionary analysis skills.

Recommended Readings

Burmeister, Lou E. *Words—From Print to Meaning*. Reading, Mass.: Addison-Wesley, 1975.

———. *Reading Strategies for Middle and Secondary School Teachers,* 2nd ed. Reading, Mass.: Addison-Wesley, 1978, chap. 5.

Canney, George, and Schreiner, Robert. "A Study of the Effectiveness of Selected Syllabication Rules and Phonogram Patterns for Word Attack." *Reading Research Quarterly* 12 (1976–77): 102–24.

Cunningham, Patricia M. "Decoding Pollysyllabic Words: An Alternative Strategy." *Journal of Reading* 21:7 (April 1978): 608–14.

Dale, Edgar, and O'Rourke, Joseph. *Techniques of Teaching Vocabulary*. Palo Alto, Calif.: Field Educational Publications, 1971.

Dillner, Martha H. and Olson, Joanne P. *Personalizing Reading Instruction in Middle, Junior, and Senior High Schools*. New York: Macmillan, 1977, chaps. 2 and 10.

Hafner, Lawrence E. *Developmental Reading in Middle and Secondary Schools—Foundations, Strategies, and Skills for Teaching*. New York: Macmillan, 1977, chap. 5.

Herber, Harold L. *Teaching Reading in Content Areas*. Englewood Cliffs, N.J.: Prentice-Hall, 1970, chap. 8.

Hittleman, David R. *Developmental Reading: A Psycholinguistic Perspective*. Chicago: Rand McNally, 1978, chap. 9.

Lee, Joyce W. "Increasing Comprehension Through Use of Context Clue Categories." *Journal of Reading* 22: 3(December 1978): 259–62.

Miller, Wilma H. *Teaching Reading in the Secondary School*. Springfield, Ill.: Charles C Thomas, 1974, chap. 4.

Pachtman, Andrew B., and Riley, James D. Teaching the Vocabulary of Mathematics Through Interaction, Exposure, and Structure." *Journal of Reading* 22:3 (December 1978): 240–44.

Pyrczak, Fred. "Knowledge of Abbreviations Used in Classified Advertisements in Employment Opportunities." *Journal of Reading* 21:6 (March 1978): 493–97.

Robinson, H. Alan. *Teaching Reading and Study Strategies—The Content Areas*. Boston: Allyn & Bacon, 1975, chap. 4.

Roe, Betty D.; Stoodt, Barbara D.; and Burns, Paul C. *Reading Instruction in the Secondary School*. Chicago: Rand McNally, 1978, chap. 5.

Shepherd, David L. *Comprehensive High School Reading Methods*. Columbus, Ohio: Charles E. Merrill, 1973. chap. 3.

Strang, Ruth, McCullough, Constance M., and Traxler, Arthur E. *The Improvement of Reading,* 4th ed. New York: McGraw-Hill, 1967, chap. 6.

Taylor, Wilson J. "Recent Developments in the Use of the Cloze Procedure." *Journalism Quarterly* 33 (Winter 1956): 42–48, 99.

Thomas, Ellen L., and Robinson, H. Alan. *Improving Reading in Every Class*. Boston: Allyn & Bacon, 1977, chap. 2.

Trela, Thaddeus. *Fourteen Remedial Reading Methods*. Belmont, Calif.: Fearon Pubs., 1968.

4

Comprehension

A thorough discussion of reading must include a description of the three levels of comprehension—literal, interpretive, and critical/creative. A close relationship exists between the development of reading comprehension skills and the learning of content. This chapter will present comprehension tasks for reading in English, history, science and mathematics to illustrate that close relationship.

Comprehension is the goal of reading.

The three levels of comprehension are literal, interpretive, and critical/creative.

Literal comprehension is understanding explicit meaning.

Interpretive comprehension is understanding implicit meaning.

The four kinds of critical/creative comprehension are: application, analysis, synthesis, and evaluation.

Ms. Morales, who teaches algebra, asks students to explain the procedures they follow in solving problems.

Mr. Salvatore, an industrial-arts teacher, asks students to write out plans for working on a mechanical project after reading the technical manual.

Mr. Woolsey, who teaches English, asks students to role play characters in a short story.

Ms. Washington, a history teacher, gives students a chart listing the main ideas in the chapter. As they read, students can write in key details which support these ideas.

COMPREHENSION: READING TO UNDERSTAND

Comprehension is the main goal, purpose, or aim of reading. Word-recognition skills are a means to an end, the end being understanding or comprehension. The reader uses his or her word-recognition skills to decode the printed symbols or to translate them into meaningful patterns. Comprehension occurs when the reader gains an understanding of these patterns. The implication for content-area teachers is that comprehension should be stressed above all other skill areas of reading.

Comprehension occurs at different levels of understanding. These levels differ in the degree of difficulty, of sophistication in thinking, and of thoroughness in reading. The lowest level is commonly designated *literal comprehension.* The next level is *interpretive reading* or *inferential reading.* The highest level is sometimes called *critical* or *creative reading* and includes reading for application, analysis, synthesis, and evaluation.

Content-area teachers should consider what level of comprehension they expect of their students when they select or write questions for them to answer—whether in assignments, discussions, or on tests. Teachers must also consider the level of difficulty of the content, style, and structure of the text. For example, readers of this book would have no difficulty operating at the highest level of comprehension with a simple, straightforward story of an everyday experience, such as going to a supermarket. On the other hand, many successful readers would have difficulty at even the literal level with a heavily symbolic poem or with a discussion of advanced mathematics. That is, they would have difficulty if they had had no previous exposure to either that particular style of poetry or that area of mathematics.

Comprehension is similar to thinking. Comprehension is considered to be a cognitive process; that is, a process of knowing and understanding, as described by Benjamin S. Bloom and his associates.[1] Norris

---

[1] Benjamin S. Bloom, et al. *Taxonomy of Educational Objectives. Handbook I: Cognitive Domain* (New York: David McKay, 1956), p. 62.

Sanders and Lou Burmeister believe that the different levels of comprehension correspond to levels of cognition.[2] Comprehension can be simply defined as *thinking* in response to text, or, to use Charles Perfetti's definition, "thinking constrained by print."[3]

Content-area teachers should realize that in learning reading comprehension skills, students are also learning cognitive skills for acquiring and understanding content. Simple strategies can help develop cognitive skills in any learning experience whether the learning experience involves reading, discussion, the viewing of films, or firsthand experiences, like field trips and experiments. These strategies help students learn to ask and answer questions at different levels of understanding.

Comprehension involves both explicit and implicit meaning. In writing and speaking, individuals communicate *explicitly* by stating exactly what they mean, and *implicitly* by suggesting what they mean. Comprehension is the ability to grasp both kinds of meaning, often simultaneously.

To illustrate the differences, read the following statements and be prepared to answer some questions.

> Joe walked into his room and saw his brother going through his things
> on the top of the dresser. James looked up and blushed.

What did Joe do? What did he see? What was his brother doing? To answer these questions, the reader need only grasp explicit meanings—in this case, stated actions.

To answer other questions, the reader must infer implied meanings: Who is James? (Joe's brother) Did James see Joe? (Yes) Whose things were on the dresser? (probably Joe's) Though fairly obvious, none of these answers is explicit. To answer the remaining questions, the reader must make further inferences and must call upon his or her experiences. Why did James blush? What was James up to? Had this happened before?

If the passage were written differently, answers to those questions would not call for inferences.

> Joe walked into his room. He found his brother James going through his
> things on the dresser. James had opened Joe's wallet. James looked up,
> saw Joe, and blushed. He felt guilty because he was trying to steal some
> money, as he had done twice before.

Comprehension at the higher levels involves more than the text. As this chapter will show, higher-level comprehension tasks typically go

---

[2]Norris Sanders, *Classroom Questions—What Kinds?* (New York: Harper & Row, 1966); and Lou E. Burmeister, *Reading Strategies for Middle and Secondary School Teachers,* 2nd ed. (Reading, Mass.: Addison-Wesley, 1978).
[3]Charles A. Perfeffi, "Language Comprehension and Fast Decoding: Some Psycholinguistic Prerequisites for Skilled Reading Comprehension," in John T. Guthrie, ed., *Cognition, Curriculum, and Comprehension* (Newark, Del.: International Reading Association, 1977), p. 21.

beyond the text. Even at the literal level, readers must bring some experience to the text—at the very least, their knowledge of the spoken language. At higher levels, comprehension is possible only if readers have access to information and ideas beyond that which is in the text itself.

For example, in a literature course, a teacher may require students to interpret a story in light of their own experiences or in light of biographical information about the author. Or in history, the teacher may expect students to recognize similarities and differences between the French and American Revolutions even when they are discussed in different chapters. And a mathematics teacher may demand that his or her students read and analyze a theorem statement, while making use of previously learned concepts and procedures of formal logic. A common task in any content area requires students to relate what they have read to what is presented in lectures, discussions, or films. A common problem is that teachers, who have gained knowledge from many different sources, often read more into a text than students can possibly understand with their limited knowledge.

LITERAL COMPREHENSION

At the literal level, the reader comprehends or understands explicit meaning. Understanding results from the successful recognition of words and their semantic and syntactic relationship to one another. Literal understanding of a single sentence such as the following is a remarkable process:

The dog ran into the street and was hit by the car.

Without having to do a conscious, grammatical analysis, the reader knows instantly that: 1) *dog* is both a performer and recipient of action; 2) *running* is the action performed by the dog; 3) *was* is an auxiliary verb (for hit), not a linking verb; 4) *into* has a specific semantic relationship to *street* which gives *into* a different meaning than what is found in *into the ground* or *into a house*.

With literal comprehension, the reader gains knowledge of details, ideas, and relationships which are explicitly presented. Details can include specific facts, such as dates, events, persons, and places, as well as other pieces of information, such as details presented to describe a character or quantities in a mathematics problem.

Ideas can include definitions of terms, minor points (such as those developed in paragraphs), and major ideas (such as a theme or thesis). Relationships can include simple time sequences, as in the events in a story; relationships in space (spatial order); the steps and stages in processes; the ways phenomena are classified, categorized, analyzed, or judged.

The following literal-comprehension tasks ask the student to pro-

Figure 4.1
A Page from an English Textbook

The Larger View

The selections below are from the works of the various writers studied in this unit. Determine how each selection is typical of the writer and what aspects of romanticism it shows. In your analysis consider such points as subject matter, the writer's treatment of the subject, the implicit or explicit purpose of the passage, the construction, and other technical aspects of the selection.

And hark! how blithe the throstle sings!
He, too, is no mean preacher:
Come forth into the light of things,
Let nature be your teacher.

She has a world of ready wealth,
Our minds and hearts to bless—
Spontaneous wisdom breathed by health,
Truth breathed by cheerfulness.

One impulse from a vernal wood
May teach you more of man,
Of moral evil and of good,
Than all the sages can.

—William Wordsworth

It was a lovely sight to see
The lady Christabel, when she
Was praying at the old oak tree.
    Amid the jagged shadows
    Of mossy leafless boughs
    Kneeling in the moonlight,
    To make her gentle vows;
Her slender palms together prest,
Heaving sometimes on her breast;
Her face resigned to bliss or bale—
Her face, oh call it fair not pale,
And both her eyes more bright than clear,
Each about to have a tear.

—Samuel Taylor Coleridge

There is no flavor comparable, I will contend, to that of the crisp, tawny, well-watched, not over-roasted, *crackling*, as it is well called—the very teeth are invited to their share of the pleasure at this banquet in overcoming the coy, brittle resistance—with the adhesive oleaginous—O call it not fat!—but an indefinable sweetness growing up to it—the tender blossoming of fat—fat cropped in the bud—taken in the shoot—in the first inno-cence—the cream and quintessence of the child-pig's yet pure food—the lean, no lean, but a kind of animal manna—or, rather, fat and lean (if it must be so) blended and running into each other, that both together make but one ambrosian result or common substance.

—Charles Lamb

Waken, lords and ladies gay,
On the mountain dawns the day,
All the jolly chase is here,
With hawk and horse and hunting-spear!
Hounds are in their couples yelling,
Hawks are whistling, horns are knelling,
Merrily, merrily, mingle they,
"Waken lords and ladies gay."

—Sir Walter Scott

I have not loved the world, nor the world me;
I have not flattered its rank breath, nor bowed
To its idolatries a patient knee,
Nor coined my cheek to smiles, nor cried aloud
In worship of an echo; in the crowd
They could not deem me one of such; I stood
Amongst them, but not of them; in a shroud
Of thoughts which were not their thoughts,
    and still could,
Had I not filed my mind, which thus itself
    subdued.

—Lord Byron

Music, when soft voices die,
Vibrates in the memory;
Odors, when sweet violets sicken,
Live within the sense they quicken.

Rose leaves, when the rose is dead,
Are heaped for the beloved's bed;
And so thy thoughts, when thou art gone,
Love itself shall slumber on.

—Percy Bysshe Shelley

A thing of beauty is a joy for ever:
Its loveliness increases; it will never
Pass into nothingness; but will keep
A bower quiet for us, and a sleep
Full of sweet dreams, and health, and quiet
    breathing.

—John Keats

408   *The Triumph of Romantic Revolt*

Source: R. Dooley, et al, *England in Literature* (Glenview, Ill.: Scott, Foresman & Co., 1968), p. 408. Used with permission.

Figure 4.2
Two Pages from a History
Textbook

can be preserved for the use and advantage of the largest number of people? A third problem concerns attitudes toward peace and war: Why do Americans go to war, and with what aims and methods have they conducted the fighting itself? A fourth problem is: How can life in cities be improved? (This is an increasingly grave question in the United States. This country began as a nation of farmers, developed enduring rural values, and then became a country where over 70 percent of the people live in urban areas.) A fifth problem is: How can all Americans make a living and share in the nation's prosperity?

EUROPEAN SETTLERS FORCE AMERICAN INDIANS TO MOVE OVER

The story of the United States begins in Asia, and Asian affairs have remained a remarkable concern of Americans. Many thousands of years ago, Asian hunters began to move into North America by crossing Bering Strait. Gradually they and their descendants spread out and occupied large areas reaching from the polar regions of the North to the southern portion of what we call South America.

Adventurous men and women must also have dared to leave Europe and Africa and to travel to the American continents. Of none of these likely journeys do we have any certain proof. Yet we are sure that Vikings from northern Europe were in America in the tenth and eleventh centuries. They made no permanent settlements, and they probably saw no reason to announce a "discovery."

EUROPEAN BREAKOUT

In the 1400's, many western and southern Europeans worked themselves into a state of excitement stemming from their efforts to reach Asia by water. Sailing the high seas in many directions, they found—"discovered"—many peoples that had not known about earlier. Most of them were living in what Europeans called the "New World." They were the descendants of the Asians who had entered North America from the west.

The pull of Asia. A number of European leaders were eager to find a way to trade with Asia by sea instead of by land, since land trade was slow and expensive. Asian goods were popular and brought great profit to merchants who imported them.

The desire to reach Asia by a sea route developed at about the time that nations began to appear on the Atlantic coast of Europe. Large groups of Europeans were beginning to band together under various kings. A group of people felt loyal to their king, and they had feelings of being close to one another. They spoke the same language and shared a common history.

The kings of the nations that were forming rivaled each other for wealth and power. Unfortunately, the people of one nation often regarded those of another as enemies—instead of looking on them simply as fellow human beings. These nations waged fearful wars against one another—wars made more deadly by the advancing military technology.

Mariner Columbus. The rivalry among the European nations took a new turn after the voyages of Christopher Columbus. An Italian who sailed for the rulers of Spain, Columbus reached what we know as American soil in 1492. Dreaming of finding China by sailing west, he found only poor areas inhabited by people living chiefly on tropical plants. Deciding that he had reached the East Indies, he called the people he saw "Indians." Columbus had no way of knowing that he had come upon a people and continent completely unknown to Europeans.

Invasions from the sea. The chief effect of Columbus' "discoveries" was to arouse even greater rivalry among the kings of the Atlantic nations. Explorers were sent out to find "new" regions, examine their resources, and claim them in the name of the sponsoring king. In general, Europeans had little concern for the Indians, who were already living in the "new" lands and whose ancestors had been inhabiting

7

Source: H. E. Geoff and J. A. Krout. *The Adventure of the American People,* Teacher's Edition. (Chicago, Rand McNally, 1973) pp. 7–8. Used with permission.

them for thousands of years.

One important reason why Europeans carried on this aggression was that they were used to a system of property-holding in which an individual could own a piece of land outright. The Indians, on the other hand, had a system in which they shared with others the right to land and its use. The Europeans never understood the Indian point of view about the use of land. They saw nothing wrong in taking over land they had "discovered."

Better weapons. Because Europeans had learned how to manufacture iron, they could make very destructive swords. Men from Spain wore iron armor that could protect them from the arrows and slingshots of the Indians. Also, Europeans had horses, and the Indians did not. Europeans could move much faster and with greater force than the Indians, who fought on foot.

If the Indians had lived together in groups large enough to plan and carry on guerrilla war-

fare, they might have been able to wear down the invaders. But the Indians lived in separate tribes and never organized the kind of cooperative effort that would have been required to repel the invaders.

Missionary work. The Europeans came to America filled with a great desire to make Christians out of Indians. Europeans looked upon this missionary work as a duty they must not shirk even if they could.

False views. The Europeans had another strong desire—to find gold and silver in America. They needed these metals to pay for the things they wished to buy from Asians.

The Indians had almost nothing else—except their land—that the Europeans wanted. For two hundred fifty years, Indians would be pushed about by white men whenever the whites wanted the tribesmen's land. The Europeans felt that they were much superior to the Indians—even though they intermarried with them.

The Spanish explorer Hernando de Soto meets for the first time a group of American Indians. Two cultures are represented. What contrasts can you see here?
New York Public Library

This drawing of the Christianizing of Indians by the Spaniards appeared in a book published in Europe in 1534. What ideas would it give the Europeans?
John Carter Brown Library, Brown University

Figure 4.3
Two Pages from a Biology
Textbook

2   THE WORLD OF LIFE: THE BIOSPHERE

CHAPTER

The Web of Life

RABBITS AND RASPBERRIES

Rabbits. They keep turning up, in nursery tales and comic strips, in candy shops and cabbage patches. They are a part of our folklore and our literature because they are common animals. In most parts of our country, even in parts of our cities, they are abundant. So all of us know about rabbits, which makes them a good thing to start with. And we all know about raspberries—at least about the jam or about the bushes along the roadside, which tear skirts and trousers and make a fine place for rabbits to hide.

A FIRST GLANCE

A rabbit and a raspberry bush: One is an animal; the other, a plant. One moves around; the other is rooted in a particular place. All of us can tell an animal from a plant, a rabbit from a raspberry bush!

This looks clear enough. But if we try to work out precise and inclusive definitions, we get into trouble. Everyone who has looked into the matter agrees that corals and sponges are animals. Yet they are as fixed in position as any plant. Then there are things called slime molds, which are sometimes classed as plants but do a great deal of creeping about. And in the microscopic world there are many creatures that move about actively, as most animals do, but use the energy of sunlight for building up foods, as do most plants. Presently we find ourselves in a state where we no longer know the difference between *all* plants and *all* animals.

Source: the American Institute of Biological Sciences Curriculum Study, *High School Biology: BSCS, Green Version* (Chicago: Rand McNally, 1963) pp. 2–3. Used with permission.

The world of living things may be more complicated than it appears at first glance. But our rabbit certainly *is* an animal, and our raspberry bush a plant. So we can postpone worrying about the exact meaning of "animal" and "plant."

PRODUCERS AND CONSUMERS

Let us try another way of looking at the matter. The rabbit is hiding under the raspberry bush. This is important, for most animals must have some place to hide, some kind of shelter. Even more important, the rabbit must have food. Rabbits usually do not eat raspberry bushes, though they would not scorn the young shoots in time of need. But rabbits and raspberry bushes do not live alone. Around the raspberry patch are many other kinds of green plants that rabbits like.

We can call such green plants the *producers* of the living world, since they build up foods by using the energy of sunlight, and the rest of the living world depends on this production. Rabbits, which cannot make food in this way, are *consumers*—that is, "eaters." Because they feed directly on the green plants, they are called first-order consumers. Foxes, cats, wolves, hawks, all sorts of things, eat rabbits. Besides these larger animals, there are fleas in a rabbit's fur, worms in its intestine, and mosquitoes seeking out its pink ears. These are second-order consumers. But the wolves, also, may have fleas, which are then third-order consumers. Even higher orders of consumers may be found, each order a step farther from the food producers.

Thus, the producers are the basis of a complicated network of consumers.

BALANCE

The rabbits live off the green plants, and many other things (including men) live off the rabbits. At first sight this seems rather hard on the rabbits. But rabbits breed fast. We get a pair of rabbits, and presently the place is overrun with them. If rabbits multiplied in nature without check, they would soon become numerous enough to eat up all the avail-

Figure 1 · 1

Lion, giraffe, and acacia tree in East Africa. Use the text to explain the relationships among these organisms.

Figure 4.4
Two Pages from an Algebra
Textbook

---

4 *Chapter 1*

1-2 Variables and Expressions

> **OBJECTIVE**   To learn how to evaluate variable expressions.

The Ecology Club is having a car wash to raise money for a field trip. They can wash 10 automobiles in one hour. Therefore, they can wash

in one hour:	10×1
in two hours:	10×2
in three hours:	10×3

Each of these numerical expressions fits the pattern

$$10 \times n,$$

where the letter n may stand for "1", "2", or "3". n is called a *variable*. The *domain* of n here is

$\{1, 2, 3\}$ (read "**the set whose members are** one, two, and three").

The *values* of n are 1, 2, and 3. The symbols $\{\ \ \}$ are called **braces**.
  In general:

> A **variable** is a symbol used to represent one or more numbers. The **set,** or collection, of numbers that the variable may represent is the **domain,** or **replacement set,** of the variable. The numbers in the domain are called the **values of the variable.**

An expression, such as "$10 \times n$", which contains a variable is called a **variable expression** or an **open expression.**
  When you write a product that contains a variable, you usually omit the multiplication symbol. Thus,

"$10 \times n$" is usually written "$10n$",
"$y \times z$" is usually written "yz".

Such a product is considered to be *grouped*. Thus,

"$10n + 6$" means "$(10 \times n) + 6$"

and

"$yz \div 10n$" means "$(y \times z) \div (10 \cdot n)$".

Source: M. P. Dolcani et al, *Algebra: Structure and Method.* Book 1. Teacher's edition (Boston: Houghton Mifflin, 1976) pp. 4–5. Used with permission.

But notice that in writing "10×2" or $10(2)$, you must use symbols such as "$\times$", or "$\cdot$", or "$(\ \ )$" in order to avoid confusion.

> The process of replacing each variable in an expression by the numeral for a given value of the variable and simplifying the result is known as **evaluating the expression** or **finding its value.**

Example If the value of x is 6 and the value of y is 2, find the

value of $\dfrac{4x + 3y}{x - 2y}$.

Solution

1. Replace "x" with "6" and "y" with "2", and insert the necessary multi-plication and grouping symbols:

$$\frac{4x + 3y}{x - 2y} = \frac{(4 \times 6) + (3 \times 2)}{6 - (2 \times 2)}$$

2. Simplify:

$$= \frac{24 + 6}{6 - 4} = \frac{30}{2} = 15 \quad Answer$$

It is a useful shortcut to write

"If $x = 6$" for "If x has the value 6".

Here "$=$" means "has the value".

Oral Exercises

In each of Exercises 1–12, the given expression indicates one or more operations to be performed. Describe the operation(s) for each expression. (More than one answer may be possible.) A. = add, S. = subt., M. = mult., D. = divide

Sample $5 + 3c$ *Solution* "Multiply 3 and c, and then add the product to 5."
or   "Add to 5 the product of 3 and c."

M. 3 and a	M. 7 and b	S. 2 from b	S. c from 8	D. 20 by c	D. 46 by a
1. $3a$	2. $7b$	3. $b - 2$	4. $8 - c$	5. $\dfrac{20}{c}$	6. $\dfrac{46}{a}$

D. 16 by prod. of   D. 24 by prod.

7. $\dfrac{16}{ac}$ a and c 8. $\dfrac{24}{bc}$ $\begin{smallmatrix}\text{of } b\\ \text{and } c\end{smallmatrix}$ M. 3 and sum   S. 1 from a;   D. sum of a S. a from b;

9. $3(c + 1)$ 10. $5(a - 1)$ 11. $\dfrac{a + c}{b}$ 12. $\dfrac{c}{b - a}$

  of c and 1   M. 5 by this diff.   and c by b D. c by this diff.

13–24. In Exercises 1–12, if $a = 2$, $b = 3$, and $c = 4$, find the value of each expression. **13.** 6   **14.** 21   **15.** 1   **16.** 4   **17.** 5   **18.** 23

  19. 2   **20.** 2   **21.** 15   **22.** 5   **23.** 2   **24.** 4

vide details, ideas, or relationships. These tasks were written for the textbook passages in Figures 4.1, 4.2, 4.3, and 4.4. Figure 4.1, taken from an English text, illustrates how necessary careful literal reading is for making reasonable interpretations of poetry. Questions could include:

1. What kind of sight did the poet see?
2. Why were the women's palms "prest" together?
3. The odors come from _____ .
4. What would be a good phrase for *heaped?*
   a. placed in a pile
   b. thinly spread
5. List four things a thing of beauty will keep for us.

Figure 4.2 is an example of narrative prose in a history text. Literal-comprehension questions could ask:

1. Where does the story of the United States begin?
2. List the areas of the world discussed here.
3. People of one nation regarded those of another as:
   a. enemies
   b. fellow human beings
4. Which statement is not true about Columbus?
   a. He reached American soil.
   b. He reached the East Indies.
   c. He reached Asia.
   d. He reached the Indians.
5. Number these events in the order in which they happened.
   _____ Columbus reaches America.
   _____ Vikings reach America.
   _____ Asian hunters cross the Bering Straits.
   _____ Nations appear in Europe.

Figure 4.3 is a passage of expository prose from a science textbook: The following would test literal comprehension:

1. List three ways by which plants are distinguished from animals.
2. What animals are mentioned in this passage?
3. Describe the rabbit.
4. Give examples of consumers and producers.
5. Define "first-order consumer."

Figure 4.4 shows expository prose from an algebra text. It presents concepts and procedures to be applied in solving problems. Questions could include:

1. What is the objective of this chapter?
2. What is the Ecology Club doing?

3. What can n stand for?
4. Match these terms with their meanings
    1 variable   a. the numbers the variable may represent
    2 domain   b. a symbol used to represent one or more numbers
    3 value   c. numbers in a domain
5. Describe how to evaluate $\dfrac{4x + 3y}{x - 2y}$

Students can perform successfully on a literal comprehension task without understanding the material. Consider the following example:

> Harvey lost his framusillator.
> What did Harvey lose?

It is obvious that the framusillator was what Harvey lost. The reader might suspect that a framusillator is some sort of instrument or tool because of its suffix. To demonstrate his or her understanding, the reader would have to be able to answer the question: "What is a framusillator?" The reader would have to translate the word into a synonym or statement of definition: "A framusillator is an instrument which measures the. . . ."

Translation tasks insure that students actually understand the text. Frank Guszak prefers the term *organizing* to *translating,* but uses the terms synonymously: "The reader organizes when he translates the printed message into a different form of communication—verbal (paraphrase, summary, synopsis), picture, or graphic."[4]

The following examples of translation tasks were also written for the textbook passages in Figures 4.1 to 4.4. By comparing these tasks with the other literal comprehension tasks, the reader will see that both translation and nontranslation tasks ask for some of the same information.

English:

1. Read the poem about Christabel aloud.
2. Draw a sketch of the scene in "Christabel."
3. In the first line of Shelley's poem
    a. singers have stopped singing
    b. singers have died
4. In your own words describe what happens to rose leaves.
5. Which statement summarizes Keats's poem?
    a. A thing of beauty gives pleasure forever.
    b. A thing of beauty will be lost.

---

[4]Frank J. Guszak, *Diagnostic Reading Instruction in the Elementary School* (New York: Harper & Row, 1972), p. 53.

History:

1. Write a one-paragraph summary of the section that begins on page 7, "European Settlers Force American Indians to Move Over."
2. On a world map, point to the areas of the world from which people came to what is now the United States.
3. Construct a time line to show the sequence of events discussed.

---

4. In your own words describe what Columbus did.
5. Outline key points discussed on p. 7.

Science:

1. In your own words state why it is difficult to define "plant" and "animal."
2. Fill in the following chart:

Producers	Consumers

3. Explain the relationships of the organisms in Figure 1.1.
4. Place these pictures of organisms under their proper designations.

Producers	First-Order Consumers	Second-order Consumers

5. Outline key points discussed in this chapter.

Mathematics:

1. Rewrite these mathematical symbols as words:
   $x, n, +, 10$.
2. Rewrite these words into mathematical symbols: multiply, variable, ten
3. $5n - 4$ is the same as
   a. $(5 \times n) - 4$
   b. $(5 + n) - 4$
4. In your own words state what finding a variable's value involves.
5. Describe the operation(s) for these expressions.
   a. $3a$ b. $7b$ c. $b - 2$

Readers must learn to interpret implicit meanings from their reading. A low-level interpretation involves relatively simple inferences, those by which the reader recognizes the unstated relationships between sentence clauses or between sentences in a paragraph. The story of Joe and James on page 57 provides an example of this level of reading. Higher-level interpretations usually involve larger pieces of material and sometimes more than one source of knowledge. For example, readers may interpret a poem in light of biographical information about the poet. Higher-level interpretations generally include identifying unstated ideas (minor or major points), implied motivation of people presented in the work, the author's purpose, the author's attitude toward the subject, and the mood of the text.

INTERPRETIVE COMPREHENSION

Figurative language by its very nature requires interpretation. Generally speaking, figurative language involves comparisons. The reader must understand what two things are being compared and what the basis is for the comparison. With similes, for example, the stated comparisons are signaled by "like" or "as."

The following interpretive-comprehension tasks refer to the sample textbook pages found in Figures 4.1 to 4.4.

English:

1. What is the mood in Coleridge's poem?
2. Why are Christabel's eyes "about to have a tear"?
3. In your own words, describe how music would vibrate in the memory?
4. In Shelley's poem to what could "love" refer?
5. What is good about a thing of beauty?

History:

1. In a paragraph, discuss the importance of Asia to the history of the United States.
2. For what reasons do you think people from Asia, Europe, and Africa came to America?
3. Why did North and South America become known as the "New World"?
4. In a paragraph, summarize the reasons Europeans came to America after 1400.
5. How did advances in military technology make war more deadly?

Science:

1. Contrast producers and consumers.
2. What would happen if there was a great destruction of plant life?
3. Distinguish between first-, second-, and third-order consumers.
4. Give an example of an organism which has characteristics of both plants and animals.
5. Explain how an animal could be both a second- and third-order consumer.

Mathematics:

1. What is the difference between a variable and a domain of a variable?
2. In the example on page 4, could n stand for 4?
3. How could the Ecology Club increase the money it raises?
   a. work more hours
   b. wash more cars each hour
   c. both a and b
4. In which of the groups would you need to use x, $\cdot$, or ( )?
   a. ten times n plus six
   b. ten times two plus six
5. Explain how the solution to the example on page 5 follows the process of finding a value.

CRITICAL AND CREATIVE COMPREHENSION

The four kinds of critical and creative comprehension are: application, analysis, synthesis, and evaluation. It is often quite difficult to make distinctions between these four kinds of higher level tasks because they seem to overlap. A critical response may involve the application of techniques for an analysis as well as the analysis itself, and a creative act may involve evaluation. The higher levels also involve operation at the lower levels of literal and interpretive reading. Sometimes the wording of the question clearly signals the specific type of comprehension: "Evaluate the behavior of the main character. . . ." or "Apply this story to your own experience by. . . ." The wording of other questions may signal a wide range of possible student responses: "What do you think of the main character?"

Teachers should try to be aware of what types of comprehension they are requesting. One way to accomplish this is for them to answer their own questions and to analyze their answers. The teacher should also be open to a variety of student responses, even though some responses may not be exactly what the teacher expected.

Reading for Application

When students learn some generalization or principle in their reading, they can gain understanding of how the idea works in practice by working problems with guidance from the text or their teacher. Reading for application is demonstrated when the student can apply the generalization or principle to a new situation. The new situation might occur in a discussion or in a subsequent reading assignment or on a test. In the following examples of application tasks, the student must go beyond the text passages in Figures 4.1 to 4.4 for the answers:

English:

1. In a paragraph, apply Keats's theme to your own experience. What "thing of beauty" have you experienced? What were its effects on you?

2. Read the next set of lines from "Christabel." Discuss how Coleridge continues to develop the loveliness of Christabel. Point out the similarities to the passage you have just read.
3. Meet in small groups and compile a list of images which illustrate the same point Shelley makes with his images of melodies, odors from violets, and rose leaves.

History:

1. Read the following account of the Spanish conquest of the Aztec empire. In what ways does it illustrate the motives and perspectives of Europeans discussed in the chapter (the teacher provides the account from another source)?
2. Given the discussion of the Europeans' explorations of the New World, predict the effects on the "Indians."
3. We will be watching a film about the history of Africa since the second World War. As you watch the film, consider the similarities between situations in Africa involving Europeans and the exploration of the New World in the 15th and 16th centuries.

Science:

1. In the exercise in Figure 1.1., you are to apply the ideas presented in Chapter 1, by explaining relationships of the organisms.
2. This chapter discusses the relationships of organisms in nature. Apply the ideas to a manmade situation. For example, how would you categorize the following: workers in a factory which produces automobiles, dealers who sell the cars, and customers who buy them?
3. After each numbered pair of items, write the letter A if an increase in the first might lead to an increase in the second. Write the letter B if an increase in the first might lead to a decrease in the second.
    1. Number of small animals
       Number of second-order consumers
    2. Frequency of fires which destroy plant life
       Number of first-order consumers
    3. Amount of water in an area
       Number of first-order consumers
    4. Number of large first-order consumers
       Number of small first-order consumers

Mathematics:

1. (a) Write a variable expression for the following sentences or phrases:
   Fred is 3 times as heavy as John.
   Express Fred's weight in terms of John's.
   (b) Find Fred's weight if John weighs 80 pounds.
2. The formula for changing Fahrenheit temperature to Centigrade is $C = \frac{5}{9}(F - 32)$. What Centigrade temperature corresponds to 212°F?

3. Tom spent half as much money as Bill, Bill spent half as much as Fred. Bill spent $4. How much did they spend all together?

Reading for Analysis   Critical reading requires analysis—analysis of the content of the text or the ways the content is presented. There are several different types of analysis, all of which apply to reading: 1) Readers can analyze elements of the text. For example, readers can distinguish conclusions from supporting statements, factual from nonfactual statements, and stated from unstated assumptions. 2) Readers can analyze relationships between ideas or between ideas and details. For example, they can discover cause-and-effect relationships. 3) Readers can analyze the structure and purpose of material. Recognition of the form (or the purposes authors have in particular sections of text) contributes to comprehension. Paragraphs and multiparagraph sections may have one or more of the following organizational patterns: cause-and-effect, comparison, ennumeration, and chronological sequence.

The following tasks require that students understand the concepts important to the ways of analysis, such as the concepts of poetic image, modes of developing ideas, and cause-and-effect relationships.

English:

1. What is Coleridge's purpose in the passage from "Christabel?" Support your answer with words from the passage.
2. What are the key images in Shelley's poem? How are they related?
3. Which of the following statements identifies the way Keats develops the idea of a "thing of beauty"?
   a. He ennumerates examples.
   b. He compares/contrasts beauty with ugliness.
   c. He defines "a thing of beauty" in terms of what it does.

History:

1. Which statement is *least* consistent with the discussion of the Europeans?
   a. They wanted to convert Indians to Christianity.
   b. They wanted to learn from the culture of Indians.
   c. They wanted to conquer land.
2. List the reasons which explain why Indians were not successful in resisting the Europeans.
3. Complete the chart by identifying cause/effect relationships with attention to multiple effects.

Causes	Effects
1. Appearance of nations	a. Wars in Europe
	b. Rivalry in exploring New World

Science:

1. Why does the author devote so much discussion to rabbits and raspberries?
2. Discuss how balance is achieved through interaction of producers and consumers.
3. What is the primary mode of development in the first two pages?
   a. chronological
   b. comparison/contrast
   c. classification and division

Mathematics:

1. If $C = \frac{5}{9}(F-32)$ is the relationship between Fahrenheit and Centigrade, find the relationship expressing F in terms of C.
2. Using $C = \frac{5}{9}(F-32)$, find F given that C is 100°. (In this problem, students must apply the concept of *variable* to the relationship between Fahrenheit and Centigrade, which they have previously studied.)
3. Ticket A costs half as much as Ticket B and B costs one third as much as Ticket C. Buying one each of tickets A, B, C would cost $9. Find the cost of each ticket.

Activities calling for *synthesis* are also occasions for creative reading. A synthesis task requires the student to relate pieces of information or ideas and present them in a new, coherent form.

Reading for Synthesis

A key word in the definition is "new." The student's response may not be original as far as the teacher is concerned because many others may have come up with the same response. The response, however, may be considered original for the student if it represents a new way by which that student views or organizes experience.

A library research project could fit the definition of synthesis. Students could select information and ideas from two or more sources, and then present their material in hopefully well-integrated reports. Neither the material nor the thesis might be original, but the particular presentation would be new for the student. Other examples of creative activities include paintings or drawings which illustrate understanding of a text (such as a portrait of a main character in a story); construction of scenes from fiction or nonfiction (such as a map of a historical battle); construction of models which illustrate concepts (such as a model of the solar system); role playing (spontaneous or planned) fictional or historical characters; or the rewriting of a text to present a different point of view. The following examples of synthesis tasks, like the application tasks, require more knowledge than the text itself provides.

English:

1. Respond to the task presented on page 408. Determine how each selection is typical of the writer. Explain what aspects it shows of romanticism.

2. Meet in small groups and list five questions which could be used to explore romanticism in poetry.
3. Select some recorded music appropriate to one of the poems being studied. Present a reading with musical accompaniment.

History:

1. Write a brief fictional account of Columbus's "discovery" of America. What would Columbus think and say when he reached land?
2. Select a topic suggested by the discussion of European exploration and write a 1,000-word research paper, using at least five sources.
3. Write a essay comparing and contrasting the exploration of the New World and the recent exploration of the moon.

Science:

1. Illustrate the concepts of producers and consumers, using organisms not discussed in the chapter.
2. In a small group, develop a plan for investigating organisms to determine if they are plants or animals.
3. Write a fictional account of the discovery of a new world by space explorers. Your account should relate to the ideas in the chapter. Examples: Organisms are not easily classified as plants and animals. The balance of nature is maintained in a different way than on earth.

Mathematics:

1. A variable expression has the following values $\{6, 12, 18\}$ when $\{1, 2, 3\}$ is used as the replacement set for the variable. Which of the following is a likely candidate for the variable expression?
   a. $3x$
   b. $x + 5$
   c. $6x$
2. The variable expression $kn + 1$ produces the following set of values, $\{4, 7, 10\}$ using a replacement set of $\{1, 2, 3\}$ for n. What is the value of k?
3. $A = S^2$ and $a^2 + b^2 = c^2$ are variable expressions which relate to squares and right triangles. Use these to solve the following problem.
   The length of the diagonal is 6. Find the area of the square and one of the triangles.

Reading for Evaluation   The highest form of reading comprehension and cognitive behavior involves making judgments. Evaluation requires the application of criteria or standards for judging the content, form, or style of the text. The criteria may be provided by the teacher or developed by the students themselves.

A key term is *criteria*. Evaluative reading is not a quick, subjective response to a text, such as "I didn't like it. I don't know why." Students are expected to apply given criteria or develop and apply their own. The teacher may present the concept of realism in literature, then ask students to judge stories as being realistic or unrealistic. Or students can read a series of stories, then stop and develop their own criteria—for example, the students could use the criteria of whether plots are relevant or suspenseful to judge stories.

In many cases, evaluative reading will require more than one text. For example, a history teacher may ask students to read official documents after reading a historical account of an event, or a teacher may ask students to read two versions of a fictional story and consider which is more satisfying. Different kinds of criteria are stated or implied in the following evaluation tasks:

English:

1. Select a contemporary poem or song and discuss it as an example of romanticism. You should apply the criteria discussed in class.
2. Select one of the poems from the Romantic Period. Write an essay of from 250 to 500 words, describing and evaluating the poem. Your criteria for judging the poem should be clear.
3. In a small group, outline an argument in favor of preserving beautiful works of art (or architecture).

History:

1. Discuss the advantages and disadvantages of the systems of "property-holding" and "property-sharing."
2. On what bases could we try to prove that the Vikings reached America?
3. Read the following account of the treatment of Indians by English explorers. Which of the following propaganda techniques are used?
   Loaded words   Card stacking
   Transfer   Plain folks
   Band wagon

Science:

1. Read the following descriptions of authors. Which would be the best authority on ideas about the balance of nature?
2. Read the following definition of plants and animals. Which is the most precise and exclusive?
3. Identify your criteria for judging the development of "nature parks."

Mathematics:

>Evaulation is a difficult area in mathematics. Some examples of its use
>are as follows:
>1. To choose a procedure that is best.
>   An extension of the study of variable expressions might be the study
>   of quadratic expressions. The student might choose to use *(a)* fac-
>   toring *(b)* completing the square, or *(c)* the quadratic formula to
>   solve for x in $ax^2 + bx + c = 0$.
>2. Evaluate your answer by checking your work and using the key for
>   problems 1–12.
>3. *(a)* Bill did the following problem. Evaluate for $x = 2, y = 4$.
>
>$$\frac{3x + y}{y - x} \rightarrow \frac{3(2) + 4}{4 - 2} \rightarrow \frac{6 + 4}{2} \rightarrow \frac{10}{2} = 5.$$
>
>   *(b)* Jane did it this way $\dfrac{3x + y}{y - x} \rightarrow \dfrac{3x}{-x} \rightarrow -3.$

STRATEGIES FOR DEVELOPING COMPREHENSION

Thorough discussions of comprehension are both difficult and abstract. Happily, however, there are several fairly simple strategies for helping students to develop good comprehension skills. Given the importance of comprehension, there will be many examples of comprehension tasks throughout this book. The following strategies, which are applicable to any content area, are of particular benefit at the beginning of a course when the teacher has little or no knowledge of a student's abilities.

Sequencing Comprehension Tasks

Prospective and new teachers often ask questions such as these: "At what level should I present instruction?" "What types of questions should I ask?" "How much can I expect my students to know?" Many experienced teachers would admit: "You *don't* really know at the beginning of the course, before you've had a chance to learn something about the students." With experience, a teacher gains a "feel" for the types of questions that would be appropriate for particular groups of students. But, until a course is underway, a teacher cannot know precisely what tasks are appropriate for *individual* students.

There are at least two reasons for this state of affairs. First, individuals come to secondary schools with a great range of ability. Second, given the state of flux which characterizes school curricula, a teacher cannot readily predict the experiences students have had. In one class, some students may have had systematic training in different levels of comprehension; others may have had no direct instruction but may have done a variety of reading. The experience of some may have been limited to literal-level tasks; others may have been frustrated by tasks that were too difficult for them.

One instructional strategy has two benefits: 1) it gives students a successful introduction to the content and 2) it gives the teacher an opportunity to diagnosis strengths and weaknesses in comprehension. The teacher uses a scheme of comprehension to sequence comprehension tasks. With the first reading assignment, the students respond to literal comprehension tasks, locating details and explicit ideas. If they respond successfully, the teacher adds a sequence task to the next assignment. Interpretation tasks come next, and so forth. The teacher can provide direct instruction in those skills which students do not successfully demonstrate.

Some teachers might wonder: "Don't students need to be challenged with difficult tasks?" "Will they get the wrong idea if they start with easy literal tasks?" It is true that for comprehension to develop, students need to be challenged; however, challenges are good only when students can meet them.

This first strategy provides challenge because there is a steady increase in difficulty. A thorough reading at the highest levels of comprehension is viewed as one of the goals students can work toward. Teachers can explain this strategy to students so they will expect more difficult tasks.

What about students who can already read beyond the literal level? Though literal comprehension is described as the lowest, easiest level, it is not a worthless task for good readers. As discussed earlier, when students are confronted with new or difficult material, even literal tasks will not be that easy. Furthermore, on some occasions at least, readers might want to check their literal understanding before moving on to higher levels.

Successful interpretation of a poem, for example, demands close attention to the actual words in the text. It is usually unnecessary for students to spend a lot of time answering many literal-level questions. Five or so well-chosen questions from one or two pages of text is often enough to check a student's literal understanding.

A traditional teaching practice is to provide study-guide questions for students. These questions establish purposes for the reading and give guidance. Content-area teachers who have used this procedure may not have realized that they were facilitating the development of reading skills.

Providing Purpose and Guidance

Teachers can use certain procedures to focus students' attention as they read. Ernst Rothkopf and Lawrence Frase call these methods orienting procedures because they orientate the reader to the way he or she should respond.[5] These procedures include general and specific

---

[5]Lawrence T. Frase, "Effect of Question Location, Pacing, and Mode Upon Retention of Prose Material," *Journal of Educational Psychology* 59 (1968): 244–49; and Ernst Z. Rothkopf, "Some Theoretical and Experimental Approaches to Problems in Written Instruction," in John Krumboltz, ed., *Learning and the Educational Process* (Chicago; Rand McNally, 1965).

questions and statements about the text presented before, during, and immediately after reading, and explicit statements of learning goals or purposes for reading. If students refer to study guide questions before, during, and immediately after their reading, the study guides should affect their comprehension positively. Different procedures will have different effects. Very specific questions presented before reading tend to help students locate specific answers but inhibit thorough reading. General questions and statements presented before and during reading tend to facilitate organized comprehension of each detail.

Ernest Kuehls conducted a study in which two groups of students read the same chapter in a mathematics textbook.[6] One group completed the exercises at the end of the chapter. For the other group, the exercises were *interspersed* or spread throughout the chapter with three results: 1) students were forced to respond actively while reading, 2) they had a smaller piece of material to read before responding, and 3) exercises were close to the relevant material in the text. When both groups were tested on the material, students in both groups who were of high or average mathematics ability showed no differences in test scores. However, lower-ability students in the "interspersed question" group performed significantly better than their counterparts in the other group.

Some teachers present materials with questions or statements positioned next to the text. Others give students a list of questions with notations about the location of the answers; that is, the page number and sometimes the column and paragraph number. Harold Herber has a variety of examples of "reasoning guides," which are exercises to be completed as or after students read. A section of one of Herber's guides for mathematics follows:

> Directions
> There are several important details in this section of Chapter 5. As you read, answer the questions assigned to you. Sometimes the page, column, and paragraph are given to help you identify the location of the answer.
> 1. Is a carpenter's straight line the same as a geometric straight line? (p. 111)
> 2. How should a line be correctly labeled?
> 3. What are parallel lines? (p. 112 #5)
> 4. Which of the figures below are simple closed figures? (p. 129)[7]

Some teachers simply present the questions or statements orally before a reading assignment or during in-class oral reading and discussion. For best results, a teacher should 1) write the guides on the board or on handouts before students begin a reading assignment so that they

---

[6]Ernest A. Kuehls, "Effect of Interspersed Questions on Learning from Mathematics Text," *Journal for Research in Mathematics Education* 7 (3) (1976): **172-75**.
[7]Harold L. Herber, *Teaching Reading in Content-Areas* (Englewood Cliffs, N.J.: Prentice-Hall, 1970), p. 267.

can see and refer to them, and 2) ask students to make an oral or written response to the guides to insure they are putting them to use.

For all the strategies discussed so far, teachers can use questions and other tasks provided in textbooks. Secondary textbooks typically include tasks at the ends of the chapters. *Using Tasks in the Text*

Teachers need to make selective use of, but not be dictated by, the tasks in textbooks. One problem with such tasks is that textbooks are written for representative groups of students, not for individuals. A second problem is that the style, content, and variety of tasks in a text are all too often, initially, too difficult for large numbers of students. A reasonable course goal would be for all students to learn to respond to a variety of tasks. At the beginning of a course, however, many of the tasks may be frustrating for many students.

In the three preceding strategies, students respond to questions. Answering questions is, in fact, the most common way to guide and measure comprehension. Three alternatives to the question-answering procedures have the following characteristics: 1) Students attempt to verbalize—to think aloud—about what is happening as they respond to the text. 2) As a result, they produce more information (for themselves and the teacher) than just answers to the questions. 3) The procedures do not make as much demand on memory as do recall questions.[8] *Students Verbalize Responses*

Retrospection. With *retrospection* students read a passage, then talk about what they have read. They may reread some or all of the passage as they speak. In some studies, students read a paragraph, talk, read the next paragraph, talk, and so forth. The teacher can provide general directions or questions to elicit the verbalizations: "Tell me what happened?" "What were you thinking about when you read?" Some students might simply retell the material, but it is better if they also try to explain their reactions. The example which follows shows a student's retrospection after reading the opening of an adolescent novel, *The Pigman,* by Paul Zindel.[9]

> Well, there were, uh, it happened in a high school. There were these two students, sophomores I think, and a man named Pignati. I think something bad happened, but I'm not sure why.

Introspection. *Introspection* occurs when the student verbalizes while responding to tasks, such as questions on the material. In a study by James McCallister, students tried to explain how they were answering

---

[8]Jill F. Olshavsky, "Reading and Problem Solving: An Investigation of Strategies," *Reading Research Quarterly* 12:4 (1976–77): 654–74.
[9]Paul Zindel, *The Pigman* (New York: Dell, 1968).

questions.[10] The following example shows a student's verbalization of his answer to the question: who are the main characters?

> The main characters are a boy and a girl, high school students, It says "sophomores" at this high school. The boy is, well, kind of strange. He starts out by saying he hates everything and he talks about how he set off bombs in the school.

Protocol Analysis. *Protocol analysis* is similar to retrospection but does not involve the use of questions. Originally, it was a procedure used in cognitive psychology to study problem-solving strategies.[11] In protocol analysis students still verbalize as they read. The student "comments about the content and problems of short segments of his reading,[12] as in the following example:

> This is a weird book. It starts off with the boy, he's a student, and he's telling the story. He says he and this girl are writing down this story about something they did. He says he hates school and everything. Sometimes I feel that way.

Using the Cloze Procedure

The cloze procedure, previously discussed in Chapter 3, can also measure and develop comprehension. The procedure calls for deleting words from the text and asking students to fill in the missing words, either orally or in writing. Educators such as Miles Zintz and John Bormuth argue that the ability to *anticipate* or *predict* what words are missing is a good indication of comprehension.[13] The activity insures that students are attempting to follow the meaning as they read.

Some teachers follow the conventional procedure of deleting every fifth word. Others delete fewer words but select words that will focus the students' attention on certain aspects of the content or structure of the text. For example, a teacher can delete words that relate to a certain topic like *energy:*

> *Source of energy.* Where does your energy _____ from? No doubt you have heard that human _____ comes from food. You have been urged to _____ in order to grow and in order to play or to work—in other words, to be _____ . Later we shall bring up the role of food in _____ , but for the present we shall stick to the role of _____ in activity, to food as an energy _____ .[14]

---

[10]James M. McCallister, "Reading Difficulties in Studying Content Subjects," *Elementary School Journal* 31 (November 1930): 191–201.

[11]Allen Newell and Herbert A. Simon, *Human Problem Solving* (Englewood Cliffs, N.J.: Prentice-Hall, 1972).

[12]Olshavsky, "Reading and Problem Solving," p. 662.

[13]Miles V. Zintz, *The Reading Process: The Teacher and the Learner* (New York: Brown, 1970), p. 293, and John R. Bormuth, "Literacy in the Classroom," in William D. Page, ed., *Help for the Reading Teacher: New Directions in Research* (Urbana, Ill.: ERIC Clearinghouse on Reading and Communication Skills, 1975), pp. 60–90.

[14]American Institute of Biological Sciences, Biological Sciences Curriculum Study, University of Colorado at Boulder, *High School Biology: BSCS,* Green Version (Chicago: Rand McNally, 1963), p. 23.

If a teacher wants to focus students' attention on a poet's selection of words to fit a rhyme scheme, the teacher can delete the rhyming words in a poem:

> They are all gone away, (a)
>   The House is shut and still, (b)
> There is nothing more to ———— . (a)
> Through broken walls and ———— (a)
>   The winds blow bleak and ———— (b)
> They have all gone ———— . (a)[15]

Teachers commonly test comprehension with recall or postquestions. The students read a passage and must then answer questions without referring to the text. Although recall is important, alternative tasks can also be helpful.

Kender and Rubenstein argue that recall tasks actually test two capacities: comprehension (in the sense of understanding the material) and memory. They propose a *reinspection task* where the reader reads the passage and answers postquestions. The reader tries to respond from memory, but is allowed to look back at the text (or reinspect) to find or confirm answers. In a study, Kender and Rubenstein found that elementary students performed with significantly higher comprehension on the reinspection task over the recall task.[16]

Hansel presents a strategy for planning a content-directed reading-thinking activity. The teacher can follow the steps to construct open-ended questions that can have a number of appropriate responses.

1. Read passage to identify important concepts.
2. (Mentally) outline passage.
3. Decide how the passage is organized.
4. Design a key question which will elicit similar organization in students' minds (or use open questions: "How many questions can you think of about this passage?" "What do you guess some answers might be?").
5. Test key question by seeing if outline (step 2) answers the question.
6. Decide what initial information (titles, graphics, summary, and so forth) will help students to guess about content of passage.

ALTERNATIVES TO RECALL TASKS

Reinspection Tasks

Selecting Questions

---

[15]E. A. Robinson, "The House on the Hill," in Chad Walsh, *Doors into Poetry* (Englewood Cliffs, N.J.: Prentice-Hall, 1962), p. 108.
[16]J.P. Kender and H. Rubenstein, "Recall vs. Reinspection in IRI Comprehension Tests," *The Reading Teacher* (April, 1977), pp. 776–779.

7. Search for ways others have applied these concepts.
8. Design open ended questions that will encourage application.[17]

Reading for Details and Main Ideas

Content-area teachers often neglect the basic skills of reading for details and main ideas. Activities stressing these skills insure that students have a basic understanding of the content before they attempt more sophisticated responses to it. The following list of activities will help students find the main idea:

1. Read a short selection and select the best title, from several listed for the selection.
2. Read a short selection and give it a title, in your own words.
3. Read the title of a chapter and attempt to predict what the author is going to say.
4. Read the introduction of a chapter and note carefully just what the author is going to say.
5. Read the summary of a chapter and tell, in a simple sentence, what the chapter covered.
6. Read a paragraph and reduce it to a simple sentence, by paraphrasing the author.
7. Rapidly skim the titles and the subheadings of a selection and attempt to list details which will give a general impression of the entire selection.
8. Read the first and last sentences of an entire selection.
9. Turn each subheading or subtitle into a question. The answer to that question will be the main idea of the paragraph or paragrahs.
10. Given a newspaper and a problem clearly stated by the teacher, skim rapidly for a solution to that problem. In the beginning, it is best to confine the exercise to a single selection from the newspaper.
11. Select a headline that best describes the narration of an incident in a newspaper.
12. Select from a series of proverbs or sayings the one that best fits a written passage.
13. Mark location of main idea sentence(s) in paragraphs. Locations of main ideas can be noted as follows:
    ∇ = Main idea at beginning of paragraph
    △ = Main idea at end of paragraph
    ⧖ = Main idea at beginning and end of paragraph
    ◊ = Main idea within paragraph
    ○ = Main idea not stated[18]

[17]T. Stevenson Hansell, "Increasing Understanding in Content Reading," in W. John Harker, ed. Classroom Strategies for Secondary Reading (Newark, Dela.: International Reading Association, 1977), pp. 44–47.
[18]Ann Neeley, *Teaching Reading in the Content-Areas* (Austin: Education Service Center, Region XIII, 1978)

The following activities guide reading for detail:

1. Ask students to note the detaile in a paragraph after you have stated the main idea.
2. Have students read a paragraph into which have been inserted some irrelevant sentences and let them identify these sentences.
3. After the students have read a paragraph, let them choose from a prepared group of sentences those that agree or disagree with the paragraph.
4. Present three paragraphs and let the students determine which of the last two supports and logically follows the first paragraph.
5. Analyze a written paragraph into its main and supporting ideas by having students make a formal outline of it.
6. Ask questions about the paragraph; multiple-choice, completion, and true-false questions are especially appropriate in eliciting answers concerning the details of a paragraph.
7. Have students develop a chart, diagram, or map of the sequence of events.
8. Have students write a paragraph describing a given object, which other students read and then try to guess the object.
9. Use exercises of completing sentences from a reading selection in which blanks have been left for words that test the comprehension of details—cloze exercises.
10. Tic-Tac-Toe for Details

Who was the main character?	Where did he live?	How was he going to travel?
Why did he go?	What would he bring back?	How long would he be gone?
Who was his friend?	Where was he going?	When would he go?

The students will read a story. Then they will answer questions about the story before they are allowed to place an X or O in a box. Three boxes across in any direction wins.[19]

Because there is no universal agreement about how people comprehend text, there are many different definitions and schemes of comprehension. Comprehension is a cognitive process that involves three different levels of understanding: literal, interpretive, and critical/creative.

SUMMARY

---

[19]Neeley, *Teaching Reading in the Content-Areas.*

Instructional strategies for helping students develop comprehension skills in content areas include 1) selecting and constructing comprehension tasks; 2) sequencing tasks in order of difficulty; 3) providing purpose and guidance during reading with study guides and interspersed questions; 4) selectively using tasks provided in textbooks; 5) asking students to verbalize their responses to the text; and 6) using the cloze procedure. (The checklists presented in Appendix B provide assistance in identifying the types and levels of tasks.)

Suggested Activities

1. Discuss one of the Key Ideas listed in the Overview at the beginning of this chapter.
2. Examine the tasks at the end of a chapter in a secondary content-area textbook. Discuss these tasks in terms of 1) the range of comprehension skills, 2) the attention, if any, to literal comprehension, and 3) the guidance, if any, for comprehending the chapter.
3. Examine commercially published material, such as a kit, laboratory, or series of readers. Discuss the instruction provided in comprehension in terms of 1) the variety of comprehension skills, 2) the mode of response, 3) the amount of practice, and 4) the variety and difficulty of text.
4. Select a piece of material for your content area, such as a textbook chapter. Write an example for each of the comprehension tasks discussed. Use the checklist in Appendix B to guide your work.
5. Select a passage of about 100 words from your content-area text. Transform the passage into a cloze exercise. Decide in advance on what aspect of the material you want students to attend to.

Alexander, Clara F. "Strategies for Finding the Main Idea," *Journal of Reading* 19: 4 (January 1976): 299–301.

Bloom, Benjamin S., ed. *Taxonomy of Educational Objectives, Handbook 1. Cognitive Domain.* New York: David McKay, 1956.

Burmeister, Lou E. *Reading Strategies for Middle and Secondary School Teachers.* 2nd ed. Reading, Mass.: Addison-Wesley, 1978, chaps. 7–9.

Dawson, Mildred, ed. *Developing Comprehension, Including Critical Reading.* Newark, Dela.: International Reading Association, 1968.

Degler, Lois S. "Using the Newspaper to Develop Reading Comprehension Skills," *Journal of Reading* 21:4 (January 1978): 339–42.

Donlan, Dan. "How to Play 29 Questions," *Journal of Reading* 21:6 (March 1978): 535–41.

Duffy, Gerald G., ed. *Reading in the Middle School.* Newark, Del.: International Reading Association, 1975.

Golinkoff, Roberta M. "A Comparison of Reading Comprehension Processes in Good and Poor Comprehenders," *Reading Research Quarterly* 11:4 (1975–76): 623–59.

Guszak, Frank J. *Diagnostic Reading Instruction in the Elementary School.* New York: Harper & Row, 1972, chaps. 5, 11, and 13.

Guthrie, John T., ed. *Cognition, Curriculum, and Comprehension.* Newark, Del.: International Reading Association, 1977.

Harker, W. John, ed. *Classroom Strategies for Secondary Reading.* Newark, Del.: International Reading Association, 1977.

Herber, Harold. *Teaching Reading in Content-Areas.* Englewood Cliffs, N.J.: Prentice-Hall, 1970.

Macklin, Michael D. "Content-Area Reading is a Process for Finding Personal Meaning," *Journal of Reading* 22: 3 (December 1978): 212–15.

Pearson, David P., and Johnson, Dale D. *Reading Comprehension.* New York: Holt, Rinehart, & Winston, 1978.

Richards, John P., and Hutcher, Catherine W. "Interspersed Meaningful Learning Questions as Semantic Cues for Poor Comprehenders," *Reading Research Quarterly* 13 (1977–78): 539–53.

Sanders, Norris. *Classroom Questions—What Kinds?* New York: Harper & Row, 1966.

Smith, Richard J., and Barrett, Thomas C. *Teaching Reading in the Middle Grades.* 2nd ed. Reading, Mass.: Addison-Wesley, 1979, chap. 4.

Thomas, Ellen L., and Robinson, H. Alan. *Improving Reading in Every Class.* Boston: Allyn & Bacon, 1972.

Wilson, Robert M. *Diagnostic and Remedial Reading for Classroom and Clinic.* 2nd ed. Columbus: Charles E. Merrill, 1972, chap. 9.

Recommended Readings

5

Study Skills and Reading Flexibility

The goal of content-area learning is the development of students' understanding at the higher levels of the cognitive domain. While keeping this long-term goal in mind, teachers should also consider the practical, immediate problems students face. Practically speaking, students read to prepare for: studying, taking notes during lectures, participating in discussions, preparing for tests, and completing writing assignments. The chapter will be divided into three sections: 1) study skills, 2) locating and using sources of information within the textbook, and 3) reading flexibility.

OVERVIEW

Through the use of SQ3R (Survey, Question, Read, Recite, Review) and other strategies, students can improve their reading efficiency and retention level.

Key Ideas

Teachers can help students increase their efficiency in note taking, discussion preparation, test preparation, and paper writing.

Students need to locate and use sources of information within the textbook to be independent learners.

Proficient readers can adjust their rate and style of reading to fit their reading goals.

Mr. Henna, a mathematics teacher, is conducting a discussion on a chapter in the textbook. Instead of asking students questions, Mr. Henna asks students to quickly look over the chapter and pose questions they think are answered in the chapter. Students are asked to share these questions with the class. Mr. Henna writes the questions on the chalkboard and leads the students in a discussion on the types of questions contributed and the ways these questions can be answered. He points out how titles, subheads, and illustrations will aid in answering the questions. Following the discussion, students select 10 questions and read the chapter individually to obtain answers to the questions on the chalkboard.

STUDY SKILLS AND STRATEGIES

Study skills are commonly taught in reading programs. However, as with comprehension skills, study skills are important to all phases of learning. Study skills can and should be taught in the context of content learning, and in fact, many educators see study skills as synonymous with learning skills.

The term *skill* may not be appropriate, because study or learning skills are actually procedures or strategies by which students consciously direct their academic performances. The strategies involve cognitive operations, reading skills, and sometimes listening, speaking, and writing skills.

SQ3R

Much of present methodology in study skills is indebted to the 1940s work of Francis Robinson and his colleagues. Robinson developed and tested a procedure called SQ3R (Survey, Question, Read, Recite, Review).[1] Variations have become common, such as PQRST (Preview, Question, Read, Summarize, Test).[2] Robinson's procedures help students increase their reading efficiency and improve retention of material.

Survey. Students survey or preview the text in order to gain a general idea of the content and organization of the material. The reader surveys textbook aids such as chapter titles, subheads, charts, graphs, and other visual aids; tables of contents, introductions and summaries; italicized words; numbered points; and the chapter exercises.

Students need the opportunity to develop their survey skills. One important survey skill is the ability to *skim*. Skimming is an efficient,

[1]Francis P. Robinson, *Effective Study*, rev. ed. (New York: Harper & Brothers, 1961), pp. 29–30.
[2]George Spache, *Toward Better Reading* (Champaign, Ill.: Garrard, 1963), p. 94.

selective style of reading by which students can identify the main points while they skip over details and minor points. Students can skim to find general ideas prior to a more thorough reading.

Question. With the general idea in mind, the readers can pose questions which they believe the text answers. These questions are then used as a reading guide. They are suggested by whatever information was picked up in the survey and by students' past experience with similar content and texts.

Read. Students read the material to answer the questions. How thoroughly or how selectively students read depends upon the difficulty of the content and the level of the questions. If the questions are at the literal level and require simple location, recall, or translation, the students can scan the material. Like skimming, *scanning* is a selective style of reading at a high rate but for the purpose of identifying specifics rather than general ideas.

Recite. The second *R* refers to reciting. To aid in understanding and retaining the material, students stop to recite or verbalize the answers they have found without looking at the text.

Review. The third *R* designates an additional step that aids retention. Before moving on to new material, the students review their answers.

Write. Donald E. P. Smith adds a sixth step to the procedure.[3] The students write the answers as a further aid to retention. In addition, the answers provide notes which can be reviewed at a later date before a test or used in preparation for a paper.

Because SQ3R was originally developed for university students and because the procedure involves a number of unusual steps, many secondary teachers have assumed that the procedure is appropriate only for high-ability, university-bound students and that it is too difficult for lower-ability students. That assumption is erroneous and unfortunate. Variations of the procedure have been very helpful to students with problems in study skills, as well as in reading (comprehension, vocabulary, and word recognition).

With colleagues in junior high schools and in a reading and learning skills clinic, Walter Lamberg and Richard Ballard have developed and tested a procedure which uses pictures to encourage comprehension development.[4] The procedure has been employed as 1) a remedial technique for elementary and secondary students, 2) an introductory

---

[3]Donald E. P. Smith et al., *Learning to Learn* (New York: Harcourt, Brace & World, 1961).
[4]Walter J. Lamberg and Richard Ballard, *Teaching the Picture and Text Survey* (Ann Arbor: Office of Instructional Services, The University of Michigan, 1974). Also in Donald E. P. Smith, *The Adaptive Classroom*, vol. 3. Donald E. P. Smith, ed. *A Technology of Reading and Writing* (New York: Academic Press, 1977), pp. 229–52. In the original version, the second step was summary. Lamberg changed this to organize to avoid the idea that students need to produce a complete summary.

Figure 5.1
Reading a Picture in a Textbook

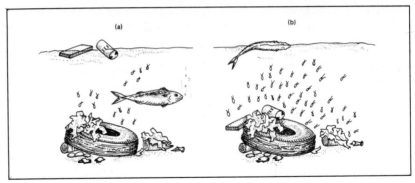

Source: Illustration from William L. Smallwood, *Challenges to Science: Life Science,* Teacher's edition (New York: Webster Division, McGraw-Hill, 1973), p. 249. Used with permission.

Figure 5.2
Graphing the Results of a Picture Survey

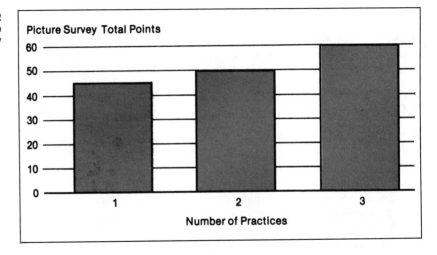

Used Graphic aid

exercise in comprehension for beginning readers, and 3) a preparatory exercise for textbook-reading techniques.

Because the Picture Survey provides practice in posing and answering both general and specific questions about pictures, students gain the opportunity to develop fluency in asking questions before encountering potential difficulties in texts. By using pictures in the textbooks, the content-area teacher can employ the procedure as an introductory activity to reading the text. The four-step procedure can be used to analyze the picture in Figure 5.1.

The Picture Survey

Survey. Students survey the picture to get the general idea. They ask the question: "What is it about?"

Organize. Students state or write an answer to the question: "What is it about?" This step insures that they *do* survey. The words or sentences students write provide an *advance organizer* (an organizing or translation response). David Ausubel and others have advocated the use of advanced organizers in teaching.[5] Teachers can present these organizers, introductions, outlines, or frames to students before they receive any specific information; students will be better able to understand and retain the specifics if they have a means of organizing them. Practice in the surveying and organizing steps helps students learn to provide their own advance organizers so that they are not dependent on teachers or textbooks for them. The picture in Figure 5.1 shows a fish dying from garbage and pollution.

Question. Students state or write questions which can be answered by carefully looking at the picture and/or by bringing their experience to the picture. These questions provide an additional means of organizing the information in the picture. For example: "What garbage is in the water?" "What happens to the fish?" "Why do people do this?"

Answers. Students state or write answers to their questions. When illustrations from textbooks are used, the "answers" in this step are ideas and details important to the content area. The answers to the three questions in the step above are: 1) tires, cans, and paper; 2) the fish dies; and 3) they are lazy and careless.

Students can practice the procedures using additional pictures from the textbook or from other sources students select. Students can keep a graph to measure their progress in developing question fluency. In the bar graph in Figure 5.2, the following point system is used: five points for the survey, five for the organizer, and five for each question and each answer. The total number of points are recorded on the graph for each practice. In this example, a student went from 45 to 60 points in just three practices.

---

[5]David P. Ausubel, *Educational Psychology: A Cognitive View* (New York: Holt, Rinehart, & Winston, 1968); and "The Use of Advance Organizers in the Learning and Retention of Meaningful Verbal Material," *Journal of Educational Psychology* 51 (October 1960): pp. 267–72.

Figure 5.3
Two Pages from an English
Textbook

Source: Glen Love: *On Purpose: Rhetoric for a Reason* (New York: Holt, Rinehart and Winston, 1974), p. R117. Used with permission.

Chapter **8**

Creating Drama

You have had some practice now in letting a character speak for himself. That is, instead of saying how a character feels ("Jim was scared"), you learned that it was more effective to let Jim *show* that he was scared through his words and actions:

> Jim crouched against the door, listening to the footsteps on the stairs. "Who—who's out there?" he called. His voice wobbled and skidded upward in a near-squeak.

If Jim were a character in a play, he would have to speak for himself. There would be no narrator on stage to explain his feelings. Instead, Jim would act out his alarm by means of startled movements, quick nervous glances, muttered words ("What's that—who's coming?"). And the audience would *watch* him grow more fearful as he listens at the door.

In other words, he would be *acting the role* of Jim, a very frightened boy.

Role-Playing

Have you ever pretended that you were somebody other than yourself? Perhaps a great detective, hot on the trail of a villain? A nurse saving hundreds of lives by her prompt action? A visitor from a strange planet, zooming in to terrify a city?

R 117

The Picture Survey is one of the few activities all students can succeed in with only a few practices. High-ability students can enjoy the activity if the pictures are interesting and if they challenge themselves and their peers with interesting questions. At first, some students may have difficulty, simply because they are not used to asking questions, but teaching the procedure is simple. Essentially, the teacher shows examples of good responses to the organize, question, and answer steps. The teacher can provide the examples or invite students to share their responses.

The Picture and Text Survey   The Picture Survey just discussed has three purposes: 1) to introduce the surveying and questioning procedures, 2) to teach students how to make use of textbook illustrations, and 3) to prepare students to use the procedure with text. With the Picture and Text Survey, students follow essentially the same steps with illustrations, text, and other text aids. The five-step procedure can be used to analyze the passage in Figure 5.3.

Survey. Students survey or look quickly over the pictures and text to preview the material, as in SQ3R.

Organize. Students tell or write a statement which provides a general view of what is in the material. For the sample in Figure 5.3, the statement could be "How drama is created."

Question. Without looking at the text, students predict the questions they believe the text will answer. They must use the organizer and their past experience. Generally, students should try for 10 questions over a page or more of text. Subheads can be transformed into the questions, as in the following:

1. How does a character speak for himself?
2. Is there a narrator in a drama?
3. What does the audience do?
4. What are some examples of role-playing?

Answers. Without looking at the text, students try to answer as many questions as they can. This step has three purposes: 1) As with the question step, students are forced to draw upon past experience. 2) They give themselves (and the teacher) a preassessment on how much, if anything, they already know about the material. 3) They receive practice in making inferences.

Read. After spending time and effort preparing themselves, students read the text selectively for these three purposes: 1) to confirm predicted questions and answers, 2) to locate answers they could not predict, and 3) to revise answers that may have been incorrect.

Instruction for this procedure is the same as the instruction for the Picture Survey. The teacher presents or invites examples for the organize, question, and answer steps. Student contributions can be writ-

Purpose	Text	Survey	Organize	Question	Answer	Confirm
	Rhetoric					
Pre-test	p. 117	1	4	5	4	5
Increase answers to 5	Rhetoric p. 118	1	7	5	5	5

Figure 5.4
Survey Chart

Source: Walter J. Lamberg and Richard Ballard, *Teaching the Picture and Text Survey* (Ann Arbor: Office of Instructional Services, The University of Michigan, 1974), p. 37.

ten on the board or shown on an overhead projector. The end result is a set of well-organized notes on the text which are also key points and particulars from the content. The procedure has an additional benefit in that it provides the teacher with the means of assessing the kinds of questions and cognition levels at which students are operating at the beginning of a course.

Students can use a chart, as in Figure 5.4, to record both their reading assignments and information on their performance in using the procedure. In the first column, students note their objective or purpose for the assignment. The second column is used to note the text and the pages to be read. In the third column, they note the number of pages covered in their survey, and in the fourth, the number of words or sentences written in the organize step. In the next column, they receive credit for all questions asked, whether or not they are answered in the text. In the sixth column, they receive credit for all answers predicted, whether or not they found them in the text, to encourage inferences. To encourage carefulness and correctness, the last column provides a record of only those answers which they found in the text. That is, at the end of the activity, students count the total answers confirmed, located, or revised after the reading. Once students show competence in using the procedure, they can move on to a more efficient procedure which will be discussed later in this chapter.

Purposefulness in Reading. Many educators believe that a sense of purpose is a characteristic of successful reading.[6] Study procedures promote purposefulness by requiring students to spend some time examining and thinking about the text before reading it. The students' questions provide particular purposes for reading a selection.

Students and teachers, when first introduced to study procedures, often consider them involved and time-consuming. With regular practice, however, the procedures take less time and become second nature to the

DEVELOPING EFFICIENCY IN STUDY

[6]Marilyn J. Taylor, "Using Photos to Teach Comprehension Skills," *Journal of Reading* 21:6 (March 1978): 514–17.

students. These study procedures are far more efficient than the study habits exhibited by many successful students.

Many students read a text very carefully and slowly but with no particular purpose in mind. They may then work the exercises at the end of chapters, and, in doing so, have to reread portions of the text. Some students take copious notes and wind up with too much unorganized information. Others use a highlighting pen to mark points and details, and again, wind up with too much unorganized highlighted material. Prior to taking a test, students may reread entire texts again slowly and purposelessly.

Problems which result from the lack of efficient, conscious strategies are found with all academic performances: reading textbooks, note taking, test preparation, and paper writing. Just as the problems are similar in different academic performances, so are the solutions. Ruth Cohen and her associates, the authors of *Quest: Academic Skills Program*, found that they could adapt the survey and question procedure of SQ3R to all basic performances.[7] *Quest* is a self-instructional text originally designed for community college students. It has been used in both senior and junior high schools.

Reading and Note Taking   The authors of *Quest* recommend that students use a variation of the SQ3R technique as their basic study procedure whenever they have reading assignments.[8]

Students begin the procedure with small amounts of material such as a single paragraph. Students then steadily increase the length of the material they cover in their survey.

Chapter 4 recommended the strategy of *interspersing* tasks throughout a textbook chapter. The survey procedure has the same benefit in that students read a small piece of material, respond to it (by answering their questions), and then move on to another piece of material.

The survey procedures previously discussed can be collapsed into a three-step procedure, which combines reading and note taking. As students survey the material, they write questions they believe to be important. Illustrations, titles, subheads, or lists of points in introductions and summaries can suggest the questions. If the assignment calls for answering questions presented at the end of chapters, students can use them to guide their reading. Students then read the text and write out the answers as they are found. At the end of the activity, students have a well-organized set of notes on the text which can be reviewed prior to lectures, discussions, and tests.

Taking Lecture Notes   The same basic procedure can be adapted to taking notes from lectures, films, or other presentations.[9] Students can use the format illustrated

---

[7]Ruth Cohen et al., *Quest: Academic Skills Program* (New York: Harcourt, Brace & Jovanovich, 1973).
[8]Cohen et al., *Quest,* pp. 3–87.
[9]Cohen et al., *Quest,* 88–152.

American History
April 3

Figure 5.5
A Note-taking Format

1. Where did the Allies go on offensive?

2. Where did the Allies attack after North Africa?

3. Where did the Allies invade Europe?

1. Allies began successful offensive by landing in North Africa. The U.S. landed in Morrocco. British fought Germans to the East.

2. After stabilizing North Africa, British and the U.S. invaded Sardinia.

3. Allies entered Europe with invasion of Normandy in France. Germans lost control of Northwest France. Allies had fooled Germans into expecting invasion somewhere in South Europe.

Source: Ruth Cohen et al., *Quest: Academic Skills Program* (New York: Harcourt, Brace & Jovanovich, 1973), p. 124.

above and follow the three steps before, during, and after the lectures.

1. To prepare for lectures, students predict questions they believe will be addressed in the lecture. Such questions can be generated from the reading assignments, handouts on the course, and previous lectures. The questions relate the reading assignments to the lectures.

2. Students take notes during the lectures, as is the usual practice, but they try to think of these notes as potential answers to questions. They should listen for explicit and implicit questions posed in the lecture. For example, a teacher may say: "Today, we will consider the economic causes of the Civil War." Students can transform that statement into the central question of the lecture: "What were the economic causes of the Civil War?"

3. Immediately following the lecture, students should make a list of questions based on their notes, as in Figure 5.5. They can use these questions to direct subsequent reading and to prepare for tests.

Discussion Participation

Many teachers prefer discussions to lectures, but fall back on lectures because of the following experiences: 1) Many students are highly reluctant to participate in discussions. 2) Students are often unprepared for the discussions. 3) Students who do participate often do not carefully consider their own responses or those of their classmates. 4) A few students dominate the discussion.

When students prepare for discussions at home or in class immediately before the discussion, these problems are reduced. If the teacher wishes to discuss particular questions, he or she provides them prior to the reading. Students are then asked to spend a few minutes prior to the discussion writing informally and freely in response to questions such as the following:

1. Who is the main character in Updike's *A & P?*
2. What kind of person is he?
3. What in the story shows you what kind of person he is?

> Sammy. He's a teenager who works in a supermarket. He's kind of a typical teenager. He gets bugged, he questions rules and adults. He sticks up for these girls who broke the rules.

This procedure gives all students an opportunity to respond actively even if they do not speak up. It also gives them a chance to reflect upon and examine their responses and to compare their responses with those of their classmates. The preparation also seems to relieve anxiety about responding orally. Walter Lamberg found that students who initially did not participate began to volunteer after a few sessions.[10]

Studying for Objective Tests   Typically, teachers tell students to study for tests but do not show them how. Often, teachers spend class time lecturing on the importance of study, or students spend time sitting around knowing they should be studying but not knowing how.

A good strategy for studying for a test is to practice responses similar to those called for in the test. Faced with an objective test, students will benefit from practicing answering objective questions. The question-answer format for note taking, discussed earlier, facilitates such practice. Students simply cover the answers in the second, wider column, as in Figure 5.5, and try to answer their own questions from memory. Students can also work in pairs or in groups with individuals taking turns reading the questions and checking others' responses to them.

Such activities also give students opportunities to compare their notes and elaborate upon or revise them if necessary. Essentially, students are functioning as peer tutors.

Teacher Guidance. Just as teachers can guide students' reading by providing tasks in advance of assignments, so they can guide study for tests by providing illustrative test items in advance of study sessions. In some cases, the tasks provided in reading assignments will be the same, or very similar to, the tasks which will appear in tests. Teachers will need to decide which modes of respones they will use on the tests—for example,

---

[10]This discussion procedure was developed for creative writing classes and is discussed in Walter J. Lamberg, "Developing the Capacity for Self-Education in Writing," *English in Texas* 6:2 (Winter 1974): 27–28.

the relatively easy matching mode or the more difficult complete-sentence answer. Common response modes for objective test items include the following:

1. underlining answers in text;
2. matching;
3. multiple-choice;
4. sentence completion (fill-in-the-blank);
5. true-or false;
6. 'short answer (word or phrase);
7. short answer (complete sentence); and
8. solution of problems.

Predicting Questions. Initially, teachers can reduce the difficulty and anxiety of taking tests by providing actual, or illustrative, test items at the beginning of learning experiences. At some point, however, students should learn to predict test items so that they will not be dependent on teachers.[11] Once students have learned to take effective notes from reading, lectures, and other sources, they can use these notes in making "educated guesses" about the tests they will face. They can examine the questions and answers they and their peers have written in the notes for two purposes. First, they should attempt to generalize; that is, to determine the types of tasks and modes of response to expect on tests. Second, they should attempt to make judgments; that is, to determine particular tasks which, because of their importance, will be likely to appear on the tests.

This activity can be done in class under the teacher's supervision. It provides an excellent way of reviewing material for tests. This activity can also develop reading comprehension and cognitive skills. To make effective predictions, students will need to analyze, synthesize, and evaluate the content.

Some teachers go a step further and ask students to actually construct their own tests. Some teachers write part of the test themselves and then invite students to contribute additional test items. Other teachers have the class vote on questions generated by individuals or small groups.

Reorganizing Notes. If students have only one source of notes such as reading and frequent short tests, the task of review is relatively simple. However, if students have notes from two or more sources (such as reading and lectures) or a great amount of material for a relatively large test, they may need to reorganize their notes to make them easier to use.

Three procedures suggested by Ruth Cohen et al are helpful for editing notes.[12] 1) Students should omit repeated or similar questions and

---

[11]The idea of students predicting test-questions is from Cohen et al., *Quest,* 144–52.
[12]Cohen et al., *Quest,* pp. 144–52.

answers. 2) Students should generate a new question which encompasses more specific questions. 3) Students should rewrite and condense information from several pages or sources into a single page or a chart:

Allied Offensives	Axis Offensives
1. Morocco	1.
2. Sardinia	2.
3. Normandy	3.

Preparing for Essay Examinations

Preparing for essay examinations involves the same basic procedures as those recommended for objective tests. First, teachers should initially provide guidance and assistance by communicating the types of responses they will expect of students. The reading guides may illustrate or actually consist of the questions that will appear on the tests. Students can study for the tests by practicing essay responses; that is, by writing or speaking essay-type answers. Students should then be able to learn to predict essay questions.

As with objective tests, it is helpful for the teacher to determine the types of questions they plan to give on tests. Questions may be categorized by the mode of development or the organizational pattern. In essence, students learn to write responses using the same organizational patterns which appear in their reading.

The authors of *Quest* identify three basic patterns of essay questions: trace, comparison/contrast, discuss.[13] The trace pattern has chronological order, as illustrated below. Students present information in a time sequence—for example, a sequence of historical events or the sequence of steps or stages in a biological process.

	"No taxation without representation":
What was the Stamp Act?	I. The Stamp Act of 1765 required stamps to be purchased and attached to all:
	A. Newspapers
	B. Legal documents
	C. Advertisements
	D. Pamphlets
When and why was it passed?	It was passed by Parliament to raise money to be used to defend the colonies

---

[13]Cohen et al., *Quest,* p. 180, p. 177, p. 172. Used with permission.

What was colonial reaction?

   II. Colonial reaction to the Stamp Act

     A. Colonials offered no alternative answer

     B. Angry mobs were formed from Mass. to South Carolina

        1. Led by Sam Adams and Jonathan Mayhew and others
        2. Burned houses of English officials

     C. Forced Americans to formulate a new theory of the empire

        1. To accommodate the American position
        2. Led by Patrick Henry, James Otis, John Dickerson

What was the new theory?

   III. The new theory—no taxation without representation

The comparison/contrast pattern requires students to point out both similarities and differences:

   I. German composers—Bach and Handel

Who was Bach?

     A. Bach (1685–1750)—personal life
        1. Lived all his life in a small town
        2. Family man—2 wives and 20 children
        3. Dealt with small problems, few adventures
        4. Family had long musical history

Who was Handel?

     B. Handel (1685–1759)—personal life
        1. Lived in many places—Italy, Germany, England
        2. Not married
        3. Had many adventures
        4. No musical heritage

How was their music alike?

C. Similarities in music
  1. Both in same historical period (Baroque period)
  2. Masters of choral music
  3. Reflected several nationalities in music
  4. Wrote a variety of music

How did their music differ?

D. Differences in music
  1. Bach's music—mainly church music
    a. Impersonal
    b. Wrote with great drama
    c. Wrote utilitarian pieces—those used for special occasions
    d. Chorales used often
  2. Handel's music—best work—operas— wrote 43
    a. Revealed his personality through music
    b. Did not use strong rhythms, chorales
    c. Did not use organ very much

The discussion response may take many forms. It may involve an *ennumeration,* that is, a listing, as in "Discuss the effects of the Civil War." A discussion response may involve a comprehensive definition which includes 1) a general statement or formal definition, 2) a synonym, 3) an example, and 4) a function.

I. Adrenal glands

What are the adrenal glands?

A. Adrenal glands—small glands attached to the kidneys.
  1. Secrete hormones which are essential to the function of certain body processes

What hormones are secreted?

B. Hormones secreted
  1. Cortin—secreted by the inner core of the gland and is essential to life

  2. Adrenine—secreted by outer layer of gland and is essential to the control of emotions

How do the hormones affect the body?

C. Effects of the adrenal glands upon the life cycle

  1. An undersecretion of cortin causes low blood pressure, muscular weakness, and general low resistance to disease

  2. Oversecretion of adrenine increases heart rate and blood pressure and interferes with respiratory and digestive processes

---

When faced with an essay examination, students should review their notes differently than they do for an objective test. Instead of focusing on smaller, more specific questions and answers, they should look for the larger organizational patterns. If necessary, they should revise their notes into those patterns, as illustrated in Figures 5.6–5.8.

A good many students, many of whom are successful readers, choke up when faced with writing an academic paper. The authors have found that many superior college and secondary students have great anxiety about writing and even select courses to avoid those requiring long written assignments.

Writing Academic Papers

Walter Lamberg's study of university students who sought help with their writing showed that the most common problems were practical academic ones, which had to do with understanding assignments, scheduling work, or getting started on papers.[14]

The use of a question-directed procedure can help students prepare for academic papers.[15] Lamberg[16] and Wolter[17] have shown how the use of questions can guide students through the entire process of composing (from finding a topic to revising), and how the procedure can be used with both academic and creative writing assignments.

In their reading students try to identify those questions which they think the text is addressing. In their writing students identify questions they will address in their own compositions. They pose a large central question, which suggests the subject and topic of the paper, then break that question down into smaller related questions which suggest the main points to be developed and the means of development. In a sense,

---

[14]Walter J. Lamberg, "Major Problems in Doing Academic Writing," *College Composition and Communication* 28:1 (February, 1977): 26–29.

[15]Cohen et al., *Quest*, pp. 212–48.

[16]Walter J. Lamberg, *Design and Validation of Question-Directed Narrative Writing* (ERIC Clearinghouse on Reading and Communication Skills, ERIC Document No. 097 689); also summarized in Charles Cooper. "Research Roundup," *The English Journal* 65:6 (September 1976): 83–86; and Walter J. Lamberg, *"Creativity and Skill in Writing:* An Instructional Program, 4–13" (mimeographed text for The Texas Hill Country Writing Project, Austin, Texas, 1978).

[17]Daniel R. Wolter, "Effect of Feedback on Performance of a Creative Writing Task." Ph.D. diss., The University of Michigan, 1975).

students conduct a dialogue with themselves, posing and answering questions, as a means of thinking about the paper. By jotting down their questions, they produce a rough, but helpful, outline for the first draft.

For example, the science teacher may want students to write a discussion on the balance in nature (a concept presented in Chapter 4). Students could pose a general question such as the following: "What is the balance in nature?" Or, "How is the balance maintained?" Smaller, related questions could be "What aspects of nature are in balance?" (consumers and producers) "What do producers do?" "What do consumers do?" "What is an example of the interaction between consumers and producers?" Additional questions could be "How could the balance be disturbed?" "How do humans affect the balance?" Following are some additional examples of the question-directed procedure for different types of writing:

1. Explicaton of a Poem:
   What is the theme? How is the theme revealed through the literal situation? (What happened?) The persona? (Who is speaking?) Imagery? Metaphor? Symbol? Form?
2. Discussion of Character:
   Who is the character? What is his or her role?
   What does the author say that tells about him or her?
   What does the author show about him or her?
   (What does _____ do? Say? What do other characters do or say to _____ ? What do other characters say about _____ ?)
3. Essay in Definition:
   What class does _____ belong to? How does _____ differ from members of its class? What are examples of _____ ? How does _____ function?
4. Persuasive Essay (Student-Selected Subject and Topic):
   How should the school respond to student rights (topic)?
   What rights should students have? Why?
   How are they not respected?
   How should they be respected? Why?[18]

In creative writing and composition courses, students usually write from their own firsthand experience. In most academic writing, however, students base their compositions on reading materials. A simple way of relating reading and writing assignments is to use the Picture and Text Survey. The written responses to the steps in the procedure provide the material for a paper, a kind of rough draft, as illustrated in Figure 5.3. The student then transforms this material into a finished paper, such as the following summary:

---

[18]Walter J. Lamberg, "Following a Short Narrative Through the Composing Process," in Ovida Clapp, ed., *Classroom Practices in Teaching English 1977–78: Teaching the Basics—Really!* (Urbana, Ill.: National Council of Teachers of English, 1977), p. 34. Used with permission.

In creating drama, the writer must let characters speak for themselves. There is no narrator to tell the audience how the characters feel. A writer can role play. I could pretend I was a football hero.

The first section of this chapter discussed the academic performances expected of students in all content areas: studying, note taking, test preparation, discussion participation, and paper writing. Variations of the question-directed procedures, based on SQ3R, can be used to direct all these performances.

In most courses, the primary source of information is the text itself. However, there are additional sources of information both within and beyond the textbook, which students need to use effectively to become independent learners.

LOCATING AND USING DIFFERENT SOURCES OF INFORMATION

A textbook has two kinds of aids: graphic aids and other textbook aids. (Textbook aids were initially discussed in Chapter 2, as one aspect of content-area reading.)

Most texts will have one or more of the following types of graphic aids: actual graphs, charts, tables, and maps. (A major exception is literary works.) Each graphic aid will call for particular responses to the information and concepts presented, the medium of presentation, and the symbols and abbreviations employed. Students will need experience, and often assistance, with a variety of each type of aid.

Graphic Aids

Students need to be able to translate graphic or nontextual communication into words to demonstrate an understanding of the graphic aids. For example, in geography a student may be asked to explain the climatic conditions of certain areas of a country by using a map.

Before making a translation response, students should first make lower level literal responses to demonstrate their ability to identify features and items in the aid. For example, students might be asked to identify the different lines in a map (those that are horizontal or those that are vertical). Students can also be asked to go beyond literal responses. Having explained a map showing climatic conditions, students can be asked to decide on the area of the country which has the best climate. Such a response involves application, synthesis, and evaluation. Perhaps the best test of a student's ability to understand a graphic aid is a creative response. For example, a teacher could provide information on the climate of another country and then ask students to construct their own map as an individual or group project.

Maps. Figure 5.6 presents a map from a geography text. Identification tasks would include "What is the title of the map?" "Locate New York City." "What symbol is used to designate places where lead can be found?" "Which areas of the United States have the highest concentrations of oil wells?"

Figure 5.6
A Map from a Geography Textbook

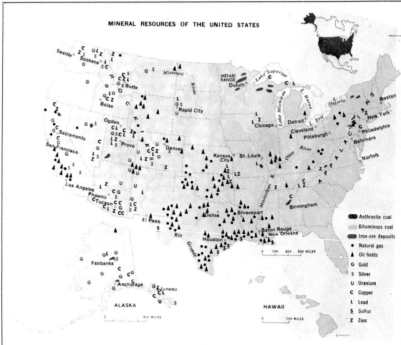

furnaces where the iron was smelted.

The greatest American iron-ore resources were still unknown in 1800. The Alabama ores, for instance, were not discovered until 1812. The Mesabi, the greatest of all American iron deposits, was not found for almost another eighty years. The Mesabi Range and its neighboring iron ranges are located in an area south and west of Lake Superior.

By the time the Mesabi ore was discovered, a waterway had already been opened by a canal at Sault Ste Marie. Thus there was a way for the ore to be taken east to areas where it could be used. When the United States had developed sufficiently to need them, the Mesabi and other Lake Superior ores became the backbone of the American steel industry.

The young nation was rich in mineral fuels, too. Early explorers made frequent mention of the black stones of the Appalachians, some of which would burn if you piled them carefully on a campfire. In fact, a seam of coal was found in a hillside across

97

Source: Stephen B. Jones and Marion F. Murphy, *Geography and World Affairs* (Chicago: Rand McNally, 1971), p. 97. Used with permission.

Figure 5.7
A Circle Graph from a Mathematics Textbook

Student Enrollment

College 8.1%

High School 21.3%

Elementary School 70.6%

Source: E. T. McSwain et al, *Mathematics 7* (River Forest, Ill.: Laidlaw Brothers, 1963), p. 212. Used with permission.

A map calls for many translation responses such as: "What is meant by landform regions?" "What does 44°N mean?" "Point to the place on the map that shows a temperate continental region." An analysis response would be "What are the similarities and differences between the Maritime and Mediterranean regions?"

Graphs. There are many forms of graphs, but all serve to illustrate a comparison/contrast among items. The pie graph in Figure 5.7 compares student enrollment at different levels by illustrating percentages. Students would have to understand 1) the percentage symbol (%) and 2) the idea that the pieces of the pie are meant to illustrate the relative sizes of the percentages.

Figure 5.8
A Bar Graph from a Geography Textbook

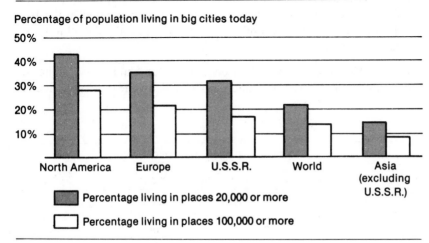

Percentage of population living in big cities today

- ▓ Percentage living in places 20,000 or more
- ☐ Percentage living in places 100,000 or more

Source: Angus M. Gunn, *Patterns in World Geography* (Toronto: W. J. Gage, 1968), p. 41. Used with permission.

Figure 5.9
Frequency-Line Graph

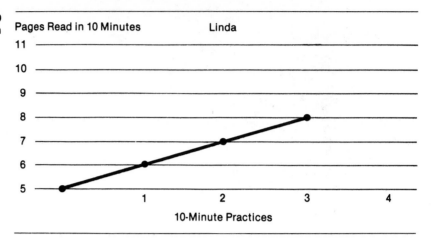

Figure 5.8 presents a bar graph in which key information is illustrated in the form of bars. In this example, students must understand that the focus is not on population per se, but on population in big cities. Several comparisons are illustrated: 1) within areas of the world, 2) among areas of the world, and 3) between areas of the world and the world as a whole. Figure 5.9 shows a frequency-line graph. It illustrates changes in frequency from one occasion to another—in this case it shows the number of pages read in a ten-minute session.

A pictograph was presented earlier in Chapter 2. (See Figure 2.4 on page 22.) That graph illustrated the number of cars in different cities. The pictograph is easy to understand, since, as the name indicates, the information is illustrated in picture form.

Charts. Charts can be used to display the same information presented in graphs. Figure 5.10 shows the same information presented in the bar graph in Figure 5.8. Charts and diagrams are especially useful in illustrating relationships.

Time lines. Time lines are widely used in the natural and social sciences. They provide a helpful aid to students in visualizing the time sequence of

Figure 5.10
Chart

Areas	Percent in Places 20,000 or more	Percent in Places 100,000 or more
North America	42%	28%
Europe	36	21
USSR	32	18
World	22	13
Asia	13	8

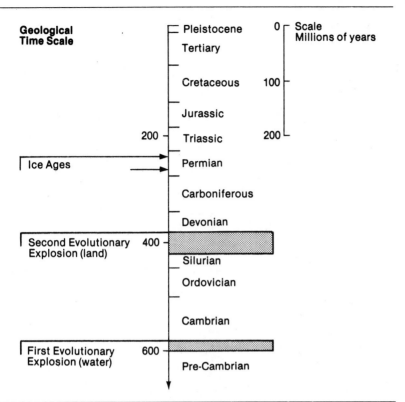

Figure 5.11
A Time Line in a Geography Textbook

Source: Angus M. Gunn, *Patterns in World Geography* (Toronto: W. J. Gage, 1968), p. 71. Used with permission.

events. The time line in Figure 5.11 illustrates the sequence of major geological changes.

Flow Charts. Other graphic aids can illustrate processes. For example, the diagram in Figure 5.12 illustrates the operation of a steam engine as well as the concept of steam as an energy source. Unlike other graphic aids, the diagram cannot be understood without a careful reading of the accompanying text.

Flow charts are often an effective means of illustrating the intricacies of a process. They show not only the steps or stages in the process but also key events (or decisions) and the different effects or outcomes of different events. The flow chart in Figure 5.13 illustrates the process of the steam engine represented earlier in the diagram in Figure 5.12.

As shown in this discussion, graphic sources, though intended as student aids, can sometimes involve difficult reading tasks. Except for very simple illustrations of low-level abstractions, graphic aids call for slow, careful reading and many translation responses. It would be best

Figure 5.12

A Diagram in a Physics Textbook

laws of physics before they could be successful engineers. In fact.
the sequence of events was just the opposite; steam engines were
developed first by men who cared less about science than about
making money – or at least about improving the effectiveness and
safety of mining. Later on. men who had both a practical knowledge
of *what* would work as well as a curiosity about *how* it worked.
made new discoveries in physics.

The first commercially successful steam engine was invented
by Thomas Savery (1650-1715). an English military engineer.
Follow the explanation of it one sentence at a time. referring to the
diagram below. In the Savery engine the water in the mine shaft
is connected by a pipe and valve D to a chamber called the cylinder.
With valve D closed and valve B open. high-pressure steam from
the boiler is admitted to the cylinder through valve A, forcing the
water out of the cylinder and up the pipe. The water empties at
the top and runs off at ground level. Then valve A and valve B are
closed and valve D is opened. allowing an open connection between
the cylinder and the water in the mine shaft.

When valve C is opened. cold water pours over the cylinder.
cooling the steam left in the cylinder and causing it to condense.
Since water occupies a much smaller volume than the same mass
of steam. a partial vacuum is formed in the cylinder. allowing the
pressure of the air in the mine to force water from the mine shaft
up the pipe and into the cylinder.

The same process. started by closing valve D and opening
valves A and B. can be repeated over and over. The engine is in
effect a pump. moving water from the mine shaft to the cylinder
and. in another step. pushing it from the cylinder to the ground above.

A model of Heron's aeolipile. Steam produced in the boiler escapes through the nozzles on the sphere, causing it to rotate.

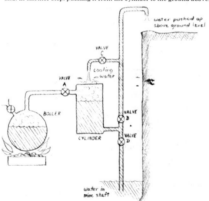

Schematic diagram of Savery engine.

Source: F. James Rutherford et al., *The Project Physics Course* (New York: Holt, Rinehart and Winston, 1970). p. 430. Used with permission.

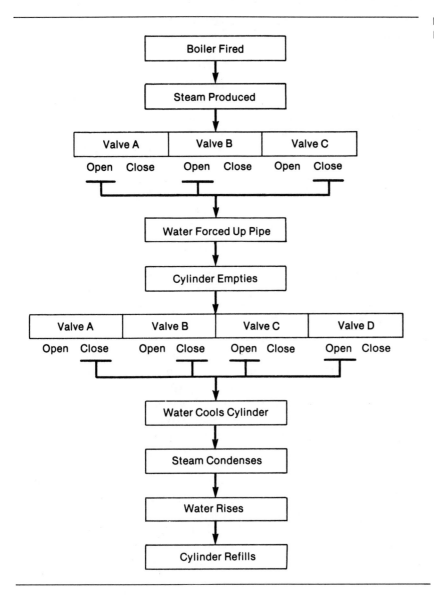

Figure 5.13
Flow Chart

for teachers to introduce graphic aids with relatively simple examples, such as the pie graph shown in Figure 5.7

Other Textbook Aids Chapter 2 included a discussion of textbooks aids which can be divided into three categories: 1) those which help to locate information within the text but are also sources of information in themselves, 2) those that provide information beyond what is in the textual material, and 3) those which help students establish purposes for reading.

The first category includes the table of contents and the index, which aid in locating information within the text itself; and titles, subheads, introductions or overviews, and transitional paragraphs, which aid in locating information within the chapter. These aids also provide information in the sense that they either state directly or imply the subject, topics, and key points addressed in the text. They also show the organization of the material and, in a sense, represent an outline of the text.

The second category of aids are intended to help students with terminology and concepts. These include graphic aids, glossaries, pronunciation keys, italicized words, and, most important, helpful context clues, such as explicit definitions.

The third category helps students to establish conscious purposes for reading. These include 1) questions and other tasks at the end of chapters, 2) study-guide or preassessment questions presented at the beginning of chapters, and 3) sometimes explicit statements of purpose or of objectives that appear at the beginning of a chapter or a text (as in a how-to-use-this-text section). Suggested activities and readings can also provide guidance for study beyond the textbook.

Effective teaching requires more than making students aware of these aids. Teachers should provide tasks within the context of the content learning that call for use of the aids. For example, prior to a reading assignment, the teacher can ask students to survey the table of contents and the introduction to a chapter and then state (or write) five key purposes for which they will read the chapter. To check students' ability to use the glossary, the teacher can ask for definitions which use actual glossary words. The key terms to be defined in a chapter can be divided among individuals or groups.

INCREASING READING FLEXIBILITY As discussed in Chapter 1, reading rate and rate flexibilty are often categorized as one aspect or skill area of reading. Commonly, development of rate and flexibility are provided for in study-skill and developmental reading courses, as was discussed in Chapter 2. Many educators believe that the proficient readers have flexibility; they can adjust their reading to various factors.

Reading style is characterized by the rate, by the degree of thoroughness and selectivity, and sometimes by the number of reread-ings necessary for thorough understanding. Readers make adjustments according to 1) the comprehension purpose, 2) the readability of the text, and 3) the amount of familiarity with the content and form.[19] In a study by S. Jay Samuels and P. R. Dahl, students were given two purposes and a chance to practice reading for each. The students read faster for general information and slower for details.[20]

Reading rate refers to the amount of information processed and the amount of time spent reading. Rate can be expressed and measured in a variety of ways: by average words per minute (WPM) or by the number of lines, half-pages, or pages read in a constant amount of time (such as 10 minutes or an hour). To measure *rate of comprehension;* the words per minute are multiplied by the percentage of comprehension. A student who covers an average of 500 words a minute with only 70 percent comprehension would have a comprehension rate of 350.

Minimum Rates

Researchers have attempted to establish some guidelines for minimum rates which would indicate a minimal level of reading proficiency. Typically, students regarded as average readers are given rate tests, and their scores are used to determine an average rate. An average rate for secondary students is considered to be 250 to 300 WPM for silent reading and 125-150 WPM for oral reading.

H. Alan Robinson recommends several guidelines for flexibility in reading. He suggests a rate of 100 WPM for relatively difficult materials, a rate of 250 WPM for studying content-area materials, a rate of 500 WPM for pleasure reading, and a rate of up to 1,000 WPM for highly selective reading.[21]

Fluency

Reading fluency can generally be defined as the speed and ease of reading. However, Frank Guszak has identified several other characteristics.[22] Fluency in silent reading also means a smooth and rhythmic eye movement. Fluency in oral reading requires expressiveness, attention to punctuation, and appropriate intonation. Fluency affects, and is in turn affected by, proficiency in word recognition and comprehension.

Many secondary students do not have sufficient fluency. Exactly how many is not known, because most testing programs do not directly measure fluency. Many students classified as disabled readers have a below-average fluency rate. Roberta Golinkoff indicates that one char-

---

[19]Phyllis A. Miller, "Considering Flexibility of Reading Role for Assessment and Development of Efficient Reading Behavior," in S. Jay Samuels, ed., *What Research Has to Say About Reading Instruction* (Newark, Del.: International Reading Association, 1978), pp. 73–74.

[20]S. Jay Samuels and P. R. Dahl, "Establishing Appropriate Purpose for Reading and Its Effect on Flexibility of Reading Rate," *Journal of Educational Psychology* 67 (1975): 38–43.

[21] H. Alan Robinson, *Teaching Reading and Study Strategies* (Boston, Mass.: Allyn & Bacon, 1975).

[22]Frank J. Guszak, *Diagnostic Reading Instruction in the Elementary School,* 2nd ed. (New York: Harper & Row, 1978), pp. 70–78.

acteristic of poor comprehension is a slowness in the processing of information.[23]

Weaknesses in word recognition or comprehension will inhibit fluency. At the same time, a lack of fluency interferes with effective word recognition and comprehension. The nonfluent reader becomes bogged down in a laborous identification of the least meaningful types of information—single words, parts of words, or single letters. The relationships between words, which yield meaning, are not grasped. Frank Smith argues that nonfluent readers will be more successful if they speed up.[24] With a sense or expectancy of larger patterns (phrases and sentences), individual words become easier to analyze, and the reader can employ both context analysis and phonic or structural analysis.

Increasing Rate and Flexibility   Teachers can use the same instructional procedures both to help students increase their rate to minimum or average levels and to help students achieve flexibility. Effective procedures have four characteristics: 1) Students start with tasks with which they can succeed. 2) Students have repeated systematic practice to gradually increase their rate up to, then beyond, minimum levels. 3) Students have a means of measuring their progress. 4) Students do a variety of reading for different purposes. The following illustrates one basic procedure for increasing rate while still maintaining or improving comprehension: Students practice by reading material of the same length (250-, 500-, or 1,000-word selections) and the readings are timed. For the first task, students read at a comfortable rate to achieve sufficient comprehension (at least 75 percent comprehension). The teacher keeps track of the time on the chalkboard in 15-second intervals (1:00, 1:15, 1:30, etc). Students record the amount of time they spent reading the selection, then answer from five to ten questions. Each time students practice, they try to reduce slightly the amount of time needed to read the same amount of material. They record time and percentage of comprehension on a graph.

SUMMARY   The three areas of skills important to independent reading and learning in the content areas are: 1) study skills important to taking notes, reading textbooks, discussion preparation, test preparation, and paper writing; 2) the ability to locate and use information sources within textbooks, such as graphic aids; 3) the development of minimal levels of fluency and flexibility in reading. A teacher can incorporate instructional procedures for developing these abilities into effective teaching of the content area.

---

[23]Roberta M. Golinkoff, "A Comparison of Reading Comprehension Processes in Good and Poor Comprehension," *Reading Research Quarterly* 11:4 (1975–76): 623–59.
[24]Frank Smith, *Understanding Reading* (New York: Holt, Rinehart, & Winston, 1971), p. 103. Smith explores the differences between fluent and nonfluent readers throughout his book and in chapter 14 in particular.

1. Discuss one of the Key Ideas listed in the Overview at the beginning of this chapter.
2. Plan a lesson for teaching students to use the Picture and Text Survey procedure. Choose a selection from a content-area text and identify aids students might use in their survey and question steps.
3. Select or compose three to five key questions students could respond to in a discussion of a chapter in a content-area text. Read the chapter and write an informal response to the questions.
4. Read a chapter in a content-area text and think about how you could prepare a test on the chapter. Consider the type of test and types and samples of questions.
5. Evaluate a content-area textbook in terms of the helpfulness of textbooks aids. Decide on a criteria for evaluating the text, such as the variety of aids, the provision of aids to illustrate key concepts, and the instruction, if any, in using the aids.

Suggested Activities

Burmeister, Lou E. *Reading Strategies for Middle and Secondary School Teachers,* 2nd ed. Reading, Mass.: Addison-Wesley, 1978, Chapter 11.

Cohen, Ruth et al. *Quest: Academic Skills Program.* New York: Harcourt, Brace & Jovanovich, 1973.

Cottier, Susan, and Koehler, Shevi A. "A Study Skills Unit for Junior High Students," *Journal of Reading* 21:7 (April 1978): 626–30.

Dillner, Martha H., and Olson, Joanne P. *Personalizing Reading Instruction in Middle, Junior, Senior High Schools: Utilizing a Competency-Based Instructional System.* New York: Macmillan, 1977, Chapter 4.

Dunkeld, Colin, "Students' Notetaking and Teachers' Expectations," *Journal of Reading* 21:6 (March 1978): 542–46.

Hanskins, Joseph A., Jr., "How Should Reading and Study Skills Test Scores Correlate?" *Journal of Reading* 20:7 (April 1977): 570–72.

Herber, Harold L., ed. *Developing Study Skills in Secondary Reading.* Newark, Del.: International Reading Association, 1965.

Hunkins, Francis P. *Involving Students in Questioning.* Boston: Allyn & Bacon, 1976.

Jensen, Poul E., "Theories of Reading Speed and Comprehension," *Journal of Reading* 21:7 (April 1978): 542–46.

Karlin, Robert. *Teaching Reading in High School.* Indianapolis: Bobbs-Merrill, 1972.

Larsen, Janet J., and Guttinger, Helen I. "A Secondary Reading Program to Prevent College Reading Problems," *Journal of Reading* 22:5 (February 1979): 399–407.

Miller, Phyllis A. "Considering Flexibility of Reading Rate for Assessment and Development of Efficient Reading Behavior," in S. Jay Samuels, ed. *What Research Has to Say About Reading Instruction.* Newark, Del.: International Reading Association, 1978, pp. 72–83.

Robinson, Francis P. *Effective Study,* rev. ed. New York: Harper & Brothers, 1961.

Samuels, S. Jay, and Dahl, P. R. "Establishing Appropriate Purpose for Reading and Its Effect on Flexibility of Reading Rate," *Journal of Educational Psychology* 67 (1975): 38–43.

Schachter, Sunner W. "Developing Flexible Reading Habits," *Journal of Reading* 22:2 (November 1978): 149–52.

Shepherd, David, *Comprehensive High School Reading Methods.* Columbus, Ohio: Charles E. Merrill, 1973, Chapter 5.

Smith, Donald E. P. *The Adaptive Classroom,* Volume 3 of *A Technology of Reading and Writing:* New York: Academic Press, 1977.

Smith, Richard J., and Barrett, Thomas C. *Teaching Reading in the Middle Grades,* 2nd ed. Reading, Mass.: Addison-Wesley, 1979, Chapter 5.

Steiner, Karen, "ERIC/RCS: Speed Reading Revisited," *Journal of Reading* 22:2 (November 1978): 172–76.

Walker, James, "Techniques for Developing Study Skills," in Gerald G. Duffy, ed., *Reading in the Middle School.* Newark, Del.: International Reading Association, 1975, pp. 175–82.

Walter, Tim, and Siebert, Al. *Student Success: How to Be a Better Student and Still Have Time for Your Friends* New York: Holt, Rinehart, & Winston, 1976.

Recommended Readings

6

Basic Instructional Strategies

Strategies for planning and conducting instruction which are applicable **OVERVIEW** to all content areas can integrate content-area learning and reading development. First, the teacher should provide structured learning experiences but with choices available to students that have different abilities and interests. Second, the teacher should provide assistance when students have difficulty but, at the same time, should encourage students and help them to develop independence.

The strategies that this chapter will present counter some widespread weaknesses in secondary-school education. Harold Herber believes that many teachers tend to assume too much about students' abilities and interests and, as a result, provide insufficient structure and assistance. He characterizes such instruction as "assumptive teaching" and identifies the often erroneous assumptions:

> that students have sufficient maturity and skill to handle the assignments, that they have sufficient command of skills to ferret out the significant points on which to report; that they have sufficient organizational skills to marshall all of the information and present it in coherent form. Frequently, structure is lacking in lessons and assignments; students occasionally are uncertain *what* they are to do; they are often uncertain *how* to do what has been assigned. . . . That is, the teacher assumes students already have the skills and already know the concepts he is supposed to teach them.[1]

This chapter will present a view of the whole learning experience by discussing the steps of the Directed Reading Activity, an approach to planning and conducting instruction.

---

[1]Harold L. Herber, *Teaching Reading in Content-Areas* (Englewood Cliffs, N.J.: Prentice-Hall, 1970), pp. vii–viii.

Key Ideas   The five-step Directed Reading Activity relates content learning to reading instruction.

An effective learning experience includes preassessment, identification and production tasks, teaching by demonstration, and confirmation tasks.

Mr. Hightower is conducting a lesson on the German words for numbers in first-year German. To prepare the students, Mr. Hightower asks them to consider situations they might encounter on a trip to Germany in which numbers would be important. He then states the goal of the lesson: students should be able to spell the word for each German number correctly and to pronounce each one correctly in short dialogues. Students begin reading the chapter silently. The teacher stops them, pronounces the words, discusses their structures, and asks for questions. After students finish reading, they practice dialogues in small groups. As an extension activity, students compose their own dialogues.

THE DIRECTED READING ACTIVITY

The Directed Reading Activity (or Directed Reading Lesson) is widely recommended for relating instruction in both content and reading.[2] It is used at the elementary, middle, and secondary levels in both content-area and reading courses. The DRA is not a specific method of teaching; rather, it is a systematic approach to planning and conducting instruction, which can encompass a variety of methods and learning activities for students.

There are five steps in the DRA, which can be spread over a few class periods, a week, or more than a week of instruction.

The following is an example of a DRA in English:

Goals:

1. Students will be exposed to short stories.
2. Students will develop understanding of plot.
3. Students will improve ability to read for inferences.

Materials:

1. *A & P*, by John Updike.
2. Annotated list of short stories for self-selection.

---

[2]Martha H. Dillner and Joanne P. Olson, *Personalizing Reading Instruction in Middle, Junior and Senior High Schools* (New York: Macmillan, 1977), pp. 144–50; Lou E. Burmeister, *Reading Strategies for Middle and Secondary School Teachers*, 2nd ed. (Reading, Mass.: Addison-Wesley, 1978), pp. 94–100; and Herber, *Teaching Reading in Content-Areas*, pp. 31–39.

Step 1. Preparation

1. For interest, the teacher can relate the plot to the student's experience by having students discuss rules and conflicts between adolescents and adults over rules.
2. For purpose, the teacher can define *plot* as the interaction between incidents in the story and characters.
3. For procedure and skills, the teacher can review the steps in the survey procedure and make a list on the chalkboard showing a variation students can follow.

Step 2. Silent Reading

After students read the first third of story, they can stop and write informal answers to "What has happened so far?" and "What do you think will happen next?"

Step 3. Oral Reading and Discussion

The teacher asks students to share answers in this step. If a student disagrees, he or she has to refer to words in the text. Predictions are listed on chalkboard.

Step 4. Follow-up

1. At home, students read to the middle of the story, stop and answer questions as in Step 2, and then finish the story.
2. In class, students discuss their predictions in small groups, then each group reports to the whole class.
3. Students select a story from the list and repeat the process.

Step 5. Extension

Students select a third story and either write a discussion of the plot or an essay discussing criteria for effective plot. They can also write an original ending to one of the stories or an original story.

Step 1. Preparation

The first step in conducting instruction prepares the students for the learning experience and for the accompanying reading assignments. Dillner and Olson have identified five tasks for the teacher in Step 1: 1) motivating the student; 2) setting purposes for reading; 3) developing concepts involved; 4) identifying problem words; and 5) creating an awareness of the necessary reading skills needed.[3] Burmeister adds a sixth task—that of relating the new assignment to previous learning, by exploring and building upon a student's background.[4] These tasks can overlap.

---

[3]Dillner and Olson, *Personalizing Reading Instruction*, p. 144.
[4]Burmeister, *Reading Strategies*, p. 94.

Motivation. Motivation can be instilled in a variety of ways and can be aided by the other tasks. Knowing the purpose of the assignment and the skills to be stressed can contribute to motivation. At the very least, students' anxiety about the new assignment will be reduced by the knowledge of what is expected of them and by their feeling that the teacher has given some consideration to organizing the learning experience.

Setting Purposes. Often teachers have fairly specific expectations of what they want students to gain from their reading. These can be translated into prequestions. If the English teacher wants students to focus on the behavior of the main character in a story, he or she can provide a general question (How does the main character behave?) or more specific questions (Who is the main character? Why do you think so? What does he or she do? Why?) If the industrial-arts teacher wants students to read a handout carefully enough to operate machinery, it might be appropriate to ask the students to read the handout on the hacksaw and construct a chart with the steps for operating the saw.

In many situations, teachers may not have specific expectations. They may simply want students to read thoroughly or to discover their own purposes for reading. In both cases, use of the survey procedure is appropriate. The practical purpose for reading is to perform the survey and question steps (read to gain an overview, write at least five questions, and find the answers), as discussed in Chapter 5. The following chart illustrates the relationship between the DRA and the survey procedure.

- Directed Reading Activity
  Teacher tasks
  Step 1. Preparation
  Teacher prepares students for assignment.
  Step 2. Silent Reading
  Teacher assigns selection.

  Step 3. Oral Reading/Discussion
  Teacher invites contributions.

  Step 4. Follow-up
  Teacher determines evaluation.

- Survey Procedure
  Student tasks

  Students survey text for preview.

  Students pose questions and read to find answers.

  Students contribute their questions and answers.

Step 5. Extension

Teacher provides choices for activities.	Students use notes to prepare for activities.

Introducing Concepts. A teacher can emphasize particular concepts by identifying and illustrating them. A motivating introduction relates the concepts to students' immediate experiences. Often the concept can be related to an actual problem students might face; for example, an English teacher could translate the plot of a story into a situation students could encounter. The mathematics teacher could give students a problem which requires application of the new concept: "Here is 10 dollars (in play money). Let's say you found it and plan to spend it at an amusement park. Decide what items you'd like to spend it on, then we will figure out what *percentage* of the money you'll need for each item."

Identifying New Terminology. In presenting new concepts, teachers are also introducing new terminology. An alternative to immediate illustration is preassessment, where students are asked to respond to new terms before they are discussed. The test is then reviewed, and students check their own or each others' responses. During the review, concepts are illustrated.

Stressing Reading Skills. An important part of the Directed Reading Activity is the emphasis on only one skill or on a few related skills. The skills being stressed should be consistent with the purposes for reading. Reading to locate details about characters and to make inferences about characters would be appropriate if the purpose were to interpret the characters' motivation. In mathematics, literal comprehension and reading for application would be relevant to a selection which explicitly presented steps for solving a problem.

Following the preparation step, students read the selection silently. *Step 2. Silent Reading*
Typically, students are expected to read an entire selection on their own as homework. Some modifications have proved more effective.

First, the purpose should be translated into a task (or a set of questions), which is copied by the students or given as a handout. Second, students start the assignment in class then stop to have their understanding checked either individually or as a group. The teacher will then know 1) if students have started the assignment; 2) if they can read it independently; and 3) if they have paid attention to the directions and can understand them. Students then finish the reading at home or during subsequent classes.

Dillner and Olson note that oral reading and discussion can follow the *Step 3. Oral Reading and*
silent reading. An alternative would be to intersperse occasions for oral *Discussion*
reading and discussion between periods of silent reading. Either way,

the teacher uses this step to clarify a student's understanding of the reading purposes, the new concepts, and the skills to be developed.[5]

Oral reading in the Directed Reading Activity, whether by the teacher or by student volunteers, serves two purposes:

First, the teacher can use oral reading to clarify the purpose of a lesson. For example, if the teacher is stressing character interpretation, the teacher or a student volunteer can read and discuss a passage that describes a particular character.

Second, students can read a passage that will support their responses to questions. For example, a student might read a passage from a mathematics chapter to justify procedures he or she used in solving a problem.

Herber recommends a procedure that takes the students through the process of comprehension[6] and is similar to the strategy of sequencing comprehension questions by level (see Chapter 4). The teacher provides a set of questions on the passage which move from literal comprehension to the higher levels of comprehension. Examples of questions for a short story would be "List some incidents in the story," "Summarize the plot," or "What do these incidents and the plot show about the characters?" In responding, students can read selectively from the story to support their answers.

Step 4: Follow-up   When the class has completed and discussed the entire selection, they may still need some follow-up activity. If the assignment has been spread out over a long period of time and interspersed with oral reading and discussion, a summary discussion would pull the material together. A test to evaluate the students' understanding of the material would also be appropriate.

Teachers could provide further practice in the skill stressed during the DRA for those students demonstrating a need for it. Similarly, students may show a need for additional reading, discussion, or other activities for developing further understanding of the concepts already presented.

Step 5: Extension Activities   An optional step in the DRA is an extension activity.[7] As the term suggests, the activity takes the students beyond what was covered during earlier steps, but it will not be an entirely new lesson. Dillner and Olson recommend supplementary reading, dramatization and other creative activities, rereading the material for a different purpose, and the use of games.[8] Burmeister further recommends opportunities for stu-

---

[5]Dillner and Olson, *Personalizing Reading Instruction*, p. 146.
[6]Herber, *Teaching Reading in Content-Areas*, p. 92.
[7]Dillner and Olson, *Personalizing Reading Instruction*, p. 147.
[8]Dillner and Olson, *Personalizing Reading Instruction*, pp. 147–50.

dents to experience the content through sources other than reading, such as with an interview or film or television show.[9]

Whatever the form, extension activities typically require students to operate at a higher skill and cognitive level than the earlier steps required. Application, synthesis, and evaluation responses would be appropriate extension activities as would expression of these responses in creative and challenging tasks. If the previous instruction has been effective, students will have a sufficient knowledge base and will have demonstrated some degree of understanding of the content, the text, and the skills they were to employ. They will therefore be ready for higher level responses.

Since a variety of activities is possible, the extension step is an excellent occasion for the teacher to provide a choice of activities for students with different interests and abilities. By making a choice, students have the opportunity to exercise independence. Students can also make their own suggestions for extension activities.

The steps of the Directed Reading Activity provide a structured view of the learning experience. The following discussion will stress ways teachers can plan and conduct effective instruction in various phases of the learning experience.

Educators such as Edgar Dale and Joseph O'Rourke recommend pre-assessing students' knowledge of vocabulary at the beginning of instruction.[10] Preassessment can also be used to measure comprehension, study skills, library skills, and various content-area skills and knowledge.

With preassessment the teacher collects information about students which is pertinent to the goals or purposes of the learning experience, such as a week's series of lessons or a multiweek unit. The teacher collects this information at the beginning of the learning experience, in Step 1 of the DRA or at the start of Step 2 (silent reading). The information is used to make decisions about the nature and quantity of instruction students need. The responses to the preassessment can be compared to responses to a similar postassessment to evaluate both the student's achievement and the effectiveness of the instruction. For example, a student might respond to only two key terms on a preassessment, but at the end of the week he or she would be able to respond to all ten key terms. This change is a good indication of the week's accomplishments.

The tasks used in pretests can be similar to the tasks provided for practice. Teachers do not have to feel they are neglecting instruction

COMPONENTS OF THE LEARNING EXPERIENCE
Preassessment

---

[9]Burmeister, *Reading Strategies*, p. 100.
[10]Edgar Dale and Joseph O'Rourke, *Techniques of Teaching Vocabulary* (Palo Alto, Calif.: Field Educational Publication, 1971), pp. 20-26.

when they are giving tests. In fact, the preassessment can be viewed as the first practice students do or their first attempt at the response. In addition, the tasks for preassessment and practice can be written for the content-area material; students are reading their assignments while taking the preassessment and practicing. This process is illustrated below:

Preassessment:

Read pp. 13-14, chapter 1., *Modern Grammar and Composition*. Try to do the following:
1. Survey the pages for a general idea.
2. Write at least five questions for the pages.
3. Find and write answers to your questions.

Instruction:

Teacher Instruction:
The teacher reviews pp. 13-14 and presents appropriate questions and answers.
Student Practice:
Read pp. 15-17 and
1. Survey the pages for a general idea.
2. Write at least five questions for the pages.
3. Find and write answers to your questions.

Postassessment:

Read pp. 18-19 and
1. Survey the pages for a general idea.
2. Write at least five questions for the pages.
3. Find and write answers to your questions.

Identificaton and Production Tasks students perform in both assessment and instruction can be categorized as *identification* or *production* tasks. In identification tasks, several responses are provided and the student must identify the most appropriate. In production tasks, the student must supply the appropriate answer. Generally, production tasks are more difficult and more meaningful than identification tasks. In many cases, teachers can provide both types. With the identification responses, students learn to recognize an appropriate response and then learn to produce their own appropriate responses.

Matching and Multiple Choice. Identification tasks commonly use either matching or multiple choice exercises. Examples of both were provided for vocabulary skills in Chapter 3 (see pages 45-47). Both can also be used for developing comprehension and study skills. The following selection presents an example for assessing the ability to read index entries:

Use the entries from the *Reader's Guide to Periodical Literature*.
Match the type of information with the appropriate items in the entries.

HOUSE decoration
   Dear House & Garden. . . ; questions and an-
     swers. House & Gard 149:24 O; 38-9 N; 54+ D
     '77
   Imagination, country style; house of S. Parish
     in Maine. il House & Gard 149:110-15 D
     '77
   Rethinking closets, kitchens, and other forgot-
     ten spaces. S. Torre and others. il Ms 6:54-5 D
     '77
      See also
   Christmas decorations
HOUSE decoration, Exterior
    See also
   Christmas decorations, Outdoor
HOUSE guests. See Guests
HOUSE plant
   Easy to grow house plants:
     Dwarf palm. E. McDonald. il House B 119:
      80 D '77
   Plants around the house:
     How to keep your holiday plants blooming.
     R. Langer. il House & Gard 149:30+ D '77
HOUSES, Remodeled
   Old house spreads its wing; R. Stern. il House
   & Gard 149:122-7 D '77
HOUSING

1. The subject	a. House plants
2. The topic	b. House & Gard
3. The name of a magazine	c. D
4. The month of the issue	d. House
5. The pages	e. 30

The following task assesses a student's ability to use an encyclopedia:

- Read the following and decide where to look for information in an
  encyclopedia. Circle the letter of the correct answer.
  1. Jerry was surprised to hear that the Los Angeles area is a major
  center for agriculture. What main topic should he look under first?
     a. Los Angeles   b. Agriculture
  2. Jerry found little information about agriculture in Los Angeles.
  Where might he look next?
     a. Farming   b. California
  3. What subtopic would he look for in an entry in California?
     a. Cities   b. Agriculture

Production Tasks. Production tasks can take a variety of forms which
range in difficulty. Students can supply words from the text (simple
literal comprehension) or respond in their own words (translation). The
tasks can call for the higher levels of comprehension and cognition:
interpretation, application, analysis, synthesis, and evaluation. The
same tasks presented as examples in Chapter 4 can be used for either

assessment or practice. Students can express their answers in increasingly difficult ways: words or phrases, complete sentences, a multisentence informal response, or a well-composed, polished paragraph or essay.

Teaching by Demonstration While students can profit from taking a pretest, often they will need something more. What they require is not further explanation but a demonstration; they need to be shown rather than told. In learning theory, this idea of teaching by example means providing a model of what is to be learned. These models can be presented during Step 3 of the DRA (oral reading and discussion).

In many cases, the model can be examples of the types of answers students are to find in the text in response to guiding questions. The teacher can present the sample answers underlined or circled in the text. Or, the teacher can read the appropriate words in the text, as was discussed earlier in Step 3 of the Directed Reading Activity. The teacher can also invite students to contribute answers and write them on the chalkboard. Such a procedure is important when there may be more than one appropriate answer or different way of expressing the answer.

In many cases, students are to learn multistep procedures, such as study-skill procedures or a computation procedure in mathematics. It is sometimes helpful for the teacher to take the students through the entire performance by demonstrating (or inviting demonstrations of) each step. As an example, the SOQAC procedure can be used as follows:

1. Survey:

   First I will survey or quickly look over this chapter. Notice that I'm not reading word by word. I'm looking for main points, subheadings, and illustrations. (Teacher surveys the chapter.)

2. Organize:

   Did I get anything from my survey? To find out, I'll try to write an organizing statement: "There are important rules that influence our federal government's decision making." (He or she writes on chalkboard.) I got that partly from the title, on page 260, and the subheadings, on pages 262 and 264.

3. Questions:

   Here are some questions I think would be answered in this chapter: "What are the important rules?" "Where are they stated?" "What is a federal system?" "How is power separated among branches of government?" (These and other questions are written on the chalkboard.)

4. Answer:

   Now before I read, I want to see how much I already know so I'll try to answer these questions. "What are the important rules?" That's a tough one. I would think the rules have to do with how our federal government works. One rule is that branches of government have separate powers. (This statement is written on the chalkboard with the other answers.)

5. Confirm:

Now I want to confirm, complete, or revise my answers; so I'll read with my questions in mind. For my first question I'll go right to that subheading: "Some Important Rules that Influence Government."

Lillian Putnam recommends the use of models in showing students how to read for main ideas.[11] In this case, the student's assignment is to produce a good outline. After the students have read five to six paragraphs, the teacher presents three statements: one good example and two poor ones. Students try to pick the best statement for an outline.

Subsequent activities require students to complete partial outlines. If the teacher presents an outline with major points listed in order, the students must read to find supporting ideas or key details. The process can also be reversed with the teacher presenting the supporting ideas or key details. The final task is for students to write a complete outline on their own. All these exercises can be used for regularly assigned selections from the content-area text.

Models and Attention. One reason models may not be effective is a lack of attention. Students need to pay attention, in general, to the teacher's demonstration; that is, they cannot be talking, daydreaming, or looking around the room. More than that, they need to attend to the specific distinctive features of the model, those features that distinguish one type of response from other types.

To illustrate, if the English teacher wants students to learn to recognize and interpret similes, he or she reads a stanza and notes the simile: "'My love is like a red, red rose.' That's a simile. It would be different if the poet had said, 'My love is like a dying rose.' Now you read this poem and find some similes." Students must attend to the comparison signaled by "is like." A student might, however, attend to what is being compared. He or she might conclude that similes are any image of flowers. In spelling, if a student attends only to the letters but not to their order, he or she might spell *their* as *thier* and *there* as *theer*.

Multiple-Choice Tasks. One way to help students attend to distinctive features is by providing a multiple-choice task. Initially the task should be relatively simple; only one or two inappropriate answers will be included because they differ in a distinctive way from the appropriate answer. In selecting the right answer, the student must attend to the key

---

[11]Lillian R. Putnam, "Don't Tell Them to Do It . . . Show Them How" in W. John Harker, ed. *Classroom Strategies for Secondary Reading* (Newark, Del.: International Reading Association, 1977), pp. 70–73.

Figure 6.1
A Page from a History Textbook

THE SEARCH FOR PEACE

cussion." Russia's request, finally, that Germany surrender to Poland the area east of the Oder and Neisse rivers was also left undecided. All that the Western Allies conceded was that Poland "must receive substantial accessions of territory in the North and West." As far as Germany was concerned, the Yalta meeting was thus notable for the postponement rather than the solution of issues. The only firm agreement was on the postwar division of the country into four occupation zones (including one for France) under an Allied Control Council. The capital of Berlin, situated within the Soviet occupation zone, was to be occupied and administered jointly; but no specific agreement was made guaranteeing Western access to the city.

Most of the time at Yalta was spent trying to establish Poland's postwar frontiers and to agree on her provisional government. The Soviet Union, for reasons of her own security, claimed a special interest in the Polish question. The fact that she was in actual possession of the country greatly strengthened her position. The problem of what territory Russia was to receive caused few difficulties. Prior to Yalta the Western leaders had already consented to the "Curzon Line" (drawn up after World War I, but subsequently ignored), and with some modifications this boundary was approved at Yalta. Russia thus received about 47 per cent of Poland's prewar territory. Her effort to compensate Poland at Germany's expense, as we have just seen, though recognized in principle, was postponed for the time being.

The real headache developed over the formation of Poland's future government. There were at the time two provisional governments, the Polish government-in-exile in London and the Soviet-sponsored Committee of National Liberation at Lublin. The Russians insisted that a new government be formed by enlarging the Lublin group. Despite protests from the London Poles, the Western powers finally gave way on this crucial point. Their decision was made easier because the new Polish government was to hold "free and unfettered elections on the basis of universal suffrage and secret ballot." A similar promise of free elections for the other liberated peoples in central and eastern Europe was embodied in a simultaneous "Declaration on Liberated Europe." Having already resisted Soviet aims in Germany and hoping to gain Russian participation in the Pacific war and in the United Nations, the Western powers obviously shrank from making too much of an issue over a region which was so clearly within the Russian orbit.

7

Source: Hans W. Gatzke, *The Present in Perspective: A Look at the World Since 1945*, 2nd ed. (Chicago: Rand McNally, 1961), p. 7. Used with permission.

difference or distinctive features. Putnam's exercise on outlining main ideas operates as a multiple-choice exercise. The following exercise shows a set of multiple-choice exercises on the features of similes:

1. This is a simile:
   "My love is like a red, red rose."
   Which is a simile?
   a. A fragile orchid.
   b. My love is like a fragile orchid.
   a. My brother thinks he's a movie star.
   b. My brother acts like a movie star.

2. This is a simile:
   "He is crazy as a loon."
   Which is a simile?
   a. She is slow as ketchup.
   b. She is slow as can be.
   a. They are as close as a bandaid on skin.
   b. They are as close as possible.

A rationale for the use of such multiple-choice tasks can be found in a theory of discrimination learning developed by Donald E. P. Smith.[12] Smith recommends discrimination tasks which consist of a model and a choice between the desirable item (which matches the model) and other items. To make the appropriate choice, the student must compare items to the model and in so doing discover the distinctive features.

Instructional tasks which ask for a confirmation response also help students attend to distinctive features. In this type of task, the teacher presents a statement or piece of information to the student. The student reads the text to confirm the correctness of the item. The student points to, reads aloud, underlines, or circles words in the text to confirm the item. The task can consist of 1) a statement to be confirmed; 2) a question with the answer; or 3) a multiple-choice question with the correct answer circled. An example of a confirmation task for the passage in Figure 6.1 follows:

The Confirmation Task

Teacher:

Which issue about Poland caused the most difficulty at Yalta? I think the answer is "Poland's future government rather than its borders." What words on page 7 confirm my answer?

---

[12]Donald E. P. Smith, *Learning to Read and Write: A Task Analysis*, Volume 1. *A Technology of Reading and Writing* (New York: Academic Press, 1976).

Students:

> "The real headache developed over the formulation of Poland's future government."

Harold Herber and Joan Nelson[13] argue that questions alone are ineffective if students have not already developed the skills required to answer the questions. Instead, students should be given key statements, phrases, or terms which are the same as, or similar to, words in the text. After reading the text, students make a response which demonstrates some form of comprehension. The following is an example of a confirmation task:

> Of the following statements about government, only some are true about our form of government. Read pages 260–66. Circle the ones that are confirmed by the text.
> 1. A federal system has a division of powers.
> 2. A federal system is a unitary system.
> 3. The federal and state governments share some powers.
> 4. The federal government has totally different powers from the states.
> 5. The branches of the federal government share the same powers.
> 6. Each branch has its own powers.

Once students can respond to these tasks, the teacher can then give them questions to answer.

SUMMARY This chapter presented some strategies for planning and conducting instruction within the framework of the five steps of the Directed Reading Activity. With procedures for preassessment, direct instruction, and student practice, teachers clarify their expectations for student performance, both in understanding content and in applying particular reading skills. Teachers can then provide instruction that will guide students in meeting those expectations.

---

[13]Harold L. Herber and Joan B. Nelson, "Questioning Is Not the Answer," in W. John Harker, ed., *Classroom Strategies for Secondary Reading* (Newark, Del.: International Reading Association, 1977), pp. 48–54

1. Discuss one of the points listed in the Overview at the beginning of this chapter.
2. After selecting a goal for content-area learning, pick an appropriate text selection and outline a Directed Reading Activity.
3. Describe procedures for developing motivation for study of your content area.
4. Write tasks which can be used in pre- and post-assessment of a reading skill important to your content area.
5. Describe procedures for demonstrating appropriate responses to a reading task relevant to your content area. Relate the procedures to a reading selection.

Aukerman, Robert C. *Reading in the Secondary School Classroom.* New York: McGraw-Hill, 1972.

Bruner, Jerome S. *Towards A Theory of Instruction.* Cambridge, Mass: Harvard University Press, 1967.

Burmeister, Lou E. *Reading Strategies for Middle and Secondary School Teachers,* 2nd ed. Reading, Mass.: Addison-Wesley, 1978, chap. 5.

Dale, Edgar, and O'Rourke, Joseph. *Techniques of Teaching Vocabulary.* Palo Alto, Calif.: Field Educational Publication, 1971.

Dillner, Martha H., and Olson, Joanne P. *Personalizing Reading Instruction in Middle, Junior, and Senior High Schools: Utilizing a Competency-Based Instructional System.* New York: Macmillan, 1977, chaps. 7, 9, and 10.

Duffy, George G., ed., *Reading in the Middle School.* Newark, Del.: International Reading Association, 1975.

Dunkeld, Colin. "Students' Notetaking and Teachers' Expectations," *Journal of Reading* 21:6 (March 1978); 542–46.

Earle, Richard A., ed. *Classroom Practice in Reading.* Newark, Del.: International Reading Association, 1977.

Gartner, Alan. *Children Teach Children: Learning by Teaching.* New York: Harper & Row, 1976.

Herber, Harold L. *Teaching Reading in Content-Areas.* Englewood Cliffs, N.J.: Prentice-Hall, 1970, chaps. 2 and 3.

Herber, Harold L., and Nelson, Joan B. "Questioning Is Not the Answer," in W. John Harker, ed., *Classroom Strategies for Secondary Reading.* Newark, Del.: International Reading Assocation, 1977.

Marrogenes, Nancy A., and Galen, Nancy D. "Cross-Age Tutoring: Why and How." *Journal of Reading* 22: 4 (January 1979): 344–53.

Provenmire, E. Kingsley. "Advantages of Verse Choir for Reading." *Journal of Reading* 30:7 (April 1977): 761–64.

Rickards, John P., and Hatcher, Catherine W. "Interspersed Meaningful Learning Questions as Semantic Cues for Poor Comprehenders," *Reading Research Quarterly* 13:4 (1977–78): 539–53.

Smith, Donald E. P. *Learning to Read and Write: A Task Analysis.* Volume 1. *A Technology of Reading and Writing.* New York: Academic Press, 1976.

Smith, Richard J., and Barrett, Thomas C. *Teaching Reading in the Middle Grades,* 2nd ed. Reading, Mass.: Addison-Wesley, 1979, chap. 8.

Steiner, Karen. "ERIC/RCS: Peer Tutoring in the Reading Class." *Journal of Reading* 21: 3 (December 1977): 266–69.

Thomas, Ellen, and Robinson, H. Alan. *Improving Reading in Every Class: A Source Botk for Teachers.* Boston: Allyn & Bacon, 1972.

Widmann, Victor F. "Developing Oral Reading Ability in Teenagers through Presentation of Children's Stories," *Journal of Reading* 21: 4 (January 1978): 329–34.

Assessing Content-Area Reading

As teachers plan and conduct instruction in their content areas, they need to collect information about students' reading abilities which will be relevant to instructional goals. Part 2 discusses a variety of approaches to reading assessment. Chapter 7 presents procedures for measuring the readability of materials used in testing and instruction. Chapter 8 examines standardized tests. Chapter 9 presents procedures for designing, using, and interpreting informal assessment instruments. Chapter 10 discusses the related concepts of the role of feedback in instruction and self-assessment by students.

7

Readability

One goal of teaching is to provide instruction appropriate to each student's abilities. To meet this goal, teachers need to consider: the students' reading abilities, the difficulty of the materials students will read, and the difficulty of the task students will perform in response to the reading. This chapter recommends a systematic approach in which the teacher assesses both the potential difficulty of the material and student ability and then uses both assessments to make decisions about the tasks. The three steps for assessing material include: 1) estimating the difficulty level with a readability formula; 2) examining the material for other potential difficulties not measured by the formula; and 3) examining the material for potential reading aids.

OVERVIEW

Readability is an objective measurement of the difficulty of reading materials.

Teachers can use readability formulas as a guide 1) for selecting materials for classes and 2) for rewriting materials to change the reading level.

Textbook aids improve readability by making material more interesting and by reducing the difficulty.

Teachers can modify the difficulty of reading assignments according to the student's reading ability.

Key Ideas

The following three teachers are effectively dealing with readability problems. All three examined their textbooks to identify potential reading difficulties and modified their instruction to help their students meet these difficulties.

Mr. Henna, who teaches math, was busily preparing overhead transparencies which presented numerous examples of mathematic concepts. His students were working in small groups on elaborate models of various geometric shapes. Mr. Henna had discovered that the textbook had two major difficulties. It introduced new concepts at a relatively high rate and it had very few illustrations of these concepts.

Ms. Simmons had a reputation of being very effective in helping students with reading in her literature courses. Visitors to her class were somewhat disappointed to find her using traditional methods: presenting study-guide questions; going over key vocabulary before assigning selections; and asking students to read some selections aloud. She explained to her visitors that she did not choose these methods haphazardly or simply for variety. Rather, she based her choices on an assessment of the readability of selections and on an informal assessment of the students' ability to read the selections. For example, one of the stories had difficult vocabulary, so she chose certain methods of teaching it.

Mr. Horton, a social-studies teacher, was using three versions of a U.S. history text in his ninth-grade class. At the beginning of the year, he used a readability formula on the text, which was labeled a ninth-grade text. However, he found the text had a 12th-grade readability level. The standardized reading test scores for his students indicated that the text would be too difficult for three fourths of the class. Happily, the school district had lower levels of the same text.

READABILITY: A DEFINITION

When people describe something as *readable,* they are usually making a subjective response to either the style or the content. They find the material easy or interesting to read. More technically, *readability* refers to an objectively measured level of difficulty, usually measured by a *readability formula.* A readability formula measures style not content. The most widely used formulas measure only two aspects of style—word difficulty and sentence difficulty.

READABILITY SORMULAS

Readability formulas have been developed for three purposes: as a research tool to measure particular variables in reading, such as sentence length; as a guide for publishers in preparing materials for particular grade levels; and as a guide for teachers in determining the appropriateness of materials. The more than 30 formulas differ in: 1) the kind and number of variables they measure; 2) the degree of difficulty and amount of time required to use them; 3) the computational procedures, and 4) the grade levels of materials they are designed to measure. Most formulas measure only word and sentence length as functions of word and sentence difficulty and are comparatively easy to use. Among these are the Fry Formula, which can be used with materials from first-grade through college; the Flesch Formula, for fifth-grade through college; and the Wheeler and Smith Formula, for preprimer to fourth grade.

Formulas are useful in making predictions about difficulty of material and in ranking materials according to their difficulty. Most formulas are limited in the factors they measure. They all fail to measure student ability; therefore, it is necessary to evaluate the results of the formula against the actual student responses in reading the material. As Mary Monteith notes, "The ultimate test of readability lies with the individual student."[1]

Most formulas are based on one of two theoretical assumptions about the reading process. The first is that the successful reader can respond effectively to a variety of linguistic units, which Walter MacGinitie identifies as "phonemes, syllables, words, phrases, and sentences."[2] The process of responding is complex in itself, requiring the reader to "recognize, analyze, combine, and recombine" the units.[3] It is generally believed that the longer and more complex the unit, the more difficult the reading. Therefore, a passage with many long and complex words and sentences ought to be more demanding than an equally well-written passage on the same content with shorter and simpler words and sentences.

The second assumption is that the successful reader interacts with the text and does not just passively receive information from it. This interaction requires the reader to bring his or her knowledge and experience to the act of reading. The more knowledge and experience the reader has of the language and content of a passage, the easier the task should be. Stated in a negative way, the greater the number of unfamiliar words and concepts, the more difficult the task. As this chapter will show, most formulas are used to measure either familiarity or length and complexity.

The Fry Formula, developed by Edward Fry, is in wide use because of the range of levels it can measure and because of its reliability. Figure 7.1 gives directions for using the formula.[4] The directions specify the following seven steps.[5] *The Fry Formula*

---

[1]Mary K. Monteith, "ERIC/RC: Readability Formulas," *Journal of Reading* 19:7 (April 1976): 604–7.
[2]Walter H. MacGinitie, "Children's Understanding of Linguistic Units," in S. Jay Samuels, ed., *What Research Has to Say About Reading Instruction* (Newark, Del.: International Reading Association, 1978), p. 43.
[3]MacGinitie, "Children's Understanding of Linguistic Units," p. 43.
[4]Edward Fry, "A Readability Formula that Saves Time," in John Harker, ed., *Classroom Strategies for Secondary Reading* (Newark, Del.: International Reading Association, 1977).
[5]Edward Fry, "Judging Readability of Books," *Teacher Education* 5 (1964): 34–39.

Figure 7.1
The Fry Formula Graph

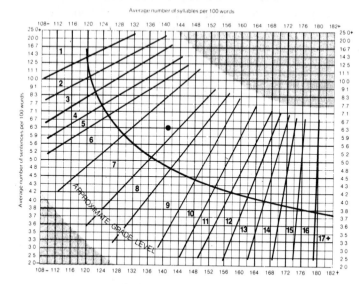

Figure 2

GRAPH FOR ESTIMATING READABILITY —EXTENDED

by Edward Fry, Rutgers University Reading Center, New Brunswick, N.J. 08904

Expanded Directions for Working Readability Graph

1. Randomly select three (3) sample passages and count out exactly 100 words each, beginning with the beginning of a sentence. Do count proper nouns, initializations, and numerals.
2. Count the number of sentences in the hundred words, estimating length of the fraction of the last sentence to the nearest one-tenth.
3. Count the total number of syllables in the 100-word passage. If you don't have a hand counter available, an easy way is to simply put a mark above every syllable over one in each word, then when you get to the end of the passage, count the number of marks and add 100. Small calculators can also be used as counters by pushing numeral 1, then push the + sign for each word or syllable when counting.
4. Enter graph with *average* sentence length and *average* number of syllables; plot dot where the two lines intersect. Area where dot is plotted will give you the approximate grade level.
5. If a great deal of variability is found in syllable count or sentence count, putting more samples into the average is desirable.
6. A word is defined as a group of symbols with a space on either side; thus, *Joe, IRA, 1945,* and *&* are each one word.
7. A syllable is defined as a phonetic syllable. Generally, there are as many syllables as vowel sounds. For example, *stopped* is one syllable and *wanted* is two syllables. When counting syllables for numerals and initializations, count one syllable for each symbol. For example, *1945* is four syllables, *IRA* is three syllables, and *&* is one syllable.

Note: This "extended graph" does not outmode or render the earlier (1968) version inoperative or inaccurate; it is an extension. (REPRODUCTION PERMITTED—NO COPYRIGHT)

Step 1: Select three 100-word passages from the beginning, middle, and end of the material. Because most texts range in readability from one section to another, a minimum of three passages are necessary for analysis. The Fry Formula does not count numbers as words, but it does count proper names as words because proper names can be a source of difficulty.[6] Below are samples of three 100-word passages from a history textbook:

Passage 1

```
      1    2  1 1    3    1    2    1   2   1    2    2
      The story of the United States begins in Asia, and Asian affairs
  1      2    1    4     2     1    4     2    2    1
  have remained a remarkable concern of Americans. Many thousands of
   1  2    2    2     2  1   1   2    1     4    1  2
  years ago, Asian hunters began to move into North America by cross-
      2   1      3    1   1  1      3      1   1  1
  ing Bering Strait. Gradually they and their descendants spread out and
      3    1   3    2    1  1   2     2   1  1  1   1 1
  occupied large areas reaching from the polar regions of the North to the
   2     2    1  1  1  1   1    4
  southern portion of what we call South America.
         4       1   1   2    1   2    1   1   1 1
      Adventurous men and women must also have dared to leave
   2   1   3   1  1   2  1 1    4       3     1  1  1
  Europe and Africa and to travel to the American continents. Of none of
   1    2     2    1  1  1   2   2    1   1  1  1  1 1
  these likely journeys do we have any certain proof. Yet we are sure that
   2    1    2      2   1   1    4    1  1  1   1
  Vikings from northern Europe were in America in the tenth and
      3       3
  eleventh centuries.[7]
```

Passage 2

```
      3     1  1 3    1  1  2    1  1   2    1    3
      Committed to the policy of the open door in China, the United
  1     3    1  2    1     3     2  2     4     1
  States directed its efforts toward preventing any nation—European or
   2   1    2    1  1  1   1    3    1    2   1 1
  Asian—from slamming the door shut. The United States also said it
```

---

[6]In one study on conducting a silent Informal Reading Inventory in secondary social studies classes, students were asked to underline words which caused them difficulty. A majority of students reading below grade level in school underlined proper names. The study is reported in William E. Miller and Walter J. Lamberg, "The Informal Reading Inventory in Social Studies: Practical Procedures" (Manuscript, The University of Texas at Austin, 1977).

[7]Henry Gnoff and John A. Krout, *The Adventures of the American People* (Chicago: Rand McNally, 1973), p. 7. Used with permission.

```
    1   1   3     2     2   2   1  1 1    5      4    1
would be vitally concerned over any threat to the territorial integrity of
    2
China.
        2      2    1   1   2      4      1   1    2   1   2
        Russia's attempt to take over Manchuria, a large region of China
    1   1       3      2   1   2   1  1    3     1   1    3
on the southeastern border of Russia, at the beginning of this century,
    1   1   2    1   1  1    3     2      4    1    3    1
was, in effect, a move to violate Chinese territory. The United States
    1   2   1   1       4          4       1   2    1  1
was alarmed by this development. Consequently, when Japan made a
    2     2   1   2   1          3       3      2      2
surprise attack on Russia in 1904, President Roosevelt quickly assured
    1   3    1   1    3    1     1    1   1  1  1    1
the Japanese that the United States would not stand in their way.[8]
```

Preamble:

```
        1   1    2  `1  1   3     1    1   2   1  1  1  1
        We, the people of the United States, in order to form a more
    2      2      3     2  ' 2     3       4        2
perfect Union, establish justice, insure domestic tranquillity, provide
    1   1   2      2       2    1   3     2   1   2   1
for the common defense, promote the general welfare, and secure the
    2     1   3    1    2     1   1    4     1   2     1
blessings of liberty to ourselves and our posterity, do ordain and
    3    1       4      1   1   3     1   1    4
establish this Constitution for the United States of America.
        1    2   1  1    3     1    1   1   1  1    1      1
        The people of the United States want to join the states more
    2    1   1   1   2   1    3    1     5        1   1
closely than they were under the Articles of Confederation. They want
    1  1  1  1  1     1   1    1    1    2    2     1   2     1
to set up fair laws. They want peace and order within their nation. They
    1   1   1     1    2     1    2    2      3
want to make their nation strong against foreign enemies.[9]
```

---

[8]Gnoff and Krout, *The Adventures of the American People*, p. 303. Used with permission.
[9]Gnoff and Krout, *The Adventures of the American People*, p. 545. Used with permission.

Step 2: Count the number of sentences in each passage and determine the average sentence length. In Passage 1, the last sentence begins with *Yet* and ends with *centuries,* but only three of the 18 words in the sentence are part of the 100-word passage. Passage 1, then, has only 5.2 sentences. Passage 2 has 4.5 sentences and Passage 3 had 5.7 (the subhead is counted as one sentence). The average sentence length for the three passages is 5.1.

Step 3: Count the total number of syllables in each passage and determine the average number of syllables. This time-consuming step is the one in which most errors occur. The easiest way to count syllables is to say each word to oneself while counting and to count one syllable for each vowel sound. For example, *history* would have a count of three because there are three vowel sounds. Passage 1 has 161 syllables; Passage 2 has 176; and Passage 3 has 166. The average number of syllables is 166.

Step 4: Plot the point on the Fry Readability Graph where the average sentence length and the average number of syllables intersect. The grade-level area where this point falls is the grade level for the material. For the three history passages above, the lines for 5.1 and 166 intersect just within college level.

English, science, and mathematics teachers can also use the Fry Formula. The Shakespearean sonnet below has 117 syllables and 2.9 sentences. If these numbers were averaged with those from two equally difficult passages, the grade level of the textbook would fall on the borderline between the seventh and eighth grades.

Sonnet 73

That time of year thou mayst in me behold
When yellow leaves, or none, or few, do hang
Upon those boughs which shake against the cold,
Bare ruined choirs, where late the sweet birds sang.
In me thou see'st the twilight of such day
As after sunset fadeth in the west,
Which by and by black night doth take away,
Death's second self, that seals up all in rest.
In me thou see'st the glowing of such fire
That on the ashes of its youth doth lie,
As the death-bed whereon it must expire
Consumed with that which it was nourished by.
This thou perceiv'st, which makes thy love more strong,
To love that well which thou must leave ere long.[10]

[10]William Shakespeare, *The Complete Works of Shakespeare,* edited by Hardin Craig (Glenview, Ill.: Scott, Foresman, 1963). pp. 483–84.

The following passage from a science textbook has a tenth-grade level:

> One statement about living things that has no exception is "They can die." Death implies life, and life implies the possibility of death. Though not all organisms die of old age, all are subject to death. Life can end in a wide variety of ways. An organism may be eaten, may be killed by parasites, may starve, or may be destroyed by natural events—frozen in a blizzard, boiled in lava, crushed in an avalanche. Obviously, since individuals are doomed, life would eventually disappear unless new individuals were continually being formed. And since the fossil evidence plainly shows that living things have been on this earth a long time and that uncountable numbers have died, it is clear that new individuals are constantly being formed.[11]

The following passage from a mathematics textbook has 6.6 sentences and 159 syllables; it also has a tenth-grade readability level.

Graphs of Functions

> By approximating by eye, we see that the instantaneous velocity at $t = 1$ is about ¾ meters per second, the slope of the line tangent to the graph at $t = 1$. The instantaneous velocity at $t = 6$ is about zero, indicating that the car has momentarily stopped.
>
> The concepts of average and instantaneous rates of change apply not only to distance-time relationships but to other functional relationships as well. The next two examples illustrate this.

Rate of a Person's Growth

The graph shows the height of a boy as a function of his age.

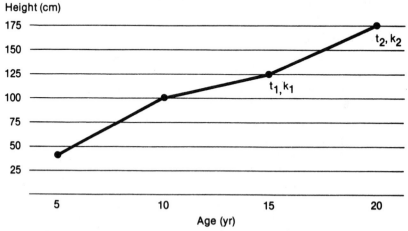

Height (cm)

His average growth rate from age 15 to age 20 can be found as follows.[12]

[11] American Institute of Biological Sciences—Biological Sciences Curriculum Study, University of Colorado at Boulder. *High School Biology—BSCS Green Version* (Chicago: Rand McNally, 1963), p. 496. Used with permission.
[12] R. G. Brown and D. P. Robbins. *Advanced Mathematics—An Introductory Course* (Boston: Houghton Mifflin, 1975), p. 293. Used with permission.

How can one label a Shakespearean sonnet as seventh- or eighth-grade material? To properly answer that question, one needs to consider what "readability level" means. Fry tested his formula on materials of different grade levels. To do this, he had to rely on estimates made by the publishers of those materials. He found that materials at different levels had a certain average number of syllables and sentences; he used those average numbers to construct his graph. To say that the sonnet is at the seventh- or eighth-grade level means that the syllable and sentence counts of the sonnet fall within the range of the counts Fry found for seventh- and eighth-grade materials.

But a readability measure is relative, not absolute. The history passages are considered college-level because they are similar to other college-level materials and are relatively more difficult than materials at the 12th-grade level.

Advantages of Formulas

Are the widely used formulas, such as the Fry Formula, good indicators of readability? Though most formulas measure only sentence and word difficulty, research does support their usefulness.

George Klare found the simple formulas to be useful, given their predictive value, their reliability, and their practicality (the amount of time required for their use).[13] Studies comparing the most widely used formulas showed that they generally agreed in the ranking of materials as to difficulty.[14] Other studies have also shown a high correlation between readability measurement and group comprehension scores of students; that is, a group of students was able to read successfully materials measured by the formula to be appropriate for them.[15]

Disadvantages of Formulas

Formulas have certain limitations that stem from the problem of generalizing from limited data. The difficulty of an entire text is generalized from the difficulty of a few passages. In turn, the difficulty of each passage is generalized from measures of two or more variables.

The problem in making a general estimate of the readability of an entire text lies in the fact that secondary textbooks commonly range in difficulty. The desire for consistency in difficulty conflicts with the desire for variety, which is expected of good writing. Variety is achieved, in part, by what T. Stevenson Hansell calls a "delicate balance" between simplicity and complexity of style.[16]

There are other reasons for the lack of consistency. In science, mathematics, and linguistics textbooks, the complexity of language may steadily increase as increasingly more complex concepts are presented.

---

[13]George R. Klare, "Assessing Readability," *Reading Research Quarterly* 1 (1974–75): 62–102.
[14]A recent study is Loyd J. Guidry and D. Frances Knight, "Comparative Readability: Four Formulas and Newbery Books," *Journal of Reading* 19:7 (April 1976), 552–56.
[15]Fry, "A Readability Formula that Saves Time."
[16]T. Stevenson Hansell, "Readability, Syntactic Transformations, and Generative Sentences." *Journal of Reading* 19:7 (April 1976); 557–62.

In a literature anthology, readability may rise and fall as different types of literature are presented. Selections by different authors and from different periods will, of course, differ. Even in a single short story, there can be a great range in readability; the narrator and characters may "speak" in different styles. It is also possible to find a fairly complex descriptive passage followed by a passage of simple, straightforward narration.

The second major limitation of widely used formulas is that they neglect many factors which can make reading more difficult for some students. If the content is familiar to a student, the vocabulary will also be familiar and therefore easier. How much interest a student has in the subject of the material also affects difficulty; content familiarity may affect interest. Lou Burmeister has identified additional factors which affect reading difficulty, including: syntax (or sentence structure), organizational patterns, the number of textbook aids, and other matters of format, like type face and type size, the kind of paper, and the type of cover.[17]

CHANGING THE LEVEL OF MATERIAL

Teachers can use readability formulas to guide and evaluate their rewriting of materials to produce versions at different levels of difficulty. If the teacher has students who differ widely in ability and if few or no multilevel materials on particular content are available, the teacher may need to rewrite selections for either instructional or testing purposes. Linda Craig notes that effective rewriting takes time and effort and is a job best shared by a group of teachers who teach in the same content area.[18] For example, the science teachers at a high school could divide up key selections to be rewritten or could take responsibility for producing or finding materials at particular grade levels.

In using a formula to guide rewriting, the teacher keeps in mind the factors measured by the formula. With the Fry Formula, the teacher would consider substituting synonyms for polysyllabic words and transforming relatively long, complex sentences into shorter sentences.

Effective rewriting involves many more considerations. For example, P. D. Pearson argues against the idea that simply shortening sentences and replacing polysyllabic words will necessarily make materials easier.[19] Joan Nelson suggests that "Arbitrarily shortening sentences may increase the difficulty of the reading task by rendering explicit

---

[17]Lou E. Burmeister, *Reading Strategies for Secondary School Teachers* (Reading, Mass.: Addison-Wesley, 1974).

[18]Linda C. Craig, "If It's Too Difficult for the Kids to Read—Rewrite It," *Journal of Reading* 21:3 (December, 1977): 212, 214.

[19]P. D. Pearson, "The Effects of Grammatical Complexity on Children's Comprehension, Recall, and Conception of Certain Semantic Relations," *Reading Research Quarterly* 10:2 (1974–75): 155–92.

relationships obscure."[20] In the following example, the first two sentences explicitly present the relationship between the two clauses (or ideas). Because the relationship is only implied in the third version, the reader would have to infer the relationship.

> The United States was very concerned over threats to China's territory.

> The United States was very concerned because of the threats to China's territory.

> The United States was very concerned. Other nations made threats to China's territory.

Many of the polysyllabic words in a content-area textbook are technical terms, which are essential to understanding the subject matter. Nelson believes it would be "foolish to suggest that teachers rewrite materials to change or eliminate these words when they represent the substance of the subject the teachers are trying to teach."[21] Other variables affecting vocabulary difficulty, such as level of abstraction, complexity of concepts, and multiple meanings, are not measured by the formulas.[22]

The following passage is an example of bad rewriting resulting from an oversimplified view of the rewriting process:

> The United States pledged itself to the idea of the open door in China. The United States guided its efforts to prevent any state from slamming the door shut. States were those of Europe and of Asia. The United States also had a vital concern. States might show a threat to the land of China.
>
> Russia tried to take over a large part of China. This part was to the south and east of the edge of Russia. Russia did this at the start of this century. The United States feared this move. Japan made a sneak attack on Russia in 1904. So, President Roosevelt told Japan the United States would not stand in its way.

This is an apparently simpler version of Passage 2 on page 139. The original was at the college level; the revision above is at the fifth-grade level. Some unnecessary polysyllabic words have been replaced by shorter words, but other key terms which students should learn, such as *policy* and *territorial integrity,* have been omitted. On the other hand, the central idea of the open-door policy, a figurative expression, remains. Some unnecessarily long sentences have been avoided, but, overall, most sentences are awkward.

Linda Craig presents some sound advice to teachers about rewriting

[20] Joan Nelson, "Readability: Some Cautions for the Content-Area Teacher," *Journal of Reading* 21:7 (April 1978); 623.
[21] Nelson, "Readability," p. 624.
[22] Nelson, "Readability," p. 621.

materials.[23] Teachers should first attend to content, then to key vocabulary, and only then to the stylistic factors measured by formulas. As a first step, the teacher should read the material and list the key points. The example below shows that a seemingly simple chronological passage has a number of key points.

1. U.S. was committed to open door policy. The open door policy was the idea that all countries should have free trade with China.
2. U.S. tried to keep one nation from preventing others from having trade with China.
3. U.S. was concerned with threats to China's territorial integrity.
4. Territorial integrity is the right of a nation to keep its own land and to be free of foreign influence.
5. Russia tried to take over Manchuria, a region of China. Japan also had disagreements with Russia and went to war.
6. President Roosevelt let Japan know he would not interfere.
7. As a result, Russia could not move freely against China.
8. U.S. action was an indirect way of furthering open door policy.
9. The situation with Russia illustrates how complex foreign policy can be.

As a second step, the teacher should decide which points he or she considers most important.

In a third step, the teacher should list key vocabulary, which, though difficult, should be retained, since students will be expected to learn them. Craig recommends trying to limit specialized terminology to about 5 words per 100. When the teacher finally rewrites the passage, he or she should attempt to make effective substitutions for polysyllabic words and longer sentences. The following passage illustrates effective rewriting: It includes simple but explicit definitions of the key concepts, which the teacher should elaborate on in discussion. These terms are underlined in the example. This version is at the seventh-grade level.

> The United States strongly believed in its policy of an open door to China. The idea of the open door was that all countries should have free trade with China. Therefore, the United States tried to keep any one nation of Europe or Asia from having all the trade. Some nations also made threats against China's territorial integrity. Territorial integrity is the right of a nation to keep its land. It is also the right to be free of foreign influence.
>
> One threat to China was from Russia. The way the United States acted shows how complex foreign affairs are.

There are many situations in which students should read, or at least be exposed to, the original texts. Such occasions occur in literature, when teachers want students to read for attention to particular styles and literary structures. In social studies, students must often attempt to

---

[23]Craig, "If It's Too Difficult," pp. 212–13.

read, or listen to an oral reading of, the original text of important documents such as the Constitution. Afterwards, they can read simpler versions to promote understanding and reading comprehension.

The prose version of the Shakespearean sonnet, which follows, cannot do justice either to the poet's style or to the characteristics of the sonnet form. But this version does help students see the logical development of ideas in the poem and the syntactic relationships of phrases and clauses:

> You may see three things in me. First, you see a season of the year, when there are few yellow leaves or no leaves at all. These leaves hang from branches which shake in the cold wind. The branches are like a bare, empty church, because the birds, who sang, have left.
>
> Second, you see in me the twilight of the day. The sunset has just faded in the west; the sky is soon to turn black. The blackness of the night is like death, which seals up everything in rest.
>
> Third, you see in me the glowing fire, which lies on its ashes. The ashes are like a deathbed. The fire must die because it is consuming itself.
>
> When you see these things in me, you will see that I am growing old. Then you will love me more, because we have more love for someone or something we will soon be losing.

USING TEXTBOOK AIDS

So far, the discussion of readability has focused on potential sources of difficulty. Teachers should also examine material for those features, called textbook aids, which may provide help to the reader. Textbook aids improve the readability of material in two ways: by making the material more interesting and by reducing or counteracting sources of difficulty.

To help students with technical language, explicit definitions may appear within the text and in glossaries. The text may also provide a pronunciation key. Various organizational features such as introductions and summaries can aid the reader in following the development of ideas. Subheadings and transitional paragraphs within the text also show the organization of the material. Good illustrations can help students visualize concepts, as does the graph in Figure 7.1.

Unfortunately, many students are not aware that these aids are intended to help them. Teachers need to make sure that students can recognize the aids and that they know how to use them. A list of these and other textbook aids follows:

1. Advance organizers—introductions and overviews
2. Purpose setting devices—study-guide questions, statements of purpose, objectives, and preassessment questions
3. Visuals—pictures, graphs, tables, and maps
4. Titles, heads, and subheads

5. Aids for terminology—explicit definitions within text, glossaries, pronunciation keys, and italized key terms
6. Transitional paragraphs
7. Summaries
8. Questions or other tasks at end of chapter
9. References for further reading
10. Table of contents
11. Suggestions for reading
12. Index

If text aids are not available, as is often the case in literary selections, teachers will need to provide them.

MODIFYING THE TASK   Teachers must consider one other factor; that is, the task or the way students are to respond to the text. Students may perform poorly on easy material because of a too difficult task. On the other hand, they may perform well on apparently difficult material, because the task reduces or avoids difficulties in the text. For example, an assignment requiring students to attend to and use textbook aids should facilitate reading (The survey procedure discussed in Chapter 5 does that).

Selective, silent reading tasks, such as skimming and scanning to answer prequestions, give students the opportunity to avoid words and sometimes whole sentences the students find too difficult. Proficient readers, when reading for pleasure, often skip over unfamiliar foreign names or even whole passages, since there is no penalty for skipping. As another means of reducing the difficulty of unfamiliar words, the teacher can present (pronounce, define, and illustrate) important abstract words prior to having the student read (see the discussion in Chapter 3).

Harold Herber, along with Martha Dillner and Joanne Olson, recommends a procedure for adjusting the difficulty of tasks, the use of differentiated assignments.[24] Students may read the same text (and the same version of it) for the same purpose, but they are given different assignments based on their general ability. The assignments differ in the amount of assistance beyond directions the teacher provides for the students.

Commonly, assignments for above-average students will consist of only the directions and perhaps an example of how they are to respond. For example:

> Read the section of the chapter on the nature of organisms. Write a rough outline of the main points and the evidence or examples presented to support those points.

---

[24]Harold L. Herber, *Teaching Reading in Content-Areas* (Englewood Cliffs, N.J.: Prentice-Hall, 1970), pp. 206–10; and Martha H. Dillner and Joanne P. Olson, *Personalizing Reading Instruction in Middle, Junior, and Senior High Schools* (New York: Macmillan, 1977), pp. 181–88.

Assignments for average-ability students may include either additional examples or some of the key points or details from the text.

Read the section of the chapter on the nature of organisms. Write an outline which includes the main points and the evidence or examples presented to support those points. The outline is started for you below.

1. All organisms must die, though in different ways.
    A. Some may be eaten.
    B.

Assignments for below-average students may include most or all of the key points or details or the page numbers of the answers to questions.

Read the section of the chapter on the nature of organisms. Write an outline which includes the main points and the evidence or examples presented to support those points. The main points of the first two paragraphs are presented below.

1. All organisms must die, though in different ways.
    A. Some may be eaten.
    B.
2. New organisms are constantly formed.
    A.
    B.

Teachers can also change the *type* of assignment for readers of different ability levels. In the following examples, all students must read Sonnet 73, but the teacher asks above-average readers to write an essay, average readers to list responses to a question, and below-average readers to perform a matching exercise:

For Above-Average Readers:

Read Sonnet 73 and write an essay showing how the theme is developed by the imagery. The theme is stated in the last two lines. The imagery in the first four lines on fall conveys the idea and mood of the passing of time.

For Average Readers:

Read Sonnet 73 to see how the theme is developed by the imagery. The theme, stated in the last two lines, can be paraphrased this way: Our love for someone grows when we realize we will be losing that person. With this theme in mind, fill out the following chart by identifying the imagery in each quatrain and the specific images in each.

1. Imagery of fall   yellow leaves, no leaves.
                            _____

2. _____   _____
                            _____

3. _____   _____
                            _____

For Below-Average Readers:

Read Sonnet 73 to see how the theme is developed by the imagery. The theme is stated in the last two lines. It can be paraphrased this way: Our love for someone grows when we realize we will be losing that person. With this theme in mind, fill out the following chart by listing the specific images that make up the imagery of each quatrain (or set of four lines). The specific images are underlined in your copy of the poem.

1. Imagery of fall   yellow leaves, no leaves _____

   _____

2. Imagery of end of day   _____

   _____

3. Imagery of dying fire   _____

   _____

SUMMARY   Assessment of the readability of materials is an important responsibility of the content-area teacher. Readability formulas which measure style, such as the Fry Formula, have practical uses but also major limitations. The formulas can provide an estimate of the difficulty of the material and guide the selection of materials for students at different grade levels in reading. Teachers should consider two other factors: 1) the parts of the material of special importance to the learning of content, such as key abstract terms, and 2) the reading aids provided in the text. A prime consideration is how students perform when reading the material. Their performance depends on their ability as well as on the degree of difficulty of the task they are to perform.

1. Discuss one of the ideas listed in the Overview at the beginning of this chapter.
2. Select some material from your content area and using the Fry Formula assess its readability. Follow the directions and use the graph provided in the chapter.
3. Rewrite a passage of content-area material to reduce its level of difficulty. Follow procedures recommended by Craig and discussed in this chapter. Check your work by using the Fry formula on the revised passage.
4. Select a passage of content-area material. Write an assessment of factors in the passage which are not measured by the Fry Formula such as familiarity of words, number of technical terms and symbols, number of abstract words referring to key concepts, complexity of sentence structure, and other factors you consider noteworthy.
5. Select a content-area textbook and make a list of the types of textbook aids provided. Write a brief evaluation of the textbook in terms of the quantity, quality, and variety of aids provided.

Recommended Readings

Bormuth, John R. "Readability: A New Approach." *Reading Research Quarterly* 1 (Fall 1966): 79–132.
_____. "The Cloze Procedure: Literacy in the Classroom," in William D. Page, ed., *Help for The Reading Teacher: New Directions in Research.* Urbana, Ill.: ERIC Clearinghouse on Reading and Communication Skills, 1975.
Burmeister, Lou E. "Judging the Difficulty of Reading Materials," in *Reading Strategies for Secondary School Teachers.* Reading, Mass: Addison-Wesley, 1974, chap. 2.
Carver, Ronald. "Measuring Prose Difficulty Using the Rauding Scale." *Reading Research Quarterly* 11: 4 (1975–76): 660–85.
Chall, Jeanne S. *Readability: An Appraisal of Research and Application.* Columbus, Ohio: Ohio State University, Bureau of Educational Research, 1958.
Dillner, Martha H., and Olson, Joanne P. "Identifying Reading Problems with Textbooks," in *Personalizing Reading Instruction in Middle, Junior and Senior High Schools.* New York: Macmilian, 1977, chap. 6.
Flesch, Rudolf, *How to Measure Readability.* New York: Harper & Row, 1957.
Fry, Edward, "A Readability Formula That Saves Time," in W. John Harker, ed., *Classroom Strategies for Secondary Reading,* Newark, Del.: International Reading Association, 1977), pp. 29–35.
_____. "Fry's Readability Graph: Clarifications, Validity, and Extension to Level 17." *Journal of Reading* 21: 3 (December 1977): 242–52.
Guidry, Loyd J., and Knight, D. Frances. "Comparative Readability: Four Formulas and Newberry Books". *Journal of Reading* 19: 7 (April 1976): 552–56.
Herber, Harold L. *Teaching Reading in Content-Areas.* Englewood Cliffs, N.J.: Prentice-Hall, 1970.
Klare, George R. "Assessing Readability," *Reading Research Quarterly* 1 (1974–75): 62–102.
MacGinitie, Walter. "Children's Understanding of Linguistic Units," in S. Jay Samuels, ed. *What Research Has to Say About Reading Instruction.* Newark, Del.: International Reading Association, 1978, pp. 43–56.
Monteith, Mary K. "ERIC/RCS: Readability Formulas." *Journal of Reading* 19:7 (April 1976); 604–7.
Pearson, David P. "The Effects of Grammatical Complexity on Children's Comprehension, Recall and Conceptions of Certain Semantic Relationships." *Reading Research Quarterly* 10: 2 (1974–75): 155–92.
Strange, Michael, and Allington, Richard L. "How to Evaluate Reading Assignments So You'll know When and How to Intervene." *Journal of Reading* 21 (November 1977): 149–52.

8

Standardized Tests

Reading educators have devoted much effort to the development of tests and testing procedures. Tests fall into two categories. Formal or standardized tests, usually commercially published, use statistical procedures to achieve consistency of results. Informal, or teacher-made tests, are designed to yield information directly related to particular aspects of instruction.

Content-area teachers rarely select standardized reading tests or analyze test results. Usually it is a reading coordinator or another administrator responsible for a school's program evaluation who performs those tasks. Often, teachers are asked to administer the tests, and, recently, some schools have given teachers individual results for their students.

Teachers should understand the nature, and in particular, the limitations of standardized tests. Familiarity with any one test is not sufficient because, as this chapter will show, reading tests differ greatly in the way they measure reading ability. The authors do encourage teachers to closely examine the tests used in their schools to understand precisely what information is and is not given about their students' reading.

Key Ideas   Standardized tests: can be norm-referenced or criterion-referenced; can be for groups or individuals; and can be used for survey or diagnostic purposes.

Assessment is the systematic collection of information about a student's reading.

Standardized tests are useful in reading-program evaluation but have limitations for evaluating particular students or groups of students.

Mr. Johnson, a content-area teacher, is concerned about the reading abilities of his students. Therefore, he gets together with the high school's reading specialist to go over standardized reading tests and individual scores for the students in his class. By doing this, Mr. Johnson gains some indication of how his students compare with certain other groups of pupils at particular grade levels. However, the information gained is not geared to particular aspects of Mr. Johnson's course. Therefore, he uses some informal tests to measure his students' abilities as they relate to his instructional goals.

KINDS OF STANDARDIZED TESTS

Standardized tests are so named because of the process by which they are developed. Test developers use broad national samples of students representing different ages, grade levels, and geographical areas. Authors of tests conduct field tests or tryouts of their tests to gather information about the responses of representative groups to the test items.

Norm-Referenced or Criteria-Referenced Tests

Standardized tests may be divided into two categories: norm-referenced and criterion-referenced. With norm-referenced tests, a student's ability is measured by comparing his or her score to scores achieved by other students; that is, educational peers. In particular, the student's score is compared to a distribution of scores, or norm, established in the field testing. With criterion-referenced tests, the student's ability is measured by comparing his or her score to a previously determined performance level. This level, or criterion, indicates acceptable performance on test items.[1]

The following provides a hypothetical illustration: The author of a norm-referenced test decides to test ability to recognize common words. In the field testing, he finds that the average score for first-grade students is 75 percent accuracy (three fourths of the words are recognized);

---

[1]Walter R. Hill, "Reading Testing for Reading Evaluation," in William Blanton, Roger Farr, and J. Jaap Tuinman, *Measuring Reading Performance*. (Newark, Del.: International Reading Association, 1974).

therefore, 75 percent becomes the norm for first-grade students. When the test is used in schools, students who score 75 percent or better are considered to be showing a first-grade level of ability on word recognition.

The author of a criterion-referenced test also decides to test recognition of common words. Based on her observation of successful first-grade readers, she concludes that 90 percent word recognition is an acceptable performance. She finds during field testing that the average score is 75 percent, but she considers this average score to be unacceptable and would argue that instruction should be revised so that most students will learn to recognize 90 percent of these words.

Standardized reading tests may be categorized by purpose as either oral or silent reading tests. *Oral reading tests* measure word-recognition skills; some tests also measure oral reading comprehension. *Silent reading tests* measure silent reading comprehension and, sometimes, other abilities such as vocabulary and silent reading rate. *Silent reading-listening tests* attempt to gather important information of several kinds. These tests may consist of a pair of parallel subtests: one is read *by* the student; the other, *to* the student.[2] The student answers questions to demonstrate silent reading comprehension and listening comprehension, respectively.

Tests can also be categorized in two other ways: 1) as either group or individual and 2) as diagnostic or survey tests. The distinctions between group and individual tests should be obvious; the primary difference is the test setting—it can be either a large-group administration or a one-to-one situation.

Group or Individual Tests

Discriminations between diagnostic and survey tests are more subtle. Diagnostic tests are intended to provide direction for specific instruction, whereas survey tests may be used only to give an estimate of performance capabilities. Because diagnostic tests are more thorough than survey tests, they can sample more skill areas.

Diagnostic or Survey Tests

Tests are a means of assessment used for purposes of diagnosis and evaluation.[3] *Assessment* in reading is the systematic collection of information about a student's reading. Assessment is usually conducted with tests of skills, but other procedures can be used such as observing

ASSESSMENT OF READING ABILITY

---

[2]Lou E. Burmeister, *Reading Strategies for Middle and Secondary School Teachers,* 2nd ed. (Reading, Mass.: Addison-Wesley, 1978).
[3]Walter R. Hill, "Reading Testing for Reading Evaluation," in William Blanton, Roger Farr, and J. Jaap Tuinman, eds., *Measuring Reading Performance* (Newark, Del.: International Reading Association, 1974).

students' written responses to reading tasks, listening to students' oral reading, and checking materials students choose to read (to assess students' interests).

Reading tests, no matter how thorough, provide only a sample of behaviors indicative of the student's reading performance and ability.[4] Information collected with tests and other means of assessment can be used for two purposes: 1) to *diagnose* or identify apparent strengths and weaknesses and 2) to *evaluate* or make judgments about the student's achievement and progress.

Validity and Reliability A valid reading test will elicit responses which give a good indication of the student's nontest performance; that is, the test should tell the teacher how well a student can read in natural situations (not just on the test). Such a test is said to have *validity*.

Good reading tests should yield consistent or reliable results. Therefore, if a student with a certain achievement level scores at the same level on different administrations of the test, the test is said to have *reliability*.

Test Results Test results can be expressed in grade-level equivalents, percentile rank, or stanines. The *grade-level equivalent* refers to the grade level for which a test score is an approximate average. It gives an estimate of the student's normal reading level in terms of grade level or year in school. *Percentile rank* gives the proportion or percentage of scores above and below the given score. *Stanine,* a standard score which takes on equal values from one to nine, is another way to describe a student's relative test performance. It divides the percentile range (0–100) into nine equal parts.

For example, a seventh-grade student scoring at the *grade-level equivalent* of 7.0 would be performing at his or her grade (or year) in school. This student performed as well on the test as the representative group of seventh graders. If this student had a *percentile rank* of 50, he or she would be in the fifth *stanine*. This rank and stanine indicate that one half of the students taking the test had higher scores and the other half had lower scores. The following chart shows samples of each of these scores.

Table 8.1

Student Name	Grade Level Equivalent	Percentile Rank	Stanine Rank
Bill Smith	10.0	50	5
Sally Jones	9.0	37	4
Charlie Edwards	11.3	92	8
Frank Hunter	7.0	10	2

[4]Roger Farr, *Reading: What Can Be Measured?* (Newark, Del.: International Reading Association, 1969.)

Martha Dillner and Joanne Olson provide a thorough list of uses for standardized reading tests.[5] Their work is based on that of R. T. Lennon and Ruth Strang.[6] Reading tests can be used to provide:

1. a statement of the status or success of the reading abilities of a group of students;
2. a statement of progress toward achieving certain goals;
3. a statement of relative status of students;
4. diagnostic information for future use;
5. an inventory of skills; and
6. data essential to an overall program of evaluation.

In addition, the tests can be used to:

1. determine individual weaknesses by analyzing small parts of the test;
2. give the classroom teacher an idea of reading range in a class; and
3. identify students in need of special reading instruction.

As with all tests, standardized reading tests have both advantages and disadvantages. Many educators believe the chief advantage of the tests is their usefulness in program evaluation. Standardized tests have the following three strengths as evaluative instruments: 1) The tests provide a national comparison of the school reading program. 2) The tests are relatively objective, because of the standardized procedures for choosing test items, for administering the test, and for scoring and interpreting test results. 3) Teachers can benefit from the expertise of professional test makers.[7]

THE VALUE OF STANDARDIZED TESTS

In recent years, many educators have expressed strong concerns about standardized tests, particularly norm-referenced tests. Some educators have called for the development and use of effective criterion-referenced tests, and others, for greater use of informal tests and assessment procedures. Weaknesses in testing programs are compounded by a lack of understanding on the part of administrators, teachers, and parents of the nature, purposes, and limitations of standardized tests. One point which is frequently misunderstood is that no single test can

LIMITATIONS OF STANDARDIZED TESTS

---

[5]Martha H. Dillner and Joann P. Olson, *Personalizing Reading Instruction in Middle, Junior, and Senior High Schools.* (New York: Macmillan, 1977).
[6]R. T. Lennon, *Selection and Provision of Testing Material.* Test Service Bulletin No. 99. (New York: Harcourt, Brace & Jovanovich, 1967) and Ruth Strang, *Diagnostic Teaching of Reading* (New York: McGraw-Hill, 1967.)
[7]Dillner and Olson, *Personalizing Reading Instruction.*

provide a complete view of the student's ability. As was discussed earlier, a test is, at best, only a sampling of important behaviors related to reading.

A severe limitation of any standardized reading test is the fact that it represents the viewpoint of only one author or team of authors. Local concerns and needs may not be reflected in the test. Students who take the test may not be adequately represented by the groups of students used to establish norms. For example, the norming group may have consisted of white, middle-class students in a large metropolitan area. Their interests and cultural and linguistic backgrounds may differ greatly from students in rural areas or students in minority groups. Some testmakers have attempted to address this limitation by expanding the field-testing process to include a greater number and variety of groups and by providing different sets of norms for use in interpreting results.

Tests may be useful to administrators concerned with overall evaluation, but they may be of little use to the classroom teacher. While these tests can show student errors, they can provide few helpful clues, if any, as to the causes. The small number of test items for each skill sampled makes it still more difficult for the teacher to know which aspects of reading students are weak in. For example, if a student misses a comprehension question, the cause of the error could be any one or a combination of the following: weakness in literal comprehension, weakness in higher levels of comprehension, a vocabulary problem, difficult material in the passage, a lack of understanding of directions for answering the question, or carelessness or anxiety on the part of the student.

Another limitation in using test results is the frequent mismatch between the test and the instructional experience of the students in a particular course. In a content-area course, the basic instructional task may be to read a multipage chapter and answer short-answer or discussion questions. Standardized tests of word recognition or vocabulary, which consist of lists of words, are very different from that instructional activity.

The differences between the test items and actual classroom reading performance often result in an incorrect assessment of student ability to read texts for instruction or pleasure. In fact, some standardized tests have been found to overestimate actual or functional ability by one or more grade levels. For example, a student may score at the tenth-grade level on the test but may not be able to successfully read material above the ninth-grade level. On the other hand, if a student is weak in the skill area stressed in a test, his or her overall ability may be underestimated. For example, a student who has developed good comprehension skills in spite of weaknesses in phonic and structural analysis should perform better on a silent reading comprehension test than on a test of oral recognition of isolated words.

Though standardized tests, along with interpretive results, do not give a **SUMMARY**
full picture of a student's reading ability, they can provide useful information for those responsible for the evaluation and development of
reading programs. Information about students' reading ability can and
should be an integral part of instructional planning by the content-area
teacher. Teachers can gain such information through a combination of
standardized and informal testing.

---

1. Discuss one of the points listed in the Overview at the beginning of this chapter. **Suggested Activities**
2. Write a comparison/contrast of subtests from two different standardized reading tests. Consider such points as 1)What skill areas are tested? 2) What specific skills (or responses) within those areas are tested? 3) What procedures are involved in adminis- tering the tests? and 4) How is the grade level determined by each test?
3. Write a comparison/contrast of two levels from the same standardized reading subtest. In what ways is one level more difficult than another?
4. Have a peer administer a standardized reading subtest to you. Write a description of your reactions to taking the test and to the test as a good or poor reflection of your interests and typical performances in reading.
5. Administer a reading test to a student or peer and score and interpret the results.

Recommended Readings

Becker, Wesley C., and Englemann, Sigfried *Teaching 3: Evaluation of Instruction.* Chicago: Science Research Associates, 1976.
Blanton, William; Farr, Roger; and Tuinman, J. Jaap, eds. *Reading Tests for the Secondary Grades: A Review and Evaluation.* Newark Del.: International Reading Association, 1972.
———. *Measuring Reading Performance.* Newark, Del.: International Reading Associa- tion, 1974.
Burmeister, Lou E. *Reading Strategies for Middle and Secondary School Teachers,* 2nd ed. Reading, Mass: Addison-Wesley, 1978, chap. 3
Buros, Oscar, ed. *Mental Measurements Yearbook.* Highland Parks, N.J.: Gryphon Press.
Calfee, Robert C.; Drum, Priscilla A.; and Arnold, Richard D. "What Research Can Tell the Reading Teacher About Assessment," in S. Jay Samuels, ed., *What Research Has to Say About Reading Instruction.* Newark, Del.: International Reading Association, 1978, chap. 8.
Della-Piana, Gabriel M. *Reading Diagnosis and Prescription—An Introduction.* New York: Holt, Rinehart, & Winston, 1968.
Dillner, Martha H., and Olson, Joanne P., *Personalizing Reading Instruction in Middle, Junior, and Senior High Schools.* New York: Macmillan, 1977, chap. 5 and appendix B.
Farr, Roger. *Reading: What Can Be Measured?* Newark, Del.: International Reading Association, 1969.
Hafner, Lawrence E. *Developmental Reading in Middle and Secondary Schools: Foun- dations, Strategies, and Skills for Teaching.* New York: Macmillan, 1977, chap. 4.
Hittleman, David, R. *Developmental Reading: A Psycholinguistic Perspective.* Chicago: Rand McNally, 1978, chap. 4.
Lennon, R. T. *Selection and Provision of Test Material.* Test Service Bulletin No. 99. New York: Harcourt, Brace & Jovanovich, 1967.
Roe, Betty D.; Stoodt, Barbara D.; and Burns, Paul C. *Reading Instruction in the Secon- dary School.* Chicago; Rand McNally, 1978, chap. 10.
Spache, George D. *Diagnosing and Correcting Reading Disabilities.* Boston: Allyn & Bacon, 1976.
Viox, Ruth G. *Evaluating Reading and Study Skills in the Secondary Classroom.* Newark, Del.: International Reading Association, 1968.

9

Informal Assessment

Standardized tests are not the only way, and are not always the best **OVERVIEW**
way, to assess reading ability in a content area. Teachers can also use
any of the following procedures for informal-assessment: the Informal
Reading Inventory (IRI), the improvised inventory, the cloze readability
test, or the modified inventory. Most informal assessment procedures
have major limitations; therefore, teachers should use a variety of approaches to collect information about a student's strengths and weaknesses as they relate to reading in a content area. The approaches
discussed in this chapter have a key advantage: they can be implemented
with actual content-area materials. (Another kind of informal assessment—collecting information about students' attitudes and interests—will be discussed in Chapter 20.)

The Informal Reading Inventory (IRI) gives a teacher information about   *Key Ideas*
a student's ability to read in a specific content area.

A teacher can use the improvised inventory for books where the readability level varies from one part of the book to another.

The cloze readability test can function as an assessment procedure.

The modified or group inventory measures comprehension levels, vocabulary, and reading rate all in one test.

Informal-assessment procedures provide teachers with the information
they need to make instructional decisions.

Mr. Harvey, a tenth-grade social studies teacher, discovered a mismatch between the level of his textbook, which according to the Fry Formula was tenth-grade level, and the ability of two thirds of his class. Informal assessment with passages from his history text indicated that 4 of his students could read the text without help, 15 could read it with help, and 7 would find the text too difficult. Therefore, he gave those 7 selected assignments from a junior-high-level text which covered most of the same content as the class text.

Because Mr. Harvey made selective assignments for only those chapters or chapter sections he considered important for students to read, he was thus able to avoid giving assignments that were either too easy or too difficult for various students. For some tests he rewrote passages so that they could be read without help by all students. He lectured only on material covered in sections of the textbook which were at a high level of difficulty and which were not available in the junior-high-level textbook.

THE INFORMAL READING INVENTORY

In recent years, the Informal Reading Inventory (IRI), has become widely used in beginning-reading and secondary remedial-reading programs. The IRI is appropriate in content-area courses because it provides an assessment of a student's abilities to read content-area material. The IRI is best thought of as a set of procedures for assessment rather than as a single test. Current procedures are indebted to the work of Emmett Betts and Patsy Killgallon during the 1940s.[1]

Simply put, the IRI consists of a series of graded passages; that is, each passage is written at a particular level of difficulty which corresponds to the equivalent grade level of reading. Teachers can use readability formulas (see Chapter 7) to verify readability levels or to guide the writing of materials to needed levels. A complete IRI will have passages from grades one to twelve. (Primer and preprimer-level materials are included at the elementary level. These are selected from materials which are of an easier level than first grade to introduce students to reading words in context.) For each of the passages, there is a set of five

---

[1]Emmett A. Betts, *Foundations of Reading Instruction* (New York: American Book, 1957); and Patsy A. Killgallon, "A study of Relationships among Certain Pupil Adjustments in Language Situations" (Ph.D. diss., Pennsylvania State College, 1942). For reviews of research on IRIs, see: Roger Farr, *Reading: What Can Be Measured?* (Newark, Del.: International Reading Association, 1969), and Jerry L. Johns et al., *Assessing Reading Behavior: Informal Reading Inventories* (Newark, Del.: International Reading Association, 1977).

to ten questions, such as the following which were developed for the sample in Figure 9.1:

1. Why was Mrs. Penn worried?
2. Who was Tom?
3. What happened to Tom?
4. What was Bill carrying?
5. Where was Bill going?
6. Why did Bill think his mother was picking on him?
7. How old is Bill?
8. Where did Bill get the money?
9. How does he plan to pay the money back?
10. How does his mother feel about Bill's behavior?

Schemes of comprehension, as discussed in Chapter 4, are employed to insure a variety of comprehension responses. Typically, questions call for literal recall of details and ideas; interpretation of implied points, causes, or feelings; and sometimes a creative response, such as supplying an appropriate title for the passage.

Questions are usually arranged in order of difficulty or by level of comprehension. Questions can also be arranged to follow the order in which the passage presents information. For example, the answer to the first question might be a specific detail in the first sentence of the passage. The last question might call for an interpretation of a phrase or statement found toward the end of the passage or for the main idea of the entire passage. Care is taken to write the questions as simply and directly as possible to avoid unnecessary difficulties in understanding the questions.

Whereas standardized tests yield a grade-level equivalent, the IRI provides three scores or levels of reading ability. At the *independent level,* students can read the material with sufficient ease to handle it on their own, independent of the teacher's help or guidance. They know almost all the words and can answer all or most of the questions. At the *instructional level,* students read with success but experience some difficulty, usually with unfamiliar words which they cannot analyze successfully. Their comprehension is good. With material at this level, students may need some help from the teacher—for example, with pronouncing and defining words or providing guiding questions. This material is appropriate for instruction; it provides problems to be overcome and, therefore, facilitates development of skills. The *frustration level* indicates that the material is simply too difficult to read. Students experience frustration and make mistakes they would not exhibit at the instructional and independent levels. There is a noticeable increase in frequency of mistakes.

Criteria have been proposed for determining the different levels, but there are two limitations. First, the criteria have been tested out on elementary-level readers; little research has been done at the secondary

Figure 9.1
Two Pages from a Literature
Anthology

EVERYBODY CRIES SOMETIMES

by Jared Jansen

Mrs. Penn was worried. Her son Bill needed some new clothes. And her pay was not enough to keep up with all the bills. She would call Tom, she thought. Bill was his son, too.

"Hello," she said into the phone. "Is Tom there? . . . Moved? Did he say where he was going? . . . No. Thank you."

She put down the phone. What could she do now? . . .

Bill came out of his room, holding a box of candy under his arm. He headed for the front door.

"Where are you going?" Mrs. Penn asked.

"Out," Bill answered.

"What is that under your arm?" his mother asked.

"It is just a box of candy," he said.

23

Source: Jared Jansen, "Everybody Cries Sometimes" in Mel Cebulash, ed., *The Fallen Angel and Other Stories* (New York: Scholastic Book Services, 1970), pp. 23–24. Used with permission.

"Are you going out with that girl again?" Mrs. Penn said. "I do not want you seeing so much of that girl. How many times do I have to tell you that?"

"There is nothing wrong with her," Bill said.

"I am not saying that," his mother said. "I am just saying that you are not going out with her tonight — or any other night."

Bill looked at his mother. Why was she always picking on him? He was 17. He had a right to do what he wanted.

"And that candy," she went on. "Is that what you do with the money I give you? Do you think I work like a dog every day so you can waste the money on a girl?"

"I will pay it back," Bill said. As soon as I find some work after school, he thought.

"Fine," his mother said. "Now call that girl and tell her you are not going to see her."

"Look," Bill said, "I am going to see her. I am not a baby any more. I am 17."

"You are just like your father," Mrs. Penn said. "If you leave here now, you can go and live with him. That is if you can find him. I have been trying to bring you up so you would not be like him. But I can see it is no use."

24

Table 9.1

	Betts		Powell	
	Word Recognition	Comprehension	Word Recognition	Comprehension
Independent	99%+	90%+	97%+	80%+
Instructional	95%+	70%+	92%+	60%+
Frustration	94% or less	60% or less	91% or less	50% or less

level. Second, different criteria have been proposed, such as the above criteria from Emmett Betts and William Powell[2]:

The best advice to teachers is to be cautious in using the criteria, to use them as a general guide, and to consider both the quantity and quality of mistakes made by students.

A student's functional reading level varies as the difficulty of the material varies. For example, John, a seventh-grade student, had these results: 100 percent comprehension at levels 1, 2, and 3; 90 percent at level 4; 70 percent at levels 5 and 6; and 50 percent at level 7. His independent level is grades 1-4; his instructional level grades 5-6; his frustrational level grade 7.

The Silent IRI   A silent IRI is conducted to assess student ability to comprehend materials at different levels of difficulty when reading silently. A teacher provides students with graded passages of at least 100 words, each accompanied by a set of questions. Students read a passage, answer the questions, and then move on to the next passage. The teacher scores the answers and interprets the scores, using the criteria to determine the grade levels at which students read at the independent, instructional, and frustrational levels. The teacher also observes the types of questions students respond to correctly and incorrectly. A ninth-grade teacher, for example, might discover that one-third of the class is experiencing frustration with passages above the seventh-grade level and that the students are missing questions calling for sequence recognition. Therefore, these students need instruction in reading for sequence with materials at their instructional level, that is, seventh grade or lower.

The Oral IRI   An oral IRI is given on an individual basis to assess student abilities in word recognition and oral reading comprehension with materials at different levels. As the student reads each passage aloud, the teacher marks miscues, or departures from the text, on his or her copy of the passage, as illustrated here:

---

[2]Betts, *Foundations of Reading Instructions;* and William R. Powell, "Validity of the IRI Reading Levels." *Elementary English* 48 (October 1971); 637–42.

Workers at the construction site went on strike, delaying comple-

tion of the building. The children had to do without having a recreation

center for the summer.

The teacher then asks questions and records the student's responses. Several categories of miscues have been established, including:

1. Variant Pronunciations: Student fails to pronounce word correctly. "Tom went *ri-git* to bed."
2. Omissions: Student fails to read a word or phrase. "Tom went _____ to bed."
3. Insertions: Student adds a word or phrase. "Tom went right *up* to bed."
4. Substitutions: Student substitutes a word for one in the text. "Tom *wanted* right to bed."
5. Repetitions: Student repeats a word. "Tom went *went* right to bed."
6. Hesitations: Student hesitates before saying the word. "Tom went *(pause)* right to bed."

Some teachers use symbols for the categories, such as *P* for mispronunciation. Others write out the responses students made—for example, *construc-tee-own* for *construction*. The authors prefer the second approach because it provides more information and aids in spotting patterns of weaknesses. In the *construction* example, the student shows a pattern of difficulty with the first sound of the suffix *tion*.

After the student has completed the reading, the teacher counts the number of miscues and determines the percentage of correct responses. In a 100-word passage, three miscues would mean 97 percent word-recognition accuracy. Seven of ten questions answered correctly would mean 70 percent comprehension. There are some unsettled questions about counting miscues and a lack of research to support particular procedures. When students omit an entire phrase, some teachers count each word omitted; others record only one miscue for the complete phrase. Some teachers do not count repetitions as miscues, and others count seven repetitions as one miscue, as a means of noting the occurrence of a large number of repetitions. Some count all substitutions as miscues; others count only those resulting in a loss of meaning.

Whatever procedures are followed, consistency is desirable, so that an objective comparison can be made of a student's reading on two or more occasions. Given the limitations of the IRI, more than one IRI should be given, and the teacher should consider other evidence, such as responses to other kinds of assessment and to actual instructional tasks.

THE IMPROVISED INVENTORY

Chapter 7 on readability noted that most textbooks have a range of readability; this is especially true with literature anthologies. This inconsistency undercuts the value of the IRI; it is entirely possible that the results of the IRI will indicate students can handle one chapter but not another in the same book. Teachers can counter this problem by applying the basic principles of the IRI with improvised inventories.

A teacher can conduct an improvised inventory whenever students start a new chapter in a text, a new selection in an anthology, or supplementary material. The teacher simply counts the first 200 to 250 words of the material and writes a set of ten questions. Students read the material and answer the questions as in a silent IRI. The answers to the questions provide the teacher with a basis for deciding how the material should be handled—for example, whether students should read the material independently or receive assistance.

When students start an assignment in class, the teacher can check whether or not they understand the directions and whether they can handle the material. The teacher should initially assess literal comprehension. If students respond well, the teacher can assess higher-level comprehension tasks after asking the students to read another passage. A discussion of the first section of the material prior to subsequent reading provides further understanding and direct instruction in concepts or ways of responding.

THE CLOZE READABILITY TEST

Chapters 3 and 4 both presented the cloze procedure as an effective instructional activity for developing context analysis and comprehension skills. William Taylor originally developed the cloze procedure for measuring readability,[3] but the cloze task is also useful for assessment.

Used in place of the IRI, the cloze test consists of a series of passages, each representing a different grade level. For group testing, students write in deleted words, and the teacher checks responses with an answer key. According to criteria provided by Bormuth, a student's independent level is indicated by at least 57 percent correct responses, instructional level by at least 44 percent correct responses, and frustration level by 43 percent or less.

Bormuth has developed and validated very specific procedures for using what he calls the *cloze readability test*. If the procedures are not followed correctly, the validity and reliability of the test may suffer. First, passages are to be 250 words in length with every fifth word

---

[3]William L. Taylor, "Cloze Procedures A New Tool for Measuring Readability." *Journalism Quarterly* 30 (Fall 1958): 416; and John Bormuth, "Literacy in the Classroom," in William D. Page, ed., *Help for the Reading Teacher: New Directions in Research* (Urbana, Ill.: ERIC Clearinghouse on Reading and Communication Skills, 1975), pp. 60–90.

deleted (50 deletions). Only those responses which are exactly the same as the words in the original text are counted as correct.[4]

The latter procedure bothers many teachers, who argue that good substitutions which preserve the meaning and syntax should also be counted as correct. Bormuth counters that his procedure avoids inconsistencies by a teacher and variability between teachers.[5] The procedure also saves time. In addition, the critieria for determining levels are much lower than those with the IRI. A reader could miss 20 words on the cloze test and still be at the independent level. To test out Bormuth's argument, the reader is encouraged to take the following cloze test with a friend. See how much time and energy you spend trying to agree on what good substitutions are.

This account of malaria 1_____ an example of a 2_____ problem and of how 3_____ problems are solved. As 4_____ most important biological problems, 5_____ has speculated about malaria 6_____ centuries. The folklore and 7_____ observations of our ancestors 8_____ hints that enabled scientists 9_____ the nineteenth century to 10_____ hypotheses about the causes 11_____ malaria. A laboratory scientist 12_____ never have thought of 13_____ possible relation between mosquitoes 14_____ malaria. But when told 15_____ malaria is more common 16_____ low, marshy places, he 17_____ set up hypotheses to 18_____. Could it be the 19_____ that promoted malaria, the 20_____ water, the decaying vegetation, 21_____ some animal associated with 22_____? Each hypothesis could be 23_____ by experiment: marsh water 24_____ be drunk, mosquitoes destroyed, 25_____ so on.

We have 26_____ now that it was 27_____ mosquitoes, not the marshes 28_____ were primarily involved. But 29_____ went by before this 30_____ was proved. How many 31_____ thought that mosquitoes might 32_____ the factor but could 33_____ prove it? No one 34_____. But we do know 35_____ the odds against success 36_____ tremendous. In all the 37_____ there are about 2,000 38_____ of mosquitoes, and we 39_____ know that only about 40_____ of these transmit 41_____. Ross failed repeatedly in his 42_____ experiments with human malaria. 43_____ now know why— he 44_____ using the wrong kinds 45_____ mosquitoes (Figure 1-7). But 46_____ had an essential characteristic 47_____ a successful scientist—perseverance. 48_____ he found that *Anopheles*— 49_____ the kind of mosquito 50_____ which the *Plasmodium* of man would grow.[6]

---

[4]Bormuth, "Literacy in the Classroom," pp. 65–66.
[5]Bormuth, "Literacy in the Classroom," p. 72.
[6]John A, Moore et al., *Biological Sciences Curriculum Study; A Biological Science: An Inquiry into Life*, 2nd ed. (New York: Harcourt, Brace & World, 1968), p. 15. Used with permission.

The answer key follows:

1. is	26. learned
2. biological	27. the
3. such	28. that
4. with	29. centuries
5. man	30. hypothesis
6. for	31. individuals
7. imperfect	32. be
8. provided	33. never
9. of	34. knows
10. make	35. that
11. of	36. were
12. might	37. world
13. a	38. species
14. and	39. now
15. that	40. 50
16. in	41. malaria
17. could	42. early
18. test	43. we
19. humidity	44. was
20. stagnant	45. of
21. or	46. he
22. marshes	47. of
23. tested	48. eventually
24. could	49. was
25. and	50. in

Students are not being punished when good substitutions are not counted. Their grades do not suffer if they lose points as on a traditional posttest. On the contrary, if the teacher overestimates the student's ability by counting substitutions, the student may suffer by having to read materials that are too difficult and by doing inappropriate assignments.

Bormuth's cloze readability test is a standardized, systematic test which reduces the possibility of teacher error. There is nothing wrong with counting good substitutions when the cloze procedure is used for instructional purposes as described in Part 1; good substitutions should be encouraged to develop context analysis.

A major argument in favor of the cloze test is that it avoids the difficulties and potential lack of accuracy when teachers write and score their own questions. A major disadvantage of the cloze test is that it places those students who are weak in context analysis but strong in other skills at a disadvantage.

Although students are faced with a quantity and variety of demands on their reading skills in any content area, the tests and assessment procedures available are severely limited in the information they can provide about students' reading abilities. Lou Burmeister offers the *modified inventory* as a way of reducing this problem[7] and David Shepherd uses similar procedures in his *group reading inventory*.[8] This type of test measures comprehension levels, vocabulary levels, and reading rate with a long passage from a textbook.

In preparing a modified inventory, the teacher chooses a representative selection from the textbook of about 1,000 words; Burmeister recommends a length of six to eight pages.[9] The first set of questions test students' understanding of key terms in the selection, particularly technical terminology. To insure that the questions call for the particular meanings of the words as used in the passage, Burmeister suggests multiple-choice questions and the inclusion of phrases from the passage.[10] In that way, the inventory is assessing the students' ability to learn meanings of terms by reading.

The remaining set of questions call for a variety of comprehension responses. The questions are arranged in order of difficulty: (1) recall of details, (2) recall of main ideas and sequence, and (3) higher-level questions relevant to the selection, such as drawing conclusions, explaining a process, or evaluating an idea.

Figure 9.2 shows the first section of a chapter in a geometry textbook. Below is a sample inventory of the chapter:

> Part 1.
> Vocabulary and concepts
> Before reading, check your understanding of the following terms. You may have studied them before. Circle the answer which gives the best definition. After you read the chapter, go back and check, and if necessary change, your answers.
> 1. A geometric point is
>   a. something that has a position
>   b. something that has length
>   c. a set
>   d. a line
> 2. A geometric line is
>   a. Something that has width
>   b. Something that has thickness
>   c. A set of points
>   d. A direction in space

THE MODIFIED OR GROUP INVENTORY

---

[7]Lou E. Burmeister, *Reading Strategies for Middle and Secondary School Teachers,* 2nd ed. (Reading, Mass: Addison-Wesley, 1978), pp. 47–59.
[8]David Shepherd, *Comprehensive High School Reading Methods* (Columbus, Ohio: Charles E. Merrill, 1968), pp. 20–21.
[9]Burmeister, *Reading Strategies,* p. 42.
[10]Burmeister, *Reading Strategies,* p. 43.

　　3. A geometric plane is
　　　　a. a set of lines
　　　　b. a set of points
　　　　c. a surface
　　　　d. a flat surface
　　4. A subset of a plane is
　　　　a. a line
　　　　b. a point
　　　　c. the surface of the plane
　　　　d. the position of the plane
　　5. A figure is
　　　　a. a set of planes
　　　　b. a design
　　　　c. a drawing of lines and planes
　　　　d. a drawing of points

Part 2.

When I tell you to begin, start reading pp. 1–3. Read at a comfortable rate. When you finish, look up at the board and write down the time. Later I'll show you how to figure out your words per minute. Then go to Part 3.

Part 3.

Noting details (Circle T or F).

　　6. T-F A line can have three points.
　　7. T-F In geometry, a line is the same as a straight line.
　　8. T-F Capital letters symbolize points.
　　9. T-F A single arrow symbolizes a line.
　10. T-F A box illustrates planes.

Main ideas (Write answers)

　11. What does it mean to say a point has the property of position?
　12. How can one name a line?.
　13. What is the difference between a double arrow and a line?
　14. What is meant by a subset of a given set?
　15. Summarize the relationships between points, lines, and planes.

Translation and higher-level comprehension (Write answers)

　16. Name this line.
　　　　$\underline{\quad R \quad\quad K \quad\quad}$

　17. Make a drawing for:　　BK
　18. How many flat surfaces are there in a box?
　19. Explain each of the symbols in

　　　$\overline{\quad\quad}$

　　　BK

　20. Name an object which would be a good illustration of a horizontal line.

Figure 9.2
Three Pages from a Geometry
Textbook

CHAPTER 1

Sets of Points

1.1   Points, Lines, and Planes

In your study of algebra you worked with sets of numbers. However, you have learned that an element of a set can be almost any kind of object. In geometry much attention is given to sets of *points*.

Point is one of the undefined terms of geometry. That is, no statement will be given that describes precisely what the word *point* means. It is necessary to leave many terms *undefined* in geometry. Usually these are very simple concepts about which people are in general agreement. These terms then form the basis for describing the meaning of many other terms that are used.

A geometric point has no length, width, thickness, weight, or color. However, a point does have one important property, that of *position*. A point is usually represented in a drawing as a dot. Points are named by capital letters. For example, the point represented in the middle of the drawing at the right is called point *O*.

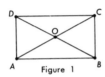

Figure 1

■ **P-1**   What other points are named in the drawing of Figure 1?

Line is another basic term of geometry that will be left undefined. A line is a set of points and is usually named by any two of its points. The word *line* will be used to mean *straight line*.

A line is shown in the drawing of Figure 2. It is called line *AB*. A symbol for "line *AB*" is $\overleftrightarrow{AB}$. The double arrow over the letters is used in place of the word "line."

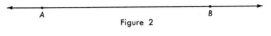

Figure 2

SETS OF POINTS   1

Source: Russell F. Jacobs and Richard A Meyer, *Discovering Geometry* (New York: Harcourt Brace Jovanovich, 1972), pp. 1–3. Used with permission.

Figure 9.2 (Cont'd)

■ **P-2**   What other name can you give to the line of Figure 2?

The two arrowheads on the drawing of a line show that the line extends without end in both directions. A geometric line has no width, thickness, weight, or color. A *drawing* of a line, like the one in Figure 2, does have these properties.

■ **P-3**   What lines can you name in the drawing of Figure 3?

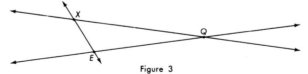

Figure 3

■ **P-4**   What different names can you give to the line in Figure 4?

Figure 4

A third important undefined term of geometry is *plane*. A geometric **plane** is a flat surface with no thickness which extends without end in all directions. Drawings of some planes are shown in Figure 5. Each plane will be named by a single Greek letter or by using the letters of three points that are in the plane. The Greek letters most commonly used are α (alpha), β (beta), and γ (gamma).

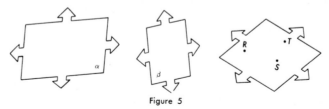

Figure 5

■ **P-5**   How can you name the planes in Figure 5?

The plane at the right in Figure 5 can be named plane *RST*.

You will note that the drawing of a plane must, of necessity, be limited in extent. The arrows are used in Figure 5 to emphasize that a plane does extend infinitely in all directions. However, these arrows will not always be used. Two common ways of drawing *horizontal*

2   CHAPTER 1

planes are shown in Figure 6. Hold a book in a horizontal position in front of you and to your left. You can see that it looks like the drawing of plane α in Figure 6. If you move it to your right, it will look like the drawing of plane β.

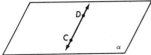 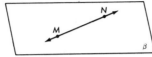

Figure 6

Each plane has a line shown which is a *subset* of the plane.

■ **P-6** What is meant by a subset of a given set?

Line CD is a subset of plane α because every point of $\overrightarrow{CD}$ is also a point of plane α. Also, every point of $\overleftrightarrow{MN}$ is a point of plane β.

> Set A is a subset of set B if every element of set A is an element of set B. You can show such a subset relation as follows.
>
> $$A \subseteq B$$

The relation of the lines and planes of Figure 6 can be shown in symbols also.

$$\overrightarrow{CD} \subseteq \alpha \qquad \overleftrightarrow{MN} \subseteq \beta$$

Two drawings of *vertical* planes are shown in Figure 7.

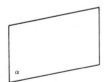 

Figure 7

Hold a book in a vertical position in front of you and to your left. You can see that it looks like the drawing of plane α in Figure 7. If you move it to your right, it will look like the drawing of plane β.

■ **P-7** What are some other examples of physical objects that look like drawings of planes?

SETS OF POINTS **3**

Burmeister recommends timing the students' reading of the selection in order to measure their rate. The teacher records the time on the chalkboard in 10- or 15-second intervals. When students complete the reading, they look up at the chalkboard and write down the time. The minutes (and fractions of minutes) are later divided into the total words to obtain an average rate in words per minute. Before computing the rate, students should close the textbooks and respond to the questions.[11]

A set of questions can also be included to test a student's ability to locate, understand, and use textbook aids. Prior to the reading students can respond to such tasks as locating the table of contents to determine the page of a chapter, locating a definition of a key term in a glossary, and using the index to locate pages on which a topic is discussed.

A teacher can score and interpret the results of a modified inventory using procedures similar to those for the silent IRI. With 20 questions, each correct response would receive 5 points. The teacher would determine the percentage of correct responses and match that percentage with a functional level: 90–100 percent, independent; 70–90 percent, instructional; and 69 percent or below, frustrational.[12]

USING THE RESULTS OF INFORMAL ASSESSMENT

The value of conducting the IRI, the cloze test, or the modified inventory is to provide information for instructional decisions. In beginning and remedial classes, teachers use IRIs for three purposes: 1) to select appropriate materials for each student's instructional level and materials for independent or free reading, 2) to identify skills in which students need instruction, and 3) to evaluate the effectiveness of instruction. To accomplish the third purpose, teachers give the IRI as a pretest (see Chapter 6) and give additional IRIs during and at the end of the instructional experience. Comparisons of a student's performance from one IRI to another should indicate whether instruction is effective. The content-area teacher can use these assessment instruments for the same purposes.

In addition, the results of the IRI, the cloze test, and the modified inventory provide the teacher with guidance in handling materials and making assignments. If students exhibit a wide range of ability, then the results of the assessment might demonstrate a need for materials at many levels. All schools do not have the resources to fully individualize reading assignments by level of material, nor do all teachers believe such a practice is necessary for all assignments.

Nevertheless, given the apparent value of independent reading in promoting both skill development and positive attitudes, all students

---

[11]Burmeister, *Reading Strategies*, p. 42–43.
[12]Burmeister, *Reading Strategies*, p. 45.

should have some independent reading assigned in every course. Informal assessment will indicate if the textbook is easy enough for students to read independently or if students need other materials. If the student cannot read the text or a portion of the text at the independent level, he or she should not be tested on such materials because a teacher cannot provide guidance during a test.

The fact that the student cannot read a text at the independent level does not prevent using that text in instruction. If the teacher knows that the material is at a student's instructional level, he or she can provide various kinds of instructional assistance. El Laissi recommends two basic procedures: 1) providing advance organizers and guiding questions and 2) asking students to use a survey/question procedure.[13] (These procedures were discussed in Part 1 and will be discussed again in Part 3 as they apply to particular content areas.) In addition, the teacher can expect students to encounter difficult words and can use various procedures for reducing vocabulary difficulties.

If the entire text is at a student's frustrational level, teachers will need to find a substitute text or will need to rewrite important passages in the text. Otherwise, the student will miss the opportunity for successful reading in that content area. If only certain portions in the text are at the frustrational level, a teacher can use any of the following four procedures: 1) the teacher can lecture on that section; 2) the teacher (or some volunteers) can read the selection aloud; 3) the portion can be taped for independent listening by students; or 4) the teacher can provide a film or other nonprint media presentation.

These procedures are, of course, not new. Teachers have traditionally provided guiding questions, shown films, done oral readings, and provided supplementary material. The key point in this discussion is that the informal assessment provides information to support these practices. Instead of making decisions about the handling of material on an arbitrary basis, the teacher uses information about each student's reading ability to make such decisions as in the following illustration:

Ms. Norton, a seventh-grade English teacher, developed a three-week unit on the short story. Her concern was not to cover specific authors and their works, but rather to help students develop an appreciation of the short-story form and an understanding of key concepts, such as the emphasis in many stories on the way the main character's problem develops through interactions with other characters. With this broad view of the unit, she was able to collect a number of stories whose difficulty levels ranged from grades one through ten. Some of the selections were high-interest, low-vocabulary materials; that is, the stories were written to appeal to adolescents but with controlled vocabulary for an elementary level of difficulty.

---

[13]Bobbie El Laissi, "Student Teachers' Assessment of Prescription for Secondary Pupils' Reading Levels" (Ph.D. diss., The University of Texas at Austin, 1978), pp. 1–9.

With a modified inventory consisting of passages taken from the stories, she determined that one-third of her class read above grade level, one third at the seventh-grade level, and one third below grade level, with two students reading at the second-grade level. All students received the same guiding questions (as discussed in Chapter 4) but with different stories. To demonstrate key concepts and to provide for large group experiences, Ms. Norton read the more difficult stories aloud, such as *The Black Cat* by Edgar Allen Poe. Each week, students had one and one-half class periods to read stories at their independent level and write brief informal responses. As a culminating activity, students were temporarily grouped by instructional level; these groups prepared and presented dramatic readings of scenes from their stories.

SUMMARY   This chapter presented procedures for several types of informal assessment including the silent IRI, the oral IRI, the improvised inventory, the cloze readability test, and the modified or group inventory. The key advantages of these methods of assessment over standardized reading tests are 1) they can be designed for use with actual materials students are reading in their content-area courses, and 2) they can assess responses which are the same as those required in instructional tasks. There are two key limitations: 1) As with any instrument for assessment they do no more than sample behavior believed to indicate reading ability. 2) Important questions about procedures, such as passage length, have not yet been sufficiently researched with secondary students.

1. Discuss one of the Key Ideas listed in the Overview of this chapter.
2. Following guidelines in this chapter, select passages from a content-area text and prepare questions for them as means of experiencing the process of constructing an informal reading inventory.
3. Following the procedures for the oral IRI, administer an oral reading test to a student (or a friend). Record, analyze, and categorize the miscues.
4. Using materials in a content-area textbook, construct one or more samples of other informal-assessment instruments, such as the cloze readability test, the improvised inventory, or the modified inventory.
5. Using a selection from a content-area textbook, select a purpose for reading (or an appropriate task in the book) and plan or describe a learning experience which incorporates informal assessment and instruction.

Betts, Emmett A. *Foundations of Reading Instruction.* New York: American Book, 1957, chap. 21.

Bond, Guy L., and Tinker, Miles. *Reading Difficulties: Their Diagnosis and Correction.* New York: Appleton-Century-Crofts, 1967.

Bormuth, John R. "Literacy in the Classroom" in William D. Page, ed., *Help for the Reading Teacher: New Directions in Research.* Urbana, Ill.: ERIC Clearinghouse on Reading and Communication Skills, 1975.

Burmeister, Lou E. *Reading Strategies for Middle and Secondary School Teachers,* 2nd ed. Reading, Mass: Addision-Wesley, 1978, chap. 3.

Durr, William K., ed. *Reading Difficulties: Diagnosis, Correction, and Remediation.* Newark, Del.: International Reading Association, 1970.

Farr, Roger, *Reading: What Can Be Measured?* Newark, Del.: International Reading Association, 1969.

————. ed. *Measurement and Evaluation of Reading.* New York: Harcourt, Brace & World, 1979.

Goodman, Kenneth S., ed. *Miscue Analysis: Applications to Reading Instruction.* Urbana, Ill.: ERIC Clearinghouse on Reading and Communication Skills, 1979.

Goodman, Yetta, and Burke, Carolyn. *Reading Miscues Inventory.* New York: Macmillan, 1972.

Hittleman, Daniel, R. *Developmental Reading: A Psycholinguistic Perspective.* Chicago: Rand McNally, 1978, chap. 5.

Johnson, Marjorie S., and Kress, Roy *Informal Reading Inventories.* Newark, Del.: International Reading Association, 1965.

Shepherd, David L. *Comprehensive High School Reading Methods.* Columbus, Ohio: Charles E. Merrill, 1979, chap. 2.

Spache, George D. *Diagnosing and Correcting Reading Disabilities.* Boston: Allyn & Bacon, 1976, chap. 6.

Wilson, Robert R. *Diagnostic and Remedial Reading for Classroom and Clinic,* 2nd ed. Columbus, Ohio: Charles E. Merrill, 1972.

10

Feedback and Self-Assessment

Assessment, or the systematic collection of information about student reading ability in a content area, has three main purposes. Previous chapters identified the first two purposes: diagnosis and evaluation. This chapter discusses a third purpose: the collection of information needed to help students evaluate their past performances and improve their subsequent performances. What many teachers call *marking, grading,* or *correcting* can also be called *feedback,* a term that encompasses both traditional and innovative practices. This chapter will discuss definitions of feedback, the role of feedback in the learning experience, different sources of feedback, and systematic ways of providing feedback.

OVERVIEW

Feedback is knowledge of the results of a performance.

Teachers can provide feedback in a variety of intentional and unintentional ways.

Feedback can affect subsequent student performance.

Feedback systems are procedures or devices that aid students in providing themselves or their peers with information.

In self-assessment, students share in the responsibility for assessment.

Key Ideas

Ms. Young, a senior-high-school science teacher, assigned a textbook chapter which presented a complex discussion of principles by which energy can be changed into different forms. She asked students to list and briefly describe the steps in a scientific process. Before collecting their papers, Ms. Young showed a sample set of responses on an overhead projector and asked her students to compare their responses to the sample. If they left out a step or incorrectly described it, they were to copy the correct response. With this procedure, students had the opportunity to evaluate their own work and provide themselves with information on how well they had performed.

FEEDBACK: A DEFINITION

W. James Popham and Eva Baker believe that knowledge of results is a key component of the learning experience. *Knowledge of results* can be defined as any kind of information which allows a student to "discover whether his [or her] responses are adequate."[1] For example, students are assigned to read a selection and then respond to a set of questions.[2] As soon as the students are finished, the teacher reviews the answers while students check their work. This review and self-check provides students with information on the results of their reading.

Popham and Baker stress that students must respond in an active way in order to learn. What they do in responding should be related to the goals or purposes of the learning experience. Stated another way, they should have "appropriate practice."[3] If, for example, the purpose of a history lesson is to identify cause/effect relationships, students should have the chance to practice reading for that purpose.

Learning by doing in itself is not sufficient. As Popham and Baker note, students may learn the wrong responses.[4] Even if they are responding appropriately, students may be uncertain of their responses. In the first instance, knowledge of results is needed so that students can correct inappropriate responses. In the second instance, knowledge of results allows students to confirm their appropriate responses.

Feedback includes any information a student receives on his or her performance. When teachers review answers or grade an assignment, they are presenting information to the students on their performance. This broad definition considers several events in the classroom as potential sources of feedback.

---

[1]W. James Popham and Eva L. Baker, *Planning an Instructional Sequence* (Englewood Cliffs, N.J.: Prentice-Hall, 1970), p. 2.
[2]Popham and Baker, *Planning an Instructional Sequence*, p. 30.
[3]Popham and Baker, *Planning an Instructional Sequence*, p. 2
[4]Popham and Baker, *Planning an Instructional Sequence*, p. 28.

Teachers have traditionally provided feedback in a variety of ways. The information may be presented orally, in writing, or in the form of grades, points, scores, editing symbols, checks, or comments. The feedback may be provided by reviewing or discussing responses; simply displaying correct answers (for example in an answer key); displaying or reading an exemplary piece of student work; checking, correcting, or scoring answers; editing students' writing; writing comments on students' papers; making verbal responses to the class or to individuals; and even smiling or frowning.

VARIETY OF FEEDBACK

In fact, teachers often present unintended feedback. For example: Ted walks up to the teacher's desk and asks where he should place his assignment. If the teacher, preoccupied with an upcoming lesson, says, "Oh, don't bother with that now," Ted might take that comment as a negative judgment of his work. Linda makes an unexpected response to a question during discussion, and perhaps the teacher doesn't know what to say. Linda might take the silence as a put-down. In another example, Gary crams the night before a test and receives a score of 100; the feedback tells him that cramming is a good thing to do.

Although the terminology may be new, the ideas discussed so far should be familiar to the reader. Teachers have traditionally elicited and checked student responses and recorded information on the responses. These practices have been carried out for three purposes: 1) to insure students are doing their work, 2) to evaluate students' learning, and 3) to influence their future performance. When students are doing well, most teachers believe they should be encouraged to continue working hard. The encouragement may take the form of a good grade or a high score. When students are doing poorly, most teachers hope the information they give on their performance will cause students to try harder, be more attentive, or spend more time on their work. When teachers write comments on students' work, they tend to believe that the comments are truly instructive and that students will learn from them.

THE ROLE OF FEEDBACK IN LEARNING
Influencing Student Performance

Effect on Performance. In their definitions of feedback, Donald Smith, Richard Olds, and Dale Brethower stress the effect of feedback.[5] Feedback is not any information on performance but only *that information which affects subsequent performance.* In the following illustration, students are asked to read the first part of a short story and record key details about the main character. One of the students, Carlos, notes only

---

[5]Donald E. P. Smith, *Learning to Read and Write: A Task Analysis.* Volume 1 of *A Technology of Reading and Writing,* edited by Donald E. P. Smith (New York: Academic Press, 1976), pp. 121-25; Richard E. Olds, "Response Frequency in Reading Tasks Under Two Schedules of Information Feedback" (Ph.D. diss., The University of Michigan, 1970); and Dale M. Brethower, "The Classroom as a Self-Modifying System" (Ph.D. diss., The University of Michigan, 1970).

a few details, either because he has not kept the purpose in mind or because he is not sure what a key detail is. When the teacher lists key details on the board and asks students to check their work, Carlos is thereby informed of what he has done successfully and what he has failed to do. When he reads the remainder of the story and notes many more key details, the information has positively affected his subsequent performance.

Spelling by Approximation Spelling by Approximation, a technique developed by Richard Ballard, provides a graphic illustration of the role of feedback in a learning experience.[6] It has been successfully used in beginning and remedial reading courses and in content-area courses in which the teacher wants students to learn to spell and define vocabulary words. According to Ballard, when students have difficulty with a word, they must try to make approximations of the word and then discover how their approximations differ from the correct spelling. Figure 10.1 illustrates the process.

Using a sheet which has three or more columns, students take a pretest on a set of words by writing their spellings in the second column (Step 1). The pretest is conducted in a traditional manner; the teacher pronounces the words and gives a sample sentence for each. The words may be key vocabulary words for the week, words students have selected from their reading or writing, or those words found in students' personal dictionaries (discussed in Chapter 3). Students can also pair up and test each other.

After the pretest, the teacher (or classmate), presents the correct spellings of the words—usually by writing them on the chalkboard. The students copy the correctly spelled words in the first column (Step 2). The teacher counts the letters in the entire set of correctly spelled words and enters the total in a box at the bottom of the first column. This total represents a perfect score for spelling all words correctly.

Students then compare their attempts at spelling (Step 1) with the correct spellings to discover which they have spelled successfully and which unsuccessfully. To insure that students make this comparison, they must count the number of letters in the pretest which are correct and in correct sequence (Step 3) and subtract points for unnecessary letters. For example, *meeter* would receive four points: five correct letters each receive one point, but one point is subtracted for the extra *e*. *Skan* would receive three points. The total is recorded in the box at the bottom of the column.

Students retake the test immediately so that they can take advantage of the information they have discovered. Students must continue to

---

[6]Richard Ballard, ''Spelling by Approximation,'' in Richard Ballard and Walter J. Lamberg, *Strategies for Individualizing Instruction in Content-Areas* (Ann Arbor: Office of Instructional Services, The University of Michigan, 1975).

Figure 10.1
Example of Spelling by
Approximation

Step 1.   meeter
                  rime
                  sceem
                  acent
                  skan

Step 2.
meter   5   meeter
rhyme   5   rime
scheme   6   sceem
accent   6   acent
scan   4   skan
         ——
         26

Step 3.
meter   5   meeter   5-1
rhyme   5   rime   3
scheme   6   sceen   2
accent   6   acent   5
scan   4   skan   3
         ——   ——
         26   17

Step 4.
meter   5   meeter   5-1   meter   5
rhyme   5   rime   3   rime   3
scheme   6   sceem   2   scheme   6
accent   6   acent   5   acent   5
scan   4   skan   3   scan   4
         ——   ——   ——
         26   17   23

Step 5.
meter   5   meeter   5-1   meter   5   meter   5
rhyme   5   rime   3   rime   3   rhyme   5
scheme   6   sceem   2   scheme   6   scheme   6
accent   6   acent   5   acent   5   accent   6
scan   4   skan   3   scan   4   scan   4
         ——   ——   ——   ——
         26   17   23   26

Source: Richard Ballard and Walter J. Lamberg, *Strategies for Individualizing Instruction in Content Areas* (Ann Arbor: Office of Instructior al Services, The University of Michigan, 1974), p. 52.

retake the test until they can spell the entire set correctly. Each time the test is taken, the other columns are folded over so that the students cannot see the correct spellings or their earlier attempts. With each test, students record total points (Step 4). The simple purpose of the activity is for students to learn to write the correct spelling without seeing the models (Step 5). The activity has some similarity to a technique developed by Grace Fernald for beginning and remedial reading, which also aims at the student's ability to write a word without having the correct spelling in view.[7] Her technique consists of the following steps:

1. The student tells the teacher a word he or she wants to learn to spell.
2. The teacher writes the word in large letters with black crayon to provide the model.
3. The student traces the word with his or her finger while slowly saying word. This step can be repeated.
4. The student tries to write the word without seeing the model.
5. The student repeats steps 3 and 4 until the word can be written correctly.[8]

Feedback on Complex Performances

The previous example of a spelling activity cannot do justice to the complexities that are involved in comprehension and vocabulary study or to the difficulties in providing effective feedback for those performances. Quite often, the feedback teachers provide has unintended and undesirable effects on reading and study. In some cases, the information students receive on one aspect of a performance has negative effects on other aspects, as the following illustrates:

Amber turns in a theme with many spelling errors. The teacher marks all the errors, assigns a *D*, and makes no comment about the content of the theme. On the next assignment, Amber has no spelling errors and the teacher is pleased. A comparison of the two compositions, however, would reveal that the second is shorter than the first, the ideas are not fully developed, and the style is less interesting. Amber avoided spelling errors by writing fewer words overall and by using words she was certain of. Content, interest, and length suffered.

A history assignment requires students to read a chapter and list the main points for each page. Don completes only three fourths of the chapter by the end of the week and receives a zero. The next week, he reads one-third of the chapter, decides he won't finish on time, and stops reading. Another classmate, Kim, who also got a zero discovers a trick; she skims through the chapter and translates each subheading into a main point. She misses the explanations of the points, but she completes the assignment on time and receives a check. In both cases, feedback on the written responses had a negative effective on the reading.

A positive example of effects of feedback on complex performances is found with the survey chart in Table 10.1 used for survey/question procedures[9] (see page 95 in Chapter 5). The chart format insures that all steps receive equal attention, so that the student will not try to improve one skill at the expense of another.

---

[7]Grace Fernald, *Remedial Techniques in Basic School Subjects* (New York: McGraw-Hill, 1943).
[8]Fernald, *Remedial Techniques in Basic School Subjects.*
[9]Richard Ballard and Walter J. Lamberg, *Teaching the Picture and Text Survey* (Ann Arbor: Office of Instructional Services, The University of Michigan, 1974) and in Donald E. P. Smith, *The Adaptive Classroom.* Volume 3: *A Technology of Reading and Writing,* edited by Donald E. P. Smith (New York: Academic Press, 1977), pp. 229–52.

Purpose	Text	Survey	Organize	Question	Answer	Confirm	
	Rhetoric						**Table 10.1**
Pre-test	p. 117	1	4	5	4	5	Survey Chart
Increase	Rhetoric						
answers to 5	p. 118	1	7	5	5	5	

To encourage improvement of the survey step, students record the number of pages covered during the survey in the third column. If students received information only on the pages covered, they might be encouraged to do a careless job and to simply flip pages. To avoid this problem, they also receive information on the number of words written in the organize step and the number of questions posed in columns 4 and 5. In other words, when surveying, they must try to gather as much information as they can. If they received information only on the number of words written, they might be encouraged to slow down, and, as a result, not improve their surveying skill.

To successfully use the survey/question procedures students must make inferences. To encourage the making of inferences, teachers give students points for every question and answer predicted, whether or not they are addressed in the text. At the same time, students need to try to predict questions and answers which are found in the text; therefore, they receive points in column 7 for answers confirmed or located in the read step. As a result, both the attempts at inference and the attention to actual words in the text are encouraged.

FEEDBACK SYSTEMS

Feedback systems are procedures or devices which aid students in providing themselves or their peers with information. They also aid teachers in providing consistent, task-related information. Feedback systems, also called *progress records,* take the form of checklists, charts, and graphs.[10] The need for feedback systems can be illustrated by the following account of learning outside of school.

Everyday after school, Ted practices shooting baskets at the playground. When he holds and shoots the ball in an appropriate way, it goes through the hoop. But when he does something wrong, he does not get a basket. The hoop serves as a feedback system, informing Ted of his performance. The hoop provides information about whether the ball goes clearly through the hoop, balances on the rim, bounces off the

---

[10]Geraldine Markel and Daniel R. Wolter, *Designing and Using Feedback Forms* (Ann Arbor: Office of Instructional Services, The University of Michigan, 1974); and Donald E. P. Smith, *The Adaptive Classroom,* pp. 27–63.

backboard, or misses the hoop by several inches. With this information, Ted begins shaping his performance. He holds the ball in more effective ways, he improves his coordination, and he attends more closely to what he is doing and to the distance and direction involved in a shot.

In most study situations, students have no "hoop." As they read they may rely on a subjective feeling as to whether or not they are successful. When they write answers to questions or write a composition, they may not even stop to reread their work. Thus, they are dependent upon the teacher for feedback. Feedback systems give them the means of objectifying their reactions to their work, of evaluating their performance in a systematic way, of discovering their successes, and of controlling their attention to what they are doing.[11]

Checklists For many of the sophisticated performances demanded of secondary students, a checklist may be an appropriate feedback system. The checklist below simply lists key questions to be answered in reading.

As you read each poem, check off the questions you can answer.

Questions	Poem 1	Poem 2	Poem 3
1. What images are used?	√	√	
2. From what area of life do the images come?		√	
3. What idea or feeling do the images all have?	√	√	
4. How do the images contribute to the theme of the poem?			

The checklist below includes a point system. Students use an answer key to record points for appropriate responses.

Give yourself 5 points for each correct detail you found in answering these questions.

Points

1. What are the powers of the President in domestic affairs?
2. What are the powers of the President in foreign affairs?
3. What are the limitations on the President's powers?
4. What are the qualifications for becoming President?

The checklist below, based on forms developed by Ruth Cohen and associates, has specific tasks to be completed in an efficient

---

[11]Smith, *The Adaptive Classroom*, pp. 7–8.

sequence.[12] This system includes a place for students to record due dates for completion of tasks. It helps students schedule their work over a period of time.

Due Dates	Tasks
Oct 1	1. Select topic for research project.
Oct 2	2. Find two sources.
Oct 3	3. Survey sources and write general question.
Oct 4	4. Turn question into at least three specific questions.
Oct 5	5. Read to find and write answers to each question.
Oct 10	6. Write draft of report.
Oct 15	7. Have classmate read draft.
Oct 18	8. Revise draft.
Oct 19	9. Proofread.
Oct 21	10. Turn in finished report.

Charts

While charts are similar to checklists, they provide a more extensive record of information. The survey chart is one example (see Table 10.1 on page 187). Students can also use a combination chart and response sheet where they record their responses as well as information on them (as with the form for Spelling by Approximation, in Figure 10.1). A teacher can design study activities to serve as feedback systems. Ruth Thomas and H. Alan Robinson suggest the type of form illustrated below for foreign language study.[13] Students record words and their meanings. They then cover the righthand part of the form and practice defining the words. By uncovering the appropriate entry in the form, they receive immediate feedback. As additional feedback, students could place a check by the words they have learned.

Word or idiom	Meaning	Illustrative sentences
magna	large	Cisterna est magna
casa	small house	Casae non surt magnae.

Graphs

Checklists and charts aid students in making necessary responses or completing certain tasks in an assignment. When students are asked to show a quantitive increase in number of responses or amount of material

---

[12]Ruth Cohen et al., *Quest: Academic Skills Program* (New York: Harcourt Brace Jovanovich, 1973), p. 267–270.

[13]Ellen Thomas and H. Alan Robinson, *Improving Reading in Every Class,* abridged 2nd ed. (Boston: Allyn & Bacon, 1977), p. 366.

Figure 10.2
Graph of Weekly Test Scores

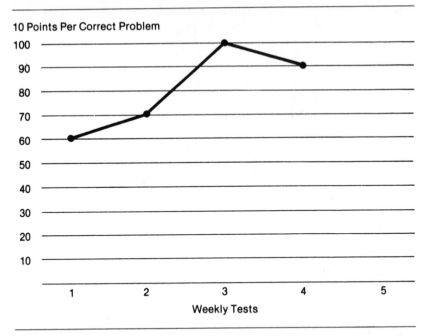

Figure 10.3
Rate/Comprehension Graph

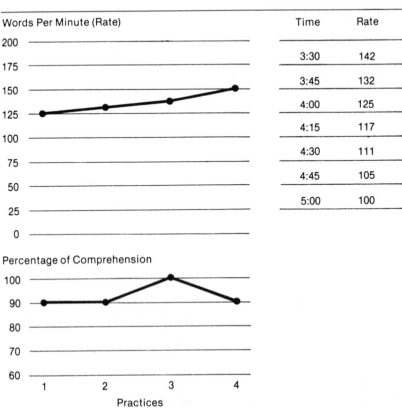

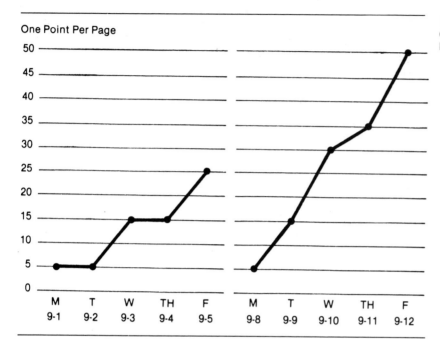

One Point Per Page

Figure 10.4
Cumulative Graph of Interest Reading

to be completed, graphs can serve as appropriate feedback systems. As illustrated in Figure 10.2, the vertical line shows the items to be completed or increased—in this case, scores on weekly mathematics tests. The horizontal line notes the number and date of study lessons or tests.

The graph in Figure 10.3 is used in exercises to improve reading rate. Increases in rate in average words per minute (WPM) are recorded in the top portion; changes in comprehension in terms of percentage are recorded in the bottom portion. The graph in Figure 10.4 provides a cumulative record of weekly reading for pleasure. Each day as the student reads, he or she records the total pages read during the session. For each subsequent session, the student adds the number of pages read; the last entry provides the total number of pages read that week.

Contracts

Contracts for student work can be considered feedback systems. As noted by Eileen Duval and her associates, contracts provide the means for teachers and students to keep track of a student's progress in completing learning activities.[14] In that sense, contracts provide students with feedback on their performance. In recent years, contracts have been used extensively in reading courses, particularly those which are individualized. Since students are doing different activities and using

---

[14]Eileen V. Duval et al., "Learning Stations and the Reading Class," in Richard A. Earle, ed., *Classroom Practice in Reading* (Newark, Del.: International Reading Association, 1977), pp. 109–19.

different materials, the teacher should have records of individual work and students should be able to operate with some independence. Contracts have also been used in content-area courses, whether or not instruction is individualized.

There is no single definition or format for contracts. At its simplest, a contract is a written record, or list, of activities to be completed by the student. Details such as specific pages to be read, descriptions of required assignments, or assignment due dates are included, as in the following:

I plan to do the following activities
    Ⓥ   1. Read chapter 7.
    Ⓥ   2. Write questions for small group.
    √   3. Discuss questions with small group.
    √   4. Participate in class discussion.
    √   5. Complete chapter exercises.
    √   6. Conduct laboratory experiment 1.
        7. Conduct laboratory experiment 2.
    √   8. Write report for 1.
        9. Write report for 2.
       10. Write summary of additional reading.

(The student checks the activities he or she has chosen and circles the check when the activity is completed.)

Some contracts take the format of a calendar. After the teacher has filled in required activities for the week, students record other activities they have chosen and scheduled for themselves:

Monday	Tuesday	Wednesday
1. Preview of week's activities.	1. Class reading—"Tornado." *Reading into the Future,* pp. 3–7.	1. Silent reading—"The Challenge," pp. 10–15.
2. Fill in contract.	2. Class discussion on questions, pp. 8–9.	2. Write answers to questions, p. 16.
3. Visit library to find materials.	3. Self-selected reading	3. Self-selected reading
4. Self-selected reading		

Thursday	Friday
1. Review answers to questions, p. 15.	1. Complete/check week's activities.
2. Lesson on recalling details.	2. Self-selected reading
3. Class reading— "Surprise," pp. 23–26.	
4. Class discussion.	

For some teachers the essence of a contract is that it is a signed agreement between the student and the teacher. The student signs his or her name as a commitment to complete certain activities, sometimes by a specified due date, as follows:[15]

Date ————————————————————————————

I agree to complete the following assignments by

Date ————————————————————————————

————————————————————————————

————————————————————————————

————————————————————————————

————————————————————————————

Student's Signature

————————————————————

Teacher's Signature

In some cases, the agreement will also note the value of the work in terms of points or a grade. The teacher may sign his or her name to indicate approval and commitment to give credit for the work. Some teachers will actually negotiate the contract with students and will discuss the particular activities to be completed and the value of the activities. This approach is sometimes described as *contingency contracting*. The teacher makes certain rewards (grades or points) or rewarding activities (free time or visits with friends) contingent upon successful completion of the learning activities.

For some teachers, a contract may be simply a handout which lists all activities for the class to complete during an instructional experience. For other teachers, the contracts are individualized to facilitate self-selection and self-pacing. The teacher provides a list of possible activities, from which students choose their assignments. Students may also schedule their own work either by selecting the order in which they will complete the assignments or by determining the amount of time they will spend on assignments.

Chapter 2 described a course contract used in a tenth-grade English class, which focuses on study, reading, and writing skills (see p. 26–27).[16] Students must complete some objectives from each of four different areas, but they can decide on the order of completion. The

---

[15]Duval et al., "Learning Stations and the Reading Class," p. 113.
[16]Audrey Gomon, *Learning Lab*, Franklin Senior High School (Lavonia, Mich.: Franklin Senior High School, 1974).

contract states objectives in relatively general terms; students, with the teacher's guidance, can decide on the specific ways they will fulfill the objectives.

A contract can serve in place of a report card for students with a record of their work for each six-week period. Completion of each objective is equated with a point value. As students record points, they are receiving feedback on their performance in meeting course objectives. In addition, students keep weekly contracts on which they record specific activities they are working on; these serve as daily and weekly feedback systems.

FEEDBACK AND SELF-ASSESSMENT   Learning contracts and other feedback systems, such as charts and graphs, promote self-assessment. Earlier chapters broadly defined assessment as the systematic collection of information. Those chapters emphasized assessment by teachers for the purposes of diagnosis and evaluation. As this chapter has shown, however, students can share in the responsibility for assessment. Students can use a feedback form for a specific instructional activity, such as the use of the survey/question procedure when reading textbooks chapters. Contracts can be designed to list a variety of activities to be completed during an instructional unit or an entire course. With the aid of these feedback systems, students can analyze their own responses and collect and record information on them. This process of self-assessment is instructive; students learn in part by doing and in part by discovering what they have done. (Part 3 will address self-assessment as it relates to reading in different content areas.)

SUMMARY   This chapter discussed the role of feedback in learning. Feedback is knowledge of the results of a student's performance. Performance information is communicated to students in a variety of ways: teachers can choose both traditional practices where the teacher is the source of the feedback or the more recent practices of peer-provided and self-provided feedback. Procedures that provide feedback can facilitate learning.

1. Discuss one of the Key Ideas listed in the Overview of this chapter.
2. Select a set of chapter questions or exercises in a content-area textbook. Describe in specific terms the feedback students would need to discover the adequacy of their responses to the activities.
3. Select a set of instructional activities, as in activity 2. Construct a checklist, chart, or other form which could be used by students for self-provided feedback.
4. Select an activity you will be engaged in over a period of time. Construct a feedback system, such as a checklist, chart, or graph, to record information on your performance in that activity.
5. Outline learning activities for an instructional unit in your content area. Then translate that outline into a learning contract for students.

Annett, John. *Feedback and Human Behavior.* Middlesex, England: Penguin Books, 1969.

Ballard, Richard, and Lamberg, Walter J. *Strategies for Individualizing Instruction in Content-Areas.* Ann Arbor: Office of Instructional Services, The University of Michigan, 1975.

Barrett, Thomas C., ed. *The Evaluation of Children's Reading Achievement.* Newark, Del.: International Reading Association, 1967.

Chapman, R. E. *"Evaluation and Feedback in Innovative School Programs."* (Ph.D. Diss., The University of Michigan, 1973) (Univ. Microfilm No. 34,1472A, 1974).

Cohen, Ruth et al. *Quest: Academic Skills Program.* New York: Harcourt Brace & Jovanovich, 1973, unit 5.

Earle, Richard A., ed. *Classroom Practice in Reading.* Newark, Del.: International Reading Association, 1977.

Fernald, Grace. *Remedial Techniques in Basic School Subjects.* New York: McGraw-Hill, 1943.

Gomon, Audrey. "Systems Communication Patterns: An Institution's Response to an Innovation."Ph.D. diss. The University of Michigan, 1974. (Univ. Microfilm No. 35, 4250A, 1975).

Hunkins, Francis P. *Involving Students in Questioning.* Boston: Allyn & Bacon, 1976.

Macrorie, Ken. *Writing to be Read.* Rochelle Park, N.J.: Hayden Book, 1968, chap. 10.

Markle, Geraldine, and Wolter, Daniel. *Designing and Using Feedback Forms.* Ann Arbor: Office of Instructional Services, The University of Michigan, 1975.

Moffett, James. *Teaching the Universe of Discourse.* Boston: Houghton-Mifflin, 1968.

Moffett, James, and Wagner, Betty Jane, *Student-Centered Language Arts and Reading, K-13: A Handbook for Teachers,* 2nd ed. Boston: Houghton-Mifflin, 1976.

Morgan, Raymond F., and Culver, Victor I. "Locus of Control and Reading Achievement: Applications for the Classroom." *Journal of Reading,* 21: 5 (February 1978): 403–8.

Popham, W. James. *Planning an Instructional Sequence.* Englewood Cliffs, N.J.: Prentice-Hall, 1970.

Resnick, Lauren B. "Motivational Aspects of the Literacy Problem," in John R. Carroll and Jeanne S. Chall, eds. *Toward a Literate Society: The Report of the Committee on Reading of the National Academy of Education.* New York: McGraw-Hill, 1975.

Smith, Donald E. P. *Learning to Read and Write: A Task Analysis.* Volume 1: *A Technology of Reading and Writing,* edited by Donald E. P. Smith. New York: Academic Press, 1976.

Thomas, Ellen, and Robinson, H. Alan. *Improving Reading in Every Class,* abridged 2nd ed. Boston: Allyn & Bacon, 1977.

Walter, Tim, and Siebert. A. I. *Student Success: How to Be a Better Student and Still Have Time for Your Friends.* New York: Holt, Rinehart, & Winston, 1976.

Wilson, Robert M. *Diagnostic and Remedial Reading for Classroom and Clinic,* 2nd ed. Columbus, Ohio: Charles E. Merrill, 1972, chap. 6.

Wolter, Daniel, and Lamberg, Walter J. "The Effect of Feedback on Writing: Research Review and Implications." *English in Texas* 8:3 (Spring 1977): 67–70.

3

Teaching Reading in the Content Areas

With a broad understanding of secondary reading and strategies for assessment and instruction, the teacher is prepared to consider specific application of those strategies to particular content areas. Part 3 discusses that application in separate chapters on reading in each of the major content areas. Each chapter includes an identification of specific problems encountered in the reading in that content area, and a discussion of procedures for helping students develop vocabulary, comprehension, and study skills for that area. Chapters 11 and 12 discuss reading in English and the social-science courses. Chapters 13 and 14 examine the reading involved in the study of mathematics and science. Chapter 15 discusses reading in foreign languages and Chapter 16 discusses reading in music, art, health, and physical education. Chapter 17 discusses reading in vocational education, home economics, industrial arts, and business education.

11

Reading in English

Perhaps the most noteworthy characteristic of the secondary English curriculum is its great variety. Students should find the study of English highly rewarding and enjoyable, but many are overwhelmed by the quantity and variety of demands in reading and writing. This chapter will examine some of the reading difficulties and procedures in the study of literature.

The English curriculum has traditionally had three components: language, literature, and composition. This model is changing.

Key Ideas

James Moffett developed a complete language-arts curriculum that relates all aspects of language and counters the fragmentation in the English curriculum.

Reading in literature has unique problems that require attention from the English teacher.

Extensive reading can stimulate interest and enjoyment and serve as a basis for literature study.

Students in a tenth-grade English class were studying imagery in poetry. Mr. Frank presented a general definition with an illustration from a short poem. Students read additional poems aloud with Mr. Frank defining unfamiliar words. After each poem was read, students responded to general questions about the overall meaning of the poems. In order to check basic comprehension, Mr. Frank asked students to identify and interpret images.

STRUCTURE AND CHANGE IN THE CURRICULUM

Since the 1950s, the dominant structure of the secondary English curriculum has been the *tripod concept*. English is presented as having three equally important components: language, literature, and composition.[1] This three-part structure has been widely criticized. Some educators are concerned about the neglect of the spoken language and have called for a fourth component—oral communication.[2] Others, who see an overemphasis on content and cognitive learning, believe a curriculum organized around the four language arts of speaking, listening, reading, and writing provides a better balance of cognitive, skill, and affective learning.

Still others see a basic lack of logic in the tripod concept. They argue that literature and composition are really aspects of language, not components that are separate from and equal to language. They prefer to view the curriculum as David Shepherd describes it: one which "consists of many parts in an interrelationship based upon the nucleic core of language itself."[3]

Variety of Materials

A great variety is available just within the literature studied. The curriculum has held on to the classics—the works of ancient Rome and Greece and British literature—while adding 18th- and 19th-century British and American literature, then early 20th-century and contemporary literature. The traditional genre include poetry, drama, the essay, and fiction. Less traditional genre include: folk music; popular songs; journalism; mythology; European, African, Asian, and Latin American literature; the electronic media, film, television, and radio; and autobiography and biography.

Variety can also be seen in student writing. This may include formal essays, creative writing, business and personal letters, applications and

---

[1] A short, but helpful, discussion of changes in the curriculum is found in Stephen N. Judy, *Explorations in the Teaching of Secondary English: A Source Book for Experimental Teaching* (New York: Dodd, Mead, 1974), pp. 3–19.
[2] A discussion of the place of oral language in the English curriculum is in Dwight L. Burton et al. *Teaching English Today* (Boston: Houghton-Mifflin, 1975), pp. 69–107.
[3] David L. Shepherd, *Comprehensive High School Reading Methods* (Columbus, Ohio: Charles E. Merrill, 1973), p. 170.

legal forms, and expressive or free writing by which students can write with great freedom to increase fluency, enjoyment, and freshness of style. Students are likely to encounter three kinds of grammars—traditional, structural, and transformational—during their schooling. Jeanne Herndon provides a very helpful, concise comparison of these three grammars.[4]

The difficulties students might experience with the various materials are compounded by the many purposes and goals for which they are expected to read and study. Also, many teachers often demand that students read each work for several purposes. The goals of sophisticated understanding, appreciation, and performance, which can be accomplished only over a period of time, are often imposed upon students at the very start of instruction.

Variety of Goals

Shepherd lists three very broad goals of language study, which are essentially the goals of all education: "1) cultivating within the student the qualities needed for a satisfying life, 2) developing social sensitivity and effective participation in the activities of society, 3) helping the student toward a vocational competence."[5] Each area of English has its own broad goals, which include:

Spoken Language:

   To improve communication
   To encourage self-expression
   To increase understanding and appreciation of spoken language

Written Composition:

   To employ writing as an outlet
   To discover what one thinks
   To gain opportunities for communication
   To gain an awareness of the world
   To gain pride, self-esteem, and satisfaction

Literature:

   To gain insight into themselves and their problems
   To gain vicarious experience
   To be exposed to different ways of life
   To observe language at work
   To discover truth and reality[6]

As might be expected, these goals and materials call for a wide range of reading skills. The skills discussed in Chapter 3 on vocabulary, Chapter

Variety of Reading Skills

---

[4]Jeanne H. Herndon, *A Survey of Modern Grammars* (New York: Holt, Rinehart, & Winston, 1970).
[5]Shepherd, *Comprehensive High School Reading Methods,* p. 169.
[6]Burton et al., *Teaching English Today.*

4 on comprehension, and Chapter 5 on study skills and reading efficiency are important to English. The following list of skills emphasizes the importance of reading in English.

Vocabulary Skills:

Word origins
Multiple meanings
Word structure
Shifts in meaning
Subject matter (technical) words
Words from other languages
Idioms
Onomatopoetic words
Denotation and connotation
Words of classification
Abstract and concrete words
Antonyms, synonyms, and homonyms
Words not common in speech but used in writing
Slang
Strange words used by an author

Comprehension Skills:

Sentences of all types
Main ideas
Sequence
Details and their relationship to main ideas
Author's organization[7]

Fragmentation in the Curriculum   To further compound students' difficulties, the English curriculum has a marked tendency toward what Shepherd calls "compartmentalization"[8] and what James Squire and Roger Applebee call "fragmentation."[9] A fragmented curriculum treats the various aspects of English as separate entities and neglects the relationships between them. This neglect undercuts both the interest and meaningfulness of the various aspects. Students may study literature as though it held no relationship to their own writing. Within literature, poetry, drama, and fiction are studied in separate units. Composition is divorced from creative writing, even though good essays and research papers are creative and good creative works must be well composed.

---

[7]Shepherd, *Comprehensive High School Reading Methods,* pp. 173–74.
[8]Shepherd, *Comprehensive High School Reading Methods,* p. 170.
[9]James R. Squire and Roger K. Applebee, *A Study of English Programs in Selected High Schools Which Consistently Educate Outstanding Students in English* (Urbana, Ill.: National Council of Teachers of English, 1966).

James Moffett has made a major contribution in attempting to counter the fragmented nature of the curriculum. He has developed a complete language arts curriculum, from kindergarten to the first year of college, that relates all aspects of language. His structure 1) divides the study of literature into the four broad modes of narration, dramatization, exposition, and persuasion, and 2) studies the role of the speaker (or writer), the subject, and the audience (or reader), and the various relationships among those components. For example, different points of view of the speaker toward the subject and different degrees of distance between the speaker and the audience are explored.[10]

Moffett's ideas can be applied to a unit on the narrative mode. Students would read various kinds of narratives: short stories, narrative poems, autobiographical sketches, and passages from history. In addition to the silent reading, they would listen to and perform dramatic readings of the works. To relate their writing to their reading, they would compose in narrative form by writing stories, narrative poems, and autobiographical and biographical pieces. They would read these writings aloud in class. These activities, along with discussion, provide equal attention to speaking, listening, reading, and writing.

MOFFETT'S LANGUAGE ARTS CURRICULUM

Students will encounter three kinds of vocabulary difficulties in reading literature: obsolete words, specialized terms, or technical terms.

First, older forms of literature will often have obsolete words or words that have undergone a change in meaning, usage, or form, as in the following passage from a Shakespearean play:

READING LITERATURE
Vocabulary

Scene II. A camp near Forres.
Alarum within. Enter Duncan, Malcolm, Donalbain, Lennox, with Attendants, meeting a bleeding Sergeant.

DUN: What bloody man is that? He can report,
As seemeth by his plight, of the revolt
The newest state.
MAL: This is the sergeant
Who like a good and hardy soldier fought
'Gainst my captivity. Hail, brave friend!
Say to the king the knowledge of the broil
As thou didst leave it.[11]

---

[10]James Moffett, *A Student-Centered Language Arts Curriculum, K-13: A Handbook for Teachers* (Boston: Houghton-Mifflin, 1968) and *Teaching the Universe of Discourse* (Boston: Houghton-Mifflin, 1968).
[11]William Shakespeare, *The Complete Works of Shakespeare,* ed. Hardin Craig (Glenview, Ill.: Scott, Foresman, 1961), p. 1047.

Students may also encounter specialized terminology that is important to the particular context of a literary work. In the following passage from *The Old Man and the Sea,* the terminology of fishing is important:

> The boy had given him two fresh small tunas, or albacores, which hung on the two deepest lines like plummets and, on the others, he had a big blue runner and a yellow jack that had been used before; but they were in good condition still and had the excellent sardines to give them scent and attractiveness. Each line, as thick around as a big pencil, was looped onto a green-sapped stick so that any pull or touch on the bait would make the stick dip and each line had two forty-fathom coils. . . .[12]

Finally, literary criticism uses many technical literary terms.

Unfamiliar Words in Literary Works. Students will meet unfamiliar words in literature, especially when they are studying an author for the first time. As discussed in Chapter 7, many commonly used readability formulas, such as the Fry Formula, do not measure the familiarity of words. In the short Shakespearean passage, at least ten words will be unfamiliar in meaning or form to most students (including some of the proper names).

All literature, whatever its age, will have words important to the particular context. One of the values found in great literature lies in its specific, concrete re-creation of experience. A story of the sea will have words familiar to sailors. A story set in a particular geographical region, such as the Deep South, or in a foreign country will have language which reflects the characteristics of those regions and of their dialects and languages.

Selectivity. Some teachers demand that students look up all unfamiliar words and be prepared to define them. As a result, students may experience so much drudgery and frustration that they will have little enjoyment or understanding of the literature. Other teachers follow a more selective approach, like the following, which still provides for vocabulary development.

Each week students are expected to learn from five to ten new words. These can be entered in their personal dictionaries (see Chapter 3). Students are to find the meanings of the words in dictionaries, glossaries, or footnotes in the text. As with other unfamiliar words, students are encouraged to use context analysis, but they can skip the words without penalty or ask the teacher for help. The teacher can provide what Ellen Thomas and H. Alan Robinson call "preventive instruction" by going over difficult words prior to student reading.[13]

---

[12]Ernest Hemingway, *The Old Man and the Sea* (New York: Scribner's, 1952), p. 31.
[13]Ellen L. Thomas and H. Alan Robinson, *Improving Reading in Every Class,* abridged 2nd ed. (Boston: Allyn & Bacon, 1977), p. 259.

Oral Reading. Oral reading will reduce some vocabulary difficulties. Many of the unfamiliar words will be more readily understood when students hear them read aloud in context. A good, dramatic oral reading will also contribute to appreciation of the work.

Technical Terminology. In literature study, technical terminology includes 1) those terms used to classify literary works, such as *short story, tragedy, comedy, epic,* and *novel* and 2) those terms used in the analysis of style and structure, such as *metaphor, simile, classical plot structure,* and *blank verse.* Many terms are also used in interpretive and analytic reading in all content areas and in literature study, such as the author's *thesis, purpose, theme,* and *tone.*

All too often, literature teachers try to cover too many terms at one time and fail to provide opportunities for students to fully develop the concepts. For example, at the beginning of a literature unit, the teacher might present a lengthy list of terms, some of which will not be sufficiently illustrated in the works to be studied. Or perhaps the teacher may devote a class period to giving formal definitions, which may be too abstract for the students, and one or two inadequate examples. Students are then often criticized because they cannot use the terms or pass a spot quiz on them.

Teachers should try to be selective in the terms they cover and should only consider those terms important to reading the literary work. For example, if only one example of *personification* will appear in the reading, that concept could be saved for a later period of instruction. The teacher can provide an entire list of the terms at the beginning of the unit or course, but students should have time to develop an understanding of the concepts throughout the entire period of instruction.

The teacher should stress only one or two terms at a time. Students should not only learn to state a general definition for each term but should also learn 1) to identify an example in context of a whole work, 2) to interpret the meaning of that example or describe its characteristics in the work, and 3) to explain the function or purpose of that example in the work; for instance, why a poet uses a particular *metaphor,* or how a scene contributes to the *rising action* in a play. Students can also produce their own examples by writing creatively in the same forms they are reading. The following lesson plan illustrates a thorough learning experience in understanding the concept of *symbolism* in poetry:

1. Focus: Reading poetry to interpret symbolism
2. Materials: Poems from anthologies and poems written by students
3. Preassessment: Students write a draft of a poem in which the key idea is communicated through a symbol
4. Teacher Procedures: Teacher presents general definition of symbolism and illustrates it with discussion of a poem

5. Student Procedures:
   a. Students are given a list of ten concrete words, such as *book, glass of wine, snake,* or *star.* Students pick five and write an abstract idea which could be symbolized for each. ("A star could symbolize eternal beauty.")
   b. Students are given a list of ten abstract ideas. They select five and write a concrete word which could be a symbol for each.
   c. Students read two poems in which the symbols are underlined. They respond to questions calling for interpretation.
   d. Students read four poems written by high school students. They respond by discussing the theme of each poem and how it is symbolized.
6. Postassessment: Students revise and complete their poem (for Preassessment) or write a new poem, which has a symbol. They then write an explanation of the symbolism in their own poems.[14]

Comprehension   In literature study, there has been a tendency to emphasize *intensive* over *extensive* reading. With the former, students are expected to analyze thoroughly every work read for content, structure, and style. In addition, students may be expected to analyze, interpret, and evaluate the work in one or more of the following contexts: the author's life, other works by the author, similar works by other authors, the author's period of history, or a literary movement, such as Romanticism.

As noted in Chapter 2, many educators in the field of adolescent literature, such as Louise Rosenblatt, are concerned with what they see as an overemphasis on literary criticism and scholarship.[15] They have a number of objections. First and foremost, intensive reading results in much time spent on relatively few works. Students miss an extensive experience and, as a result, may lack both an interest in literature and an adequate preparation for intensive reading.

Second, although analytic reading may yield aesthetic pleasure, other pleasures may be neglected. Students may not discover that they can respond to literature in an emotional, personal way; that literature can provide vicarious pleasure; or that literature can be moving, exciting, suspenseful, and humorous.

Third, intensive reading often involves greater attention to style and structure than to content. As a result, plot and character—which adolescents can more easily understand and appreciate—may be neglected. In addition, students may simply be unable or unwilling to attend to

---

[14]Audrey Gomon, "Lesson Plan for Poetry for Sophomore English" (Lavonia, Mich: Franklin Senior High School, 1975).
[15]Louise M. Rosenblatt, *Literature as Exploration,* rev. ed. (New York: Noble, 1965).

literary techniques until they have finished a work and satisfied their curiosity about what happened to the people in it.

Focus in Teaching. As an alternative to intensive reading, Stephen Dunning and Alan Howes recommend that teachers limit their aims in teaching a particular work.[16] One aspect of literature is focused upon with each work—for example, plot in one story, characterization in another, and style in a third. This approach is selective and provides sequence in comprehension questions (see Chapter 4). If the focus is on plot, the teacher would select or write questions which relate to the plot. During a discussion of the story, the questions could be presented in a sequence which will take the student from a literal understanding to interpretation: from "What happened in the story?" to "Now, why do you think it happened?"

The same principle can be applied to poetry. With narrative poems the focus can be on plot or characterization. With descriptive poems, attention to fine points of style is appropriate. In a sonnet or ode, the emphasis could be on the way the poet develops an argument. With longer works, such as novels and five-act plays, there could be different focuses at different points in the work.

Purpose Setting and Advance Organizers. When the teacher wants students to focus on one aspect of the work, he or she might present purpose-setting questions or advance organizers prior to the reading, such as the following examples for *The Old Man and the Sea:*

Purpose-Setting Questions:

> *The Old Man and the Sea* has a very interesting story line, but you should also pay close attention to the characters and to what is shown about them. As you read do the following:
> 1. Write the names of the two key characters.
> 2. Jot down important details about each. Do this with the first ten pages.

Advance Organizer and Motivator:

> How many of you have seen the movie *Jaws?* Has anyone read the book? Would someone tell us a little about the movie? Now, *The Old Man and the Sea* is quite different from *Jaws,* though there are some similarities. People struggle against the sea, and at one point, against sharks. There is much more attention to the people than to the sharks, to what is revealed about the characters in their struggle.

As discussed in Chapter 4, students might start reading in class and then stop to check their understanding of the purpose before they complete the assignment.

---

[16]Stephen Dunning and Alan B. Howes, *Literature for Adolescents: Teaching Poems, Stories, Novels, and Plays* (Glenview, Ill.: Scott, Foresman, 1975), pp. 93–97.

Interspersed Questions and Discussions. A characteristic of good literature is its development, its sense of something happening as the work progresses. Characters are not simply described; they are developed. A good plot is not simply a series of incidents; it develops through different phases. The five-part classic plot structure serves as an example:

1. *Exposition:* Introduction to characters, story line, setting, key problem
2. *Rising action:* Intensification and complication of key problem
3. *High point:* Moment of greatest intensification, sometimes called climax or crisis
4. *Falling action:* Lessening of tension; unravelling of complications
5. *Denouement:* Resolution of problem, or at least conclusion of action

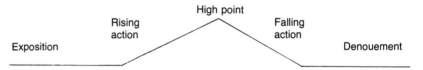

Even when the classic structure is not precisely or completely followed, there is, typically, an introduction to the problem, an intensification or complication of the problem, and sometimes, but not always, a resolution. This structure can also be found in drama and poetry as the following poem by Thomas Hardy illustrates:

> At the Altar-Rail
> "My bride is not coming, alas!" says the groom,
> And the telegram shakes in his hand. "I own
> It was hurried. We met at a dancing-room
> When I went to the Cattle-Show alone,
> And then, next night, where the Fountain leaps,
> And the Street of the Quarter-Circle sweeps."
>
> "Aye, she won me to ask her to be my wife—
> Twas foolish perhaps!—to forsake the ways
> Of the flaring town for a farmer's life.
> She agreed. And we fixed it. Now she says:
> *'It's sweet of you, dear, to prepare me a nest,*
> *But a swift, short, gay life suits me best.*
> *What I really am you have never gleaned;*
> *I had eaten the apple ere you were weaned.'* "[17]

[17]Thomas Hardy, *Collected Poems* (New York: Macmillan, 1925), p. 420.

Without intervention by the teacher, many students will read works too quickly and with too little concentration to attend to the development. An effective procedure is to interrupt the reading at appropriate places in the text and insert questions or call for discussion. Questions such as the following can be used for a play.

1. Who are the two most important characters in this act?
2. What happens to them?
3. What do you think will happen next?

By responding to such questions, students will be aware of changes occurring in the work; they will also be developing, or elaborating upon, their own responses as they read.

Many teachers have the impression that study-skill procedures are not applicable to reading literature. Francis Robinson, who developed SQ3R, did acknowledge that literary selections present problems not often found in other content-area textbooks.[18] (To review the SQ3R procedure, see Chapter 5.) One practical problem is that most literary pieces do not have textbook aids, such as subheadings, italicized key terms, and numbered points. Many secondary textbooks, however, do often include pictures, advance organizers, and footnotes to make literary selections more readable. Literary pieces also lack the direct, readily perceived organizational patterns found in textbook discussions.

Study-Skills

Nevertheless, modifications of the survey/question procedures are applicable to literature. Of particular importance is the posing of questions by students to guide and check their understanding. In a sense, the goal of literature study involves learning to ask as well as answer appropriate questions about literature. Basic questions include: "Who are the characters?" "What happens to them?" "Why does it happen?" "When and where does it happen?"

Some questions are more important to one particular type of literature than to another. In reading sonnets, two key questions might be "What problem is introduced and how is it developed?" "How is the problem resolved?" In poems which depend on imagery to communicate meaning, some appropriate questions would be "What does each image represent?" "What do the images have in common?" "What idea or feeling do the images suggest?" Some of the questions important in drama are "What is revealed about the characters in what they say?" "What action occurs off stage?" "What settings do the scenes represent?"

In learning to ask questions, students are learning ways to approach literature. They may be more motivated by, and better able to answer, their own questions than their teacher's. Also, student questions give

---

[18]Francis Robinson, *Effective Study*, rev. ed. (New York: Harper & Row, 1961) pp. 41–44.

the teacher information about the levels at which students are comprehending and about what aspects of literature they are and are not attending to.

The Picture and Text Survey discussed in Chapter 5 is usually applicable with prose literature (see pp. 94–96). Students survey the piece or the opening of the piece, pose questions and then read to answer them. If the teacher wants students to focus on one aspect of the work, students can pose questions about that one aspect. The following questions represent two approaches to guiding reading for characterization:

Approach 1:

As you read, select one important character and answer each of these questions:
1. What does the author say about _____?
2. What does _____ do that shows something about him or her?
3. What does _____ says that shows something about him or her?
4. What do others do to _____ that shows something about him or her?

Approach 2
As you read, note the names of three characters and key details about each

Names: 1. _____ 2. _____ 3. _____

Details: _____   _____   _____
           _____   _____   _____
           _____   _____   _____

Teachers can use student questions in various ways. Students can read a short selection or part of a longer selection, then pair up and ask each other questions. Or students can meet in small groups, share questions, and decide on a few key questions, which are later discussed by the class. For short but difficult pieces, such as poems and short stories, students can read the piece (or hear it read), pose and discuss a few basic questions, and then reread the piece and pose and discuss additional questions.

Poetry and poetic drama require a special modification. Given the concentrated quality of poetic writing, a quick survey may not yield suffficient meaning. In place of the survey step, students can 1) read the piece aloud, 2) try to paraphrase the overall meaning, 3) pose one key question, 4) reread the piece aloud, and 5) write their answer, as in the following example using the Hardy poem on page 208.

1. Read aloud
   "My bride is not coming. . . .
2. Paraphrase
   This groom was going to get married, but she sends him a telegram.

3. What was she actually saying in the telegram?
4. Read aloud
   "My bride is not coming. . . .
5. She says it was nice he wanted to marry her,
   but, I think, she wants a different life.

Reading Poetry

Many students do not enjoy poetry because they find it difficult to read. Their difficulties often result from the very qualities that make the poetry good: compression, suggestiveness, communication of a generalizable theme through a very concrete situation, and inventive language. If students are to appreciate these qualities, teachers must be patient and helpful.

The Literal Situation. In reading poetry, the place to start is the literal situation of the poem and not with those qualities of style and structure which demand interpretive, analytic, and evaluative reading. Teachers often skip over literal comprehension, perhaps because of their college experience which emphasized critical reading. Poems do have literal meanings which may be very simple and obvious to the teacher but not necessarily so to the students:
   "In this poem, two lovers are quarreling, and one threatens to leave the other."
   "In this poem, the poet describes an eagle perched on a cliff."
   "In this poem, the poet shows us a beach and a raging surf." Having students paraphrase the poem is often a helpful first step to insure literal comprehension.

Helpful Structural Elements. Although poetry obviously differs from prose, there are key similarities which students need to take advantage of. Poems may have the equivalent of thesis statements at the beginning, topic sentences within stanzas, and underlying logical structures of development found in prose: comparison/contrast, ennumeration, cause/effect, and chronological order. A helpful sequence would be the following: Initially, the teacher notes the presence of a structure in the poem and demonstrates how consideration of that structure aids comprehension. With a second poem, the teacher points out the structure and the students discuss it. With a third poem, the teacher notes that a particular structure is present; students must then locate and discuss it. With the last poem, students must determine what structure is in the poem and try to explain it.

Difficulties. Poetry tends to be compressed and, as a result, highly suggestive. A quality expected of good poetry lies in the ability of the poet to say a great deal in relatively few words. This quality is especially noteworthy in short forms, such as the sonnet, but it also appears in passages or lines in longer poems (like epics), in poetic drama, and in poetic prose passages in fiction.
   Compression results in suggestiveness and implication. The poet will rely on implicit meaning which he or she expresses in figurative

language, such as metaphors, allusions, and symbols. There will be more than one level of meaning. Relatively slow reading, rereading, and analytic and interpretive comprehension are necessary for understanding most poems.

Great poetry uses inventive language. It is this quality that often causes the reader problems in decoding the lines, as the following Shakespearean poem illustrates:

Sonnet 73

That time of year thou mayst in me behold
When yellow leaves, or none, or few, do hang
Upon those boughs which shake against the cold,
Bare ruined choirs, where late the sweet birds sang.
In me thou see'st the twilight of such day
As after sunset fadeth in the west,
Which by and by black night doth take away,
Death's second self, that seals up all in rest.
In me thou see'st the glowing of such fire
That on the ashes of its youth doth lie,
As the death-bed whereon it must expire
Consumed with that which it was nourished by.
This thou perceiv'st, which makes thy love more strong,
To love that well which thou must leave ere long.[19]

Usually, proficient readers are able to decode with great speed and ease by taking advantage of predictable language patterns. The poet, however, may deliberately violate these patterns. New words may be coined or familiar words may be used with unusual or older meanings. For example, in Sonnet 73, above, "choirs" refers to the place in the church where the singers sit, rather than to the singers themselves.

Successful decoding requires a grasp of syntactic relationships. Shakespeare's poem is difficult because of the play with syntax. In the first line, the direct object (time of year) occurs before the subject instead of after the verb. Two appositives are removed from the nouns they relate to: The student must see that "choirs" refers to "boughs" and that "Death's second self" refers to "black night." In the second to the last line, the referent for "This" is ambiguous: "This" can stand for all of the preceding lines or it can refer to the last line of the poem. Slow reading and rereading are often necessary to decode the text.

Teachers can help students by initially reducing difficulties both in comprehension and decoding. Stephen Dunning and Alan Howes recommend that students start with contemporary poems that have a clear narrative or dramatic situation which students can readily grasp through literal reading.[20] Contemporary poems will also, generally, present

---

[19]Shakespeare, *The Complete Works of Shakespeare*, pp. 483–484.
[20]Dunning and Howes, *Literature for Adolescents*, pp. 93–97.

fewer vocabulary problems than older poems. Sometimes oral reading can greatly reduce the problems; students can listen to the teacher read, then do a reading in unison. Later, when students are expected to perform independently, they should be encouraged to read the poem aloud at least three times: 1) to get a general sense of the poem and to tackle decoding problems, 2) to get a clearer sense of the literal situation, and 3) to do some interpretation. Comprehension with the second and third readings can be facilitated if students pose questions.

EXTENSIVE READING

From as early as the 1920s, educators have urged that extensive self-selected reading (also called *free reading*) should be a major component of the secondary language-arts curriculum.[21] Extensive reading is not possible if teachers see the literature curriculum only as one body of specific authors and works which students must read and thoroughly analyze. Extensive reading is both possible and very appropriate if teachers can see the broad learning goals of the curriculum (such as those Burton suggested) and the broad structure of the curriculum (such as that developed by Moffett).

Some teachers use extensive, self-selected reading not only to provide interest and enjoyment but also to serve as the basis for literature study. Some teachers impose a structure on the reading by asking students to select works from certain categories (such as narratives or fiction) or from a suggested reading list. Other teachers ask students to read the same work for direct instruction but then provide self-selection for additional reading. Many teachers are attempting to provide a balance between longer, more difficult adult literature and usually shorter, more readable adolescent literature. (A more thorough discussion of extensive reading programs and adolescent literature will be presented in Chapter 20.)

SUMMARY

This chapter addressed problems of reading and instruction in the context of literature. According to many educators, a major task of the English teacher is to integrate the various aspects of language and to avoid fragmented learning experiences. In literature study, teachers can use oral reading, discussion, and informal writing to help students understand literary works and develop reading skills. Extensive reading experience can also improve both appreciation and ability.

---

[21]Burton et al, *Comprehensive High School Reading Methods*, pp. 183–184.

Suggested Activities   1. Discuss one of the Key Ideas listed in the Overview of this chapter.
2. Select a long-term goal for studying an area of literature and describe learning experiences, including reading, which will move students toward that goal.
3. Select a piece of literature and describe (or write a plan for) a learning experience which provides preventive instruction to reduce vocabulary difficulties and to aid comprehension.
4. Select a piece of literature and decide on one aspect of the piece to focus on. Identify the kinds of questions the teacher or students could pose.
5. Select a poem and identify potential difficulties in understanding the syntax.

Recommended Readings   Bengleman, Fred. *The English Language: An Introduction for Teachers.* Englewood Cliffs, N.J.: Prentice-Hall, 1970.
Blanc, Robert A. "Cloze-Plus as an Alternative to Guides for Understanding and Appreciating Poetry." *Journal of Reading* 21:3 (December 1977): 215–18.
Booth, Wayne C. *The Rhetoric of Fiction.* Chicago: University of Chicago Press, 1961.
Burton Dwight L. *Literature Study in the High School,* 3rd ed. New York: Holt, Rinehart, & Winston, 1970.
Burton, Dwight L., and Simmons, John S. ed., *Teaching English in Today's High Schools,* 2nd ed. New York: Holt, Rinehart, & Winston, 1965.
Burton Dwight L. et al. *Teaching English Today.* Boston: Houghton-Mifflin, 1975.
Carter, B. Betty. "Helping Seventh Graders to Understand Figurative Expressions." *Journal of Reading* 20: 7(April 1977): 559–62.
Dominguez, Ivo, Jr. "A High School Reading Club Writes a Novel." *Journal of Reading* 21: 8 (May 1978): 698–700.
Dunning, Stephen, and Howes, Alan B. *Literature for Adolescents: Teaching Poems, Stories, Novels and Plays.* Glenview, Ill.: Scott, Foresmen, 1975.
Flynn, Peggy. "What's Black and White and Spread All Over? The Newspapers." *Journal of Reading* 21:8 (May 1978): 725–28.
Hogan, Robert F., ed. *The English Language in the School Program.* Urbana, Ill.: National Council of Teachers of English, 1966.
Judy, Stephen, N. *Explorations in the Teaching of Secondary English: A Source Book for Experimental Teaching.* New York: Dodd, Mead, 1974.
Macrorie, Ken. *Writing to Be Read.* Rochelle Park, N.J.: Hayden Book, 1968.
Moffett, James. *Teaching the Universe of Discourse.* Boston: Houghton-Mifflin, 1968.
Moffett, James, and Wagner, Betty Jane, *Student-Centered Language Arts and Reading, K-13: A Handbook for Teachers,* 2nd ed. Boston: Houghton-Mifflin, 1976.
O'Hare, Frank. *Sentence-Combining.* Lexington, Mass.: Ginn & Co., 1975.
Richards, I. A. *Practical Criticism.* New York: Harcourt ь race and Jovanovich, 1929.
Shepherd, David L. *Comprehensive High School Reading Methods.* Columbus, Ohio: Charles E. Merrill, 1973, chap. 8.
Strong, William. *Sentence Combining.* New York: Random House, 1973.
Thomas, Ellen L., and Robinson, H. Alan, *Improving Reading in Every Class,* abridged 2nd ed. Boston: Allyn & Bacon, 1977, chap. 7.

12

Reading in the Social Sciences

Reading in the social sciences (history, government, and economics) and in the behavioral sciences (psychology, sociology, anthropology) makes many of the same demands on a student. Teachers can use basic methods for developing vocabulary, comprehension, and study skills to help students to handle these reading demands.

OVERVIEW

The special demands of reading in the social sciences include understanding special terminology and symbols, following directions, and understanding the text.

Key Ideas

The goals of teaching the social sciences are: to improve behavior, to make social events relevant to student's lives, to show common themes, to develop attitudes and values in students, and to expose students to a variety of experiences.

Teachers can use directed-reading procedures to help students with difficulties in vocabulary, comprehension, and study skills necessary for reading in the social sciences.

Ms. Gonzales is a social-studies teacher who teaches several different courses including history, government, and economics. In addition to teaching specific names, dates, and major ideas, she is interested in helping students improve their behavior and develop positive attitudes towards society. In order to do this, she incorporates a selection of diverse reading materials into her overall instruction. These provide students with a broad experience base from which to make decisions about social matters.

DEMANDS OF READING
Understanding Special Symbols

Many of the social sciences use specialized symbols and present information in quantitative or numerical form. For example:

1. "3rd World"
2. Route numbers on highway signs
3. Special emphasis on dates, for example, 1066, 1776
4. Latitude and Longitude, for example, 33° N
5. Population data, for example, 3,000,000
6. Ratios such as 2,000 per capita
7. Measurement ideas such as area (square miles)
8. Economic indicators such as stocks and world oil prices

Understanding Terminology

The potential difficulties in vocabulary are those found in all content areas: common words with specialized meaning; words with multiple, specialized meaning; technical vocabulary; and abbreviations and acronyms.

Common Words with Specialized Meaning. Many words that are familiar to most readers have other special meanings in social studies. Each social-studies content area has its own special terms:

Economics	History	Sociology
stock market	third world	peer
bull	iron curtain	group
futures	cold war	community
bear		
crash		

Words with Multiple Meanings. Terms such as *state, revolution,* and *cycle* have a number of special meanings within a single social-science discipline and also different meanings in different disciplines. These words may also have different connotations depending on the particular context or writer as is often true with words like *liberal, nuclear, affirmative action, marketplace,* and *inflation.*

Technical Vocabulary. Technical terminology in social studies may present three kinds of problems. First, if the word is entirely new, the student may experience difficulty with pronounciation and other word-analysis skills. Second, the concept or idea represented by the word may be new, even though the word itself may be familiar. Third, the word may represent some idea that has no simple concrete referent; for example, *ego* or *detente*. Some examples of technical vocabulary from social-studies disciplines include:

Psychology	Politics	Economics
paranoid	communism	microeconomics
schizophrenic	bipartisan	capitalism
ego	republic	socialism

Abbreviations and Acronyms. Often in social studies, official names or titles for organizations, laws, or countries are abbreviated or are given short names or acronyms. Once understood, the new label is usually easier to remember than the full name. Some familiar examples are NATO (North Atlantic Treaty Organization), FCC (Federal Communications Commission), and CPA (Certified Public Accountant).

Following Directions

As discussed in Chapter 6, understanding and following written directions is a common problem in both reading and studying. The teacher often needs to give special attention to brief directions which may have important details students might overlook. The teacher should explain and clarify directions and help students work through them, perhaps by doing one of the exercises as a demonstration. Some examples follow:

Match the country and its capital by drawing a line between the two:
(1) Russia   (a) London
(2) England   (b) Moscow
(3) USA   (c) Washington, D.C.

Circle the best answer in the following multiple-choice questions:
(1) The *first* president of the USA was:
    (a) Lincoln
    (b) Washington
    (c) Jefferson
    (d) Hamilton
    (e) Burr

Fill in the blanks, using a word *from the given list:*
    (a) capitalism
    (b) imperialism
    (c) socialism
    (d) marxism
    (e) communism

(1) The economic system in the USA is best designated by ———.

(2) ——— is named after Karl Marx.

(3) ——— is the system of the USSR.

Understanding the Text   Understanding the small units (symbols, words, and sentences) is not the only area of potential reading difficulty in social studies. The main goal of reading in social studies is to understand the combinations of such units; that is, to gain knowledge in a rational, coherent, and organized fashion. Reading comprehension depends heavily on the ability to recognize patterns in large units of material.

The material in most textbooks can be divided into two categories: *problems* and *explanations*. The problem category includes such items as study questions, directions, and application exercises that provide new tasks to be performed. The explanation category includes demonstrations of tasks to be performed, descriptions of strategies, and, of course, explanations of concepts. These might also include explanations of how to use special materials such as maps, films, and reference aids.

WHY TEACH SOCIAL STUDIES?   Leonard Kenworthy provides one answer to the question—why teach social studies?

> To discover and develop the abilities of every student so that he or she may comprehend himself or herself and other human beings better, cope with life more effectively, contribute to society in his or her own ways, help to change society, enjoy it, and share in its benefits.[1]

As Kenworthy notes, several corollaries follow from this proposition which provide further guidance to teachers:

1. The social studies are a basic part of the education of every pupil, including the poor reader, the underachiever, and the slow and the retarded, as well as the average and the gifted.
2. The goal of all social studies learnings is improved behavior.
3. Knowledge is important, but most knowledge gained should be pertinent in the lives of students now, as well as in the foreseeable future.
4. The experiences of students should be organized to promote the discovery by them of concepts, generalizations, or "big ideas."
5. Social studies teaching should include feelings as well as facts.
6. The formation, change, and improvement of attitudes is even more important than the acquisition of knowledge.
7. The acquisition of skills and the understanding of processes is essential to any effective social studies program.
8. Students should be assisted in examining values and eventually in becoming committed to those of our democratic society, which are rooted in large part in the Judaic-Christian tradition.

---

[1] Leonard S. Kenworthy, *Social Studies for the Seventies*, 2nd Ed. (Lexington, Mass: Xerox, 1973).

9. Students should be helped in identifying with the United States and in developing a refined sense of patriotism.
10. Understanding and accepting oneself, with all one's strengths and limitations, is a first step toward accepting offers.
11. Learning to respect the wide variety of persons in our nation and on our planet should follow from self-respect. Pupils should grow toward associating strangeness with friendliness rather than hostility.[2]

The inclusion of social studies in an educational program is a necessity for all students, no matter what their background, their strengths, or their weaknesses. Teachers can use basic procedures for developing vocabulary, comprehension, and study skills to help students read more effectively. These basic procedures will help teachers meet the following goals for teaching the social sciences: improving behavior, providing relevant knowledge, showing common themes, developing attitudes and values, and providing a variety of experience.

The following activity is an example of a procedure teachers can use to improve a student's reading efficiency:

1. Subject area:
   Geography—current events
2. Grade level: 7–9
3. Name of activity: Important places in the news
4. Objective: Familiarize students with locations of important places in the news.
5. Student activity: Find five major news stories in the newspaper. Have students share their finds with class and show locations of the stories on a map or a globe.[3]

Improving Behavior

If teachers want students to improve their social behavior, they should provide students with examples of how men and women have sought to affect the behavior of society. For instance, students might read such documents as *The Constitution* or *The Mayflower Pact*, which show how society tries to regulate itself. This might encourage civic participation among students.

Finding Relevant Knowledge

In any social-studies course, one goal is to make the new material relevant to the lives of the students or to current events. In a history class studying the American Civil War, for example, after listing causes for the Civil War, the class might consider the civil wars in Lebanon or Ireland and list their causes. The students could then look for differences and similarities between the wars.

---

[2]Kenworthy, *Social Studies for the Seventies,* pp. 8–9. Used with permission.
[3]D. Piercey, *Reading Activities in Content Areas, An Ideabook for Middle and Secondary Schools,* abridged ed. (Boston: Allyn & Bacon, 1976), pp. 336–37. Used with permission.

Looking for common ideas   Students should be encouraged to look for common themes as they study in different social-studies areas. For example, as students look at the history, economics, and government of the United States, they might try to build an idea of what "American Spirit" is. The formation of such a broad and complex idea requires the ability to understand and read at the higher levels of the cognitive domain (see the discussion in Chapter 4).

Developing Attitudes   One of the prime goals of the social sciences is to provide a basis for forming attitudes or value judgments about people, institutions, countries, or ideas. Reading will play a critical role in the development of these attitudes and values. Students will be expected to read, discuss, analyze, and synthesize ideas in order to form their own opinions. Another decision social-studies teachers must make is: "How controversial can the topics be?" But different teachers have conflicting ideas about what is and is not "controversial." For example, different teachers would have different ideas about which of the following are controversial:

1. *The Bible*
2. *Mein Kampf*
3. *The Rise and Fall of the Third Reich*
4. *The Rise and Fall of the Roman Empire*
5. The books of Mao Tse-Tung
6. *The Koran*
7. A treatise on socialism as an economic system
8. Jewish and Christian accounts of events surrounding the life and death of Jesus Christ
9. Books on Watergate
10. Books on the CIA
11. Newspaper editorials
12. Campaign bumper stickers
13. The 6:00 news

Providing a Variety of Experience   All of the preceding points suggest that the social-studies teacher must provide a broad spectrum of experiences for the students. Our fast-paced society makes it crucial for students to be exposed to many different communication methods. Reading, in all of its formats, will be a necessary skill for students throughout their lives.

HELPING STUDENTS READ THE TEXTBOOK   The teacher must provide direct assistance to students as they encounter vocabulary problems, as they try to interpret different writing patterns, and as they try to use materials outside the textbook like maps, globes, and charts.

In helping students to develop new vocabulary words the teacher might follow Ellen Thomas and H. Alan Robinson's suggestions for teaching technical terminology and developing concepts in the classroom.[4] Teachers can:

Developing Vocabulary

1. use the term,
2. show the idea with pictures or diagrams,
3. point out examples,
4. point out nonexamples,
5. list characteristics,
6. analyze meaning,
7. discuss relevant situations,
8. present more complex examples,
9. ask students to find their own examples, and
10. provide instruction on a concept over time.

David Shepherd describes six different writing patterns in social-studies textbooks and other materials: 1) graphic sources, 2) cause and effect, 3) sequential events, 4) comparison, 5) detailed facts, and 6) propaganda.[5] These patterns are characteristic of the explanation mode of textbook writing discussed earlier in this chapter.

Encouraging Comprehension

Graphic Sources. Drawings, maps, and pictures aid the student by breaking up text into smaller units of meaning. However, students often skip over them, unaware of their purpose or potential benefit.

Graphic material requires two kinds of reading responses: 1) guided synthesis and 2) independent synthesis.[6] In *guided synthesis,* the text explicitly refers to or discusses the graphic aid. In *independent synthesis,* the text does not attract the readers' attention to the graphic material so the social-studies teacher should provide extra guidance. For example, the teacher's reading assignment can include explicit instructions to respond to a particular aid or type of aid.

Cause and Effect. The cause and effect pattern is common in social-studies reading. An event occurs (the cause) and a series of other events (effects) follow:

> On December 7, 1941 at dawn, the Japanese attacked Pearl Harbor in the Hawaiian Islands. They destroyed many ships and planes. Also, many U.S. soldiers were killed. Our forces retaliated. The President called for a declaration of war and the country mobilized.

---

[4]Ellen L. Thomas and H. Alan Robinson, *Improving Reading in Every Class,* abridged 2nd ed. (Boston: Allyn & Bacon, 1977).
[5]David L. Shepherd, *Comprehensive High School Reading Methods* (Columbus, Ohio: Charles E. Merrill, 1973).
[6]H. Alan Robinson, *Teaching Reading and Study Strategies—The Content Areas* (Boston: Allyn & Bacon, 1975).

Cause—Japanese attack Pearl Harbor

Effects—destruction, death, retaliation, declaration of war, mobilization.

Chronological. Quite often historical material is presented in a sequential or chronological manner. As discussed in Chapter 4, reading to identify sequence is considered a key comprehension skill. Often, dates or times are given to provide additional information. The reader can gain some idea of this pattern by again referring to the paragraph on the start of World War II on page 221. After reading the paragraph, students could respond in several ways to demonstrate their grasp of the sequence. For example, they could rewrite the paragraph in their own words, using descriptors such as first, second, etc., or they could simply list the key details in order.

Comparison. In social studies it is often desirable to compare or contrast similar events. For example, the American Revolutionary War could be compared with other wars to note likenesses and differences; the beliefs of different religions can be similarly examined. The comparison (or contrast) method can also be used to examine things that are very different. For example, the students in an economics class might use the comparison pattern to describe the differences between a bull and a bear market.

Detailed Facts. Many social-studies texts present many details or facts in a simple listing or enumeration. The following example of this type of writing is from a study of folk music in America:

> "Western Swing" is a type of American folk music. It was invented around 1900. It grew in popularity in the 1930s and 1940s. Some of the main characteristics in western swing music are fiddles, dance beat, and a western flavor. It was played at dances, festivals, and other celebrations in the Southwest United States. There has been a revival of western swing in the 1970s.

Facts about Western Swing:

1. American folk music
2. 1900
3. Popular in 1930s and 1940s
4. Fiddles, dancing, western flavor are characteristics of western swing
5. Played at social gatherings
6. Common in Southwest U.S.
7. Revived in 1970s

Such material obviously demands literal comprehension for identification and perhaps recall of details. Sometimes this pattern will also occur in combination with one or more of the other patterns noted earlier, as in a detailed comparison/contrast.

Propaganda. *Propaganda,* persuasive writing, attempts to influence the thoughts and opinions and sometimes the actions of others in a desired direction. Lou Burmeister lists and briefly identifies several propaganda techniques:

(1) Bad names—calling something by a negative name
(2) Glad names—using words like marvelous and fantastic
(3) Testimonial—personality giving endorsement
(4) Transfer—associating with something attractive
(5) Plain folks—relating to common people
(6) Card stacking—telling only one side
(7) Band wagon—everybody's doing it[7]

Typically, in both English and social science, students are taught to recognize propaganda, both its obvious use in political speeches and advertisements, as well as its more subtle use in writing which appears to be more informative than persuasive in purpose. (For an effective textbook discussion of propaganda in the social studies, see *Your Life as a Citizen.*[8]) The following activity shows students some of the different ways propaganda is presented.

> Define *propaganda* for the students and give some examples of propaganda techinques. As an assignment, have students bring examples of propaganda from newspapers, billboards, bumper stickers, TV advertising, and magazines.

Using materials outside the textbook. This chapter has already given several suggestions about the use of extra materials, such as newspapers, films, TV, charts, or pictures.

Developing Study Skills

The study-skills strategies presented in Chapter 5 apply to the study of the social sciences, in particular the SQ3R technique and its variations. In fact, much of the research on, and development of, study-skill techniques involved social-science materials. Generally, social-studies teachers will find it helpful to have students pose and answer their own questions about social-studies topics.

The lesson plan that follows focuses on a reading performance important in social studies—distinguishing facts from opinions.[9]

A SAMPLE LESSON PLAN

[7]Lou E. Burmeister, *Reading Strategies for Secondary School Teachers* (Reading, Mass: Addison-Wesley, 1974).
[8]Smith/Tiegs/Adams, *Your Life As A Citizen* (Lexington, Mass: Ginn, 1976), pp. 290–94.
[9]David L. Shepherd, *Comprehensive High School Reading Methods* (Columbus, Ohio: Charles E. Merrill, 1973).

1. Purpose: To discriminate fact from opinion
2. Materials: Newspapers
3. Preassessment: Have each student cite an example of a statement of fact and an example of an opinion. Have them tell the difference using specific details.
4. Teacher procedures: Direct discussion. Handout newspapers. Give individual help as needed.
5. Student activities: Discussion. Pick a newspaper article. Read it. List details that are facts. Write down sentences that seem to be opinion statements.
6. Postassessment: Repeat activity with new article from a magazine.

SUMMARY　This chapter addressed the problems common to the social-studies disciplines and the goals of social-science education. Using these as a foundation, a teacher can help students in social-studies classes develop vocabulary, comprehension, and study skills.

1. Discuss one of the Key Ideas listed in the Chapter Overview.
2. Select and review a social studies textbook. List the features which would aid the teacher or student in regard to reading.
3. Design (or describe) a display which will help students with vocabulary development. For example, a bulletin board display might emphasize key terms selected from a chapter in a social studies textbook.
4. Review the purposes for teaching social studies (see page 218). Then make a list of some reading activities that are designed to help promote each of them.
5. Select one of the recommended readings. After reading it, make a short outline on how it might help a social studies teacher.
6. Pick a chapter from a social studies textbook and try out the steps of the survey/question procedure. Does the procedure seem appropriate for this material?

Suggested Activities

Recommended Readings

Burmeister, Lou E. *Reading Strategies for Middle and Secondary School Teachers,* 2nd ed. Reading, Mass.: Addison-Wesley, 1978, chap. 5.

Hafner, Lawrence E. *Developmental Reading in Middle and Secondary Schools—Foundations, Strategies, and Skills for Teaching.* New York: Macmillan, 1977, chaps. 8 and 9.

Hittleman, Daniel R. *Developmental Reading: A Psycholinguistic Perspective.* Chicago: Rand McNally, 1978, chap. 10.

Howes, Virgil. *Individualizing Instruction in Reading and Social Studies.* New York: Macmillan, 1972.

Johnson, Roger, and Vardian, Ellen B. "Reading, Readability and the Social Studies." *The Reading Teacher* 26 (February 1973): 483–88.

Kenworthy, Leonard S. *Social Studies for the Seventies.* Lexington, Mass: Xerox, 1973.

Lunstrum, John P. "Reading in the Social Studies: A Preliminary Study of Recent Research." *Social Education* (January 1976).: 10–18.

Mize, John M. "A Directed Strategy for Teaching Critical Reading and Decision Making." *Journal of Reading* 22:2 (November 1978).: 144–48.

Piercey, Dorothy. *Reading Activities in Content Areas—An Ideabook for Middle and Secondary School.* Boston, Allyn & Bacon, 1976, chap. 11.

Robinson, H. Alan. "Reading Skills Employed in Solving Social Studies Problems." *The Reading Teacher* 18 (January 1965): 263–69.

———. *Teaching Reading and Study Strategies—The Content Areas.* Boston: Allyn & Bacon, 1975, chap. 7.

Roe, Betty D.; Stoodt, Barbara D.; and Burns, Paul C. *Reading Instruction in the Secondary School.* Chicago: Rand McNally, 1978, chap. 9.

Shepherd, David L. *Comprehensive High School Reading Methods.* Columbus, Ohio: Charles E. Merrill, 1973, chap. 9.

Thomas, Ellen L., and Robinson, H. Alan. *Improved Reading in Every Class,* Boston: Allyn & Bacon, 1977, chap. 6.

13

Reading in Mathematics

Students encounter problems in reading in mathematics on each level of reading development. Students may have problems: decoding mathematical letters, numerals, and symbols; recognizing technical vocabulary; following equations and formulas; or understanding the difference between mathematical explanations and problems.

Reading in mathematics makes special demands on the reader.

A teacher can help students who are having problems in mathematics by helping them to improve their reading skills.

The directed-reading procedure can help students solve mathematical word problems.

Teachers can help students develop study strategies for reading mathematics.

The following conversation took place in the teacher's lounge at a local high school.

Ms. SMITH (mathematics teacher): Mr. Jones, do you have Freddie in your class?

MR. JONES (English teacher): Yes, why do you ask?

Ms. SMITH: I'm having a little problem with him. If I pose a problem orally, he responds very well. But if I have him work by reading the text, he seems to get lost.

MR. JONES: You know, the same thing happens in my class. When we read stories aloud, Freddie does very well in discussing them. But he just doesn't do anything when he reads by himself.

This brief dialogue illustrates an all-too-common problem. Students may not be able to read their mathematics text, but yet they have mastered the concepts to the extent that they can work problems successfully. Other students have difficulties both in reading their text and in understanding concepts and operations. Both groups of students can be helped with the procedures presented in this chapter. The first step in helping is to identify some of the special demands students face in the content area of mathematics.

SPECIAL DEMANDS OF MATHEMATICAL READING

Successful reading in mathematics requires an understanding of the "two languages of mathematics": the technical vocabulary and the specialized symbols.[1] Donald E.P. Smith has identified the levels of response in reading. The reader must respond to: 1) letters, 2) words, 3) sentences, 4) paragraphs, and 5) discourse. In this hierarchical model, reading moves from small units to complete pieces of text or discourse.[2]

Letters

In general reading, students must respond to the usual alphabet (26 capitals and 26 lower-case letters). There may also be variations in letters due to different styles of print and script. Four kinds of problems can occur with letters. First, are the special mathematical symbols. These may be the more common symbols like $\div$, $+$, $-$, and $\times$ or the more highly specialized symbols such as Σ, $\#$, and $\int$.

---

[1]David L. Shepherd, *Comprehensive High School Reading Methods* (Columbus, Ohio: Charles E. Merrill, 1973).
[2]Donald E. P. Smith, *Learning to Read and Write: A Task Analysis.* Volume 1 of *A Technology of Reading and Writing* (New York: Academic Press, 1976).

General Mathematics:

+ add
− subtract
× multiply
÷ divide
% percent

Algebra:

$\sqrt{}$ radical-square root
$(x)^y$ exponents
$f(x)$ function at x

Geometry:

∢ angle
⊥ perpendicular lines
= parallel lines
° degrees

Trigonometry:

sin sine
cos cosine
π 3.14159265

Second, although numerals appear in ordinary reading, they are of special importance in mathematical reading. For example, in reading a short story, failure to note the numeral 3 in "The girl was living in Apt. #3" might have no effect on overall knowledge of the story. However, failure to note the 3 in the following problem will lead to a costly error. "The boy bought 3 loaves of bread at 42¢ each. How much did he spend?"

Third, mathematical texts use numerals in very special ways. For example, in 10^2 the numeral 2 indicates a mathematical operation—"10 squared."

Fourth, letters of the alphabet are sometimes used as mathematical symbols. For example, $2\,a = 6$ and $3 \times 2 = 6$.

In all these cases, there is something special about letter usage. In ordinary reading, with the exception of *a,* meaningful units consist of letter combinations. In mathematics, however, both single letters (and numerals) as well as letter combinations may function as nouns or verbs.[3] For example, in $A = 1 \times w$, the functions of A and $1 \times w$ are analogous to that of nouns.

---

[3] B. E. Leary, "Reading Problems in Mathematics," in N. B. Henry, ed., *The Forty-Seventh Yearbook of the National Society for the Study of Education: Reading in the High School and College* (Chicago: The University of Chicago, 1948), pp. 150–61.

Words Mathematical "words" are formed by making combinations of letters or mathematical symbols or both—for example, 22 or $2x$. Of course, the longer and more complex the combination, the more difficult the word. When presented with an unfamiliar word in ordinary reading, the reader can use word-analysis skills to break the word down into parts.

However, this process is not so easy in mathematics. The student must recognize and understand the mathematical relationship between the components of the word. For example, in reading 22, the student must see the first 2 as tens and the second 2 as ones. In $2x$, however, the 2 is ones and the juxtaposition with the x means that the two quantities are to be multiplied.

The potential problems of vocabulary in mathematics fall into five broad categories (roughly paralleling those problems at the letter level).

Words with More Than One Meaning. Many words which are familiar to most readers have special meanings in mathematics; for example, words such as *square, root, point,* and *slope. Square* can mean "outdated," "a geometric figure," or "a mathematical operation (10^2)."

Words with Special Emphasis in Mathematics. Phrases such as "how many," "how many more," or "how many less" take on special meanings in mathematics. Failure to interpret them properly could lead to faulty solution of a mathematical problem.

Technical Vocabulary. Technical terminology in mathematics may present problems of three different kinds. First, the word may be entirely new. The student may be unable to pronounce the word or to use word-analysis skills. Second, the concept represented by the word may be new. Finally, the concept represented by a word may have no simple concrete referent. Some examples are *sine, cosine, polynomial,* and *chord.*

Varied Forms. Another confusing factor in vocabulary development is that basic words can be presented in many different forms. The student will have to recognize differences in pronounciation as well as identify differences in meaning. An example of this potential problem is found in the variations of the word *multiply (multiplier, multiplication,* and *multiplicand).*

Abbreviations and Specialized Symbols. A final area of potential difficulty is the use of abbreviations and special symbols. For example, cos for cosine; and in. or " for inches. (Note that " is also used for denoting seconds in degree-measure notations.) The sample page from an algebra textbook in Figure 13.1 illustrates many of the difficulties discussed so far.

Figure 13.1
A Page from an Algebra Textbook

4 *Chapter 1*

1-2 Variables and Expressions

OBJECTIVE: To learn how to evaluate variable expressions

The Ecology Club is having a car wash to raise money for a field trip. They can wash 10 automobiles in one hour. Therefore, they can wash

in one hour: 10 × 1
in two hours: 10 × 2
in three hours: 10 × 3

Each of these numerical expressions fits the pattern

10 × *n*,

where the letter *n* may stand for "1", "2", or "3".
n is called a *variable*. The *domain* of *n* here is

{1, 2, 3} (read "the set whose members are one, two, and three").

The *values* of *n* are 1, 2, and 3. The symbols { } are called braces.
  In general:

> A **variable** is a symbol used to represent one or more numbers. The **set,** or collection, of numbers that the variable may represent is the **domain, or replacement set,** of the variable. The numbers in the domain are called the **values of the variable.**

An expression, such as "10 × *n*", which contains a variable is called a variable expression or an open expression.
  When you write a product that contains a variable, you usually omit the multiplication symbol. Thus,

"10 × *n*" is usually written "10*n*",
"*y* × *z*" is usually written "*yz*".

Such a product is considered to be *grouped*. Thus,

"10*n* + 6" means "(10 × *n*) + 6"

and

"*yz* ÷ 10*n*" means "(*y* × *z*) ÷ (10 · *n*)".

Source: M.P. Dolcani et al, *Algebra: Structure and Method.* Book 1. Teacher's edition (Boston: Houghton Mifflin, 1976) pp. 4–5. Used with permission.

Sentences   At the sentence level, there are entities called *mathematical sentences,* for example, $3 + 2 = 5$, or, more commonly, *equations* and *formulas.* The distinction between equations and formulas is a subtle one. In all cases, formulas are really equations, which describe a generalized rather than a particular situation. Formulas usually represent a well-known principle with commonly used symbols.

> Example: $A = \frac{1}{2}bh$ is a formula for the area of a triangle, where
>
> A = area,
> b = length of the base of the triangle, and
> h = altitude of the triangle.
> $A = \frac{1}{2}bh$ is also an equation.

$2x + 3 = 7$ is an equation. The word *formula* would probably not be used here, because this equation refers to a more particular situation.

In trying to draw the analogy between a mathematical sentence and an ordinary English sentence, the reader runs into three kinds of problems. The patterns found in many mathematical sentences do not conform to traditional sentence patterns. Also, prepositions, articles, and connectives which aid in identifying patterns have no parallels in the structure of a mathematical sentence. Finally, the use of context analysis often does not adequately deal with situations in mathematical text. In ordinary reading, context analysis can be used when the words surrounding the unknown words are known to the reader (see Chapter 3). For example, in the sentence "Ted fixed his bicycle chain using a *rachet* wrench." we can guess that rachet is a special kind of wrench. In a mathematical sentence, however, many of the words represent unfamiliar concepts and unknown quantities. For example, "The tangent of ϕ can be found by solving $\frac{\sin\phi}{\cos\phi} = $ _____. Context analysis can come into play if the student can use the English sentences to help understand the mathematical sentences such as in the following example:

> Square Roots
>
> The square root of a number is a different number which when multiplied by itself yields the first number. For example, the square root of four is two, because two times two equals four. The symbol for square root is $\sqrt{\ }$. $\sqrt{4} = 2$. $\sqrt{1} = 1$.
>
> Solve this problem:
>
> $\sqrt{9} = $ _____.

Discourse   Mathematical textbooks, like other kinds of textbooks, use both the explanation and the problem pattern of writing:[4]

---

[4]John H. Catterson, "Techniques for Improving Comprehension in Mathematics," in G. G. Duffy, ed., *Reading in the Middle School* (Newark, Del.: International Reading Association, 1975), pp. 153–65.

Explanation:

> To add fractions, be sure the fractions have like denominators. For example, $\frac{1}{4}$ and $\frac{3}{4}$ have like denominators because the denominators are both 4s. Then add the numerators and use the like denominator.

Problem:

> John had $\frac{1}{4}$ yard of leather string. Fred gives him $\frac{1}{2}$ yard more. How much did he have in all?

Many times students are unaware of the particular purpose for reading a section of text. Their comprehension is hindered when they read all parts of a mathematics text in the same way without realizing each part's purpose.

HELPING STUDENTS WITH DIFFICULTIES

The relationship between reading and mathematics has been discussed by educators for many years. Students having problems in the mathematics classroom may be having trouble with reading skills, especially those pertaining to mathematics.[5] In attempting to help students with reading problems in mathematics, the teacher should keep the following four points in mind: 1) Mathematical reading involves essentially the same basic responses as ordinary reading. 2) The primary difference between mathematical and ordinary reading is the amount of specific content the student will have to respond to. 3) Diagnostic practice in general reading instruction indicates that few students have general deficiencies in reading skills but lack mastery of specific responses. 4) Deficiencies are overcome by directly orienting instruction to specific responses.[6]

Some other general recommendations for helping students are:

1. Teachers should base decisions on written responses as well as on observation of students engaged in tasks. (A procedure for systematically observing students will be described later in the chapter.)
2. Teachers should talk with the students and consider their perceptions of the difficulties they are experiencing.
3. Students should assist in selection of remedial activities.
4. Many activities used to diagnose reading and mathematics ability can also be used as effective instructional activities.

---

[5]Lewis R. Aiken, "Language Factors in Learning Mathematics." *Review of Educational Research* 2 (Summer 1972): 359–85.
[6]Smith, *Learning to Read and Write.*

Symbols and Vocabulary The following teaching suggestions parallel the breakdown of potential reading difficulties. Teachers can use activities of this sort in both regular instruction and remedial instruction. By looking at the reading process in detail, it will be possible to make more instructions preventative in nature, and thereby, head off difficulties.

Letter Level In considering reading responses at the letter level, the teacher (especially in a geometry class) might draw the students' attention to the form of letters and mathematical symbols. Students should look for similarities and differences in letters and other mathematical symbols to discover the distinctive features. Some exercises to help students see similarities in symbols are:

1. Circle the symbols that are alike.

2. Circle the symbols that are alike.

   4^2 3^2 2

3. Circle the symbols that are alike.

   x   *x*   /   X

Exercises for finding differences in symbols could include:

1. Circle the ones that looks like this: 2

   2   7   Z   2

2. Circle the ones that look like this: ⌐‾‾

3. Circle the ones that look like this: $\sqrt[3]{}$

An exercise like the following requires a creative response from the student:

Make a design using this symbol:
Example:

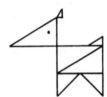

Word Level. Vocabulary development demands that the teacher use a variety of pedagogical techniques. For a lesson designed to overcome

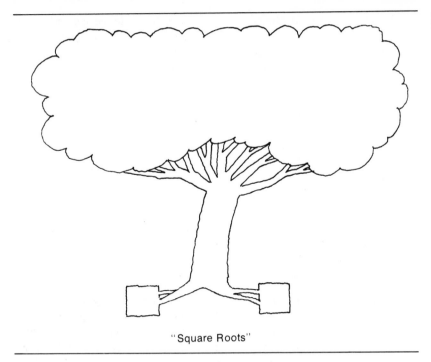

Figure 13.2
Vocabulary in Mathematics

"Square Roots"

the problem of common words with special mathematical meanings, the teacher could find pictures or other visual displays to illustrate differences in meaning as in Figure 13.2.

In regard to words or phrases which emphasize important concepts in mathematics, the teacher might provide displays of cue words with appropriate connections. For example:

Sum	$\longrightarrow$ Add
Difference	$\longrightarrow$ Subtract
Product	$\longrightarrow$ Multiply
Quotient	$\longrightarrow$ Divide
How many more?	$\longrightarrow$ Subtract
How many in each group?	$\longrightarrow$ Divide
How many in all?	$\longrightarrow$ Add or Multiply

For technical vocabulary in mathematics, textbooks commonly provide lists of new words and glossaries for student use. The teacher might provide additional help by using crossword puzzles, listing key words for the day or week, giving assignments dealing with definitions, or asking students to write sentences using technical vocabulary. Teachers can also develop exercises comparing varied forms of important words—for example, the forms of *divide*.

Directions: Using the hints provided below, complete the spelling of each of the following key words. Do only those you are certain you know. You'll learn the meanings of the rest in the next few days as we continue to study this topic.

1.   _ _ C_ _ _ _ _
2.   _ I_ _ _ _
3.   _ _ R_ _ _ _ _ _ _ _
4.   C_ _ _ _ _ _ _
5.   _ _ _ _ _ L_
6.   _ E_

Hints:

1. The numbers to be multiplied (factors)
2. The symbols 0, 1, 2, 3, 4, 5, 6, 7, 8, 9 (digits)
3. Do the operation within these first (parenthesis)
4. Another word for solve (calculate)
5. A mathematical principle (formula)
6. Used as a grouping number or base (set)[7]

Finally, students should develop facility in recognizing and understanding abbreviations and specialized symbols. One suggestion for reinforcing these skills and concepts relies on the use of flash cards. Flash cards are commonly used by reading teachers for sight-word recognition and by content-area teachers for vocabulary. Figure 13.3 provides some examples of mathematics flash cards.

Figure 13.3
Flash Cards for Vocabulary
Development

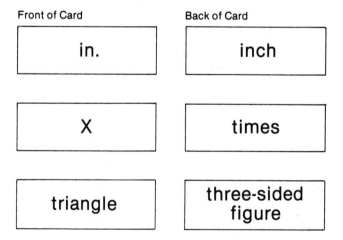

Front of Card   Back of Card

in.	inch
X	times
triangle	three-sided figure

Comprehension   **Sentence Level.** The teacher should spend enough time with students to insure proper reading and interpretation of instructions. The teacher can do this by "working through" the first exercise to make sure that

[7]R. A. Earle, *Teaching Reading and Mathematics* (Newark, Del.: International Reading Association, 1976), p. 19. Used with permission.

everyone understands what to do. In "working through" the exercise, the teacher is presenting a model of the desired response (see Chapter 6). For example, the teacher might say:

> The directions say "In the following problems, multiply the whole numbers by the fractions." Let us look at the first problem: $3 \times \frac{1}{2}$. The whole number is 3; the fraction is $\frac{1}{2}$. Multiply 3×1 and write $\frac{3}{2}$.

To aid understanding of equations and formulas, class time should be spent on exercises calling for translation responses.

> Example: $3 + 2 = 5$.
> "Three and two is the same as five."
> "Three and two is another name for five."
> "Three and two may be substituted for five."
> "Three and two is five."
> "Three and two equals five."
> "Three plus two equals five."

Note that all of the sentences convey the same mathematical meaning.

Paragraph and Discourse Level. As discussed earlier, there are two types of discourse for the student in mathematics to read—explanations and problems. Teachers should be careful to make students aware of the purposes for assigned reading in mathematics and of the relationships between the reading and other activities. For example, is the reading to be a follow-up to the teacher's lecture, a first contact with a topic, or a prelude to a written homework assignment? Telling students what they are to do will have great impact on their successful performance of assigned tasks.

The Mathematics Textbook

The mathematics textbook is often the key curriculum factor in the mathematics classroom. Since it is the primary source of content, its organization provides the structure of the course.

The textbook should be used for what it is—a valuable resource for both teacher and student. Teachers can use the book for follow-up reading on an idea, algorithm, or concept. It can also be used for introducing a topic or for providing enrichment work. Another important use is as a source for drill and practice.

The Word Problem

For many years, both mathematics teachers and their students have expressed frustration with word problems. Often the problem is with the students' failure to understand mathematical operations and/or concepts. However, several reading-related responses might also cause these problem-solving failures. Often, the difficulties with word problems are compounded by a less than enthusiastic presentation from the classroom teacher.

Students could learn to use the following approach to solving word problems:

Step 1. Read through the problem quickly.
Step 2. Examine the problem again.
Step 3. Read the problem again to note what *information* is *given*.
Step 4. Analyze the problem carefully to note the *relationship* of information given to what you are asked to find.
Step 5. Translate the *relationship* to *mathematical terms*.
Step 6. Perform the necessary *computation*.
Step 7. Examine the solution carefully.[8]

DIRECTED-READING PROCEDURES

Directed-reading procedures can help students solve mathematical problems. The procedures are an adaptation of study-skill techniques that have helped students improve reading in general (see Chapter 5). This technique also follows the general problem-solving scheme suggested by George Polya: understand the problem, devise a plan, try out the plan, and reflect on the solution.[9]

Shepherd developed one such procedure:

1. Read it slowly and carefully. Picture the scene of the problem in your mind.
2. Reread the last sentence. Decide what is asked.
3. Reread the entire problem. Determine the facts given to work with.
4. Decide what process to use.
5. Estimate the answer. Judge reasonableness of estimate.[10]

Robinson developed another approach:

1. Read the problem thoroughly, asking, "What is this all about?"
2. Reread the problem, asking, "What am I to find here?"
3. Ask yourself, "What facts are given?"
4. Next, plan your attack.
5. Estimate the answer.
6. Carry out the operations.
7. Check your work.[11]

The following procedure gives students a set of steps to respond to as

---

[8]Earle, *Teaching Reading and Mathematics,* pp. 49–50. Used with permission.
[9]George Polya, *How to Solve It* (New York: Doubleday, 1957).
[10]Shepherd, *Comprehensive High School Reading Methods,* p. 262. Used with permission.
[11]H. A. Robinson, *Teaching Reading and Study Strategies—The Content Areas* (Boston: Allyn & Bacon, 1975), pp. 182–83. Used with permission.

they read rather than a set of directions to follow before or after the reading experience. The directions are based on those tasks found to be most important for successful reading of a particular content. The procedure, which is applicable to all mathematics problems, includes steps for self-evaluation, revision, and reflection. The procedure asks students to make responses in writing because writing about mathematics increases understanding and problem-solving ability.[12] A crucial factor is the provision for feedback and correction.

The procedure also provides the teacher with a useful diagnostic tool. By using it, the teacher discovers some of the specific difficulties that a student is having in the process of reading the problem; the procedure gives a teacher more information than just an incorrect answer. This 10-step procedure will help students with each new skill or concept they encounter. As students become more proficient, they can advance to a more efficient problem-solving method.

1. Read quickly to obtain a general idea. Write a statement of the general idea.
2. Reread slowly to find details. Make a list of the important details.
3. What does the information mean? Translate the information, if necessary, into another form.
4. How does the information fit together? Draw a diagram or picture if necessary. Reread if necessary.
5. Devise and outline a plan for solution.
6. Solve the problem and write the answer.
7. Check your answers with the teacher-provided key.
8. Count and record the number of steps you completed correctly.
9. Revise any incorrect or incomplete responses.
10. Reread the problem. Briefly summarize what you have learned from working this problem.[13]

Several steps call for rereading. Accepting the necessity of rereading is crucial to successful mathematics reading. Note that rereading is always done for a specific purpose. Because of the design of the procedure, students will meet with success if they finish the task—an important motivational aspect. The three problems below illustrate how the procedure works with a simple addition problem, a problem involving a graph, and a word problem:

[12]William E. Geeslin, "Using Writing About Mathematics as a Teaching Technique." *Mathematics Teacher* 70 (February 1977): 112–15.
[13]Walter J. Lamberg and Charles E. Lamb, "A Directed Reading Procedure for Mathematics." *Illinois Mathematics Teacher* 28 (November 1977): 8–14.

Problem 1.

$$350 \atop +345$$

Find the sum

1. Finding the sum of two 3-digit numbers.
2. 350
   345
   +
3. three hundreds, five tens, zero ones
   three hundreds, four tens, five ones
   add
4. 3 5 0
   +3 4 5
5. Add the ones, then add the tens, and then add the hundreds
6. 695
7. Check steps 1–6.
8. Count correct steps—6
9. Correct if necessary. Discuss with teacher if unsure of any procedure.
10. Looking back—for example, procedures apply to other addition problems such as 4-digit problems, and so on.

Problem 2.   Average family's dollar

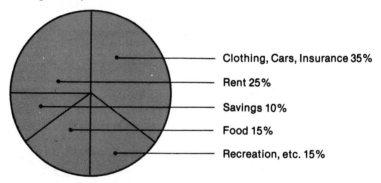

Clothing, Cars, Insurance 35%

Rent 25%

Savings 10%

Food 15%

Recreation, etc. 15%

How much of the family's budget does not go to housing and food?

1. Family budget—housing and food
2. Rent 25%, Savings 10%, Food 15%, clothing, and so on 35%, Recreation, and so on 15%, Average family's dollars, not housing and food
3. housing and food / rest

4. See picture
5. Add Housing % to Food % Subtract from 100%
6. 25% + 15% = 40%   100% − 40% = 60%
7. Check
8. 6 correct
9. Revise if necessary—with teacher's help. Teacher could use this opportunity to polish format, and so on.
10. Look back—general graph reading, and so on.

What horsepower is needed to raise 66,000 lbs. a distance of 6 ft. in 2 minutes?

Problem 3.

---

1. How much horsepower?
2. 66,000 lbs.
   6 ft.
   2 minutes
3. Weight lifted through distance in time—horsepower required.
4. 33,000 6 ft. 2 min.
5. $\text{hp} = \dfrac{\text{ft.} - \text{lb. of work per min.}}{33,000}$
6. $\dfrac{66,000 \times 6 \text{ hp.}}{33,000 \times 2} = 6 \text{ hp}$
7. Check steps 1-6.
8. 6
9. Correct
10. Horsepower problems—situations dealing with work.

STUDY SKILLS

In addition to those study strategies presented in Chapter 5, teachers can also ask students to write and answer their own questions about the mathematical text. Writing about mathematics provides students with an opportunity for cognitive involvement.

SAMPLE LESSON PLANS

A sample lesson plan illustrates some of the problems discussed in the chapter. Lesson Plan 1 deals with vocabulary development; Lesson Plan 2 works on comprehension by asking students to distinguish between problems and explanations in a specific section of the textbook.

Lesson Plan 1:

1. Purpose: To present concept of prime number.
2. Materials: Chalkboard, chalk, textbook, and handouts.
3. Preassessment: Have students circle primes in a list of ten numerals. Ask students to list three other primes. Students should write a definition of primes in their own words.
4. Teacher procedures: Teacher gives examples and nonexamples. Leads students to "All primes are odd." The teacher counters with "What about 2?"
5. Student activities: Students use a chart and circle the primes. They work selected exercises on primes in the textbook.

1	2	3	4	5	6	7	8	9	10
11	12	13	14	15	16	17	18	19	20
21	22	23	24						

6. Postassessment: Students are given a new sheet paralleling preassessment.

Lesson Plan 2:

1. Purpose: To distinguish between text which explains and text which gives problems.
2. Materials: Textbooks, paper, and pencil.
3. Preassessment: Have students survey the first three pages of a chapter introducing a new topic. Students should indicate the sections which give explanation and those which give problems.
4. Teacher procedures: Teacher goes over the same three pages with the student, giving and explaining the appropriate responses. (At the same time, the teacher is introducing the topic to the class.)
5. Student activities: In small groups, students repeat the task with the next three pages.
6. Postassessment: Students repeat task on remaining pages in chapter.

SUMMARY   This chapter presented the potential problems in reading mathematical text and several teaching methods that can help to correct the reading difficulties students encounter. Students encounter special problems when they try to solve word problems. Directed-reading procedures can reduce these problems and improve both reading and computation ability.

1. Discuss one of the Key Ideas listed in the Overview of this chapter.
2. Describe some potential problems which might be encountered in mathematical reading at the sentence level.
3. Select and review a mathematics textbook. List the features which would aid the teacher or student in regard to mathematical reading.
4. Using a directed-reading procedure outlined in the text, solve the following problem as if you were a secondary mathematics student: "John is 10-years old. His uncle is 3 years more than 4 times as old as John. How old is the uncle?"
5. Design a bulletin board to help students acquire technical vocabulary skills as related to mathematics.
6. Select and read one of the suggested readings. Write a short two- or three-page summary. Include a description of how the article or chapter could help a classroom teacher.

Recommended Readings

Bamman, Henry A. "Reading in Science and Mathematics," in Margaret Early, ed., *Perspectives in Reading.* Newark, Del.: International Reading Association, 1969.

Blankenship, Colleen S., and Lovitt, Thomas C. "'Story Problems' Merely Confusing or Downright Befuddling?" *Journal for Research in Mathematics Education* 7 (November 1976): 290–98.

Call, J., and Wiggins, Neal A. "Reading and Mathematics." *Mathematics Teacher* 59 (February 1966): 149–51.

Dunlop, William P., and McKnight, Martha Brown. "Vocabulary Translation for Conceptualizing Math Word Problems." *The Reading Teacher* 32:3 (November 1978): 183–89.

Lerch, H. H. "Improving Reading in the Language of Mathematics—Grades 7–12," in L. E. Hafner, ed., *Improving Reading in Secondary Schools: Selected Readings.* New York: Macmillan, 1967, p. 345.

Earle, Richard A. *Teaching Reading and Mathematics.* Newark: Del.: International Reading Association, 1976.

Morris, Robert W., "The Role of Language in Learning Mathematics." *Prospects* 8:1 (1978): 73–81.

Pachtman, Andrew B., and Riley, James D., "Teaching the Vocabulary of Mathematics Through Interaction, Exposure, and Structures." *Journal of Reading* 22:3 (December 1978): 240–44.

Piercey, Dorothy. *Reading Activities in Content Areas: An Ideabook for Middle and Secondary Schools,* abridged ed. Boston: Allyn & Bacon, 1976, chap. 9.

Richards, J. J. "Processing Effects of Advance Organizers Interspersed in Text." *Reading Research Quarterly* 11:4 (1975–76): 592–622.

Riley, James D., and Pachtman, Andrew B. "Reading Mathematical Word Problems: Telling Them What to Do is Not Telling Them How to Do It." *Journal of Reading* 21:6 March 1978): 531–34.

Robinson, H. Alan. *Teaching Reading and Study Strategies: The Content Areas.* Boston: Allyn & Bacon, 1975.

Roe, Betty D; Stoodt, Barbara D.; and Burns, Paul C. *Reading Instruction in the Secondary School.* Chicago: Rand McNally, 1978, chap. 9.

Shepherd, David L. *Comprehensive High School Reading Methods.* Columbus, Ohio: Charles E. Merrill, 1973, chap. 10.

Strang, Ruth; McCullough, Constance M; and Traxler, Arthur E. *The Improvement of Reading,* 4th ed. New York: McGraw-Hill, 1967, chap. 9.

Thomas, Ellen L., and Robinson, H. Alan. *Improving Reading in Every Class,* 2nd ed. Boston: Allyn & Bacon, 1972.

14

Reading in Science

Because of the nature of scientific language and study, reading in science makes special demands on the secondary student. Students have to be able to decode special symbols and understand technical terminology. They must be able to understand how scientists gather and verify information by means of the scientific method of inquiry. They need to know how to perform an experiment in a laboratory by following a lab manual. These special demands call for special kinds of instruction.

OVERVIEW

Reading in science presents problems for the student in understanding technical vocabulary and special symbols, in following equations, and in comprehending scientific problems and explanations.
To study science effectively, students must be able to follow the scientific method of inquiry and must know how to use the laboratory.

Key Ideas

As Mr. Schmidt, the local science teacher, was preparing lessons for the coming week, he thought of some of the problems his students were having. Some students were comfortable reading the explanation portions of the textbook but had difficulty reading and responding to some of the mathematical portions of the text. As a first step in solving this pedagogical problem, Mr. Schmidt met with the head of the department, Ms. Blaine, who told him about some reading tools she had used for her students. Mr. Schmidt made some minor alterations to make the exercises and examples more pertinent to his science classes and content materials.

THE SPECIAL DEMANDS OF SCIENTIFIC READING

The science teacher should remember that students will need assistance in applying reading skills to new and difficult content.[1] Donald Smith has developed a hierarchical model for reading that has five levels: letters, words, sentences, paragraphs, and discourse (or multiparagraph text).[2]

Letters

At the letter level, reading in science may present four special problems, which are similar to problems presented in mathematics. These problems include: 1) the use of special symbols, 2) the specialized use of numerals, 3) special emphasis on numerals, and 4) the use of letters as numerals or variable quantities.

The following example is taken from the field of chemistry where letters are used to symbolize elements. (Note that with a few exceptions, the letter used is the first letter of the word.)

C—carbon	P—phosphorus
F—fluorine	K—potassium
I—iodine	W—tungsten
N—nitrogen	Na—sodium
O—oxygen	Si—silicone

The teacher must remember that students may need help in learning to recognize and understand the symbols. Specific instruction may be required because of a lack of cues to the symbol's meaning as with *Na* for sodium. Just because a student learns one item, there is no reason to believe that the ideas will transfer to other symbols such as *Fe* (iron).

Words

Words are formed from combinations of letters or symbols. In science, this practice can lead to some new and interesting combinations. For

[1]David L. Shepherd, *Comprehensive High School Reading Methods* (Columbus, Ohio: Charles E. Merrill, 1973).
[2]Donald E. P. Smith, *Learning to Read and Write: A Task Analysis.* Volume 1: *A Technology of Reading and Writing* (New York: Academic Press, 1976).

example, two-letter combinations can be used to denote the combining of elements as in H_2O (water). The combinations become more and more complex and sophisticated:

NaCl—sodium chloride	pH—scale for rating presence of acidity
H_2SO_4—sulphuric acid	KCl—potassium chloride
$\triangle H$—change in H	+3—charge on an ion

When faced with an unfamiliar word in ordinary reading, the reader can use word-analysis skills. But this process may not be so easy with the more complex combinations of scientific symbols. The student may not know 1) the referent of the symbol (for example, that H_2 = a hydrogen atom with two electrons) or 2) the relationship of the referents (that H_2SO_4 = a chemical combination of hydrogen, sulphur, and oxygen).

Specific Difficulties with Vocabulary. Vocabulary difficulties fall into several categories, which roughly parallel those same problems at the letter level.

Words with more than one meaning. As with many content areas, some words in science take on different meanings than they have in ordinary reading. For example, the phrase "the expenditure of energy could be explained in terms of an *active transport*" requires thinking of more than the usual sense of *active transport*. The phrase refers to the movement of ions across a cell membrane. The following chart gives some other examples:

Biology	*Physics*
cell	acceptor
binomial	best
circulation	chain
colon	cycle
nerve	field
plant	medium
taxis	pitch

Chemistry	*Earth science*
addition	amber
base	core
boiling point	gravity
group	law
mass	streak
normal	

Technical vocabulary. Technical vocabulary in science may present three different types of problems. First, the word may be entirely new. The student may not be able to pronounce the word or use word-analysis skills on it. Second, the concept the word represents may be new. Finally, the concept represented by a word may have no simple concrete referent. Some examples of technical vocabulary include *ecological system, chemical combination,* and *relativity.*

Varied forms and meanings. Another confusing factor in science vocabulary is that key words in the text may appear in different forms, which the reader will have to recognize and relate. For example, biology uses many variations of the word *cell,* such as *cellular, celled* (as in nerve-celled), and *cellulla.* A related problem is that the same or similar words may have different meanings in each branch of science. *Nucleus* refers to the positively charged portion of an atom in chemistry, the essential element of protoplasm in biology, and the head of a comet in astronomy.

Abbreviations and Acronyms. Abbreviations and other short labels are common in science. For example, the label *DNA* is commonly used for *deoxyribonucleic acid.* Symbols for elements are actually abbreviations for the English or foreign names of the elements. For example, the symbol for iron, *Fe,* comes from the Latin word for iron,

Using Textbook Aids to Develop Vocabulary. If the text introduces many new terms, the teacher may need to pronounce, define, and illustrate them before students read the assigned selection.

At the same time, the teacher should demonstrate how to use textbook aids, such as explicit definitions and visual aids. Two additional suggestions are: to use glossaries and make illustrated science dictionaries.

Glossaries. Most science textbooks have a glossary of the key technical terminology. Teachers can provide an informal assessment that checks that students know the location and purpose of the glossary. Teachers can ask students to read a short section and look up definitions of words. The glossary exercise in Figure 14.1 directs students to relate the definitions to the particular context in which the words appeared.

Illustrated Science Dictionaries. Lawrence Hafner suggests the compiling of a class dictionary with diagrams and pictures to enhance science vocabulary development.[3] This activity is similar to the compiling of a personal dictionary (see Chapter 3). One difference is that students supply an illustration rather than a synonym for the term. Students find the definitions in their text glossaries.

Abstract Concepts. Another problem of developing vocabulary in science is understanding abstract concepts. Many new words in a science class do not have simple concrete referents. For example, consider the concept of *atom.* One cannot see an atom, one cannot feel an atom, and one cannot use any of the other five senses to find out what an atom is. Therefore, the teacher will need to use diagrams, charts, or other demonstrative aids to help students acquire the concept of *atom.*

---

[3]Lawrence E. Hafner, *Developmental Reading in Middle and Secondary Schools—Foundations, Strategies, and Skills for Teaching* (New York: Macmillan, 1977).

Figure 14.1
A Glossary Page in a Biology
Textbook

Glossary

In order to learn the correct use of these terms and their definitions in context, refer to the pages that are shown by **boldface** numerals in the Index.

abiogenesis The doctrine that life can be generated from nonliving material.

acetylcholine A chemical produced at a synapse to transfer an impulse across the synapse.

acromegaly A disease of adult life; caused by overproduction of growth hormone by the anterior lobe of the pituitary gland; characterized by enlargement of the bones.

active transport The movement of ions across a cell membrane; it requires the expenditure of energy.

adaptation An inherited structural or functional characteristic that gives an organism, or the population of which it is a member, an advantage in the environment.

Addison's disease A disease caused by insufficient secretion of the adrenal cortex; characterized by general weakness, low blood pressure, anemia, and bronzing of the skin.

adenosine triphosphate (ATP) A molecule that contains a great deal of energy in phosphate bonds and supplies energy for cell activities.

adrenal glands A pair of glands on the kidneys; help regulate blood pressure and the concentration of various mineral salts in the blood.

adrenocorticotropic hormone (ACTH) a hormone, secreted by the anterior lobe of the

pituitary gland, that stimulates the activity of the adrenal cortex.

aerobic respiration The second major step in the oxidation of glucose, in which two molecules of pyruvic acid are broken down to give a high yield of ATP and water and carbon dioxide.

afferent neuron A nerve cell that transmits a stimulus from a sensory receptor.

agglutinin The type of antibody, present in blood serum, that causes clumping of foreign antigens.

algae A group of single-celled monerans or protists that carry on photosynthesis.

allele Each of the two related factors that control a trait.

Alternation of generations A type of life cycle characterized by alternating asexually and sexually reproducing generations.

alveolus A thin-membraned air sac in the lungs, through which diffusion of gases occurs.

amino acids Organic compounds that are the building blocks of proteins.

amnion The inner wall of the sac in which the reptile, bird, and mammal embryo develops.

amphibians Members of the class of cold-blooded chordates characterized by smooth,

694

Source: W. L. Smallwood and E. R. Green, *Biology* (Morristown, N.J.: Silver Burdett Co., 1977), p. 694. Used with permission.

Figure 14.2
A Page from a Physics Textbook

charge. This equation can be rearranged and used to provide a definition of *electric field intensity* (*E*):

$$E = \frac{F}{Q}$$

Hence the intensity of electric fields is expressed in terms of force per unit charge, usually as newtons per coulomb.

This defining equation makes possible the solution of many problems involving electric fields.

Since an electric field has both *intensity* (magnitude) and *direction,* it is a vector quantity. Hence electric fields can be added vectorially.

You have already seen that field intensity varies inversely with the square of the distance from a small object. For a long rod, however, the field varies inversely with the distance, not the square of the distance. The field between two oppositely-charged plates (flat conducting surfaces) is uniform. For charged objects with rough surfaces, the field is strongest near corners and sharp points. Figure 8-14 illustrates these effects. (From Figure 8-14b, what can you tell about the field inside a metal ring?)

8-12 Electric fields can be described in terms of potential energy. Physicists, like all scientists, constantly experiment to find answers to problems and explanations for observed phenomena. Sometimes, however, the experiments they would like to do are extremely difficult, or they may be impossible. Then a good technique is a thought experiment, one which is carried out entirely in the mind—usually with the help of pencil and paper. This method was widely used by Albert Einstein and others in developing extremely abstract ideas about relativity. After all, if you want to do an experiment with an airplane traveling at half the speed of light, it must be a thought experiment.

Here is a thought experiment to help illustrate the concept of electrical potential energy. Imagine a large, negatively-charged object and a tiny, positively-charged object, as in Figure 8-15. The large, negatively-charged object is fixed in position so that it cannot move. Of course, these objects are attracted to each other by electrostatic force. Now think of them as being extremely close to each other. If you pull the positively-charged object out a distance of 0.1 m, you must exert a force through

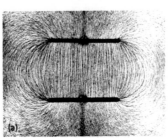 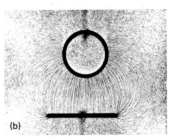

(a)   (b)

These photos, similar to those in Figure 8-1, show electric fields about (a) two oppositely-charged plates and (b) a plate and a cylinder with opposite charges.

Source: Robert Stollberg and Faith Hill, *Physics: Fundamentals and Frontiers*, rev. ed. (Boston: Houghton Mifflin, 1975), p. 265. Used with permission.

At the sentence level, science reading has similar difficulties to those found in reading mathematics. For example, sentence structures often parallel formulas. The following equation is a combination of symbols from both science and mathematics: *Sentences*

$$2H_2 + O_2 = 2H_2O$$

In science it is important for the student to be able to read and comprehend directions. The teacher should spend time with students to insure proper reading and interpretation of instructions. One way to do this is to work through the first exercise to make sure that everyone understands what to do.

Reading comprehension is heavily dependent upon recognition of patterns in large units. *Paragraphs and Discourse*

Science textbooks usually contain the two kinds of writing mentioned in previous chapters: *explanations* (descriptions) and *problems* (quantitative discourse). The explanations introduce students to new terms and concepts in the context of discussions on scientific principles and procedures. The problems test students' understanding of the concepts by asking students to apply a general concept to a particular situation. Quite often, a science textbook will present a large number of new terms and symbols in a relatively short segment of text, which makes comprehension of both the explanations and problems difficult. Figure 14.2 shows a page from a typical science textbook.

Teachers should try to make students aware of the purposes for reading a particular selection and the relationships between the reading and other activities. For example, is the reading to be a follow-up to the teacher's lecture, the first contact with a topic, or a prelude to a written homework assignment? Clarifying purposes for students will have a great impact on how successfully they perform assigned tasks.

The science textbook is usually the primary source of content, and its organization typically provides the course structure. The textbook can be a valuable resource for both teacher and student. Teachers can use the book: for follow-up reading on a concept, process, or principle; for introducing a topic; to guide enrichment work (such as a laboratory experience); or as a source for practice with problems. The teacher can encourage independent study of the textbook by selecting key terms and giving the students a guide sheet to help organize their studies. *The Textbook*

Use of Other Written Materials. In addition to the textbook, students can read other materials in conjunction with activities in the science classroom. Each of these calls for a unique style of reading behavior. Among these materials are technical journals, laboratory guides, and scientific articles.

Since most technical journals tend to be very sophisticated, teachers should caution students to read them in a careful, organized manner and make sure that students are aware of new vocabulary. Skills such as reading graphs will also be important.

The ability to follow a sequence of step-by-step directions will be crucial in using laboratory guides. Feedback and self-appraisal are also important aids and can help make laboratory experiences more fruitful. (The laboratory method is discussed in more detail under developing study skills.)

Students can often gain useful information by reading articles from newspapers or magazines that are indirectly related to class activities. Teachers should point out that it is often sufficient to skim quickly to get an overall idea of content and ideas.

DEVELOPING STUDY SKILLS

Using the Scientific Method

As students read, write, and study in their science class, they will need to know how to use the scientific method of inquiry. Briefly, the scientific method consists of the following steps: 1) presenting a problem; 2) collecting relevant data: 3) generating a hypothesis; 4) making predictions; 5) confirming or rejecting the predictions; and 6) evaluating the hypothesis.[4] The teacher should acquaint the student with this method by discussing it, illustrating it, and assigning readings about its uses.

Many characteristics of this method are inherent in reading and instructional strategies. For example, when diagnosing reading deficiencies, the teacher would proceed much as a scientist does by

1. Defining the problem,
2. Collecting student data,
3. Hypothesizing causes and effects,
4. Predicting future performance,
5. Testing predictions,
6. Evaluating hypotheses, and
7. Planning remedial instruction

In an analogous way, the student engages in scientific inquiry when employing the survey/question procedure:

- Survey: examine content
- Summarize: organize content
- Question: make predictions about points to be covered
- Read: test out predictions and confirm, reject, or revise

When students confront unfamiliar, abstract materials, they might find the steps in the SQ3R technique appropriate. Students could survey and pose questions based on titles, subtitles, and other aids and then read to answer their questions. To aid their understanding and retention,

---

[4]Alfred T. Collette, *Science Teaching in the Secondary School—A Guide for Modernizing Instruction* (Boston: Allyn & Bacon, 1973).

Figure 14.3
A Page from an Earth Science
Textbook

CHAPTER **14**

AIR PRESSURE
AND WINDS

In the previous chapter you learned that air descends in the horse latitudes and in certain latitudes of the Polar Zones. When the air meets the earth's surface, it spreads northward and southward. This surface flow is caused by a difference in pressure. Air flows from a region of higher pressure to one of lower pressure. Meteorologists use the terms **high** and **low** for areas of relatively higher and lower atmospheric pressure. In this chapter we shall investigate highs and lows.

It might be pointed out that Galileo and, to some extent, Torricelli were criticized for daring to doubt Aristotle and for putting his ideas to laboratory test. They lived and studied at the time when modern science was being evolved by men with courage enough to doubt accepted authorities.

14-1 THE MEASUREMENT OF AIR PRESSURE

In the seventeenth century an Italian physicist invented an instrument that enabled him to accurately measure the pressure exerted by a column of air. Evangelista Torricelli was educated in Rome as a mathematician and wrote a book about the branch of physics called mechanics. Galileo read this book with interest. As a result, Galileo invited Torricelli to Florence to work with him.

Galileo suggested to Torricelli that he investigate why a lift pump can lift water no more than 33 feet. To Galileo, this was contrary to Aristotle's statement, "Nature abhors a vacuum." If Aristotle was correct, there should be no limit to the height water can be raised by a lift pump.

Torricelli had performed many experiments having to do with the flow of fluids. It occurred to him that the behavior of the pump might have something to do with that subject. He had the idea that air pressing down on the surface of water pushed the water up into the tube beneath a pump.

To test this idea, Torricelli used a fluid that is much denser than water. He used mercury, which has a density of 13.6 grams per cubic centimeter. He sealed a long glass tube at one end and filled it with mercury. Then he placed the open end of the tube into a bowl of mercury, as shown in Figure

The eye of a cyclone is an area of quiet low pressure surrounded by raging winds and waterfall rain.

187

Source: F. Martin Brown, Grace H. Kemper and John H. Lewis, *Earth Science* (Morristown, N.J.: Silver Burdett Co., 1970), p. 187. Used with permission.

they could recite and review their answers. Figure 14.3 presents a typical page from a science textbook.

Using the Laboratory   The laboratory experience is inherent in the use of the scientific method, because of the observation, recording of data, and thoughtful consideration of ideas. Since much classtime will be spent in the laboratory, teachers should make sure that students 1) carefully read written directions, 2) understand key terms, 3) and realize they will be demonstrating application of key concepts.

SUMMARY   Reading in science presents special problems for students. These problems include understanding technical vocabulary and special symbols, following equations, and comprehending scientific problems and explanations. To study a science effectively, students must be able to follow the scientific method of inquiry and must know how to use a laboratory. Teachers must be able to use appropriate procedures to handle science reading problems as they arise.

1. Discuss one of the Key Ideas listed in the Overview of this chapter.
2. Select a chapter from a science text of your choice. Use SQ3R to outline it.
3. Select and review a different science text (along with its supplemental materials). Cite examples where these materials will aid the student as he or she reads.
4. Make a visual aid for helping students understand a scientific concept.
5. Select and read one of the suggested readings. Write a two or three-page summary including some key ideas that would help students develop reading skills in the content area.

Suggested Activities

Collette, Alfred T. *Science Teaching in the Secondary School—A Guide for Modernizing Instruction.* Boston: Allyn & Bacon, 1973.

Deason, H. J. *The AAAS Science Book List,* 3rd ed. Washington, D.C.: American Association for the Advancement of Science, 1976.

Dillner, Martha A., and Olson, Joanne P. *Personalizing Reading Instruction in Middle, Junior and Senior High Schools—Utilizing a Competency-Based Instructional System.* New York: Macmillan, 1977, chap. 8.

Hafner, Lawrence E. *Developmental Reading in Middle and Secondary Schools—Foundations, Strategies, and Skills for Teaching.* New York: Macmillan, 1977, chaps. 12 and 13.

Hittleman, Daniel R. *Developmental Reading: A Psycholinguistic Perspective.* Chicago: Rand McNally, 1978, chap. 10.

Lamberg, Walter J., and Lamb, Charles E. "An Analysis of Reading Difficulties in Mathematics." *Alabama Reader* 5 (1977): 33–38.

Logasa, H., and Brooklawn, H. T. *Science for Youth: An Annotated Bibilography for Children and Young Adults.* Ocean City. N.J.: McKinley, 1963.

Piercey, Dorothy. *Reading Activities in Content Areas—An Ideabook for Middle and Secondary Schools,* abridged ed. Boston: Allyn & Bacon, 1976, chap. 10.

Robinson, H. Alan. *Teaching Reading and Study Strategies—The Content Area.* Boston: Allyn & Bacon, 1975, chap. 6.

Roe, Betty D.; Stoodt, Barbara P.; and Burns, Paul C. *Reading Instruction in the Secondary School.* Chicago: Rand McNally, 1978, chap. 9.

Shepherd, David L. *Comprehensive High School Reading Materials.* Columbus, Ohio: Charles E. Merrill, 1973, chap. 10.

Thelen, Judith, *Improving Reading in Science.* Newark: Del.: International Reading Association, 1976.

Thomas, Ellen L., and Robinson, H. Alan. *Improving Reading in Every Class,* abridged 2nd ed. Boston: Allyn & Bacon, 1977, chap. 8.

Recommended Readings

15

Reading in Foreign Languages

This chapter presents a discussion of reading instruction in the context **OVERVIEW** of foreign-language study. The ideas and procedures for reading in a foreign language also are applicable to the study of English as a foreign or second language. In this chapter, "native language" refers to the dominant language of a culture or nationality. For example, English is the native language of most Americans. "Second language" refers to a language which is not dominant in a culture but which many of the educated persons in that culture study or speak. English is the second language in many European and middle-eastern countries. English is also the second language for many Americans. In the Southwest, for example, Indian languages, such as Navaho and Pueblo, are the first languages for many people; Spanish, German, Czechoslovakian, and French are the first languages of many others in this country. In areas of Arizona, Texas, and Louisiana many children do not learn English until they enter public schools.

The reading problems of the student of a foreign language or a student studying English as a foreign or second language are similar to the beginning problems of native-language readers.

Therefore, many of the instructional procedures used to teach beginning reading are applicable to teaching reading in a foreign or second language.

Key Ideas   The difficulties of reading in a foreign language parallel those of the beginning reader.

Teachers should use a variety of activities to help students develop their foreign-language vocabulary.

Teachers can use a variety of comprehension activities to improve student comprehension in a foreign language and simplify complex syntax.

Using study skill strategies and adjusting reading rate to fit the purpose are important to proficient reading in a foreign language.

When Mr. Sands, the French teacher, introduces a set of new words, he encourages his students to use their skills in phonic and structural analysis to analyze the new words. To prepare his students, he questions them about similarities and differences between structures in English and French. After the students have read the passages containing the new words silently, he holds a class discussion on how the context might suggest the meaning of the new words. He also poses questions to check his students' comprehension of the passages.

SPECIAL DEMANDS OF READING IN A FOREIGN LANGUAGE
Parallels to Beginning Reading

The difficulties most students experience in the study of a foreign language often parallel those of the beginning reader who is learning to read his or her native language. Word-recognition skills learned in beginning reading are equally important to decoding a foreign language.

When reading, the student must learn to comprehend the decoded message as well as the messages spoken by the teacher and classmates. The initial emphasis may be on translation responses as the student practices moving back and forth from English to the foreign language. To be proficient, the student must learn to process meaning directly from the foreign language without first translating it into English. Similarly, the beginning reader must learn to process meaning directly from the text in silent reading without first having to translate the text into a spoken version. Finally, the student should learn to speak, listen, and read at the higher levels of the cognitive domain: interpretation, application, analysis, synthesis, and evaluation.

To develop fluency, students will need to learn to recognize instantly a large stock of words, whether they are listening or reading. Development of context analysis is critical because students will continually be confronting unfamiliar words and unfamiliar uses of known words. Unfamiliar syntactic structures are a special difficulty, particularly long, complex structures not found in English syntax. Dictionaries have limited value here. The student must learn to generate several possible responses based on how these words function. More opportunities to read increasingly long selections without having to meet unrealistically high standards for correct pronunciation or accurate comprehension will encourage fluency.

Most students of foreign languages have one key advantage over the beginning reader. Since they have already learned to read in their native language, they can take advantage of what they have already learned in studying the new language. They have already learned word-recognition skills; they need only to transfer this learning to the new language. They can apply knowledge about language and the relationships between spoken and written language to the new language. For example, the fact that word order in written sentences usually follows word order in everyday spoken language is true for most western languages. Students have already been exposed to instructional tasks in their native language that they will use in foreign-language study such as sentence-completion, sentence-transforming, and matching tasks.

Language Similarities

At the initial stage of language study, a key aid is the widespread use of the Roman alphabet in European languages. On the other hand, in the study of Russian, middle-eastern, and Oriental languages, the student must learn a new graphemic system. Even European languages have some differences in form and use of written symbols, and some symbols have no direct correspondence in English. For example, the German language has the *umlaut,* two dots placed over vowels to signal a particular pronunciation as in schön (pretty).

Cognates—words in two or more languages that have the same or similar pronunciations and spellings and the same or similar meanings—are an important aid to vocabulary development. The following chart shows some examples of cognates.

English	*Latin*
family	familia
color	color
figure	figura
herb	herb
rose	rosa
English	*French*
arm	arme
advantage	advantage
beauty	beauté
dame	dame
grave	grave
English	*Spanish*
color	color
auto	auto
art	arte
professor	profesor
adore	adorar

English	*German*
all	alle
apple	Apfel
ball	Ball
class	Klasse
fish	Fisch

A less obvious aid is the similarity of pronunciation and structure of words with the same meanings in two or more languages. For example, notice the similarities between the following words that refer to numbers in English, German, and Spanish:

English	Spanish	German
one	uno	eins
two	dos	zwei
three	tres	drei
four	cuatro	vier
five	cinco	fünf
six	séis	sechs
seven	siete	sieben
eight	ocho	acht
nine	nueve	neun
ten	diez	zehn
sixteen	diez y séis	sechzehn
twenty	viente	zwanzig

Since both modern English and modern German evolved from the same language, similar sentence patterns appear in both. For example:

1. Subject—Transitive verb—Direct object:
   Er hat zehn Finger.
   He has ten fingers.
2. Subject—Linking verb—Predicate adjective:
   Das ist falsch.
   That is false.
3. There—Verb—Subject:
   Da sind die Schüler.
   There are the students.

Of course, some of the more complex patterns in German have no direct equivalents in English as is the case with other foreign languages.

Another important aid to comprehension is the similarity of patterns in both paragraph and multiparagraph structures. Most languages have logical patterns of organization such as: ennumerative, chronological, comparison/contrast, and cause/effect.

Many genres of literature appear to be universal like short, fictional narratives and short, highly structured lyric poems. In spite of major differences between the Japanese and English language, modern

Japanese novels can be successfully translated into English and have much in common with European and American novels. One important reason for the similarities in literature is that poets, novelists, and dramatists have studied and deliberately initiated forms from other countries. For example, both William Butler Yeats, an Irish writer, and Ezra Pound, an American writer, have experimented with the traditional Japanese verse and dramatic forms.

There are obviously major differences to consider from one language to another. One example is the difference in the structure of lyric poetry between Oriental and western literature. In both American and British poetry, the tendency is to develop patterns from rhyming words and meter (patterns of stressed and unstressed syllables). But in Oriental poetry—the Haiku, for example—structure is often based on the number of syllables in a line. Differences in writing often reflect important cultural differences. The student will confront unfamiliar values, family and social relationships, and religious and philosophical views. These are sources of difficulty in reading but are also sources of interesting and meaningful learning in foreign-language study.

Reading difficulties in a foreign language will be, in part, a function of the commonality (or lack of it) between the English language and American culture on one hand and the foreign language and culture on the other. Therefore, German, French, and Spanish should be among the easiest languages for an American student to study given the history of interaction between those nationalities. These languages have much in common in syntax, vocabulary, and in their phonemic-graphemic systems. English evolved from a Germanic language and was then heavily influenced by both Latin and Romance languages. The further removed a language is from English, both culturally and linguistically, the greater the difficulties in learning to read that language.

DEVELOPING VOCABULARY

As noted earlier, sight-word recognition and word-analysis skills are also important in foreign-language study. It is also important for students of a foreign language to be able to define words and concepts, analyze word structure and word relationships, and use a foreign-language dictionary. Most methods for assessing and teaching English vocabulary can be readily adapted to foreign language. Teachers should provide instruction in speaking, listening, reading, and writing new words.

Phonemes and Graphemes

Although the foreign language may have the same alphabet as English and may share many of the same phonemes (discrete sounds), students will still encounter differences in the phonemic and graphemic systems. These differences will cause difficulty in learning to decode the written language and to pronounce the words and recognize them when listening.

First, although words may have the same letters in both languages, they may sound differently. For example, in Spanish there is a greater tendency to pronounce the *double-s* sound, as in the English word *hiss,* when words end in a single *s*.

Second, the same grapheme may represent two different phonemes in the two languages. For example, *ie* in German is pronounced as long e and *ei* as long i. In English, the reverse is often the case, as in *receive* and *tie*. In addition, *ie* and *ei* have other sounds in English, as in *foreign, weight,* and *their*. Such differences lead to mistakes in spelling and pronunciation—mistakes which are often explained as *language interference*—the American student's previous learning of English interferes with his or her attempts to respond in the new language.

Third, physiological differences affect the production of sounds. Ruth Strang, Constance McCullough, and Arthur Traxler note that French and English have similar phonemes but they are produced with different positionings of the tongue.[1] In English, the tongue is often flat or concave; in French, it is often convex. They also note that the *rate* of sound production may differ—English is slow compared to French.

Teachers can alleviate some of these difficulties by providing experience in speaking and listening. T. P. Casaubon recommends that students 1) listen to recordings and talks by native speakers or very proficient teachers and 2) make observations about the sound characteristics of the language.[2] Lawrence Hafner recommends writing exercises as a means of reinforcing perception.[3] For example, the student who writes German words with *ie* and *ei* should become more aware of that area of difference between English and German. Many foreign-language teachers use dictation exercises. The teacher can dictate words, sentences, then paragraphs while the students record them.

Hafner also recommends use of vocabulary cards as an aid in identifying word meaning. Each card has the word accompanied by a picture of the word (see Example 1 in Figure 15.1.)[4] This is a common method for teaching phonics skills in beginning reading. As a further aid, he recommends adding a phonetic spelling of the word (see Example 2.)[5]

Cognates   According to Strang, McCullough, and Traxler, cognates are a very helpful way to introduce the vocabulary of the foreign language.[6] Because English is a Germanic language, there are many easily recognized German cognates, such as *schwine/swine, halt/halt*. Many modern German words, such as *diesel, blitz,* and *cloze,* have been borrowed by

---

[1]Ruth Strang, Constance M. McCullough, and Arthur E. Traxler, *The Improvement of Reading*, 4th ed. (New York: McGraw-Hill, 1967), p. 366.

[2]T. P. Casaubon, "A New Concept in Language Training." *Canadian Modern Language Review* 14 (Winter 1958): 14–15.

[3]Lawrence E. Hafner, *Developmental Reading in Middle and Secondary Schools: Foundations, Strategies, and Skills for Teaching* (New York: Macmillan, 1977), pp. 430–31.

[4]Hafner, *Developmental Reading in Middle and Secondary Schools*, p. 436.

[5]Hafner, *Developmental Reading in Middle and Secondary Schools*, p. 436.

[6]Strang, McCullough, and Traxler, *The Improvement of Reading*, p. 367.

Example 1.

el jarro

Example 2.

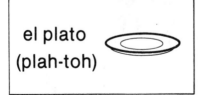

el plato
(plah-toh)

Figure 15.1
Foreign Language Vocabulary Cards

Source: Based on Lawrence E. Hafner. *Developmental Reading in Middle and Secondary Schools* (New York: Macmillan, 1977), p. 436.

English. Louise Sieberg and Lester Crocker argue that French cognates are less easily recognized because of differences in spelling and pronunciation.[7] Strang, McCullough, and Traxler give as examples *hâte*/*haste* and *dé bander*/*disband*.[8]

Common Language Experience

In the initial stages of study in a foreign language, it is especially helpful to introduce words in the context of common experiences. As a result, students can immediately grasp the meaning of the context in which the new words are used. Exercises can use common objects, actions, and situations such as asking for the time. Textbook exercises frequently follow this approach (see Figure 15.2). Teachers should actively involve students by asking questions, giving commands, and asking students to act out situations.

Instructional Tasks

Many of the instructional tasks used in beginning reading and vocabulary development in the native language apply to study of a foreign language. Teachers can use matching, sentence-completion, and multiple-choice exercises such as the following in the study of word structure and word associations.[9]

[7]Louise C. Sieberg and Lester C. Crocker, *Skills and Techniques for Reading French*. (Baltimore, Md.: Johns Hopkins, 1958).
[8]Strang, McCullough, and Traxler, *The Improvement of Reading*, p. 367.
[9]Mischa H. Fayer, *Basic Russian* (New York: Pitman, 1959).

Figure 15.2
A Page from a French Textbook

DEUXIEME LEÇON

**UNE VRAIE
PARISIENNE**

*Paul sort d'une salle de classe. Il rencon-
tre un de ses amis, Georges Leblanc, un
Français.*

GEORGES
¹Ça va, Paul?

PAUL
²Ça ne marche pas du tout. ³Je voudrais
faire la connaissance d'une jeune fille,
mais. . . .

GEORGES
⁴Comment s'appelle-t-elle?

PAUL
⁵Je ne sais pas. ⁶C'est une des étudiantes
de notre classe. ⁷Tiens! La voilà—là-bas
de l'autre côté de la rue!

21

Source: Thomas H. Brown, *French: Listening, Speaking, Reading, and Writing* (New York: McGraw-Hill, 1965), p. 21. Used with permission.

Match the French letters with the approximate sound in English.

(1) é   a. ee in see
(2) ç   b. a in gate
(3) i   c. ss in lesson

Complete these sentences by supplying the French word.

Voyez-vous _____ (the book)?

Select the proper form of the French verb *to read*.

I am reading   a. lis
                    b. lit

The study of common roots, prefixes, suffixes, and inflectional endings is a necessary component of vocabulary study. As with cognates, the teacher should help students take advantage of elements of the foreign language which are similar to the same elements in English. For example, many endings in the Germanic and Romance languages are similar to those found in English. Both French and English have the suffix *age*, as in *bandage*. German, like English, forms the comparative adjective with the inflectional ending *er*, as in *gut/besser* and *good/better*.

Teachers can present new words in the context of word relationships which have parallels in English. For example, some English words change gender with the addition (or deletion) of inflectional endings, as with *Don/Donna*, and *widow/widower*. The same phenomenon is found in other languages, often with greater consistency. For example, in Spanish, *-o* indicates male and *-a*, female as in *chica/girl* and *chico/boy*.

Flash cards are commonly used to develop sight-word recognition in beginning reading and to develop vocabulary in foreign-language study. Typically, the foreign word is printed on one side and the English equivalent on the reverse side. Teachers can use two techniques to avoid an overemphasis on isolated drill. Frank Guszak recommends including a cloze sentence with the word for beginning reading:[10]

Flash Cards

| La _____ esta en la calle Fannin. | oficina |

---

[10]Frank J. Guszak, *Diagnostic Reading Instruction in the Elementary School*, 2nd ed. (New York: Harper & Row, 1978), pp. 210-11.

Hafner, who recommends that the cards relate words in meaningful ways, offers this example: A student with one card with the German word for *egg* and another with the German word for *plate* places the egg card on the plate card in response to: "Put the egg on top of the plate."[11]

Personal Dictionary   Students can use the personal dictionary as a systematic activity for building vocabulary in a foreign language. The following example is part of the personal dictionary for a student of Latin:

Word	1. *casa*
Guess from context	house
Dictionary meaning	small house
Original sentence	Casa non est magna.

Ralph Preston developed another personal-dictionary format.[12]

Word	Phrase in Which It Occurred	Translation	Other Meaning
magna	Cisterna est magna	large	great
casa	in casas et villas	small house	cottage

Ellen Thomas and Alan Robinson recommend the following procedure as an alternative to the personal dictionary: Students divide a notebook page into three columns. In the first column they record new words or idioms they wish to study; in the second column, they record a particular meaning for the words; and in the third, an illustrative sentence.

Word or idiom	Meaning	Illustrative sentences
magna	large	Cisterna est magna
casa	small house	Casae non sunt magnae

During study, the second two columns are covered or folded over. The student reads a word in the first column, tries to respond, and then checks the response by referring to the second and third columns.[13] This procedure provides self-recitation and immediate feedback and is similar to the spelling-by-approximation exercise presented in Chapter 10 (see Figure 10.1 on page 185).

[11] Hafner, *Developmental Reading in Middle and Secondary Schools,* p. 439.
[12] Ralph Preston, "Give Students Tips on How to Get the Most from Foreign Language Books," in Lawrence F. Hafner, ed., *Improving Reading in Middle and Secondary Schools,* 2nd ed. (New York: Macmillan, 1974), pp. 420–22.
[13] Ellen L. Thomas and H. Alan Robinson, *Improving Reading in Every Class,* abridged 2nd ed. (Boston: Allyn & Bacon, 1977), pp. 365–66.

In foreign-language reading, the student's ability to respond success-   *Context Analysis*
fully to new words in the context of whole selections is very important.
Therefore, students should pay close attention to context analysis.
Foreign-language texts may have such context clues as: explicit definitions, definition by synonym or apposition, and comparison/contrast.

Thomas and Robinson strongly recommend that teachers encourage students to try context analysis before resorting to a dictionary.[14]
Students should continue reading beyond the unknown word completing
the sentence, the whole paragraph, or more. If context analysis does not
work, Thomas and Robinson recommend the use of structural analysis
before going to a dictionary.[15]

Hafner recommends use of the cloze exercise following particular
procedures which are somewhat similar to the Directed Reading Activity (see pages 118–123).[16] After the teacher prepares the students for a
selection by pretesting them on the new words, he or she attempts to
help the students learn the new words by using such methods as the flash
cards discussed earlier. The teacher then reads the selection aloud.
After students read the selection both silently and aloud, the teacher can
give them guiding questions to facilitate comprehension.

The teacher then provides a paraphrased version of the selection
with every seventh word deleted. The deleted words are listed in al-
phabetical order following the selection. Students write in the deleted
words as in the following example.

Wie viele Schuler hast der Lehrer? _____ Lehrer hast zwanzige
schüler. Hier sind _____ zwanzige schüler in Zimmer. Nein, das
_____ falsch. Anna und Peter sind hier, _____ sie studieren
nicht.

aber   der   die   ist

How many students does the teacher have? The teacher has twenty
students. Here are the twenty students in the room. No, that is false.
Anna and Peter are here, but they do not study.

As an extension activity, students can read an additional selection on a
related topic or dictate a new selection using some of the new words.

To develop independence, students must learn to use a foreign-language   *Dictionary Analysis*
dictionary as well as the glossaries in the text. Glossaries are generally
easier to use, since they are limited in both the number of words and
word meanings (see Figure 15.3).

Strang, McCullough, and Traxler note that the dictionary will not

---

[14]Thomas and Robinson, *Improving Reading in Every Class*, p. 362.
[15]Thomas and Robinson, *Improving Reading in Every Class*, pp. 363–64.
[16]Hafner, *Developmental Reading*, pp. 444–45.

Figure 15.3
A Glossary Page in a French
Textbook

---

fabriquer to manufacture
face f. face; **en — de** opposite, across the
    street; **faire — à** to face
fâcher to anger; **se —** to get angry
facile easy
facilité f. ease
façon f. way
facteur m. postman
faible weak
faillir to fail, to be on the point of
faim f. hunger; **avoir —** to be hungry
faire to do, to make; **Cela fait 3 francs.** That
    comes to (will be) 3 francs.
fait m. fact; **en —** in fact
falloir to be necessary
fameux, –euse famed
famille f. family
fatigué tired
faute f. error, mistake
fauteuil m. armchair
faux, fausse false
féminin feminine
femme f. woman, wife; **— de chambre** maid
fenêtre f. window
fer m. iron
fermer to close
fermier m. farmer
féroce ferocious
fertilité f. fertility
fête f. festive occasion, holiday
feu m. fire; **donner du —** to give a light
feuillage m. foliage
feuille f. leaf
février m. February
se fiancer to become engaged
fidèle faithful
fidélité f. faithfulness
fier, –ère proud
fièvre f. fever
figure f. face, mathematical figure
filet m. net
fille f. daughter; **jeune —** girl
fils m. son
fin f. end

final last, final
finir to finish, to end
fixer to fasten
flâner to stroll
flèche f. spire, arrow
fleur f. flower
fleuve m. river
foi f. faith
fois f. time, occasion; **une —** once; **à la —**
    at the same time
fonctionnaire m. officeholder, government
    worker
fonder to found
fontaine f. fountain
football m. soccer
forcer to force
forêt f. forest
forme f. shape, form
former to form
formidable terrific, formidable
formule f. form
fort strong
fortifier fortify
fouiller to rummage
foule f. crowd; **une — de** many
fourchette f. fork
fourmi f. ant
foyer m. home
frais, fraîche fresh, cool, cold
fraise f. strawberry
framboise f. raspberry
franc m. franc
français n. and adj. Frenchman, French
France f. France
frappant striking
frein m. brake
fréquenter to frequent, to visit often
frère m. brother
frites f. pl. French fried potatoes
froid cold; **avoir —** to be cold (of persons);
    faire — to be cold (of weather)
fromage m. cheese
frontière f. frontier, boundary
fruitier, –ère fruit merchant

632   APPENDIX 3

Source: Thomas H. Brown, *French: Listening, Speaking, Reading, and Writing* (New York: McGraw-Hill, 1965), p. 632. Used with permission.

always be a sufficient aid.[17] Many of the difficulties students encounter in using a foreign-language dictionary are the same as those beginning readers encounter using dictionaries in their native language.

Students may have trouble finding the word or the particular form of the word which appears in the text. Another problem is selecting the appropriate English equivalent from those listed in the dictionary entry. Other difficulties occur when the word appears in the context of an idiomatic expression or a nonstandard dialect form. Students can alleviate these problems to some degree by combining context and structural analysis with dictionary use.

The comprehension activities discussed in chapter 4 provide the basis for improving comprehension in a foreign language. These comprehension activities include: writing questions which move students from literal to higher levels of comprehension, providing guiding or purpose-setting questions, interspersing questions throughout the text, providing opportunities for verbalizing, and the cloze exercise.

IMPROVING COMPREHENSION

Teachers can rely on confirmation tasks in initial instruction since they are usually easier than other comprehension tasks. For example, the teacher could read a story aloud, then have students respond to ten statements by indicating 1) if the statement is true or false and 2) if they could understand the statement.[18] Essentially, teachers can use the same task for silent or oral reading and could supply the statements before or after the reading.

A major source of difficulty in comprehension is unfamiliar, long, complex syntactic structures, particularly those that do not have direct equivalents in English. To aid students, Grant Brown recommends sentence-combining exercises, such as the following:[19]

> Combine these sentences into one sentence:
> Viae sunt Romanae
> Viae sunt antiquae
> Viae sunt stratae
>
> The roads are Roman.
> The roads are old.
> The roads are paved.
> Answer: The paved Roman roads are old.

---

[17]Strang, McCullough, Traxler, *The Improvement of Reading,* p. 367.
[18]Hafner, *Developmental Reading,* p. 439.
[19]T. Grant Brown, "How to Apply Linguistics to Language Learning Without Scotch Tape." (Unpublished study, Florida State University, 1975).

Capua est urba.

Via est strata.

Via ad Capuan ducit.

Capua is a city.

A highway is paved.

A highway leads to Capua.

Answer: A paved highway leads to the city of Capua.

The same type of exercise is recommended by Frank O'Hare and William Strong for use in composition and grammer study.[20]

Brown also recommends that teachers rewrite complex sentences from reading passages into simple sentences. After readingsthe original passage, students then try to recombine the simple sentences into more complex ones. Traditionally, teachers in foreign language have employed a similar approach. When students encounter a complex structure in a passage, they are asked to analyze it by identifying the simpler patterns.

BUILDING STUDY SKILLS AND READING FLEXIBILITY

Using study-skill strategies and adjusting reading rate to fit the purpose of the reading are important to proficient reading in a foreign language, particularly when students are confronted with increasingly longer selections (see Chapter 5). Generally, students will benefit from using a survey/question procedure when reading textbook chapters. They will have gained a preview of the chapter and done some selective reading prior to attempting to learn new words or work on chapter exercises.

Asking Questions

Textbook chapters commonly include short selections which present new words in context. In more advanced study, the text may be a literature anthology or a series of literary selections. In some cases, but not all, these materials will have various aids, such as glossaries, pronunciation keys, and study questions.

Hafner and Thomas and Robinson recommend that teachers give students guiding and motivating questions prior to reading assignments.[21] Teachers will initially be giving these in English, but at advanced levels, they may give them in the foreign language.

To develop independence, students should pose their own questions to guide their reading, as in The Picture and Text Survey (see

---

[20]Frank O'Hare, *Sentencecraft: An Elective Course in Writing* (New York: Ginn & Co., 1975); and William Strong, *Sentence Combining: A Composing Book* (New York: Random House, 1973).
[21]Hafner, *Developmental Reading*, p. 445; and Thomas and Robinson, *Improving Reading in Every Class,* pp. 357-58.

Chapter 5).[22] Students could pose questions on the illustrations, title, study questions, and English introduction, if available. If no aids are available, the teacher can help by giving a brief introduction to the situation in the selection, then asking students to pose questions based on the introduction. Students can also read the opening passage of a selection and then stop and predict questions. Finally, students will profit from posing questions at the end of the reading to check their own or their peers' comprehension.

When students encounter a difficult selection which contains many unfamiliar words, they commonly follow one of two time-consuming and frustrating strategies. Either they continually interrupt their reading to look up every new word, or they slow their rate and laboriously analyze every new word. Both approaches inhibit development of fluency and comprehension. W. K. Jones recommends that students first skim through a selection to locate unfamiliar words. Students should look up the more important ones in the dictionary if they can not make a good guess as to meaning.[23]

Selective and Fluent Reading

Jones recommends an alternative approach which calls for three readings of the selection at different rates. In the first, students read quickly, skipping unfamiliar words, and attending to key words. In the second reading, students read more slowly and attempt to analyze the unfamiliar words, using context, structural, and perhaps phonic analysis, and, if necessary, dictionary analysis. The third reading is done very rapidly with attention only to meaning.

Strang, McCullough, and Traxler question the value of this procedure with students who are not proficient readers in English. They note that whereas good readers apparently know how to attend to essential words, poor readers are apt to skip them.[24]

Another rereading strategy has been effective with remedial readers in native-language reading.[25] In an initial reading at a comfortable rate, students may skip unfamiliar words or ask the teacher to say those words. But on the second and third readings, they must attempt to increase their rate. With a better understanding of the context and repeated practice with the same passage, students are often able to attack the unfamiliar words. Over a period of time, the gain in fluency seems to have a positive effect on both comprehension and word recognition. To insure students try to increase their rate, they can keep a graph to record the fastest rate in each session:

---

[22]Walter J. Lamberg and Richard Ballard, "Teaching the Picture and Text Survey," in Donald E. P. Smith, ed. *The Adoptive Classroom.* Volume 3: *A Technology of Reading and Writing* (New York: Academic Press, 1977), pp. 229–52.
[23]W. K. Jones, "Cultivating Reading Speed in Spanish." *Modern Language Journal* 41 (March 1957): 126–30.
[24]Strang, McCullough, Traxler, *The Improvement of Reading,* p. 368.
[25]Richard Ballard, "The Talking Dictionary," in Smith, *The Adaptive Classroom,* pp. 204–12.

Figure 15.4
Rereading Graph

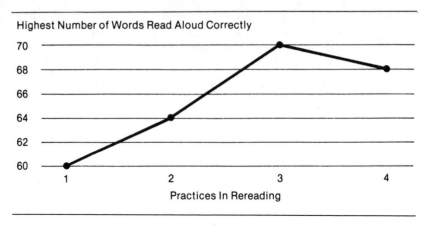

Highest Number of Words Read Aloud Correctly

Practices In Rereading

SUMMARY   This chapter addressed reading instruction in the study of foreign language. Procedures for developing vocabulary, comprehension, and study skills apply to the reading of foreign languages and the reading of English when it is studied as a foreign or second language. Students can benefit from direct, systematic instruction as well as extensive reading for interest and enjoyment.

1. Discuss one of the Key Ideas listed in the Overview of this chapter.
2. Examine a textbook used in foreign or second language study to discover what emphases are used in goals and instructional activities.
3. Examine the first chapter of a foreign language textbook. In what ways does it attempt to relate the language to English? Are similarities between the languages taken advantage of?
4. Using a textbook or other material, select a list of ten words and plan (or describe) an introductory lesson for introducing the words. Use one or more of the methods discussed in this chapter and chapter 3.
5. Select a reading selection of one or more paragraphs from a foreign language text. Plan (or describe) an activity using one or more comprehension or study-skill strategies discussed in this chapter and chapters 4 and 5.

Allen, Edward D., and Valette, Rebecca M. *Classroom Techniques: Foreign Languages and English as a Second Langage.* New York: Harcourt Brace Jovanovich, 1977.

Chastain, Kenneth. *Developing Second Language Skills: Theory to Practice,* 2nd ed. Chicago: Rand McNally, 1976.

Combs, Warren E. "Sentence-Combining Practice Aids Reading Comprehension." *Journal of Reading* 21:1 (October 1977): 18-24.

Dale, Edgar, and O'Rourke, Joseph. *Techniques for Teaching Vocabulary.* Palo Alto, Calif.: Field Publications, 1971.

Disick, Renee S. *Individualizing Language Instruction: Strategies and Methods.* New York: Harcourt Brace Jovanovich, 1975.

Feeley, Joan T. "Bilingual Instruction: Puerto Rico and the Mainland." *Journal of Reading* 30:7 (April 1977): 741-44.

Franke, Thomas L. "English as a Second Language: The Role of the Reading Teacher." *Journal of Reading* 20:3 (December 1976): 232-36.

Hafner, Lawrence E. *Developmental Reading in Middle and Secondary Schools: Foundations Strategies, and Skills for Teaching.* New York: Macmillan, 1977, chap. 18.

Hall, Mary Anne. *Teaching Reading as a Language Experience.* Columbus, Ohio: Charles E. Merrill, 1976.

Hayden, Louise. "Dialogues in Action: A Multisensory Approach to Language and Content Learning." *Journal of Reading* 22:1 (October 1978): 55-59.

Mackey, William F. *Language Teaching Analysis.* Bloomington: Indiana University Press, 1975.

Strang, Ruth; McCullough, Constance M.; and Traxler, Arthur E. *The Improvement of Reading.* 4th ed. New York: McGraw-Hill, 1967, chap. 11.

Strong, William. *Sentence Combining: A Composing Book.* New York: Random House, 1973.

Temperley, Mary S., and Rivers, Wilga M. *A Practical Guide to the Teaching of English as a Second or Foreign Language.* New York: Oxford University Press, 1978.

Thomas, Ellen L., and Robinson, Alan H. *Improving Reading in Every Class,* abridged 2nd ed. Boston: Allyn & Bacon, 1972, chap. 12.

Ziros, Gail I. "Language Interference and Teaching the Chicano to Read." *Journal of Reading* 19:4 (January 1976): 284-88.

16

Reading in Music, Art, Health, and Physical Education

OVERVIEW

This chapter will look at the particular demands of reading in music, art, health, and physical education. Content-area teachers in these special fields can help their students gain skills, knowledge, and interests that students can develop in lifelong education.

Key Ideas

The special demands of reading in music include: learning the special symbols of musical notation and learning to appreciate music.

The special demands of reading in art include: learning a technical vocabulary, learning to follow directions for doing art work, learning to read and comprehend background literature, and learning to interpret art.

The special demands of reading in health and physical education include: mastering a technical vocabulary and interpreting graphic materials.

Mr. Sims is the band director at a metropolitan high school. He leads a music program large enough to support several elective music courses. Most of the students who are motivated by and interested in music do very well in these courses. As a result, Mr. Sims decided to offer a basic course in music theory. This was a tough decision for him because he remembers how hard the course was for him in college. As he ponders why this was the case, he realizes that music uses a special symbolic and technical language. Only after understanding the language and symbolism can one decipher the theory it represents. This understanding will help Mr. Sims do a better job of teaching music theory to his students.

READING IN MUSIC The specialized reading required of a student in a music class may be very difficult and may, in fact, be the reason the student has trouble. The problem may not be the student's lack of intelligence, interest, or ability in music at all. As a student reads and studies a music book, he or she must both grapple with the special symbolic and technical language and try to digest the theory it represents.[1]

Specialized Symbols The symbols used in musical compositions or musical notation present the reader with problems that are similar to problems of reading symbols in mathematics (see Chapter 13). Figure 16.1 gives some examples of musical symbols.

Teachers should direct students to look for similarities and differences in symbols to discover the distinctive features.

Vocabulary A primary difficulty with musical vocabulary is the use of new or technical words. As these words are introduced, the reader needs to develop a utilitarian knowledge of the word and be able to use the word in all its contexts. Examples of technical vocabulary are presented in Table 16.1.

The student should be encouraged to use vocabulary skills and concepts, including word-analysis skills. However, as with other content areas, there are cases in music where context analysis will not help the reader. Many musical terms such as *allegro* and *vibrato* may present special difficulties because they have their origins in a foreign language (see Chapter 15).

---

[1]Frank Tirro, "Reading Techniques in the Teaching of Music," in H. Alan Robinson and Ellen Lamar Thomas, eds., *Fusing Reading Skills and Content* (Newark, Del.: International Reading Association, 1969), pp. 103–107.

For Notes

For Time (Beats)

For Phrasing

For Keys

For Chords

Am   Dm   E⁷

Figure 16.1
Specialized Symbols in Music

Ellen Thomas and Alan Robinson outline the following steps for studying musical vocabulary:

1. Students should look for new words which will often be set off in boldface or italic type.
2. Students should consider new terms as they are presented and reread as necessary.

Table 16.1

Forms	Tempo	Periods	Aspects of form
symphony	vivace	Baroque	cadence
fugue	allegro	Classical	chords
opera	moderato	Romantic	chorus
art song	andantino	Impressionism	melody line
ballad	largo	Expressionism	motif

Techniques	Instruments	Types of music	Harmony
atonality	winds	solo	key
contrapuntal	strings	ensemble	major
dissonance	percussion	chamber	minor
polyphonic	reeds	symphonic	natural
variations	keyboard	choral	diminished

Figure 16.2
A Page from a Music Textbook

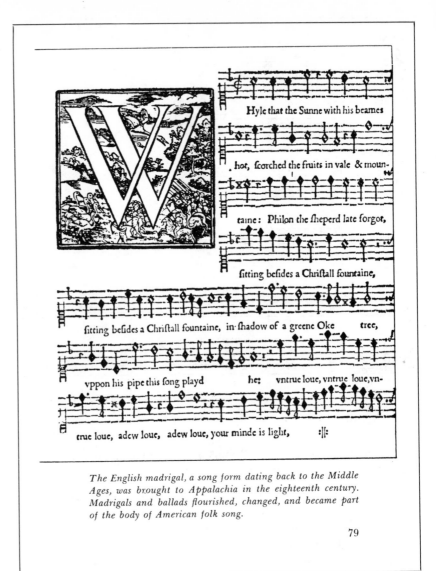

The English madrigal, a song form dating back to the Middle
Ages, was brought to Appalachia in the eighteenth century.
Madrigals and ballads flourished, changed, and became part
of the body of American folk song.

79

Source: John Rublowsky, *Music in America* (New York: Crowell-Collier Press, 1967), p. 79. Used with
permission.

3. Students should use textbook aids such as the glossary, the dictionary (for pronunciations and definitions), and the index (to locate further discussions).
4. When words (along with their definitions) are followed by illustrative examples, students should consider these in depth.
5. Students should use paper and pencil to ponder the examples or to create new ones.
6. Students should ask questions to help clarify the terms. (The survey/question procedure discussed in Chapter 5 might be helpful here.)
7. Students should use the new terms in class discussion and writing.[2]

In reading musical text, the reader must be able to integrate explanations and symbols. Musical text may appear to the secondary student in any one of the following three forms: 1) a musical excerpt only, 2) a musical excerpt and explanation, or 3) explanation only. In the case of explanation only, the reader (after learning appropriate vocabulary) will read in a way similar to several other content areas, such as history or English.

Reading Musical Text

In the case of a musical excerpt, such as that in Figure 16.2, the student has new reading problems to cope with. The student can take several approaches including:

1) considering new words in the lyrics,
2) discussing the song's meaning,
3) looking at words with or without symbols,
4) singing or humming the song a few times, and
5) considering the song's musical characteristics.[3]

Figure 16.3 shows another short piece of music with explanatory material. The teacher might help the students read this piece by asking questions such as: "Where might the composer have gotten the idea for this song?" "Were composers usually performers?" "Were people concerned with originality?"

Reference sources and textbook aids, such as dictionaries and glossaries, may be necessary when reading musical text. Survey/question procedures such as the following might be used with textbook discussions. (These questions refer to the selection in Figure 16.3.)

Developing Study Skills

Organize: This page is about *the writing of popular songs.*

---

[2]Ellen L. Thomas and H. Alan Robinson, *Improving Reading in Every Class*, abridged 2nd ed. (Boston: Allyn & Bacon, 1977).
[3]Lawrence E. Hafner, *Developmental Reading in Middle and Secondary Schools—Foundations, Strategies, and Skills for Teaching* (New York: Macmillan, 1977).

Figure 16.3
A Page from a Music Textbook

A manuscript of "Dixie," autographed by its composer, Daniel Decatur Emmett.

Performers picked up likely material wherever they heard it, modified melody and lyrics, and used it in their acts, more often than not claiming both as original.

Emmett's most popular song was unquestionably

92

Source: John Rublowsky, *Music in America* (New York: Crowell-Collier Press, 1967), p. 92. Used with permission.

Questions: 1. What is the title of the song?
            2. What is the song about?
            3. Were popular songs always original?

Answers: 1. "Dixie Land"
           2. The South
           3. No. Composers would take melodies and
              words from other songs.

The following is a sample lesson plan suitable for use in the reading of *A Sample Lesson Plan* musical material. It outlines the study of a musical selection along with its historical background.

Objective: To gain knowledge concerning background of the song "Dixie."

Materials: Copies of sheet music to "Dixie" (see Figure 16.3) and history books containing Civil War articles on American folk music.

Procedures: 1. Have students look over music.
             2. Ask how many recognize it.
             3. Discuss historical background.
             4. Sing the song.
             5. Check facts with resource materials.
             6. Discuss the song's social impact.

READING IN ART

Much of the reading in the art classroom is similar to reading in other classes. David Shepherd establishes three categories of skills for reading in art: 1) the acquisition of new technical vocabulary, 2) the ability to read and follow directions for doing art work, and 3) the ability to read and comprehend the background literature concerning art works.[4] In addition to being able to read *about* art, the student should learn to view, analyze, and interpret works of art.

Vocabulary

Art has a technical vocabulary for concepts important to the study and appreciation of art. Some examples appear in Table 16.2.

Many technical art terms are derived from foreign languages. A variety of activities, including games, can help students develop vocabulary. Students, for example, can play a game that involves the technical names for colors. As the teacher calls out a technical name, the student marks his or her game card in the appropriately colored square. This would be an adaptation of Bingo and might be called Color Bingo.

---

[4]David L. Shepherd, *Comprehensive High School Reading Methods* (Columbus, Ohio: Charles E. Merrill, 1973).

Table 16.2

Techniques	Forms	Qualities
arabesques	arcade	chroma
broken color	collage	flamboyant
emboss	cornace	intensity
engraving	facade	order
woodcut	fresco	volume

Aspects of Design	Materials	Periods
axis	enamel	Classicism
contour	glaze	Renaissance
relief	lacquer	Baroque
scale	medium	Realism
perspective	primary colors	Impressionism

Following Directions The ability to read and follow directions is crucial in all content areas, not only the arts. However, in art a special situation exists because the student must often transform what he or she reads into physical performance—for example, drawing, painting, sculpting, and making jewelry.

In helping students to follow directions in the art classroom, it is often necessary for the teacher to model the desired behavior; that is, to work through the activity with students. For example, a teacher might demonstrate how to follow written directions in mixing paints.

Reading Background Text Often, the student is asked to read about the background of a work of art. This reading may include historical accounts or biographical information and is closely related to the types of reading responses required in the social sciences (see Chapter 12).

The textbook and supplementary texts are valuable in both study and motivation. Many students who are poor readers in other classes may be interested in art or art-related topics. Using art as the motivating theme, it may be possible to develop a strong interest in reading.

Interpreting Art Work In many art classes, the teacher will present a picture or other graphic with accompanying textual material. As in dealing with graphics in social studies, the student is expected to translate and interpret the pictorial information and integrate it with the written text. The following is a sample lesson plan for presenting the art piece in Figure 16.4.

Objective: To interpret art pictures in relationship to written material.

Materials: History books and picture

Figure 16.4
A Page from an Art Textbook

Procedures: 1. Have students read the text concerning the picture and events.
2. How does the picture relate to the written text?
3. Is there information in the picture not given in the text?
4. Would the picture be different if painted by an Indian or an Anglo? Why?
5. Does the picture help you learn about events? How?

Developing Study Skills

The study skills discussed in Chapter 5 also apply to the study of art materials. The teacher will find that the survey/question procedures, such as the following for the picture in Figure 16.4, will help students to read and work on their own.

Survey: (Both the text and the picture)

Organize: This section is about *Indian art*.

Questions: 1. What does the picture show?
2. Who is winning the battle?
3. Why would Indians make this picture?

Answers: 1. Cowboys and Indians
2. Indians
3. Maybe to celebrate victories.

READING IN HEALTH AND PHYSICAL EDUCATION

Instruction in health and physical education may proceed with or without the use of a textbook. Even without a text, students must do some reading both inside and outside the classroom. For example, in health, students will need to read pamphlets, bulletin boards, and other possibly technical literature. In physical education, students will be reading such materials as the rules of games or techniques needed to perform certain physical acts.[5]

Symbols and Vocabulary

In the field of health and physical education, much of the material about the human body may be quite technical and scientific. As a result, the student will face difficulties that parallel those presented in Chapter 14 on reading in science. In addition to these skills, the reader must learn technical vocabulary peculiar to games and sports, and understand the techniques and physical skills used in the games and sports. A list of such terms follows. Students might find the use of personal dictionaries and study guides with preselected words particularly helpful.

Table 16.3

Tennis	Football	Baseball
service court	offside	fair
service	foul	foul
love	end	umpire
fault	guard	base
deuce	kick	plate
ace	goal	mound
net	umpire	
	field goal	

Basketball	Soccer	Table tennis
foul	goal	service
guard	kick	deuce
field goal	offside	service court
umpire		

Interpreting Graphic Materials

In health and physical education, students must read pictures, drawings, and other graphic materials to comprehend them. The skills for reading art and social-studies graphics will be helpful. Students must be able to follow picture sequences depicting specialized actions to understand particular athletic activities.

Teaching for Special Aims

Reading in health and physical education can be useful to students in later life in three important ways. This area of reading can: 1) help

[5]Betty D. Roe, Barbara D. Stoodt, and Paul C. Burns, *Reading Instruction in the Secondary School* (Chicago: Rand McNally, 1978).

students learn good health habits; 2) motivate students to read broadly in many related areas; and 3) help students develop the ability to follow complex sequences (such as in a football game). In the area of good personal health habits, students might learn about the advantages of good food, exercise, and regular medical check-ups, or they might read to become familiar with the negative effects of overeating, drug abuse, and lack of sleep. Shepherd sees physical education as a field ripe for motivational reading which may in turn improve reading skills in other fields. There are so many related areas that certainly every student can find something in which he or she is interested.[6] For this reason alone, the physical-education department should acquire a large variety of books and related materials. The following lesson plan deals with motivational reading outside the classroom.

      Objective: To motivate outside reading related to physical education.

      Materials: Newspapers

      Procedures: a. Have students read sports pages in local newspapers.
               b. Encourage them to select a story they like.
               c. Have them tell the class about it.
               d. Have them write a similar story about either their own experiences with or dreams about the sport involved.

Betty Roe, Barbara Stoodt, and Paul Burns see the study of sequences, such as those used in complex games and sports activities, as an important area of development.[7] The student can use these skills in later life as a spectator. The skills also serve the immediate purpose of making the student a better performer at the time. In studying game sequences, the teacher might ask students to read the material, act out the game, watch the game being played, and finally reread for further understanding and clarification. These activities would be especially profitable for a student's first formal contact with a sport.

Reading in the content areas of music, art, and physical education is similar in many ways to other secondary-school reading. However, much of this reading may have a lifelong effect on the student's hobbies or vocations. For those students with strong interests in these areas, opportunities to read can lead to more positive attitudes toward reading as a vehicle for learning.

SUMMARY

---

[6]Shepherd, *Comprehensive High School Reading Methods.*
[7]Roe, Stoodt, and Burns, *Reading Instruction in the Secondary School.*

Suggested Activities

1. Discuss one of the Key Ideas listed in the Overview of this chapter.
2. Select a chapter from either a music textbook, an art textbook, or both. Review the chapters by noting the potential problem areas students might encounter as well as the textbook aids which are available.
3. Select a piece of sheet music and outline the steps you would use to help your students study the musical selection.
4. Plan a field trip to a local art museum for your students. Take into account the reading responses necessary for the trip to be a profitable educational experience.
5. Select and review one of the recommended readings. Make notes as to how it could assist the teacher of music, art, or health and physical education in the reading of content-area materials.
6. Prepare a list of readings that could be used as motivational readings in physical education.

Recommended Readings

Burmeister, Lou E. *Reading Strategies for Middle and Secondary School Teachers,* 2nd ed. Reading, Mass.: Addison-Wesley, 1978, chap. 5.

Davis, Mary K. *Music Dictionary.* New York: Doubleday, 1956.

Dillner, Martha H., and Olson, Joanna P. *Personalizing Reading Instruction in Middle, Junior, and Senior High Schools—Utilizing a Competency-Based Instructional System.* New York: Macmillan, 1977, chap. 8.

Feldman, Edmund B. *Becoming Human Through Art—Aesthetic Experience in the School.* Englewood Cliffs, N.J.: Prentice-Hall, 1970.

Forgan, Harry W., and Mangrum, Charles T. *Teaching Content Area Reading Skills.* Columbus, Ohio: Charles E. Merrill, 1976.

Hafner, Lawrence E. *Developmental Reading in Middle and Secondary Schools—Foundations, Strategies, and Skills for Teaching.* New York: Macmillan, 1977, chap. 19.

Hennings, D. G. *Communication in Action—Dynamic Teaching of the Language Arts.* Chicago: Rand McNally, 1978, chap. 11.

Hittleman, Daniel R. *Developmental Reading: A Psycholinguistic Perspective.* Chicago: Rand McNally, 1978, chap. 10.

Laffey, James C. *Reading in the Content Area.* Newark, Delaware: International Reading Association, 1972.

Roe, Betty D.; Stoodt, Barbara D.; and Burns, Paul C. *Reading Instruction in the Secondary School.* Chicago: Rand McNally, 1978, chap. 9.

Rublowsky, John. *Music in America.* New York: Crowell-Collier Press, 1967.

Shepherd, David C. *Comprehensive High School Reading Methods.* Columbus, Ohio: Charles E. Merrill, 1973, chap. 12.

Strang, Ruth; McCullough, Constance N.; and Traxler, A. E. *The Improvement of Reading,* 4th ed. New York: McGraw-Hill, 1967, chap. 11.

Thomas, Ellen C., and Robinson, H. Alan. *Improving Reading in Every Class,* abridged 2nd ed. Boston: Allyn & Bacon, 1977, chaps. 14 and 16.

West, Gail B. *Teaching Reading in Content Areas: A Practical Guide to the Construction of Student Exercises.* Orlando, Fla.: Sandpiper Press, 1974.

17

Reading in Vocational Education: Home Economics, Industrial Arts, and Business Education

This chapter discusses reading problems students often encounter in vocational education. The method of attacking problems presented here should prove equally successful for teachers of home economics, industrial arts, and business education.

OVERVIEW

The special demands for reading in vocational areas include: developing a new vocabulary, learning to follow directions, using graphical information and technical literature, reading for main ideas and details, and using career-oriented reading material.

Key Idea

Ms. Martin, an industrial shop teacher, is thinking of doing a special unit on industrial careers. This would require very specialized and technical literature that might cause reading problems for some of her students. She prepares a pretest of necessary vocabulary and finds that most students are unfamiliar with the terms. Therefore, prior to each reading assignment, she discusses the terms and provides definitions and illustrations.

TEACHING STRATEGIES FOR READING IN VOCATIONAL EDUCATION

Problems for the reader of vocational material often result from the technical nature of the material. One major problem is vocabulary. Another is that this material is often interspersed with graphic information, which the reader must integrate to follow the specified directions.

David Shepherd summarizes the skills needed for reading in the vocational areas: 1) developing vocabulary; 2) following directions; 3) using graphic information, 4) understanding technical literature; 5) reading for main ideas and details; and 6) using career-oriented reading.[1]

Developing Vocabulary

Technical vocabulary is an important component of vocational materials as is shown by the following word lists for home economics, industrial arts, and business education.

Home Economics	Industrial Arts	Business Education
acidity	electricity	interest
caffeine	resistance	percent
carbohydrate	conductor	compound
protein	mechanical drawing	double-entry
fat	horsepower	draft
fermentation	perspective	affadavit
curdle	meter	dividend
crystallize	phillips screwdriver	elite type
marinate	awl	pica type
cholestrol	plane	voucher
vitamins	lathe	foreclosure
minerals	insulator	subsidiary

Some students will encounter problems with 1) familiar words with new meanings; 2) technical vocabulary; and 3) the use of specialized abbreviations and acronyms.

Lawrence Hafner, using business education as an example, suggests the use of home-study work sheets in a systematic study of

---

[1]David L. Shepherd, *Comprehensive High School Reading Methods* (Columbus, Ohio: Charles E. Merrill, 1973).

Figure 17.1
A Page from a Home Economics Textbook

BROILED LIVER WITH BACON

4 Servings

4 slices calf or lamb liver, ⅓ to ½ inch thick
2 tablespoons melted butter or margarine
Salt and pepper
4 slices bacon

1 Brush liver on both sides with melted fat.
2 Place on rack in broiler pan, and place pan in oven with liver 3 inches from broiling unit.
3 Broil for 6 minutes on one side.
4 Turn, and broil for 3 minutes on other side.
5 Season with salt and pepper.
6 Serve on hot platter with Broiled Bacon.

BROILED FISH

4 Servings

1½ pounds fish steaks or fillets
1 teaspoon salt
⅛ teaspoon pepper
3 tablespoons butter or margarine
1 tablespoon hot water
Lemon wedges

1 Rub fish with salt and pepper.
2 Melt butter or margarine in the hot water.
3 Place fish, skin side up, on greased rack in broiler pan, and place in broiler, 3 inches from heat unit.
4 Brush with melted butter or margarine, and broil for 11 minutes on one side.
5 Turn, brush with melted butter or margarine, and broil for 3 to 7 minutes on other side.
6 Serve with lemon wedges.

TUNA FISH CASSEROLE

4–6 Servings

1 teaspoon salt
1 quart water
1 cup uncooked noodles
1 tablespoon butter or margarine
½ cup chopped onion
1 can cream of celery soup, undiluted
½ cup milk
1 cup canned tuna fish, drained and flaked
½ cup cooked peas
½ teaspoon salt
Few grains pepper
½ cup grated American cheese

1 Add 1 teaspoon salt to water, and bring to rapid, rolling boil.
2 Add noodles gradually so water does not stop boiling.
3 Cook, uncovered, stirring occasionally to prevent sticking, for 10 minutes, or until fairly tender.
4 Drain in colander.
5 Melt butter or margarine in skillet over low heat, add onion, and cook until brown.
6 Add soup, milk, tuna fish, peas, ½ teaspoon salt, pepper, and noodles.
7 Pour into greased baking dish, and sprinkle with grated cheese.
8 Bake in moderate oven (350° F.) for 25 minutes.
9 Serve hot in dish in which it was baked.

VARIATION
Add 2 hard-cooked eggs, sliced or chopped, to mixture before baking.

483

Source: Reprinted from *Teen Guide to Homemaking*, 3rd ed. by M. S. Barclay and F. Champion, Copyright © 1972 with permission of Webster/McGraw Hill, p. 483.

vocabulary.[2] Since they provide definitions, pronunciation guides, and use of the terms in the context of sample sentences, students can use these work sheets much like a dictionary. An alternative is to have students compile a personal dictionary in which they write down 1) 5–10 new words each week, 2) a guess at the meaning of each word from the context, 3) an appropriate dictionary definition for each word and 4) an original sentence using each word. For terms related to practical performances, equipment, or tools, students can substitute a graphic illustration for Step 4.

Following Directions

The student of home economics, industrial arts, or business education will be expected to read and follow directions as he or she carries out a particular task. Figure 17.1 gives one example of directions from a home-economics class. In industrial arts, the directions might guide the safe operation of expensive equipment such as a hacksaw (see Figure 17.2). In business education, the directions might guide the computing of an income-tax form (see Figure 17.3). Although the situations are different, the general reading techniques and responses are the same since they involve interpretation of directions and the carrying out of subsequent physical actions.

Using Graphic Sources for Information

The ability to comprehend and follow sources of graphic information is often crucial to vocational education. Graphic displays include graphs, tables, pictures, maps, and other symbolic presentations such as the example from business education given in Figure 17.3.

Assigning Technical Literature

Technical material from journals, pamphlets, and manuals can present potential problems for the student because of the new concepts and technical vocabulary. However, because of the abundance and importance of technical literature, the teacher of vocational education should use this material to give students a broader and deeper understanding of the content area.

Reading for Main Ideas or Details

Learning when to read for the main idea and when to read for specific details will help the student accomplish the specific task at hand. For example Figure 17.2 presents a guide for how to use the hacksaw safely. At one time, a student might read this page for the main idea of shop safety, while at another time he or she might read for specific details important to the safe use of the tool.

Teachers should direct students to read a particular selection several times and orient their reading either toward main ideas or toward specific details by the questions they ask students prior to reading.

---

[2]Lawrence E. Hafner, *Developmental Reading in Middle and Secondary Schools—Foundations, Strategies, and Skills for Teaching* (New York: Macmillan, 1977).

Hacksaw Safety

23. Why is it unsafe to use a dull hacksaw blade?
If a saw does not cut efficiently it seems practical to apply more pressure. However, this is wrong. More pressure, with poor cutting action will cause the blade to break.

24. What is the best procedure to follow if the hacksaw blade breaks before the cut is completed?
Start the new blade on the opposite side of the job so that it will run into the first cut only when the piece is sawed through. Starting a new blade in the first cut will result in another broken blade.

25. How should the hacksaw blade be mounted in the saw frame?
The teeth of the hacksaw blade should be pointed away from the handle and towards the front of the frame. Tension should be sufficient to prevent the blade from bending, and the blade should be straight, not twisted.

26. Is there a proper speed for hacksawing?
The kind of metal being cut and the shape of the job will have much to do with the number of strokes per minute of the hacksaw. The average speed when sawing cold rolled steel that does not spring or chatter should be 50 to 60 strokes per minute, slower when sawing harder and cast metals. The heat of the saw blade will indicate the need to slow down.

27. Why is it good practice to slow down just before the saw blade completes the cut?
When the cut is almost completed it is good practice to reduce both speed and pressure because when the saw clears the stock, forward motion will be actually greater. Many knuckles have been skinned and hands cut because this practice was forgotten.

28. What other rules should be observed for the practice of safety when hacksawing?
(A) Grip the work in the vise so that the saw cut will be near the jaws (Fig. 1-23).
(B) Only apply pressure on the forward stroke.

FIG. 1·23. **The saw cut should be close to the supporting vise jaws.**

(C) Start the saw cut with a light, even forward stroke, holding the saw frame at an angle. When the cut is established hold the frame level and saw the full width of the job.
(D) Take the longest stroke possible, but do not permit the blade-supporting pins to touch the job.
(E) Use a blade having the proper number of teeth per inch to suit the job; fine pitch for thin metal, coarse pitch for solid pieces.

Drill Press Safety

29. What is the most common cause of accidents on a drill press?
Most drilling accidents are caused by the work not being securely fastened. The job must be securely held, clamped, or bolted down, whatever size hole is being drilled.

9

Figure 17.2
A Page from an Industrial Arts Textbook

Source: J. Anderson and E. E. Tatco, *Shop Theory,* 5th ed. (New York: McGraw-Hill, 1968), p. 9. Used with permission.

Figure 17.3
A Page from a Business Textbook

A retail installment contract.

Merit's   600 MAIN STREET
MADISON, WIS. 53705

Contract No. _4328_

RETAIL INSTALLMENT CONTRACT

The undersigned (herein called Purchaser, whether one or more)
purchases from _Merit's_ _____ (seller)
and grants to _the seller_ _____
a security interest in, subject to the terms and conditions hereof,
the following described property.

QUANTITY	DESCRIPTION	AMOUNT
1	Stereo phonograph	294 95

Description of Trade-in: _None_

	Sales Tax	11 80
	Total	306 75

Insurance agreement

The purchase of insurance coverage is voluntary and not required
for credit _Group Credit_
Insurance coverage is available at a cost of $ _5.54_
for the term of credit.

☐ I desire insurance coverage.

Signed _____ Date _____

✓ I do not desire insurance coverage.

Signed _William R. Darby_ Date _Dec. 10, 19--_

PURCHASER'S NAME _William R. Darby_
PURCHASER'S ADDRESS _24 Maple Ave_
CITY _Madison_ STATE _Wis._ ZIP _53704_

1. CASH PRICE $_294.95_
2. LESS: CASH DOWN PAYMENT $_29.50_
3.   TRADE-IN _____
4.   TOTAL DOWN PAYMENT _____ $ _29.50_
5. UNPAID BALANCE OF CASH PRICE $_265.45_
6. OTHER CHARGES:
   Sales tax $ _11.80_
7. AMOUNT FINANCED $_277.25_
8. FINANCE CHARGE $ _58.55_
9. TOTAL OF PAYMENTS $_335.80_
10. DEFERRED PAYMENT PRICE (1+6+8) $ _365.30_
11. ANNUAL PERCENTAGE RATE   _21_ %

Purchaser hereby agrees to pay to _Merit's_ _____
_____ at their
offices shown above the "TOTAL OF PAYMENTS" shown above
in _24_ monthly installments of $_14.00_ (final
payment to be $_13.80_) the first installment being
payable _January 10,_ 19--, and all subsequent installments
on the same day of each consecutive month until paid in full.
The finance charge applies from _December 10, 19--_

Signed _William R. Darby_

Notice to Buyer: You are entitled to a copy of the contract you sign. You have the right to pay in advance the unpaid balance of this contract
and obtain a partial refund of the finance charge based on the "Actuarial Method." (Any other method of computation may be so identified,
for example, "Rule of 78's," "Sum of the Digits," etc.)

Three-Pay, or 90-Day, Account

Many furniture, department, and clothing stores offer three-pay, or 90-day,
accounts, sometimes called *budget accounts.* These are much like regular, or 30-day, charge accounts, but the debt is repaid in thirds. You might
call them installment charge accounts. For example, suppose you bought
a coat costing $75 on a 90-day account. Each month you would pay $25,
or one-third of the cost of the coat. At least that is the way the plan works
at one store. Each seller makes his own rules. Some treat 90-day accounts

Source: R. G. Pine, V. A. Musselman, and J. C. Hill, *General Business for Everyday Living,* 4th ed. (New
York: Gregg Division, McGraw-Hill, 1972), p. 263. Used with permission.

With the emphasis today on career planning and training, the teacher should provide students with pamphlets and other materials about job opportunities which relate to the content area. This could serve as a useful motivator to improve reading. *Career-Oriented Reading*

Study skills can also apply to career-oriented reading. For example, the survey/question procedure would prove effective for reading textbooks, manuals, and technical literature, most of which will have textbook aids (see Chapter 5). The following is an illustrative lesson plan for relating job information to the class:

1. Objective: To relate job information to the class
2. Materials: Magazines and newspapers
3. Procedures: Have students, as an outside assignment, find articles on two different jobs that relate to their home economics, industrial arts, or business education classes. Students pose and answer questions about each article.
4. Evaluation: Write a paragraph or two designed to convince a prospective employer of your job qualifications and how you acquired them.

This chapter showed the importance of developing vocabulary and understanding technical literature and graphics to reading in the content areas of home economics, industrial arts, and business education. The content-area teacher should adapt general reading techniques and skills to his or her special area of vocational education. These skills include following directions and reading technical and career-oriented materials. **SUMMARY**

Suggested Activities

1. Discuss one of the Key Ideas listed in the Overview of this chapter.
2. Select and review material relevant to home economics. Determine two activities that could be used with students to facilitate their reading.
3. Obtain a copy of IRS Form 1040 and determine ways this form could be used in a business education course to help students read and respond to reading directions.
4. Using a how-to manual as a guide, what kinds of reading responses does one have to make in order to use the manual to do general repairs around the home for example? Suggest three activities to facilitate this reading.
5. Select one of the recommended readings. Use it to make a list of suggestions for aiding the reading process in home economics, industrial arts, or business education.
6. Design a bulletin board or other display to draw students' attention to safety in the shop or home economics lab. What special reading skills could you concentrate on?

Recommended Readings

Anderson, James, and Tatro, Earl F. *Shop Theory,* 5th ed. New York: McGraw-Hill, 1968.

Barclay, Marion S., Champion, Frances; Brinkley, Jerome H.; and Funderbuk, Kathleen W. *A Guide to Teen Homemaking,* 3rd ed. New York: McGraw-Hill, 1972.

Burmeister, Lou E. *Reading Strategies for Middle and Secondary School Teachers,* 2nd ed. Reading, Mass.: Addison-Wesley, 1978, chap. 5.

Carney, John J., and Losinger, William. "Reading and Content in Technical-Vocational Education." *Journal of Reading* 20, (October 1976): 14–17.

Dillner, Martha H., and Olson, Joanne P. *Personalizing Reading Instruction in Middle, Junior, and Senior High Schools—Utilizing a Competency-Based Instructional System.* New York: Macmillan, 1977, chap. 8.

Hafner, Lawrence E. *Developmental Reading in Middle and Secondary Schools—Foundations, Strategies, and Skills for Teaching.* New York: Macmillan, 1977, chaps. 16 and 17.

Hittleman, Daniel R. *Developmental Reading: A Psycholinguistic Perspective.* Chicago: Rand McNally, 1978, chap. 10.

Johnson, Joyce D. "The Reading Teacher in the Vocational Classroom." *Journal of Reading* 17 (October 1974): 27–29.

Piercey, Dorothy. *Reading Activities in Content Areas—An Ideabook for Middle and Secondary Schools,* abridged ed. Boston: Allyn & Bacon, 1976, chaps. 3, 7, and 8.

Price, Ray G.; Musselman, Vernon A.; and Hale, J. Curtis. *General Business for Everyday Living,* 4th ed. New York: McGraw-Hill, 1972.

Robinson, H. Alan. *Teaching Reading and Study Strategies—The Content Areas.* Boston: Allyn & Bacon, Inc., 1975, chap. 11.

Roe, Betty D.; Stoodt, Barbara D.; and Burns, Paul C. *Reading Instruction in the Secondary School.* Chicago: Rand McNally, 1978, chap. 9.

Shepherd, David L. *Comprehensive High School Reading Methods.* Columbus, Ohio: Charles E. Merrill, 1973, chap. 12.

Strang, Ruth; McCullough, Constance M.; and Traxler, Arthur E. *The Improvement of Reading,* New York: McGraw-Hill, 1967.

Thomas, Ellen L., and Robinson, H. Alan. *Improving Reading in Every Class,* abridged 2nd ed. Boston: Allyn & Bacon, 1977, chaps. 10, 11, and 13.

Organizing Instruction and the Curriculum

Part 4 goes beyond instruction for specific problems in reading and considers strategies for developing the entire schoolwide reading program. Chapter 18 provides guidance in designing effective units and courses in content areas. Chapter 19 discusses ways teachers can work cooperatively to improve the school program. Chapter 20 presents procedures teachers can follow in courses and in the entire program for developing positive attitudes toward reading. Chapter 21 examines procedures for meeting individual needs, with emphasis on the needs of special students.

18

Organizing Units for Instruction

This chapter will address strategies for planning effective units and courses. With these strategies, the teacher can go beyond day-to-day planning to more effective learning experiences that help students achieve long-range goals in reading and content learning.

Educators have long accepted the advisability of advance planning. By looking ahead at the educational goals to be achieved, teachers—and students—have a sense of direction in their work. Well-planned units will allow for flexibility in handling new situations or difficulties that arise.

Key Ideas

Effective unit planning gives both students and teacher a sense of direction and allows for greater flexibility in instruction.

The two basic approaches to unit planning are: to plan around reading skills and to plan around the key concepts in the content area.

Effective units provide balance, variety, and active student participation.

The five stages of the Directed Reading Activity can serve as the overall structure of the unit.

Assessment procedures can follow three approaches to diagnosis and evaluation: pre/post assessment, continuing assessment, or a combination of the two.

Teachers can use the same planning guidelines for planning a course that they use for planning a unit.

Two teachers are chatting in the lounge at Palm High School. It is two days before the start of a new school year, and they are discussing the task of planning their instruction. They quickly discover that their approaches differ drastically. Ms. Blaine uses the textbook as an exclusive guide and plans lessons on a day-to-day basis. She readily admits that this sometimes leads to minor problems when other scheduling conflicts occur (for example, assemblies, bad weather, and holidays). And some lessons do not seem to relate meaningfully to each other. But even with these drawbacks, she continues to use this method of planning for two reasons: 1) The planning doesn't take up as much time at one sitting, and 2) it appears to be very flexible because it is not necessary to plan very far in advance.

Ms. Williams uses the unit-planning approach to her instruction. While she realizes that this takes a lot of teacher effort and planning before each unit, she likes the security it provides throughout the year; a quick glance will redirect her tasks back to the desired goals. Her units are flexibly planned to allow for unseen scheduling problems as well as any unexpected educational opportunities that might present themselves during the course of the school year.

REASONS FOR UNIT PLANNING

Some teachers view a unit as a series of lesson plans, which each cover one day's lesson. The major weakness in this approach is that the material and activities may not be meaningfully related to each other; they fail to set worthwhile learning goals for the students. Such goals would identify the key concepts to develop, the relationships between these concepts and the key reading or study performances expected of students.

Broad planning allows the teacher more flexibility in considering differences in pupils' abilities and needs. Also, the teacher can use school and community resources as an integral part of the teaching and learning experience for his or her students. In terms of pedagogy, a broad unit plan will permit a variety of teaching methods. Teachers can use methods diverse enough in nature to accommodate the many different learning styles that their students bring to the learning experience.[1]

A unit is an organized period of instruction; it may be as short as a week or as long as a month. The unit plan integrates a series of daily lesson plans with overall instructional goals or aims.

---

[1]David R. Hittleman, *Developmental Reading: A Psycholinguistic Perspective* (Chicago: Rand McNally, 1978).

Unit plans may be developed around several themes or topics, such as "the hero in American history" or "the individual against society." Another plan might focus on a topic like "careers" or "weather." In English, units are often organized around a genre, such as poetry, the novel, short stories, or plays. A unit could also focus on developing a performance or set of skills, such as the operation of particular machinery, the use of library reference aids, or multiplication of rational numbers.[2] Units can lead to the development of a major class project, such as the performance of a play, the writing of a class magazine, or the conduct of a scientific study. (A scientific study could be the cultivation and crossbreeding of plants, an oral history of the community, or a survey of slang expressions used by the student body.)

In planning the unit, the teacher should consider how to relate reading instruction to the content. The two basic approaches to unit planning are: 1) to focus on reading skills and 2) to focus on the content area.

APPROACHES TO UNIT PLANNING

Martha Dillner and Joanne Olson discuss the four key steps for planning around reading skills.[3]

1. *Start with a scope and sequence of reading skills and abilities.* Teachers should list the overall reading skills the reading program should develop in the areas of vocabulary, comprehension, and study skills.
2. *Select one or more skills to teach.* From the list of skills, the teacher should select one or two skills to address in the instruction. For example, the teacher might choose to focus on reading 1) to identify details, 2) to identify main ideas, or 3) to identify ideas and supporting details.
3. *Relate skills to content.* Following the selection of one or two important skills, the teacher should look for ways to relate these skills to the aspect of the content area under study.
4. *Select appropriate materials.* After selecting skills and making the appropriate connections to the content area, the teacher should use instructional resources to find appropriate materials for instruction.

An alternative approach to unit planning also uses a four-step sequence, but planning centers around the content area instead of around reading skills:

---

[2]Lou E. Burmeister, *Reading Strategies for Middle and Secondary School Teachers,* 2nd ed. (Reading, Mass.: Addison-Wesley, 1978).
[3]Martha H. Dillner and Joanne P. Olson, *Personalizing Reading Instruction in Middle, Junior, and Senior High Schools—Utilizing a Competency-Based Instructional System* (New York: Macmillan, 1977).

1. *Start by analyzing the content area.* The teacher should analyze the content area to determine the broad topics or principles to be covered.
2. *Identify key concepts.* The teacher should then identify the key concepts to be developed and choose certain ideas to be the central focus of the content unit.
3. *Identify relevant reading skills.* Using the identified content ideas as a guide, the teacher looks for reading or study skills needed by the students for successful study of the key concepts.
4. *Find appropriate materials.* As a last step, the teacher will select appropriate materials to implement instruction. These materials serve four purposes: 1) they introduce the concepts; 2) they provide activities for developing the concepts; 3) they serve as assignments or tests on which students can demonstrate understanding, and 4) they provide practice in the reading skills.[4]

QUALITIES OF EFFECTIVE UNITS

Educators in the different content areas and in the field of secondary reading instruction tend to agree on general qualities of effective units. One key quality is the selection of broad, meaningful goals. Other qualities are balance and variety.

Balance

A unit needs to "balance" learning experiences and emphases. There should be a balance between 1) skill and concept learning, 2) cognitive and affective learning, 3) large and small-group learning, 4) group and individual learning activities, 5) teacher and student direction of instruction, and 6) structured and creative activities.

Variety

Implicit in the need for a balanced instructional unit is the need for variety in instructional methodology. Variety can be accomplished in a number of ways including: 1) using a variety of materials in addition to the textbook, 2) using a variety of teaching methods appropriate to the goals and the needs of students, and 3) asking for a variety of responses from students (reading, writing, listening, and speaking).

Active Student Participation

Another quality of effective units is an emphasis on active student participation in the learning experience. An effective unit would not consist mainly of class periods devoted to lectures and whole-class discussions (in which actually only a few students participate). Rather, the variety of learning activities would include small-group experiences during which all students have the opportunity for active participation,

---

[4]Richard A. Earle, *Teaching Reading and Mathematics* (Newark, Del.: International Reading Association, 1976).

and periods of independent individual work. Units can also stress active involvement by providing the student with choices and with an opportunity for planning.

In unit planning, teachers should identify a variety of activities and materials and then allow students to select those most suitable to their individual interests and abilities. Many teachers ask students to assist in unit planning by making choices or at least expressing preferences. Some teachers plan the aims, topics, and subtopics and ask students to help plan the activities. Others identify just the aims and perhaps basic learning activities and ask students to plan topics and subtopics to address. Still other teachers use a more structured approach by giving students an incomplete list of aims, topics, activities, and materials and asking them to suggest additions. Other teachers provide less initial direction and set aside the first days of the unit for student planning which they consider a learning experience in itself.

David Shepherd provides an outline for comparisons between the Directed Reading Activity as applied to content areas and the unit plan.[5] The five stages of the Directed Reading Activity can serve as the overall structure of the unit with each stage occupying one or more class periods or the five stages can serve as the structure for each week of the unit. (For a review of the DRA, see Chapter 6.) The DRA can be related to the unit in several different ways:

THE DIRECTED READING ACTIVITY AND UNIT STRUCTURE

One-Week Unit

Monday	Tuesday	Wednesday	Thursday	Friday
Preparation	Oral reading/ discussion	Silent reading	Follow-up activities	Extension activities
Silent reading	Other activities	Oral reading/ Discussion		

Two-Week Unit

Monday	Tuesday	Wednesday	Thursday	Friday
Preparation	Silent reading Oral reading/ Discussion	Other activities	Silent reading Oral reading/ Discussion	Follow-up activities

Monday	Tuesday	Wednesday	Thursday	Friday
Preparation Silent reading	Oral reading/ Discussion	Other activities	Follow-up activities	Extension activities

[5]David L. Shepherd, *Comprehensive High School Reading Methods* (Columbus: Charles E. Merrill, 1973).

2 Week Unit—Major Projects for Extension Activities

Monday	Tuesday	Wednesday	Thursday	Friday
Preparation	Preparation (library research)	Oral reading/ Discussion	Silent reading Oral reading/ Discussion	Follow-up Independent projects

Monday	Tuesday	Wednesday	Thursday	Friday
Silent reading Oral reading/ Discussion	Independent projects	Follow-up	Extension activities	Extension activities

Stage 1.
The introduction to the unit parallels the introductory or preparation stage of the DRA. The teacher may spend one or more class periods for an overview of the unit, motivation, and identification of key reading purposes and key concepts.

Stage 2.
In the DRA, stage two consists of a silent reading. In a unit of more than one week, the teacher should provide a number of occasions for silent reading and for class discussions to check comprehension during the silent reading.

Stage 3.
Teachers should intersperse oral reading and discussion with the silent reading to check understanding, to assist students with the reading, and to develop skills and understandings. This approach avoids many of the problems that occur when teachers give students one long reading assignment (for example a novel or multichapter unit in the textbooks) and expect them to complete it in one or more weeks and then perform well on a single occasion in a class discussion or on one large test.

Stage 4.
As in the DRA, periodic follow-ups to a series of reading and discussion activities are necessary. These follow-up activities 1) help students understand the materials they have read, 2) provide additional assistance if necessary, or 3) provide periodic, short tests. In a multiweek unit, a follow-up activity might occur at the end of each week and might cover the materials in a textbook chapter, a few chapters in a novel, or a few short selections in a literature anthology.

Stage 5.
As in the DRA, the extension stage could be a culminating activity directed by the teacher, a research project, or other creative activities for individual students or small groups. In the last few days of a multi-

week unit, one or more class periods can be set aside for students to complete and share their projects. To avoid incomplete or poor-quality assignments, teachers should start students on their projects early in the unit and should provide periodic progress checks. A teacher can provide a checklist of tasks to be completed such as the following early in the unit and periodically review it:

1. Select topic for project
2. Decide on type of report
3. Identify key questions to research
4. Find appropriate sources
5. Take notes from one source
6. Take notes from second source
7. Finish note taking
8. Write rough draft
9. Write finished draft
10. Make class presentation

ASSESSMENT STRATEGIES

Assessment procedures can follow one of three approaches to diagnosis and evaluation: 1) pre/post assessment, 2) continuing or formative evaluation, and 3) a combination of 1) and 2). Most educators do not recommend the traditional practice of relying on a single, large posttest.

Pre/Post Assessment

In this approach to evaluation, the teacher would pretest the unit to determine what students already know about the topic and their level of competence in the reading skills. Given this information, the teacher is better able to plan his or her instructional unit giving emphases to those areas of indicated weakness. At the same time, the unit plan would give less emphasis to the areas of indicated strength. Following the presentation of the unit, the teacher would retest the students to determine the effectiveness of the instruction.

Continuing Assessment

The formative-evaluation strategy employs a continuing system of evaluation. The teacher provides several opportunities throughout the unit for students to exhibit their ability on desired skills and their understanding of content. The teacher uses this information to plan specific instruction. With this strategy, the teacher gives a series of short tests or relies on student responses to frequent learning activities.

Pre/Post and Continuing Assessment

The most desirable and workable system for assessment within a unit structure usually involves a combination of the two strategies. The teacher collects information at the beginning of the unit for initial planning and adds the information gained during the unit to determine if and how instruction should be modified.

SAMPLE UNITS   The sample instructional units, presented in this section, illustrate the guidelines for effective unit planning. The units vary in length from one week to one month and show some of the different formats that teachers can use, including a daily calendar of teacher and student procedures and an outline of key unit components.

The first plan is a week-long unit on the study of poetry. This is one of a series of week-long units on literature. Students have previously read poems for basic understanding and for personal responses and have done free prose writing. The teacher's main concern is to develop understanding and enjoyment of poetry. To provide a focus, the teacher emphasizes reading to interpret and explain similes as one type of figurative language.

In this unit, the pretest is spread over the week. The first two skills (or test items) are presented, responses are reviewed, and students are temporarily assigned to groups according to their performances. Later, the teacher does further testing and regroups the students as necessary. Students also read a variety of poems in independent, small-group, and whole-class activities. All students read from the same collection of poems, but some read independently and some for instructional purposes.

Unit 1.

1. *Unit title:* Poetry: Figurative language
2. *Aims:*
   a. Develop enjoyment, understanding, and critical appreciation of poetry
   b. Develop skills and understandings in interpretation and analysis of poetry
3. *Performance objectives*
   a. Identify, interpret, and explain the use of similes in the context of a complete poem
   b. Write poems with effective use of similes
4. *Pre/post assessment:* Students read short poems and attempt the following responses.
   a. Underline all similes
   b. Write a brief interpretation of each simile
   c. Explain how the poet used each simile
   d. Write a poem using similes effectively
5. *Time:* one week
6. *Schedule:*

Monday
Teacher provides orientation for week's activities
Students do free writing as preparation for writing poems (activity is related to test item 4).
Students take pretest on items 1 and 2
Teacher reviews test
Students listen to recordings of poems and songs and volunteer personal reactions

Tuesday
Students do free writing
Group A. Students who responded well to pretest read poems to identify one to share with class
Group B. Students who could not respond to pretest meet with teacher for direct instruction

Wednesday
Writers' Workshop. Different groups meet to read each others' free writings and make suggestions for poems
Whole class composes short poems with emphasis on using similes (Happiness is like_____)

Thursday
Group A. Students meet in small groups and share chosen poems
Group B. Students meet with teacher for direct instruction
Group A. Teacher meets with students for informal discussion of selected poems
Group B. Students read poems to consider use of similes

Friday
Students revise/complete their poems
Volunteers read their own poems or poems selected from text

The advanced unit on the study of important events and trends in the history of 19th-century America that follows is a month-long plan:

1. *Unit title:* America after the Civil War: The Growth of Industry and the Railroads **Unit 2.**
2. *Goals:*
   a. Develop ability to analyze historical events and trends for complex cause/effect relationships
   b. Gain knowledge and develop understanding of major events and historic trends in 19th-century America
   c. Develop understanding of present problems in light of history
   d. Improve skills in reading to identify details, ideas, sequence, and cause/effect relationships
   e. Improve skills in map reading
   f. Improve skills in library research
3. *Time of unit:* 4½ to 5 weeks
4. *Schedule and topics:*

Week 1
Topic: Growth of industry and the railroads
Subtopics: Nature of the factory
            Causes of the growth of industry
            Causes of the growth of railroads
            Effects on groups and individuals
            Effects on the development of the nation
Reading skills: Reading to answer cause/effect questions
                 Reading maps with special symbols

Week 2
Topic: Settlement of the west
Subtopics: Effects of the expansion of railroads
            Wars with the Indians
            Effects on Indians
            Growth of the cattle industry and of mining
Reading skills: Reading to pose and answer cause/effect questions
                 Reading maps with special symbols
                 Using library reference aids

Week 3
Topic: Economics and politics
Subtopics: Effects of the growth of industry and the railroads on
            national politics
            Interest and involvement in foreign affairs
Reading skills: Reading to pose and answer questions in analyzing
                 historic events for multiple causes and effects
                 Reading detailed maps of small areas
                 Using library reference aids

Week 4
Topic: The growth of labor unions
Subtopics: Effects of the growth of industry and railroads on labor
            unions
            Setbacks and successes of unions
            Effects of unionism on the American people
Reading skills: Reading to pose and answer questions in analyzing
                 cause/effect relationships in a historical trend.
Culminating activities: Reports of short research projects conducted
                 by small groups.

   5. *Materials*
      a. Selected chapters from three textbook levels for independent
         reading
      b. Selected passages from three textbook levels for use in pre-
         and post-assessment of reading for cause/effect
      c. Articles from newspapers and magazines used for instruction
         in reading skills and for enrichment

　　d. Self-selected materials for research projects:
　　　Historical writings, Biography and autobiography of histori-
　　　cal figures, Fictional and nonfictional accounts of events,
　　　Articles from newspapers and magazines, Articles in profes-
　　　sional history journals, Indian stories, poems, and songs,
　　　Folk songs about the railroads and unions, and Federal and
　　　state laws and treaties
　　e. Maps in the textbook and related materials for instruction
6. *Reading activities*
　　a. Weekly assignments from textbooks
　　b. Weekly map-reading exercises
　　c. Use of reference aids to locate sources for projects
　　d. Self-selected reading for projects
7. *Topics for research and creative projects*
　　a. Modern day leaders of industry
　　b. Foundations established by 19th-century leaders of industry
　　c. Recent problems of the railroads
　　d. Railroads in other countries
　　e. Technological development of the railroads
　　f. Conditions in modern factories
　　g. Modern "cottage industry" and crafts
　　h. Famous battles with Indians
　　i. Indian culture before the coming of the white man
　　j. Recent developments in Indian life
　　k. Different perspectives of Western heroes
　　l. Current problems in Latin American countries
　　m. Treaties with the Indians
　　n. Recent labor union legislation
　　o. Recent developments in labor unions
　　p. Literature, art, or music about Indian life,
　　　frontier life, factory life, the railroads, or the unions
8. *Research and creative projects*
　　a. Small groups choose a topic; individuals choose and research
　　　subtopics; the group prepares a written report and makes an
　　　oral report.
　　b. Small groups choose, research a topic, and write a brief
　　　summary of their findings. Group prepares, rehearses, and
　　　performs a dramatic presentation (role-playing of encounter
　　　between historic personages. Panel discussion of an issue, or
　　　"playlet" on an historic event).
　　c. Small group or individual chooses and researches a topic and
　　　writes a brief summary of findings. Group or individual pre-
　　　sents a "media" presentation (slide-tape show; exhibit of art
　　　work, tools; prepared recording of songs and dramatic read-
　　　ings; or performance of songs and/or dramatic readings).

The unit above is intended for a class who has previously studied this period of history and is ready for an intensive look at certain topics (although weekly textbook assignments provide a basic knowledge of the period). The unit lasts from four-and-one-half to five weeks with the last few class periods devoted to student reports on research projects and creative presentations. In this case, the basic structure of the unit is based on a four-chapter unit in the course textbook.

The plan emphasizes developing students' understanding of the causes and effects of historical events and trends. The reading skills emphasized are reading for cause/effect relationships and identifying details, ideas, and sequence. In a previous unit, the teacher provided instruction in map reading. In the present unit, there are additional exercises which require students to read maps with special symbols (those referring to the unit topics, such as symbols for railroad lines, industry, and population). Class reviews of materials from weekly assignments, small-group discussions, small-group planning of projects, and oral presentations of research and creative activities provide opportunities for listening and speaking.

Donovan Johnson and Gerald Rising developed the following outline, which gives the skeleton around which a formal unit could be developed.[6]

Unit 3.   Unit on graphing:

1. Objectives
   a. Locate points, segments, and intervals on a one-dimensional graph
   b. Locate points, lines, and regions on a two-dimensional graph
   c. Translate in both directions
      algebraic statement . . . coordinate representation

2. Pretest
   Instructions: This test will not be counted toward course grade. It is designed to supply information for planning purposes only. Some of the content has not yet been taught in this course. Try your best on each item but do not guess. The pretest will evaluate ability to perform on tasks related to stated objectives.

3. Learning activities
   a. Locating points represented by ordered pairs using the rows and columns of seats in a classroom
      Playing the game Battleship®
      Using a state highway map
      Using a rectangular coordinate grid

---

[6]Donovan A. Johnson and Gerald R. Rising, *Guidelines for Teaching Mathematics,* 2nd ed. (Belmont, Calif.: Wadsworth, 1972).

b. Drawing graphs of sets of ordered pairs
   Have students at seats identified by ordered pairs stand to
   show conditions that give lines of students
   Graph the ordered pairs collected by measurement and ex-
   perimentation
   Graph the ordered pairs produced by a guessing game
   Graph the ordered pairs produced by a function machine
   Graph the ordered pairs of the truth set of a linear equation

4. Special teaching procedures and techniques: Stress working in
   pairs, especially on checking homework, to develop student
   interaction and to improve preparation

5. Materials
   Overhead projector transparencies; textbook selections

6. Daily lesson plans: Daily lesson plans will reflect the overall
   goals of the unit

7. Posttest: The posttest like the pretest will reflect the unit's goals
   and objectives[7]

The development of total courses requires use of the same sound educational practices as do units and daily lesson plans. By planning a course
in the same general ways, the teacher can insure effective instructional
experiences for his or her students, which provide balance and variety.
In particular, plans for a content-area course can follow the same five
planning steps:

DEVELOPING COURSES

1. Analyze content to be taught.
2. Select key topical areas and key concepts.
3. Identify relevant reading and study skills.
4. Break content and skills into unit sections.
5. Select appropriate instructional resources and materials to develop the units.

[7]Adapted from Donovan A. Johnson and Gerald R. Rising, *Guidelines for Teaching Mathematics*, 2nd
ed. © 1972 by Wadsworth Publishing Co., Inc., Belmont, California 94002. Reprinted by permission of
the publisher.

SUMMARY   This chapter looked at the process of developing instruction units (and courses). The chapter included discussions of 1) the desirability of unit planning, 2) processes for doing unit planning, 3) processes for carrying out the plan, and 4) samples of unit plans. The reader should now recognize the desirability of long-term advance planning in teaching content-area topics. This planning process should focus on the reading and study skills needed for successful learning by students in the classroom.

Suggested Activities

1. Discuss one of the Key Ideas listed in the Overview of this chapter.
2. Select a topic or reading selection for your content area and either identify key reading skills or key concepts in planning your approach to unit planning. Which approach seems more appropriate for a content-area teacher?
3. Describe how one or more of the stages in the Directed Reading Activity could be provided for in a multiweek unit in your content area.
4. Select a textbook from your content area which is organized in multichapter units. Evaluate one unit in light of the guidelines presented in this chapter. What could a teacher do to supplement or reorganize the textbook unit to make it more effective?
5. Select a topic or reading selection for your content area. Describe how you could achieve one of the qualities of an effective unit.

Bloom, Benjamin S. *Taxonomy of Educational Objectives: Handbook 1, Cognitive Domain.* New York: McKay, 1956.

Burmeister, Lou E. *Reading Strategies for Middle and Secondary School Teachers,* 2nd ed. Reading, Mass.: Addison-Wesley, 1978, chap. 5.

Dillner, Martha H., and Olson, Joanne P. *Personalizing Reading Instruction in Middle, Junior and Senior High Schools—Utilizing a Competency-Based Instructional System.* New York: Macmillan, 1977, chaps. 3 and 11.

Duchastel, Philippe L., and Merrill, Paul F. "The Effects of Behavioral Objectives on Learning: A Review of Empirical Studies," *Review of Educational Research* 43 (1973): 53–69.

Fry, Edward, *Reading Instruction for Classroom and Clinic.* New York: McGraw-Hill, 1972.

Harris, Theodore L. "Making Reading an Effective Instrument of Learning in the Content Fields," *Reading in High School and College.* NSSE 47th Yearbook, Part II. Chicago: University of Chicago Press, 1949, chap. 7.

Hittleman, David R. *Developmental Reading: A Psycholinguistic Perspective.* Chicago: Rand McNally, 1978, chap. 7.

Horn, Thomas D. *Reading for the Disadvantaged—Problems of Linguistically Different Learners.* New York: Harcourt, Brace, and World, 1970.

Lopp, Diane. *The Use of Behavioral Objectives in Education.* Newark, Del.: International Reading Association, 1972.

Myer, R. E., and Torrance, Paul E. *The Idea Book Series in Creative Development: Can You Imagine? Invitations to Speaking and Writing Creatively. Invitations to Thinking and Doing.* Waltham, Mass.: Ginn, 1966.

Roe, Betty D.; Stoodt, Barbara D.; and Burns, Paul C., *Reading Instruction in the Secondary School.* Chicago: Rand McNally, 1978, chap. 3.

Sanders, N. *Classroom Questions: What Kinds?* New York: Harper & Row, 1966.

Shepherd, David L. *Comprehensive High School Reading Methods.* Columbus, Ohio: Charles E. Merrill, 1973.

Spache, George D. *Diagnosing and Converting Reading Disabilities.* Boston: Allyn & Bacon, 1976, chap. 12.

Strang, Ruth; McCullough, Constance M.; and Traxler, Arthur E. *The Improvement of Reading,* 4th ed. New York: McGraw-Hill, 1967, chap. 6.

Taylor, B. J. *When I Do, I Learn.* Provo, Utah: Brigham Young University Press, 1974.

Vargs, Julie S. *Writing Worthwhile Behavioral Objectives.* New York: Harper & Row, 1972.

Zintz, Miles V. *The Reading Process—The Teacher and the Learner.* Dubuque, Iowa: William C. Brown, 1975, chaps. 2, 6, and 15.

Recommended Readings

19

Working Effectively with Others

Many persons are pessimistic about the possibilities for improving **OVERVIEW** reading instruction. Some believe that large numbers of students are simply incapable of learning how to read or improve in reading. Others believe insufficient resources are available to teachers and schools. However, failures to improve reading instruction are not the result of a lack of effective methods or materials, a lack of understanding of the learning-to-read process, or a lack of dedicated teachers. Many effective programs exist now, many more promising programs are on the way.[1]

These programs are usually limited to one or only a few classrooms and may, in fact, be special-reading programs whose existence depends on temporary funding from the federal or state governments or from local school districts. When the funds run out, the programs disappear. Even if the programs are maintained, their impact is limited because too many content-area teachers believe that someone else has the responsibility for secondary reading and that separate reading courses can adequately address reading problems.

---

[1]Summaries of elementary, secondary, and adult-education programs are found in *Effective Reading Programs: Summaries of 222 Selected Programs* (Urbana, Ill.: National Council of Teachers of English, 1975).

This chapter will discuss the need for schoolwide reading programs which stress reading instruction in content-area courses. The term "program" is used broadly to discourage the idea that a secondary reading program must be a specialized operation distinct from the academic curriculum. Rather, structures, processes, and roles already available in traditional school settings have the potential to affect change in classrooms. The program leader, the coordinating committee, and in-service and other staff-development activities all play an important role in a schoolwide reading program.

Key Ideas   In a schoolwide reading program, content-area teachers have a major responsibility for the development of reading skills.

The program leader and coordinating committee can promote change by providing in-service programs, models of effective courses and procedures, demonstration lessons, and involvement in effective classroom programs.

The program leader and coordinating committee can begin a schoolwide reading program by focusing on a few skills and procedures.

For a schoolwide program to be truly successful, it must be extended and maintained.

Ms. Bowers develops an effective ninth-grade English course and is working harder than most teachers to provide a variety of materials for students of differing reading abilities. She enlists the help of other ninth-grade language-arts teachers in collecting multilevel materials which they can share. Two teachers, who tutor in Ms. Bowers's class during their conference period, learn the value of multilevel materials and learn to use Ms. Bowers's methods, which include teaching study-skill techniques.

The group of four ninth-grade teachers begin planning their courses together. When Ms. Bowers takes a leave of absence, the other three teachers are able to maintain the program. During the second year, the teachers begin using some of the methods they learned from Ms. Bowers in their English courses. When one of the teachers becomes chairperson of the English department, she visits other teachers' English classes in other grades and presents demonstration sessions on study skills. Now, when students leave ninth-grade English, they will benefit from the same procedures they experienced in ninth grade in other courses.

In this example, the program (in the sense of particular procedures) extended beyond one classroom and one subject, English, to the entire school curriculum. This extension, in turn, allowed for the maintenance of the program when there were personnel changes.

A SCHOOLWIDE READING PROGRAM

Most reading educators agree on the need for a schoolwide reading program at the secondary level—one in which content-area teachers have a major responsibility for the development of reading skills. Special reading programs have been implemented with dramatic success but often fail to have sufficient impact on overall reading improvement. Effective remedial programs have helped students overcome severe problems and make major gains in ability, but these students still need—and often fail to receive—further assistance and patience from their content-area teachers. Similarly, teachers introduce students to study-skill procedures in developmental reading courses, but these procedures go unused in other courses because content-area teachers fail to require and guide their application to actual study situations.

Three trends in secondary education have impeded progress in developing schoolwide reading programs. First, the training and responsibilities of teachers have become increasingly specialized. It is not uncommon, for example, to hire English teachers solely as composition teachers. Such teachers would, understandably, question the requirement that they teach reading when they do not even have the opportunity to teach other areas that have traditionally been within their field, such as literature and language study.

Second, the movement toward "short courses," particularly at the senior high level, has also encouraged specialization. Recently, many senior high schools have adopted a quarter system, with 12-week courses. During the 1960s, many schools offered six-week minicourses largely to make a greater number and variety of electives available. Many teachers feel they are already facing difficult demands to cover specified content within short periods of time and impossible demands to meet individual differences in ability and background just within the content area, to say nothing of differences in reading ability.

A third trend has been increased expenditures for reading at the secondary level, which has followed the other trends toward specialized training and courses. Federal funds have supported reading specialists and extracurricular remedial-reading programs. Some local school systems have added developmental reading courses and hired reading teachers. Other large school districts have separate reading departments. A few states have required special certification for secondary reading teachers, and more commonly, some states have required courses in reading for English teachers.[2] One positive result is that many secondary students who need help with reading are now receiving it. The negative result is that content-area teachers have received added encouragement for the idea that reading is not their responsibility but is rather the sole responsibility of either the reading specialist or the language-arts teacher.

---

[2]Walter J. Lamberg, "Required Preparation in Reading for Secondary Teachers." *Reading Horizons* 18, 4: 305–307.

Schools can make little progress toward developing schoolwide reading programs as long as teachers view reading as a set of skills that students should have developed in elementary schools or as a separate subject in secondary schools. Rather, as David Shepherd argues, reading must be seen simply as one aspect of language and language as the "basic tool of learning."[3] Competence in reading can be defined, in Shepherd's words, as the ability "to gain ideas independently."[4] Teachers must see vocabulary, comprehension, and study skills, often identified as the skill areas of reading, as the essence of study.

Shepherd's conception of the secondary reading program places emphasis on reading instruction within content-area courses:

1. Reading instruction is provided in each of the subject fields as it applies to each.
2. The central library of the school provides opportunity to the students for both research and pleasure from reading.
3. Supplementary classroom libraries must be available to provide opportunities for enrichment.
4. Elective courses are offered in the mechanics of reading for those students who wish to sharpen their reading-study skills.
5. Remedial courses are available for those students who need help in addition to the content-reading instruction in each classroom.[5]

The Program Leader   A. Sterl Artley argues that development of a schoolwide reading program demands that one or more individuals assume a leadership position.[6] The key responsibility of this individual, who should be a faculty member, is not to design and implement the program but to elicit cooperation and commitment from other faculty members. The expertise of a consultant or of a reading coordinator who works at the school-district level may be undercut by the feeling that this individual is an outsider with no long-term commitment to the program. Principals or assistant principals who have the authority to institute program change may be viewed as imposing a program on the teachers.

Leslie Burg and his associates note that the leader or supervisor of the program may not have an official administrative position in reading but may be an "administrator, another teacher, or persons with such disparate titles as consultant, resource teacher, coordinator, director, or supervisor."[7] A reading or language-arts teacher would be the logical

---

[3]David L. Shepherd, *Comprehensive High School Reading Methods* (Columbus, Ohio: Charles E. Merrill, 1973), p. 293.
[4]Shepherd, *Comprehensive High School Reading Methods,* p. 293.
[5]Shepherd, *Comprehensive High School Reading Methods,* pp. 293–94.
[6]A. Sterl Artley, "Implementing a Developmental Reading Program on the Secondary Level," in Margaret Early, ed., *Reading Instruction in Secondary Schools* (Newark, Del.: International Reading Association, 1964), p. 5.
[7]Leslie A. Burg et al., *The Complete Reading Supervisor: Tasks and Roles* (Columbus, Ohio: Charles E. Merrill, 1978), pp. 3–4.

person to assume such a leadership role. In some schools, the position of reading specialist involves instruction in remedial reading as well as supervisory functions. The strongest advocate of a reading program is often a social studies or science teacher who has seen the results of teaching study techniques or a mathematics teacher who has been successful in individualizing instruction. Therefore, a content-area teacher often assumes the leadership role in improving the reading program.

Formalizing the involvement of several school personnel facilitates the program's development. Many educators recommend the establishment of a coordinating committee which represents faculty, administrators, and other staff. Typically, the committee consists of one person with training in reading (a reading teacher or specialist or a language-arts teacher), one teacher from each content area, one administrator (the principal or an assistant principal), the school librarian, and a guidance counselor. Both Lou Burmeister and David Shepherd recommend the addition of a media or audiovisual specialist, who can assist teachers in preparing materials to aid or supplement reading, and a school nurse, who will have knowledge of visual, hearing, or other physical problems which may affect reading.[8] Burmeister further recommends the committee include a member of the school board, a student, and a parent.[9]

The Coordinating Committee

Work of the Committee.   Generally, the committee serves to elicit cooperation and involvement, inform school personnel, and, by its composition, avoid feelings on the part of faculty that the reading program is either an imposition on them or the private domain and sole responsibility of one teacher or one group of teachers. Regular committee meetings should be held to identify and assign tasks to be accomplished and to keep members informed of progress. An important responsibility of the program leader during meetings is to facilitate identification of and agreement on general goals and functions of the committee and specific, useful tasks for individuals, teams, or small groups to complete. The committee must avoid meeting merely to discuss problems and "kick around" vague solutions without taking concrete action.

Coordinating committees can begin their work in a variety of ways. Some start by agreeing upon general duties or responsibilities. Burmeister identifies the following ten duties, which would be carried out over a period of time. They begin by formulating a philosophy of reading and then move to determining recommendations and ways to communicate those recommendations for assessment and instruction in reading.

[8]Shepherd, *Comprehensive High School Reading Methods*, pp. 297–98; and Lou E. Burmeister, *Reading Strategies for Middle and Secondary School Teachers*, 2nd ed. (Reading, Mass: Addison-Wesley, 1978), p. 341.
[9]Burmeister, *Reading Strategies*, p. 341.

1. Determining a philosophy of reading
2. Determining ways of diagnosing students' needs in reading skills
3. Deciding what kinds of materials teachers should be encouraged to purchase
4. Deciding on recommendations for schoolwide grouping plans
5. Determining ways of helping teachers group students and individualize instruction in the classroom
6. Determining ways of showing teachers how to recognize the need for specific types of skill development and ways of showing them how to satisfy these needs
7. Determining ways of showing teachers the value of the directed reading activity, SQ3R
8. Determining how the schoolwide reading program can be coordinated and providing for such coordination
9. Determining methodology and materials to be used in evaluating successes and failures of the program
10. Determining policies to be used in in-service training.[10]

Some committees are able to reach immediate agreement on key goals of the new or expanded reading program, such as the following goals identified by Ruth Strang and Donald Lindquist:

1. To try to help the most seriously retarded readers
2. To introduce a developmental reading course for all students in addition to their regular schedule
3. To help teachers of every subject give more effective instruction in the reading of his subject
4. To set up a reading clinic for helping complex cases
5. To work on all these fronts at once in a whole-school reading program.[11]

Other committees postpone identification of program goals and their functions until they have conducted a thorough *needs assessment*. As Leslee Bishop notes, a needs assessment can be thought of as a diagnosis of the current school program.[12] The committee diagnoses the program to identify its strengths and weaknesses in a way analogous to the way the classroom teacher identifies strengths and weaknesses in the knowledge, skills, and attitudes of his or her students.

Some committees have used checklists and questions which focus on reading instruction, student performance, or student or teacher atti-

---

[10]Burmeister, *Reading Strategies,* pp. 342–43.
[11]Ruth Strang and Donald M. Lindquist, *The Administrator and the Improvement of Reading* (New York: Appleton-Century-Crofts, 1960), p. 26.
[12]Leslee J. Bishop, *Staff Development and Instructional Improvement* (Boston: Allyn & Bacon, 1976), pp. 27–33.

tudes toward reading. Lois Bader recommends a set of questions like the following, which require collection and analysis of data on student performance.

1. Standardized test results
   a. Are there large numbers of very poor readers beyond the expectancy of the normal curve?
   b. Are the students with high-verbal intelligence achieving their potential?
   c. Is progress fairly steady through the grades?
   d. Does item analysis indicate areas of general weakness?
   e. What are the component skills related to these deficiencies?
   f. What are the students' attitudes? Are they doing their best? Do they finish? Do they guess?
2. Informal test results
   a. How are students' achievements in reading capabilities not tested by the standardized tests?
   b. What are the students' content-area reading skills?
3. Development of broader interests
   a. Are students given time to read?
   b. Do they have access to materials?
   c. Are the materials suitable to the interests of the children?
   d. Are the children capable of reading the materials available?
4. Instructional efficiency
   a. Do teachers possess effective and efficient instructional strategies?
   b. Do they have materials necessary to teach the skills they need to develop?
   c. Do teachers have efficient record-keeping systems?
5. Other investigations
   a. Reports on very poor readers have revealed high absenteeism (if children are not in school, they can hardly be taught); low energy levels; and poor health, in addition to other factors inhibiting achievement.[13]

Joseph Vaughan offers the following questionnaire on teacher attitudes toward their responsibilities for teaching reading in content areas.[14]

Directions: On the separate answer sheet, indicate your feeling toward each of the following items.

---

[13]Lois Bader, "The Reading Coordinator: Key to An Effective Program," in Gerald G. Duffy, ed., *Reading in the Middle Schools* (Newark, Del.: International Reading Association, 1975), p. 39–40.
[14]Joseph L. Vaughan, Jr., "A Scale to Measure Attitudes toward Teaching Reading in Content Classrooms," *Journal of Reading* 20:7 (April 1977): 607. Used with permission.

1. A content-area teacher is obliged to help students improve their reading ability.
2. Technical vocabulary should be introduced to students in content classes before they meet those terms in a reading passage.
3. The primary responsibility of a content teacher should be to impart subject matter knowledge.
4. Few students can learn all they need to know about how to read in six years of schooling.
5. The sole responsibility for teaching students how to study should lie with reading teachers.
6. Knowing how to teach reading in content areas should be required for secondary teaching certification.
7. Only English teachers should be responsible for teaching reading in secondary schools.
8. A teacher who wants to improve students' interest in reading should show them that he or she likes to read.
9. Content teachers should teach content and leave reading instruction to reading teachers.
10. A content-area teacher should be responsible for helping students think on an interpretive level as well as a literal level when they read.
11. Content-area teachers should feel a greater responsibility to the content they teach than to any reading instruction they may be able to provide.
12. Content-area teachers should help students learn to set purposes for reading.
13. Every content-area teacher should teach students how to read material in his or her content specialty.
14. Reading instruction in secondary schools is a waste of time.
15. Content-area teachers should be familiar with theoretical concepts of the reading process.

Specific Tasks. Once needs are identified, the committee must find specific tasks to address those needs. Some of the tasks are for committee members; most, however, should be accomplished by other content-area teachers with support and guidance from the committee. Strang and Lindquist provide some examples of these tasks: identifying reading skills important to any content area, identifying teachers who have already effectively combined instruction in reading and content, analyzing the readability of textbooks, identifying consultants who can provide expertise for particular problems, and identifying practical reading performances students will be faced with, such as the drivers-license test.[15] A list of other tasks important to program improvement follows:

---

[15]Strang and Lindquist, *The Administrator and the Improvement of Reading,* pp. 44–45.

1. Writing relatively specific goals to be worked toward during the first year of the program
2. Agreeing on ways of measuring progress toward those goals
3. Developing procedures for scheduling; for example, for students who will be excused from regular classes for tutoring
4. Developing an instrument for evaluating materials
5. Examining materials to determine which to order for the program
6. Conducting an inventory of materials already available
7. Identifying ways of informing persons about the program
8. Identifying a tentative list of workshop topics
9. Identifying special problems and expertise needed to solve those problems
10. Designing a referral form to be used by classroom teachers in identifying students who may need special help

STRATEGIES FOR PROMOTING CHANGE

The program leader and other members of the coordinating committee must see their essential role as that of a change agent, as one who assists others in changing. Bader identifies five principles to be followed in promoting change:

1. Change originating within the school that is based on group diagnostic efforts is more acceptable than changes brought by outsiders;
2. Change will be more acceptable when endorsed by formal and informal leaders within the school;
3. Change that does not increase workloads or threaten security and status is more acceptable than change that does;
4. Change that offers interesting, novel experience in harmony with the values and goals of those within the school is welcome; and
5. Change, open to evaluation and modification, is more acceptable than irrevocable commitment to an unknown course.[16]

Bader also stresses the importance of communication in promoting change. The remainder of this chapter will present four strategies for communicating to teachers new views of reading and effective assessment and instructional procedures: in-service programs, model classrooms and courses, demonstration lessons, and involvement in effective classroom programs.

---

[16]Bader, "The Reading Coordinator," p. 38.

In-Service Programs   Most faculty members have had no preservice training in the teaching of reading—that is, course work while they were completing degree and certification requirements. Those faculty who have had course work may not have had the opportunity or the support to apply what they have learned to their teaching. Therefore, committees should provide in-service programs, consisting of workshops for experienced teachers, presented by fellow teachers, reading or content-areas coordinators, or outside consultants. Workshops should be held at the beginning of the school year, after school hours or on weekends, and on days set aside for staff or curriculum development.

Planning Workshops.   Administrators often design in-service workshops without any input from teachers. Sometimes, teachers are not even informed of the subject of the workshop until they meet for it. In such circumstances, teachers are understandably unreceptive. An obvious improvement is to inform teachers of the content and purposes of the in-service program well in advance of the workshops. Administrators and the coordinating committee can involve teachers in planning the program. If teachers participate in the needs assessment, the identified needs can become the topics for the workshops. The committee can circulate a list of tentative topics and ask teachers to indicate those they consider valuable and to add others. If a variety of topics are offered, teachers can select those of special interest. For example, a three-hour workshop can consist of four one-and-one half hour sessions. Participants can then choose two out of the four to attend.

Practicality.   Burmeister and many others involved in in-service programs have observed that teachers often demand very practical workshops.[17] Teachers tend to be unreceptive to what they perceive as theoretical discussions or reviews of research. Workshops can address major questions or issues, such as the relative merits of standardized and informal assessment, but participants will want to come away from the presentation with something practical to use. An effective approach is to design the workshop to allow time for a practical, guided exercise. For a workshop on readability, teachers can analyze a passage in a textbook they are using. Similarly, during a workshop on study-skill techniques, teachers can try out the techniques again with actual materials they use in the classroom. The following list provides some possible practical topics for workshops:

1. Writing performance objectives for a future lesson
2. Designing a pre- and post-test for a future lesson
3. Rewriting textbook exercises to provide appropriate models and practice

---

[17]Burmeister, *Reading Strategies*, p. 346.

4. Designing a feedback system for a future lesson
5. Assessing readability of textbooks currently used
6. Constructing an IRI for a current textbook
7. Identifying ways of presenting the text and content to students who have difficulty reading the text independently
8. Constructing a complete IRI (all levels)
9. Constructing a modified IRI of textbook aids
10. Reading, scoring, and interpreting the results of the standardized test used by the school
11. Writing a scope and sequence of key concepts for a particular content area
12. Planning a Directed Reading Activity
13. Using procedures to facilitate comprehension
14. Using procedures to reduce vocabulary difficulties
15. Teaching study-skill procedures

Model Courses and Procedures

Chapter 6 on basic instructional strategies discussed the idea of providing models or demonstrations. Simply stated, teachers can show, as well as explain, desired responses and ways of arriving at these responses. The same idea applies to in-service programs. During workshops, the presenter can demonstrate a recommended procedure—for example, by showing participants how to perform a study-skill technique or how to write guiding questions for a reading assignment. Visits to effective classrooms or demonstration lessons are also effective models.

One of the tasks of the coordinating committee is to identify teachers who are effectively combining reading and content instruction. The committee can ask these teachers to invite other faculty members to observe their classes. Teachers can also visit reading classes to see how to follow particular assessment or instructional procedures. During staff-development days, administrators can give teachers released time to visit other schools which have developed effective programs.

Audrey Gomon has demonstrated and documented the effect of model classrooms on the school and school district. With a team of language-arts teachers, Gomon designed and implemented an innovative course to replace the first-semester sophomore English course at a senior high school. The class, called a language laboratory, emphasized study, reading, and writing skills. Gomon encouraged observations of the classroom and interaction among other faculty members. Over a five-year period, she recorded responses to the innovation and reported that other faculty within and outside of her school exhibited what she termed ''initiative responses''; that is, they applied some of the procedures in the model course to their own teaching. For example, a social-studies teacher in her school designed a similar course which stressed study skills in a social-studies context. A social-studies teacher at another high school followed the model in designing psychology courses.[18]

Demonstration Lessons   A third strategy consists of demonstration lessons that are presented by the program leader to students of other faculty. According to Burg and his associates, such lessons may teach vocabulary, comprehension, or study skills, such as employing context analysis for new words in the textbook, identifying structures of paragraphs, and using survey/question procedures.[19] These demonstration lessons are presented in the other teacher's classroom using his or her materials. As Bader notes, they serve to counter a frequently voiced reaction to new procedures: "That sounds good, but it won't work with my kids."[20]

The most effective in-service program will employ all three strategies logically related to particular needs. Workshops could serve to introduce procedures and also prepare teachers either for observations of model classrooms or demonstration lessons in their classrooms. For example, a workshop on study-skill procedures could precede visits to classes to observe the procedures, or the workshop could take place during one of those classes, with the presenter giving a demonstration with his or her own students. Those teachers who are not entirely comfortable with the procedure can then request a demonstration lesson for their students.

Active Participation   A fourth strategy involves teachers not only observing but actually participating in model classrooms or in some phase of a program. Teachers who direct reading centers or laboratories can invite fellow teachers to tutor in their programs during a free period. The other teachers have the opportunity to try out procedures with one student—in some cases, one of their own students who needs extra help. The director of one reading tutorial program invited content-area teachers to provide written guidance for instruction in important academic performances—for example, a set of directions and examples for solving mathematics and chemistry problems.

A simple but effective way of gaining teacher involvement is through referral procedures. Many schools have established reading or writing laboratories or centers to which students are referred for special help. Directors of these programs have designed referral forms which the classroom teacher is to fill out. The forms require the teacher to specify the student's difficulty and attempt to identify the nature of the difficulty. As a result, in an indirect way, classroom teachers are receiving training in diagnosing student reading and writing skills in the context of their content areas.

---

[18]Audrey Gomon, "Systems Communication Patterns: An Institution's Responses to an Innovation" (Ph.D. diss., The University of Michigan, 1975).
[19]Burg et al., *Complete Reading Supervisor,* pp. 179–81.
[20]Bader, "The Reading Coordinator," p. 42.

Many of the more successful schoolwide reading programs were initiated in modest ways. Rather than attempting to solve all problems related to reading instruction, programs leaders and coordinating committees initially focused on a few skills and procedures. As Shepherd, Burmeister, and Burg and his associates note, the focus is typically on study-skill procedures.[21] Of all aspects of reading, these procedures are most readily perceived by teachers as directly applicable to content-area instruction. Also, many teachers have used one or more of the procedures, such as outlining, to some extent and, as a result, are pleased to discover they have already been assisting students with reading.

Burg and his associates have identified the following study skills which they believe content-area teachers will recognize as being "inextricably tied to their own disciplines:"

1. Previewing
2. Classifying
3. Selecting main ideas and related or subordinate details
4. Outlining
5. Summarizing
6. Using key words
7. Using guide or signal words
8. Skimming and scanning
9. Locational and reference skills
10. Reading maps, charts, graphs, diagrams, and other visual aids[22]

The list also includes some key comprehension and vocabulary skills, such as identifying main ideas and key words.

Shepherd emphasizes that teachers must directly apply study skills to the particular content area and that students should then practice the skills under the teacher's supervision.[23] Stated another way, all teachers must include relevent procedures as part of their assignments. Burmeister has developed and implemented in-service programs which stress study skills and key comprehension skills.[24] Workshops scheduled throughout the year introduced these skills to teachers in different content areas, as Table 19.1 shows.

STRESSING STUDY SKILLS

The current program is evaluated to identify needs related to reading instruction. The needs are then translated into goals for a revised or new program and into specific tasks to be accomplished by teachers. In-service programs present information and skills needed to implement new

MAINTAINING AND EXTENDING PROGRAMS

---

[21]Shepherd, *Comprehensive High School Reading Methods*, pp. 295–96; Burmeister, *Reading Strategies*, pp. 346–47; and Burg et al., *Complete Reading Supervisor*, pp. 84–85.
[22]Burg et al., *Complete Reading Supervisor*, pp. 84–85.
[23]Shepherd, *Comprehensive High School Reading Methods*, pp. 295–96.
[24]Burmeister, *Reading Strategies*, p. 347.

Table 19.1 Sample In-Service Program

Skill	English	Social Studies	Science	Mathematics	Other
SQ3R	November April	September February	October March	January May	
Sequence and main idea	December January	October March	November April	September February	
Interpretations: a) anticipation b) cause-effect c) motives of characters and real people	October (anticipation) February (motives)	December (motives) April (cause-effect)	September (cause-effect) May (anticipation)	November (cause-effect) March (anticipation)	
Following directions: a) literal level; b) critical-creative level	November April	September February	October March	December May	
Analysis level: a) fallacies of reasoning; b) propaganda analysis; c) syllogistic reasoning; d) fact-opinion	October (propaganda) March (fallacies)	December (fallacies) April (propaganda)	September (fact-opinion) February (syllogistic reasoning)	November (syllogistic reasoning) January (fact-opinion)	
Synthesis level: a) unique communication; b) inductive/ deductive reasoning	September May	November February	December March	October April	
Interest: emphasis on building interest, *per se*	September May	November February	December March	October April	
Developing flexibility of rate	whenever appropriate	whenever appropriate	whenever appropriate	whenever appropriate	

Source: Lou E. Burmeister, *Reading Strategies for Middle and Secondary School Teachers,* 2nd ed. (Reading, Mass: Addison-Wesley, 1978), p. 347. Used with permission.

policies and procedures. Many schools have carried out this phase of program development and implemented effective, or at least, promising programs. Quite often, new or revised programs are not effectively extended throughout the school and ultimately cease to be maintained.

Many schools have received special funds to implement programs, which may achieve impressive results. But if the funds are not available the following year, the program will often disappear. Part of the problem may be a lack of patience. The "reading problem" has existed for as long as there have been schools. Yet administrators, teachers, and parents often expect an innovative program to solve the "problem" immediately. If it does not, the school attempts another innovation, or the school system goes back to the old way of doing things.

The development of an effective program takes time—years, not months. The program must be designed and then tried out. Information about student achievement and behavior must be collected and analyzed. Problems will be identified and possible solutions must be generated and tried out. Many of the problems will be management problems: scheduling, location of materials, seating arrangements, use of aids, and recording of test scores. One school found that their major problem involved giving pre- and post-tests. Students had to wait until the teacher had the time to give a test and score it before the students could go on to the next phase of instruction. The problem was solved by parents who served as volunteer aids, doing nothing except handling the tests. After that solution, the program worked beautifully.

During the second year, the program might have to be modified to meet new conditions: a new group of students, changes in teaching personnel, changes in school policy and procedures. The results of the two years of tryouts should be compared to identify long-range improvement. If the new program had been tried out in only a few classes or content areas, it should then be extended and adapted to other classes and subjects.

SUMMARY

Both content-area teachers and reading teachers or specialists are naturally more immediately concerned with their own students and courses. One teacher may be particularly effective in helping his or her students with reading, but these efforts will have limited value if the students fail to receive assistance from other teachers and if most of the other students in the school receive no assistance at all. Effective content-area or reading teachers must assume formal or informal leadership roles and serve as agents of change for their entire school. A key step is gaining and formalizing the cooperation of administrators and other faculty and staff in evaluating, developing, extending, and maintaining a schoolwide reading program.

Suggested Activities

1. Discuss one of the Key Ideas listed in the Overview of this chapter.
2. Observe a school situation and look for five specific ways teachers are—or could be—cooperating, for example, in finding or preparing multilevel materials.
3. Select one of the tasks recommended for a coordinating committee and discuss how each member can contribute to the successful completion of the task.
4. Select one instructional procedure and write a description of it which will be understandable to someone (parent or teacher, for example) who has no knowledge of teaching reading.
5. Observe a school situation in which reading is taught. Identify five specific questions about the situation which relate to program development.

Recommended Reading

Aukerman, Robert. *Reading in the Secondary School Classroom.* New York: McGraw-Hill, 1972, chap. 15.

Bishop, Leslee J. *Staff Development and Instructional Improvement: Plans and Procedures.* Boston: Allyn & Bacon, 1976.

Burg, Leslie A. et al. *The Complete Reading Supervisor: Tasks and Roles.* Columbus, Ohio: Charles E. Merrill, 1978.

Burmeister, Lou E. *Reading Strategies for Middle and Secondary School Teachers,* 2nd ed. Reading, Mass: Addison-Wesley, 1978, chap. 12.

Carlson, Thorsten R., ed. *Administrators and Reading.* New York: Harcourt Brace Jovanovich, 1972.

Crisculo, Nicholas P. "Quality Reading Programs at Bargain Basement Prices," *Journal of Reading* 18 (November, 1974): 127–30.

Dillner, Martha H., and Olson, Joanne P. *Personalizing Reading Instruction in Middle, Junior, and Senior High Schools.* New York: Macmillan, 1977, chap. 12.

Duffy, Gerald G. *Reading in the Middle School.* Newark, Del.: International Reading Association, 1975).

Early, Margaret, ed. *Reading Instruction in Secondary Schools.* Newark, Del.: International Reading Association, 1964.

Jefers, Pearl B. "Guidelines for Junior High Reading Programs," *Journal of Reading* 15 (January 1972): 264–66.

Olson, Arthur V., and Ames, Wilbur S. *Teaching Reading Skills in Secondary Schools.* Scranton, Pa.: Intext Educational Publishers, 1972.

Palmer, William L. "Toward a Realistic Rationale for Teaching Reading in Secondary School," *Journal of Reading* 22:3 (December 1978): 236–39.

Robinson, H. Alan. "Reading in the Total School Curriculum," in J. Allen Figurel, ed. *Reading and Realism.* Newark, Del.: International Reading Association, 1969.

Roe, Betty D.; Stoodt, Barbara D.; and Burns, Paul C. *Reading Instruction in the Secondary School.* Chicago: Rand McNally, 1978, chap. 11.

Rorie, I. LaVerne. "Analysis and Validation of the Revised Inventory of Teacher Knowledge of Reading," *Journal of Reading* 21:7 (April 1978): 606–7.

Rossman, Jean F. "How One High School Set Up a Reading Program for 500 Students," *Journal of Reading* 20 (February 1977): 393–97.

Rossoff, Martin. *The Library in High School Teaching,* 2d ed. New York: H. W. Wilson, 1961.

Shepherd, David L. *Comprehensive High School Reading Methods.* Columbus, Ohio: Charles E. Merrill, 1973, chap. 13.

Smith, Richard J., and Barrett, Thomas C. *Teaching Reading in the Middle Grades.* Reading, Mass.: Addison-Wesley, 1974.

Wood, Phyllis Anderson. "Judging the Value of a Reading Program," *Journal of Reading* 19 (May 1976): 618–20.

20

Developing Positive Attitudes Toward Reading

Why do some students read as a habit, willingly and enthusiastically complete assignments, read on their own initiative, and read a variety of materials outside of school? Why do other students read only when assigned to and then only when the assignments "count" for grades? Why do others refuse to read anything—at least anything in school—and sometimes exhibit highly negative behaviors (disrupting the class, or destroying books) when asked to read?

Motivation for reading is a highly complex subject. Differences in motivation are as varied and extreme at the secondary level as are skills and abilities. The first group of students are obviously highly motivated; they read for the sake of reading. The second group is motivated to the extent that they will do academic assignments. Members of the third group lack any motivation to read but they also have a strong motivation to avoid reading.

This chapter will present principles and procedures for developing positive attitudes toward reading. One goal of the secondary curriculum is the encouragement and expansion of interest in reading. Teachers in all content areas can contribute to that goal. Beyond the acquisition of reading skills, growth in reading requires that: students read for a variety of reasons; they discover both intrinsic and extrinsic rewards of reading; they read on a regular basis; they expand their interests both in the subjects they choose to read about and the types of materials they choose to read; and they increase the level of sophistication of their response to reading material.

OVERVIEW

Key Ideas   Students read for a variety of reasons including: for pursuit of interests, for learning, for information, for vicarious pleasure, for social and emotional experiences, and for the enjoyment of literature.

Teachers can provide motivation for students by allowing them to choose their own materials, by encouraging regular reading of a variety of materials, by administering interest inventories, and by monitoring the reading.

Teachers should encourage students to increase the variety of the material they read.

Teachers can help students develop their ability to respond to what they read.

Ms. Jefferson, a senior-high social-studies teacher, devotes each Friday's class period to a "read-in." Students spend the entire period reading silently from materials they have selected from the class library. The library, actually two book cases, includes: newspapers and magazines; fiction, biography, and autobiography related to periods of history being studied; articles from professional journals; and research reports written by former students. At the end of the class, students count the pages or articles they read and note the total along with the title and author in their reading logs. Every two weeks, students meet in small groups to discuss their reading experiences.

REASONS FOR READING   Although the obvious reason most students read is to complete assignments, educators hope students also develop other reasons for reading. What teachers believe are the goals for secondary-school reading, in fact, could become the reasons students read. The main goal is that students become balanced readers; that they read for *positive* reasons. Particular people will differ on the particular reason that is primary for them. Rather than identifying one reason as more important than others, a curriculum might best give equal weight to all the following reasons to read: 1) for pursuit of interests, 2) for learning, 3) for information, 4) for vicarious pleasure, 5) for social and emotional experiences, and 6) for the enjoyment of literature.[1]

Some educators prefer to use the word "reasons" in discussing motivation in reading; others use the word "rewards" for the same kinds of things. The six reasons above are intrinsic rewards of reading; those

---

[1]This discussion is indebted to a discussion of reasons for reading in Lou E. Burmeister, *Reading Strategies for Middle and Secondary School Teachers,* 2nd ed. (Reading, Mass: Addison-Wesley, 1978), pp. 64–90.

that are a part of, or inherent in, the reading experience. Extrinsic rewards, such as money, good grades, praise from peers or teachers, honor pins, special responsibilities or privileges for the ''honor student,'' scholarships, and acceptance in college or better universities, are *external* to the experience.

Many educators are suspicious of extrinsic rewards and believe intrinsic rewards should be the primary motivators. They fear that students will no longer be motivated when extrinsic rewards are no longer available, and that extrinsic rewards can even destroy intrinsic rewards that are already available. But what happens to the student who has never discovered the intrinsic rewards? What happens to the student with reading problems who finds reading hard work, and who experiences few if any rewards?

The extrinsic rewards all serve as concrete symbols of achievement or success. Most educators seem to agree that the learner must experience success or achievement if he or she is to be motivated. Ideally, the feeling of success will be intrinsic; perhaps it should be unconscious, so that the reader's attention can focus on other reasons for reading.

Successful readers have the best of both worlds: rewards that are both intrinsic and extrinsic. Their positive attitude toward reading probably started before school when they discovered that the books their parents read to them were interesting. These students also learned to associate books with other positive experiences—for example, the attention, affection, physical warmth, and security of sitting near their parents as they listened to the stories. After continual exposure to books as children, one day students felt the sense of achievement when they could remember certain letters or say certain words. The recognition of parents and, later, teachers strengthened this feeling of achievement.

Students with reading problems miss both kinds of rewards. Each year, reading becomes more and more difficult. Whatever success they have is diminished by the fact that their peers are more successful and by the criticism of their teachers. If they have found they can read about subjects they are interested in, chances are that these subjects are not found in the textbooks assigned to them. As they grow older and develop more and more mature interests, they find fewer and fewer rewards and more and more frustration. They see a film that moves them, but they are not able to read the novel on which the film is based. They respond in a mature way to a character in a story but are criticized because the teacher wants to discuss the author's style. They read a high-interest, low-vocabulary book (one written for mature students but with a controlled vocabulary to produce a lower-reading level) and like it, but they cannot meet the requirements of the written report. Reading becomes so punishing that some students generalize their negative feelings to all reading—magazines and paperback books as well as textbooks—and become actively opposed to reading.

DEVELOPING MOTIVATION TO READ

Students with reading problems need the opportunity to read about their immediate interests; that reading must be respected and acknowledged. Daniel Fader, a professor of literature, advocates quantity before quality in allowing students to select whatever they want to read.[2] Students must have a chance to read widely and regularly and to pursue their interests if they are to reach a point at which they can appreciate literature.

Students need the opportunity to develop and expand their interests over a period of time. Students with seemingly narrow interests will grow if given the opportunity to do so. The stronger the student's negative feelings, the more a teacher must resist the temptation to force materials on the student.

Fortunately, ways to improve motivation are very simple, very inexpensive, and very powerful. They include: 1) allowing self-selected reading, 2) encouraging regular reading, 3) providing a variety of materials, 4) administering interest inventories, and 5) monitoring student reading.

Self-Selection

How does the teacher know what materials will interest the student? At the beginning of the year, he or she does not know. The student is a stranger. The student with reading problems will probably be a student who does not readily participate or give the teacher an opportunity to learn about him or her. The best judge of what a student is interested in is the student.[3]

Students should have some choice in what they read. For some of their reading experiences, they should be able to select any subject and any type of material, within reason, such as comics, magazines, how-to manuals, paperbacks, biographies, novels, short stories, or newspapers. The teacher can exercise some control over the material by limiting the source of materials to the public library, the school library, or the classroom library. Whatever the case, there should be a wide variety of types of materials, subjects, and reading levels.

Grover Mathewson developed a theoretical model of reading to support the practice of self-selection.[4] According to Mathewson, most

---

[2]Daniel Fader and Elton B. McNeil, *Hooked on Books: Program and Proof* (New York: Berkley Publishing, 1968).
[3]A recommended discussion of self-selected reading is found in Marvin E. Oliver, *Making Readers of Everyone* (Dubuque, Iowa: Kendall/Hunt, 1976), pp. 51–99. Oliver calls his method "High Intensity Practice (HIP)," and notes its similarity to "Uninterrupted Sustained Silent Reading (USSR)."
[4]Grover C. Mathewson, "The Function of Attitude in the Reading Process," in Harry Singer and Robert B. Ruddell, eds., *Theoretical Models and Processes of Reading,* 2nd ed. (Newark, Del.: International Reading Association, 1976), pp. 655–76.

people do not have a positive attitude toward reading in general but rather have positive attitudes toward particular subjects, forms, or formats. For example, a student's positive attitude may be limited to only news accounts of basketball in magazines. The reader's acceptance or lack of acceptance of what he or she reads affects performance. Little acceptance may negatively affect attention to the text and comprehension. Lack of acceptance may result in the reader's ceasing to read the particular text. With self-selection, differences in positive attitudes and acceptance are taken into account.

Self-selected reading will work if (1) the activity is done on a frequent, regular basis, and (2) class time is provided. How much time can be provided will depend on the particular course, the needs of the students, and the class schedule. In content-area courses, some teachers put aside one day of every week for a full class period of self-selected reading. Another common approach is to put aside the first ten minutes of each class period at least three days a week for reading. In addition, if students finish class work early, they can spend the remaining time reading. *Regular Reading*

  Besides being of enormous benefit to the students, self-selected reading makes the teacher's job much easier. Since students differ so much in skills, all teachers face the almost impossible task of perfectly timing activities so that all students finish at the same time. With the reading, the teacher can always have available a meaningful activity for students to do when they finish their other activities.

Immediate Feedback. Some students, because of highly negative, if not hostile, attitudes toward reading, will not read unless they receive immediate, positive, and quantitative feedback. These students may need to keep a cumulative graph of their reading as an instrument by which they can measure and manage their own behavior. A weekly graph can serve this purpose (See Figure 20.1 on page 334).

  The graph is set up according to the number of days the students would have opportunities for reading. If they can read every day, the graph would be, essentially, a calendar for the week. If reading is less often and not always regular, then the student can record the date of each day's reading. The graph is cumulative so that if a student fails to read, he or she will not receive negative feedback. In addition, the cumulative graph avoids problems that might result when the reading period is not always the same amount of time or when the student selects a different book that has more or fewer words on a page. In the example in Figure 20.1, the student read two pages on Monday and two on Wednesday but did not read on Tuesday and Thursday. She read four additional pages on Friday.

Figure 20.1
Weekly Cumulative Graphs for
Self-Selected Reading

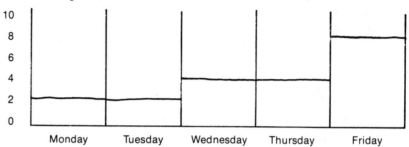

Weekly Reading (Fixed, Daily Schedule)

Name _Mary L._

Week of _Sept. 13-17_

Number of Pages Read

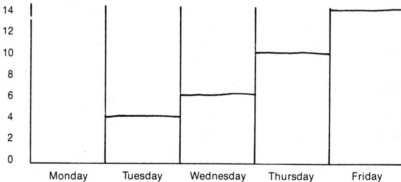

Week of _Sept. 20-24_

Number of Pages Read

Measurement.   The cumulative graphs also provide a basis for measuring the effectiveness of a self-selected reading program. The graphs show gains in, and maintenance of, silent, sustained reading in terms of the number of pages read per week and the number of class sessions students read.

In most content-area courses, the classroom textbook serves as the students' primary reading material. Traditionally, many teachers have supplemented the textbook to update information, elaborate upon key concepts, provide additional instructional activities, meet differences in ability, or promote interest and enjoyment. Although their main concern may have been to enrich the study of the content area, these teachers have to some extent addressed differing reading interests.

Variety in Reading

Martha Dillner and Joanne Olson demonstrate the need for a variety of materials for effective content-area teaching.[5] A. Burron and A. Claybough divide the materials into the following types: a fundamental source of information, an introductory source, supplementary sources, alternative sources, reference sources, and review sources.[6]

In most courses there will be one fundamental source of information, usually the class textbook. This material will develop a knowledge base and help the student understand key concepts. At the beginning of an instructional experience, teachers will provide *introductory material.* The textbook may serve the purpose of introduction, but often teachers bring in other more interesting or immediately relevant material. In both the social and natural sciences, newspaper or magazine articles can demonstrate the current, widespread interest in a topic to be studied. In English, contemporary literature or songs can introduce the study of literary forms. A mathematics teacher might present materials which show very practical applications of concepts, such as those involving finances.

Supplementary materials, provided during or at the end of the learning experience, can enrich the study or provide further practice beyond the activities in the textbook. Even if the textbook is adequate, teachers may rely to some extent on alternative sources of information, such as a library research project in which students can select either the research topic or particular sources for an assigned topic.

Teachers can use the last two types of material selectively. They can ask students to either consult various *reference sources,* such as general or specialized dictionaries, encyclopedias, and atlases or use *review sources,* particularly if the textbook has inadequate review sections. Dillner and Olson note that review sources are especially common in foreign-language study.

---

[5]Martha H. Dillner and Joanne Olson, *Personalizing Reading Instruction in Middle, Junior and Senior High Schools* (New York: Macmillan, 1977), pp. 180–81.
[6]A. Burron and A. Claybough, *Using Reading to Teach Subject Matters: Fundamentals for Content Teachers* (Columbus, Ohio: Charles E. Merrill, 1974).

While textbooks can often serve all six purposes above, content-area teachers may also need to use a variety of other materials. The greater the variety of materials, the more likely differences in both interests and abilities will be addressed. Some materials may be supplements or alternatives to text selections. Other materials may be less directly related to the particular content under study but may still be relevant. The following list provides a good starting point:

1. News articles
2. Editorials, profiles, and human interest stories in newspapers
3. Magazine articles
4. Articles in professional journals
5. Selections from easier or more difficult textbooks
6. Autobiographies or biographies of contributors to field of study
7. Historical novels
8. Student compositions and creative projects
9. Writings by contributors to the field of study, such as letters, articles, and journals
10. Humorous pieces, such as satire and parodies
11. Screenplays for television and motion pictures
12. Contemporary literary works
13. Short selections written for adolescents
14. Comic books
15. Maps
16. Pamphlets
17. Manuals

Besides providing additional sources of information, such materials may have more intrinsic interest to students.

Interest Inventories Chapter 9 discussed informal procedures for assessing skills such as the informal reading inventory. The affective area of reading can also be informally assessed by means of interest inventories. The inventory helps both students and teachers. It gives students a chance to identify and evaluate their own interests and guidance for extending their interests. It benefits the teacher by providing information about what range of materials to provide for a student's self-selection. Walter Lamberg describes how to design inventories to provide information about students' 1) general interests, 2) desired activities, 3) reading interests, 4) problems and goals, and 5) content-related interests.[7]

The Interest Inventory. In an interest inventory students identify the kind of experience or subject they are interested in and give the teacher clues about what materials they might like to read. The student who enjoys spy movies and television shows is an obvious candidate for reading spy novels. The student who loves basketball will usually enjoy sports

---

[7]Walter J. Lamberg, "Helping Reluctant Readers Help Themselves: Interest Inventories." *The English Journal,* 66:8 (November 1977): 40–44.

magazines or biography, autobiography, and fiction about basketball players. A sample inventory of subjects or experiences follows:

1. What kinds of shows do you like to watch on television?
2. What kinds of shows do you like to listen to on the radio?
3. What kinds of motion pictures do you like to see?
4. What hobbies do you have or would you like to have?
5. What sports do you like to participate in or see?
6. What kind of work do you do (or have you done)?
7. What kind of work would you like to do?
8. If you could be anyone for a day, what people would you like to be?
9. If you could travel anywhere, what places would you like to visit?
10. If you would like to live in the past or future, what period of time would you like to live in?
11. What animals would you like to raise or see or know more about?
12. What problems or subjects would you like to understand better or know more about?[8]

Activities Inventory.   Another kind of inventory can determine the type of school activities a student would enjoy. At first, some students have such strong negative feelings about reading that they will read only for some obvious reward. Ideally, they—rather than the teacher—should choose the reward. Reading, they feel, is hard, unpleasant work, and they want some "pay" for it. With the information from an inventory of activities, the teacher can provide a "reinforcement menu." Students can then select both their own reading and the reward or reinforcement that will follow. The teacher still controls the relationship between the two. For example, for each ten minutes students spend on reading (or other skill work), they can spend one minute on their chosen activity. In other words, students and teachers make contracts (see Chapter 10). A sample activity inventory follows:

These are activities you can do when you complete assignments. Check the ones you would like to do. Then double-check three you would like to do most:
1. Sit by yourself and do nothing.
2. Talk to your friends quietly.
3. Do homework for a different class.
4. Work out in the gym.
5. Practice in the music room.
6. Write stories, poems, or letters.
7. Play checkers or chess.
8. Play games, such as *Scrabble*® and *Monopoly*®.

---

[8]Lamberg, "Helping Reluctant Readers Help Themselves," p. 42. Used with permission.

9. Play sports games.
10. Draw or paint.
11. Learn a hobby or craft.
12. Work as an aide in the office or as a teacher's aide.[9]

Inventory of Problems and Goals. After administering the interest and activity inventories, the teacher can begin students on a self-selected reading program and start collecting information that will help to expand the students' reading interests. Teachers can administer another inventory to identify students' goals and problems in reading.[10] For many students, the goals will involve overcoming particular problems. This inventory is not given at the beginning of the program since students may be reluctant to consider such matters. However, once students begin to experience success and pleasure they will be ready to open up. A sample inventory of problems and goals follows:

A. Which of these are problems for you in this class? Check them.
B. Which one would you like to work on as a goal for the next two weeks? Double-check that one.
  1. Do you have trouble understanding what you are reading?
  2. Do you have trouble figuring out what you are supposed to do with a reading assignment?
  3. Do you have trouble understanding many of the words in the reading assignment?
  4. Do you have trouble paying attention to what you are reading?
  5. Do you have trouble completing assignments on time?
  6. Do you feel that you spend too much time on the reading for the amount of pages you finish?
  7. Do you seldom like what you are reading?
  8. Do you have trouble finding the section in a book you are supposed to read?
  9. Do you have trouble finding books or magazines you would like to read in the library?
  10. Do you have trouble remembering important information or ideas for tests?
  11. When there is a discussion about the reading, do you have trouble following it?
  12. Are you reluctant to participate in discussions?
  13. Do you have trouble relating the lecture to the reading?
  14. When you have to write about what you have read, do you have trouble getting started?
  15. When you write, do you have trouble spelling many of the words?[11]

---

[9]Lamberg, "Helping Reluctant Readers Help Themselves," p. 42. Used with permission.
[10]This inventory is based on self-assessment questions in Ruth Cohen et al., *Quest: Academic Skills Program* (New York: Harcourt Brace Jovanovich, 1973).
[11]Lamberg, "Helping Reluctant Readers Help Themselves," p. 42. Used with permission.

Reading Interests Inventory.   Once students have an opportunity to satisfy their immediate interests, they will be ready to expand their interests. The expansion may involve reading about subjects they do not usually read about or reading types of materials they have rarely or never read. The following inventory can serve as both a guide (for teacher and student) and as a feedback system for the students' expansion of interests:

> Rate these types of reading. Put an A before the ones you read a lot. Put a B before the ones you sometimes read. Put a C before the ones you never read (or hardly ever read).
>
>   1. News stories
>   2. Sports stories
>   3. Editorials
>   4. Comic strips
>   5. Advice columns
>   6. Reviews of books, theater, films, and T.V.
>   7. Society pages
>   8. Ads
>   9. Comic books
> 10. Sports magazines
> 11. News magazines
> 12. Movie magazines
> 13. Science magazines
> 14. "Mechanical" magazines
> 15. "Social" magazines
> 16. Biographies
> 17. Autobiographies
> 18. How-to-books
> 19. Religious books
> 20. Science fiction
> 21. Short stories
> 22. Novels
> 23. Poems
> 24. Plays
> 25. Essays[12]

The inventory can also serve as a pre- and post-assessment of the students' progress.

Content-Area Interest Inventories.   In content-area courses, interest inventories can focus on a particular aspect of the content area and still include a variety of relevant materials. A teacher can design such an inventory for an entire course or for each unit of instruction. In de-

---

[12]Lamberg, "Helping Reluctant Readers Help Themselves," p. 43. Used with permission.

veloping two- to four-week units, many teachers provide choices of projects (see Chapter 18). The following inventory was written for an English unit on people and the sea:

Reading about people and the sea

Read through the list of materials and check three you would like to read during our two-week unit on "Man and the Sea."

1. 19th-century novels
2. 20th-century novels
3. 19th-century short novels
4. 20th-century short novels
5. 19th-century short stories
6. 20th-century short stories
7. Poems and songs about the sea
8. Historical accounts of famous sailors and explorers
9. Magazine profiles of modern sailors and explorers
10. Autobiographies by sailors and explorers
11. Biographies of sailors and explorers
12. Accounts of seagoing peoples
13. Myths of the sea and sea creatures
14. Adventure stories about the sea
15. Essays on important issues involving the sea (pollution, conservation of whales and porpoises, and laws of the sea)
16. Scientific articles on the sea or on sea life
17. Science fiction on the sea.
18. News articles or stories about the sea
19. Articles or stories on sea sports
20. Pamphlets about careers involved with the sea[13]

Next is a sample inventory for a unit on mathematics:

Read through the list of materials and check two you would like to read during our two-week unit on measurement.

1. Short pieces on cultures which help to develop measurement ideas (such as foot, inch, and mile)
2. Articles from journals which are in favor of adoption of the metric system
3. Articles which are opposed to the adoption of the metric system
4. Material which contrasts our system to the Imperial measure previously used in Canada
5. The history of metrication in the U.S.
6. Lists of "odd ball" measures used in the world today
7. Technical journals which point out the need for accuracy in measurement

[13]Lamberg, "Helping Reluctant Readers Help Themselves," p. 43. Used with permission.

8. Discussions of professions which require skill in mathematical measurement, such as architecture, technical drawing, and medicine
9. Materials on Olympic contests involving metric measurement
10. How-to-books involving problems in measurement, such as making kites

Finally this inventory was used in a one-semester social-studies course:

World War II (History)

Name_____

Would you like to read a book or article about the following? (circle Yes or No)

1. Yes-No: Norwegian children who helped smuggle millions of dollars out of Norway to America to keep it from their German captors (Marie McSwigan: *Snow Treasure*)
2. Yes-No: A Jewish girl who spent several years in an attic room in Amsterdam to escape the Nazis (Anne Frank: *Diary of a Young Girl*)
3. Yes-No: A hunchback who sailed the British Channel to rescue stranded soldiers in Dunkirk who were being forced into the sea by the Nazis (Paul Gallico: *Snow Goose*)
4. Yes-No: Five men who lived through the atomic attack on Hiroshima and tell their story (John Hersey: *Hiroshima*)
5. Yes-No: The dilemma of a Japanese girl who saw her mother die in the atomic attack on Hiroshima and later fell in love with an American soldier (Edita Morris: *Flowers of Hiroshima*)
6. Yes-No: An insane genius who feared he was part Jewish (one grandparent) and was determined to exterminate the Jews and rule the world (John Toland: *Hitler*)[14]

Monitoring Student Reading

Both students and teachers need some overt or observable feedback to see that the reading program is working. The inventory chart provides one kind of monitoring device. As students read different types of materials, they check them off.

Contracts. A more immediate form of monitoring (and feedback) would be a weekly contract and schedule. Students fill out the schedule on Monday and then check off each day's activities as they complete them. Chapter 10 showed a schedule and contract written for an English class in which students select three different types of materials.

---

[14]Burmeister, *Reading Strategies*, pp. 76–77. Used with permission.

The teacher fills out, in advance, the activities he or she wants all students to do for the week and leaves blank spaces for students to fill in their self-selected reading. The teacher can duplicate copies of the weekly schedules and hand them out at the beginning of each week. (Or the teacher can put the schedule on the board for the students to copy in their notebooks.) The form serves as both a schedule for the week and a contract. The students contract, or make an agreement, to complete certain activities that week, some chosen by the teacher and some by the student.

The teacher can require written responses along with the contract/schedule. Their advantage is to insure students respond to what they are reading and reflect upon their responses. The written responses must be appropriate to the abilities of the student. Since they are serving as a means to an end, they should be relatively easy. If the written responses seem like a difficult chore, or, worse, if students can not do them, they will stop reading to avoid the writing.

The Journal. The place to start with written responses is a journal or a diary. The content of this writing, as Fader and McNeil recommend, should be absolutely free.[15] The students should write whatever they wish and do not necessarily have to respond to what they read (What was it about? Did you like it? Why?). Some students will take advantage of the experience to release their negative feelings about school, reading, their teachers, their family, and themselves. The teacher should be prepared, therefore, for expressions of hostility and for profanity. The best way to handle such expressions is to ignore them. Students may expect some response; if it does not come, they will cease such expressions on their own as their negative feelings dissipate and as their positive reaction to reading and feeling successful begins to influence their writing.

Although the content of the journal should be up to the student teachers should place some control on the amount of writing, mainly to relieve the students' anxieties about what is expected of them. Fader and McNeil recommend that the students write at least four pages a week. If students cannot think of anything to say, they can copy material. Since expressing one's self is more rewarding than copying, the latter will soon diminish. For students with very weak writing skills, copying can provide needed practice in letter printing, spelling, and punctuation.

Teachers can choose other types of written response or activities like speaking, oral reading, drawing, and painting, to supplement or substitute for the journals. The range of possible activities is unlimited, but all should provide some kind of observeable response. A variety of choices are necessary to address differences in interest and ability.

---

[15]Fader and McNeil, *Hooked on Books.*

Teachers who provide self-selected reading have found that many students will read, on their own initiative, a variety of materials (textbooks, literary works, magazines, newspapers, and "how to" books). Teachers can use a four-step-approach to make sure that all students do, eventually, increase the variety in their reading.

At the beginning of a course, students can select any type of material from types provided by the teacher. The only requirement is to read on a regular, frequent basis. The only goal, at this point, is for *all* students to read and enjoy reading.

After one or two weeks, the students select three different types of materials. They can, but they are not required to, select types they have never read before. The goal is for all students to read with some variety.

Later in the course, students must again select at least three types of materials, but now they must choose one type they have rarely or never read.

At any point in the course, the teacher selects one type of reading from types students have not selected themselves and devotes a unit to introducing this type of reading. For example, in one class, students had chosen autobiographies and biographies but not novels. Therefore, the teacher presented a two-week unit on novels which stressed similarities and differences between the fictional and nonfictional works.

Developing Reading Responses

Once students are reading regularly and writing freely and regularly in their journals, the teacher can use the journal to increase the variety and sophistication of their responses to reading. The teacher can simply provide several open-ended questions for each week's writing. Open-ended questions permit a variety of responses and insure success. The teacher should also limit the number of questions: one good question may be enough; ten should probably be the maximum. Students can select the number of questions and the particular questions they will respond to. They can also learn to write their own questions to guide their reading and stimulate their responses (see Chapter 5).

For guidance in providing questions, the teacher can use a scheme of developmental stages from the works of Dwight Burton and Margaret Early, two educators in the area of adolescent literature.[16] Burton's and Early's ideas apply to any kind of reading, from literary works to content-area texts to mass media. They have identified three stages through which they believe adolescents pass as they develop into sophisticated readers: 1) "unconscious enjoyment" or "imaginative entry into the work," 2) "self-conscious appreciation" or "perception of meaning and central purpose," and 3) "conscious delight" or "perception of artistic unity and purpose."

INCREASING READING VARIETY

---

[16]Dwight L. Burton, *Perspectives in Reading: Reading Instruction in Secondary Schools* (Newark, Del.: International Reading Association, 1964); and Margaret Early "Stages of Growth in Literary Appreciation." *English Journal* 49 (March 1960): 161–67.

Stage 1—Unconscious Enjoyment At this stage students are subjective, uncritical readers. They must be able to relate to, or become engaged with, the work immediately and easily. Their likes and dislikes are ''unconscious''; that is, they cannot or will not readily examine their reasons for liking or disliking a work. At this stage, students are able to respond to the following type of questions:

1. What was this story (or poem, play, article or section) about?
2. What happened in this story?
3. Who was the story about?
4. Who else was in the story?
5. What is the main idea or point of this story?
6. How did the story start?
7. What happened in the middle of the story?
8. How did it end?
9. Did you find this story interesting?
10. Did you like what happened?
11. Did you like the people in the story?
12. Did you like the way the story ended?
13. What kind of people are in the story?
14. What kind of animals are in the story?
15. Did you think the story was funny?
16. Did the story remind you of something that happened to you? What?

Stage 2—Self-Conscious Appreciation At this stage, readers begin to look objectively at the work and at their responses to it. They begin to compare their own experiences and values with those of the people in the story and those of the author. They begin to look below the surface of the writing and evaluate the writing beyond a simple positive or negative response. Students can now respond to the following type of questions:

1. Why did it happen this way?
2. Why did the person act the way he or she did?
3. How did the person change?
4. What was good about the person?
5. What was bad about the person?
6. In what ways are you like the person?
7. In what ways are you different?
8. Could the person have behaved differently? How?
9. Could the story have ended differently? How?
10. What does this story say about people?
11. Why do you think the author wrote this?
12. How do you think the author felt about the people he or she wrote about?
13. What did you like about the way the story was presented?
14. What did you like about the author's style?
15. What did you like about the way the people were presented?

Stage 3—Conscious Delight   At this stage, readers reflect upon and critically examine their responses and view the work according to some criteria for judging a piece of writing. On first reading, they still might be unconsciously engaged in the work, but after reading they can then reflect upon their responses with some detachment. These students can respond to the following type of questions:

1. What is the significance of this work?
2. What is the author's purpose?
3. How well did he or she accomplish his or her purpose?
4. What is the author's perspective?
5. Where or how does the author's perspective reveal itself?
6. Who is the main person (or character)?
7. Who are the secondary people (or characters)?
8. What do the people represent?
9. How well are they presented?
10. What is the plot of the story?
11. Why does the author choose this plot?
12. What is the setting of the story?
13. Why does the author choose this setting?
14. What does the setting contribute to the overall effect of the work?
15. What is the mood of the work?
16. How does the author achieve the mood?
17. What is distinctive about the author's style?
18. What type of literature is this?
19. How is it similar to other works of its type?
20. How is it different from other works of its type?
21. What works have influenced the author?
22. What is the relationship between the author's life and this work?

SUMMARY

Many secondary students have highly negative attitudes toward school reading, which result from years of frustration and failure in reading as well as a lack of opportunity to satisfy immediate interests by reading. Many other students have sufficient motivation to read to complete assignments but have developed neither a strongly positive attitude toward reading nor a variety of reading interests. Both categories of students can benefit from a program of regular, self-selected reading, which provides for gratification of immediate interests and pleasures in reading and gradual expansion of interests and sophistication of response. Such programs can also enrich the reading experiences in content-area courses.

Suggested Activities

1. Discuss one of the Key Ideas listed in the Overview of this chapter.
2. Assess your own interests by responding to the inventory of interests and the reading interests inventory, or assess the interests of a student or peer with these inventories.
3. Describe (or write a plan for) a self-selected reading program within a content-area course. Consider such matters as the amount of time for, and frequency of, reading, the source of selections, and the subjects and types of materials to be provided.
4. Observe a secondary school class with a focus on three students and their reactions to the reading for the course. Do their behaviors suggest positive or negative attitudes toward reading? Consider such matters as their participation in reading discussions, the amount of time they sustain silent reading, their attention to lectures or comments about the reading, and their positive or negative expressions about particular selections.
5. Select and read one piece of material. Respond to at least three questions for each stage of response (as based on Burton's and Early's schemes). What is your reaction to responding to different levels of questions?

Recommended Readings

Burmeister, Lou E. *Reading Strategies for Middle and Secondary School Teachers,* 2nd ed. Reading, Mass: Addison-Wesley, 1978, chap. 4.

Burton, Dwight L. *Perspectives in Reading: Reading Instruction in Secondary Schools.* Newark, Del.: International Reading Association, 1964.

Carlsen, Robert. *Books and the Teenage Reader,* rev. ed. New York: Bantam, 1971.

Criseuolo, Nicholas P. "Convincing the Unconvinced to Read: Twelve Strategies." *Journal of Reading* 21:3 (December 1977): 219–21.

Dillner, Martha H., and Olson, Joanne P. *Personalizing Reading Instruction in Middle, Junior, and Senior High Schools.* New York: Macmillan, 1977, chap. 11.

Dunning, A. Stephen, and Howes, Alan B. *Literature for Adolescents: Teaching Poems, Stories, Novels, and Plays.* Glenview, Ill.: Scott, Foresman, 1975.

Fader, Daniel, and McNeil, Elton B. *Hooked on Books: Program and Proof.* New York: Berkley Publishing, 1968.

Haimowitz, Benjamin. "Motivating Reluctant Readers in Innercity Classes." *Journal of Reading* 21:3 (December 1977): 227–30.

Halpern, Honey. "Contemporary Realistic Young Adult Fiction: An Annotated Bibliography." *Journal of Reading* 21:4 (January 1978): 351–56.

Krathwohl, David. *Taxonomy of Educational Objectives: Handbook II, Affective Domain.* New York: David McKay, 1964.

Mason, George E., and Mize, John M. "Twenty-two Sets of Methods and Materials for Stimulating Teenage Reading." *Journal of Reading* 21:8 (May 1978): 735–41.

Moffett, James, and Wagner, Betty Jane. *Student-Centered Language Arts and Reading, K-13: A Handbook for Teachers,* 2d ed. Boston: Houghton-Mifflin, 1976.

Oliver, Marvin E. *Making Readers of Everyone.* Dubuque: Kendall/Hunt, 1976.

Pell, Sarah-Warner J. "Asimov in the Classroom." *Journal of Reading* 21:3 (December 1977): 258–61.

Purves, Alan C., and Beach, Richard. *Literature and the Reader: Research in Response to Literature, Reading Interests, and the Teaching of Literature.* Urbana, Ill.: National Council of Teachers of English, 1972.

Resnick, Lauren B., and Robinson, Betty A. "Motivational Aspects of the Literacy Problem," in John B. Carroll and Jeanne S. Chall, eds., *Toward a Literate Society: The Report of the Committee on Reading of the National Academy of Education.* New York: McGraw-Hill, 1975), pp. 257–77.

Rosenblatt, Louise. *Literature as Exploration.* New York: Noble & Noble, 1938.

Smith, Richard J., and Barrett, Thomas C. *Teaching in the Middle Grades,* 2d ed. Reading, Mass.: Addison-Wesley, 1979, chap. 6.

Strickler, Darryl J. "Planning the Affective Component," in Richard A. Earle, ed., *Classroom Practice in Reading.* Newark, Del.: International Reading Association, 1977.

21

Working with Special Students

At a time when more and more students with different backgrounds and **OVERVIEW** needs are being placed in the regular classroom, teachers are especially interested in how they can do better for their students. For example, a mathematics teacher explains that she would like to further individualize her instructional program to provide enrichment for the gifted students. Unfortunately, she is limited by time constraints and the availability of resource materials.

At the same time, a junior high social-studies teacher talks about several students in his class who have special needs, ranging from cognitive to emotional or affective needs. With only a traditional education, he has feelings of inadequacy about dealing with these new pedagogical demands.

Teachers should encourage students to develop reading skills at their   *Key Ideas* own individual rates.

The teacher must be able to modify instruction to handle both major and minor individual differences.

To individualize instruction, the teacher can modify: instruction goals, materials, the task, the amount of time, the amount of practice, or the number of examples.

Teachers should modify instruction for gifted students, remedial students, and linguistically different students.

INDIVIDUAL DIFFERENCES A goal of all education, and certainly of reading instruction, is to encourage all students to proceed at their own individual rates toward the achievement of necessary skills. By looking for individual differences, the teacher becomes aware of both a pupil's strengths and weaknesses. The teacher can use this knowledge to implement instruction best suited to his or her students. Respect for individual differences is necessary for a totally literate society. The goal of universal literacy is based on the assumption that all students are capable of achieving some level of competence in reading.

The fact that schools group students for instructional purposes by age and overall ability makes it difficult for teachers to provide for individual differences. Teachers, as well as administrators, who believe that all instruction should be presented to the whole class and that instruction must be geared to an average level, will often react negatively to individual differences. Even when students are grouped by ability and presumably have much in common, there will be differences which affect their performance.

How Students Differ The most common source of difference among students is their previous educational experiences. Curricula in all content areas have been in a state of flux throughout the century. The 1960s, in particular, saw much experimentation and innovation in conceptions of the curriculum as well as in teaching methods and materials. As a result, secondary students will differ simply in the content they have been exposed to.

The quality of previous educational experiences, particularly in reading, will also differ greatly. Some schools will have emphasized reading instruction in content areas, and others will not. Since the preparation and effectiveness of teachers varies, differences in the quality of education can occur within the same school. Community resources and the quality of school or school-district administration will also vary from one area to another.

Different students are influenced by different psychological factors, which affect achievement and rate of learning both in general and in particular content areas. Students will differ in levels of intelligence as measured by standardized intelligence tests. Their interests will vary in degree and range. For example, some students will express a strong interest in a variety of reading in several content areas, whereas other students will react negatively to any reading (see Chapter 20). Finally, in the area of psychological differences, any number of emotional, personality, or perceptual problems may be apparent.

Sociological factors are another potential source of individual differences. Cultural, value, and attitudinal differences are associated with the students' social, economic, and ethnic backgrounds. Finally, physical factors—problems in hearing, vision, speech, and general health—can have a negative effect on a student's performance.

The Special Student

If teachers view differences positively, then, in a sense, all students are special for their individuality. However, the term *special* is often used to designate those students who exhibit major differences from most of their peers. It includes both the unusually able or gifted student as well as the less able or remedial student, who functions well below average. Special education is concerned, then, with both categories of students.

A number of other labels are also applied to less able students, particularly those who demonstrate reading difficulties. Labels such as *slow, retarded,* or *disabled,* by their very nature, represent gross generalizations about the students and neglect their many strengths. All too frequently, the persons who use these labels do not fully understand their meanings or implications and are not trained to make psychological and medical diagnoses. In fact, training in diagnosis, special education, and remedial and clinical instruction stresses the importance of resisting labels or fixed conclusions about a student's abilities and capabilities.

The term *mainstreaming* refers to the current practice of putting special education students into a regular classroom situation. In this case, "special" refers to those students with severe handicaps or learning difficulties. Mainstreaming has become prominent in the past few years and has even been mandated by many states. It attempts to both respect individual needs and guarantee all children the access to a quality education. It assumes that all students will benefit from interaction with students who differ from them.

INDIVIDUALIZING INSTRUCTION

The teacher needs to be aware of ways to modify instruction to handle both major and minor individual differences. Gabriel Della-Piana identifies three important requirements for implementing an individually prescribed instructional program.[1] 1) teachers need adequate testing materials along with a keyed system of materials for student use; 2) student materials should be varied and should include independent activities allowing for self-direction; and 3) teachers must have sufficient organizational management training to be able to run the system without resorting to less individualized teaching practices.

Testing materials that are broad in scope and varied in format will allow the teacher to pretest for diagnostic purposes and to posttest the impact of instruction. The tests should also be keyed to available in-

---

[1]Gabriel M. Della-Piana, *Reading Diagnosis and Prescription—An Introduction* (New York: Holt, Rinehart, & Winston, 1968).

structional materials. Having identified deficiencies in certain tested skill areas, the teacher knows exactly which instructional materials should be used with a particular student.

Materials used in an individually prescribed instructional program must be of sufficient diversity to permit different learning styles and different teaching styles. Some of the materials should be of a self-instructional nature to allow students to work independently and to free the teacher to work with other students who need special help.

A point often overlooked in setting up an instructional program is the fact that teachers need training in the overall management of the program. A teacher's confidence in his or her ability to manage the system will minimize the tendency to revert to less individualized methods.

Management and Grouping   When faced with students of different abilities and interests, many teachers use various forms of small-group experiences. As Martha Dillner and Joanne Olson[2] and Lou Burmeister[3] note, teachers commonly group students by achievement level, by specific skills or needs, or by interest. The small-group experience gives all students more opportunities to participate than is possible in a whole-class experience.

Achievement Groups.   Achievement or ability groups group students according to their overall ability level. Frequently reading ability, as measured on standardized tests or informal inventories, is the basis for grouping. For example, a social studies teacher who regularly uses a textbook available in three different levels would be inclined to divide the class into three ability groups, for students reading at grade level, above grade level, and below grade level.

Achievement grouping has several harmful consequences. First, the basis for assigning students to groups is imperfect. A standardized reading-test score may not be an accurate indication of a student's reading abilities in the content area. Second, groups do not adequately address individual differences. Students in the same lower-level group, for example, may have very different needs. Some may require attention to vocabulary skills; others, to comprehension skills. Third, once students have been assigned to a particular level, it is far too easy for them to be permanently tracked at that level. The so-called low-ability student may remain in that group even though he or she has demonstrated the capacity to do higher-level work. On the other hand, students in higher-level groups may be denied assistance because they are always expected to perform at an above-average level.

[2]Martha H. Dillner and Joanne P. Olson, *Personalizing Reading in Middle, Junior, and Senior High Schools* (New York: Macmillan, 1977), pp. 380–81.
[3]Lou E. Burmeister, *Reading Strategies for Middle and Secondary School Teachers*, 2nd ed. (Reading, Mass.: Addison-Wesley, 1978), pp. 90–91.

Temporary Ability Groups.   An alternative to the traditional practice of grouping by ability is to establish temporary ability groups, based on specific needs or skills which are being addressed in a unit of instruction. The use of preassessment or continuing assessment facilitates this approach to grouping. During a unit, the teacher discovers that some students have more difficulty with particular skills or concepts than other students. The teacher temporarily groups students together who need more assistance or more direct teacher instruction, while other students either work independently or meet in groups to share more sophisticated responses to the content.

Interest Groups.   The fact that students differ in ability, particularly in reading ability, does not mean that they will not have similar interests. They may also share the same level of sophistication in studying the content area because of similar educational experiences. Grouping students by interests will usually result in groups of mixed ability and counter the potentially negative effects of ability or achievement grouping. Interest groups work best for units which provide a variety of projects on a number of topics.

An illustration is literature courses organized around the production of a class literary magazine. The teacher divides the class into groups or committees with specific responsibilities. One group produces or selects short stories and another, poems. Or, if the magazine is organized around subject matter, one group would produce or choose selections on school, and another on the family. Students with a special interest in the fine arts might serve on the committee responsible for format and design.

To individualize instruction, the teacher does not necessarily have to plan several, very different learning experiences. Rather, students can work on essentially the same learning activities and work toward the same general goals. The teacher should modify any of the following elements to provide for individual differences: the goals or purposes of instruction, the materials, the task, the amount of time, the amount of practice, or the number of examples. In modifying these elements, the teachers make adjustments in the particulars of instruction, either to reduce difficulties or to increase the challenge. Adjustments in one element may affect another as shown in the following sections.

MODIFYING INSTRUCTION

Chapter 6 stressed the need for teachers to clarify their expectations for student performance by clearly defining and communicating the goals, objectives, or purposes of a lesson or reading assignment. Such clarification does not necessarily mean the teacher must establish highly specific objectives. As many educators have noted, stating specific objectives will be inappropriate for many students. The particular per-

Goals of Instruction

formance may be far beyond the current abilities of some students; it may also be inappropriate for other students who are already capable of more sophisticated performances.

An alternative to specific objectives is a general performance goal. Such a goal indicates the type of performance expected in sufficiently general terms to permit a variety of ways to meet the goal. Study-skill procedures can serve as the basis for establishing general performance goals. The steps in the procedure serve to define the performance; for example, the desired performance could be to survey for general ideas and pose and answer questions appropriate to the selections.

To modify goals, teachers first need to go beyond the specifics of instruction, such as the pages to be read in a textbook, and determine the essential understanding and performances they desire of students. The teacher must look for a variety of ways students could demonstrate success in meeting the goals. The teacher will discover that students do not always have to read the same selections or read a selection in only one way, that they can provide different amounts of time to complete the assignments, or that different students can make different responses.

Suppose a teacher is planning a unit on short stories as a literary form. The school curriculum does not require that students study particular selections or authors, but only that students learn key understandings about the short-story form. Therefore, the teacher decides that unit goals do not have to specify particular selections or numbers of stories to be read. Students can still study such concepts as plot, character development, and theme, but they can choose from a variety of stories that the teacher will provide.

In another school, the English teachers decide that students should be exposed to particular authors. Their goals identify particular authors and characteristics of their writing. In this situation, all the students will have to read some of the same selections. To modify the goals, these teachers consider and provide a variety of tasks which range in difficulty. The tasks include reading a few pieces by the same author and writing an essay, reading stories and writing short answers to questions, reading stories and responding to interspersed questions, and listening to a recorded reading of stories and making an informal response.

Materials   Chapter 7 discussed the factors which affect the readability of materials. Materials used in a course will differ in the degree of difficulty or ease students experience in reading them. The teacher with students of widely differing abilities must expect that 1) a selection may not be appropriate for all students or 2) the selection cannot be read in the same manner by all students.

The teacher can, therefore, modify instruction by providing material of different levels of difficulty. Students can work toward the same goal and study the same concepts while reading different selections. In a social-studies class, students can read about the same historical event using different versions of the same selection. A science teacher who wants to provide a successful introduction to a study-skill procedure can use a great variety of materials including passages from lower-level textbooks and articles from magazines and newspapers.

The kind of reading response a teacher asks students to make can have a major effect on their performance. Therefore, the teacher needs to consider the difficulty of both the materials and the instructional task (assignment or exercise). A teacher can adjust the difficulty of a task by adjusting any of these three things: the amount of assistance, size of task, and complexity of task. *The Task*

Chapter 9 defined three functional levels of reading: independent, instructional, and frustrational. When teachers know that the materials will offer few or no difficulties, they need not plan to provide assistance; students can read independently. If the material is at the students' instructional level, the teacher can plan to give assistance. Teachers can use the procedures discussed in Chapters 3 and 4 to help students read material at this level.

Chapter 4 discussed the effect of the size of a task on student performance. Some teachers commonly rely on the format of the textbook to establish the length of reading assignments. The chapter discussed ways of modifying the size of the task to better meet student abilities—for example, by breaking up the selection into shorter segments and inserting questions after each segment. As students demonstrate success, the teacher can then make gradually longer assignments.

Finally, the teacher can consider the complexity of the task. Any instructional task involves many responses. Teachers, who mastered the tasks years before, may see them as terribly simple. Students new to the tasks may find them terribly complicated and perhaps overwhelming. The teacher can modify the task and facilitate success by temporarily cutting out some of the responses students must make.

Chapter 7 presented a differentiated assignment for reading poetry. The most difficult version of the assignment required students to make four responses: read the poem to identify theme, identify images, discover how images were related, and interpret the meaning of related images (or the imagery). The lower-level version of the assignment presented students with the theme, with the ways images were related, and with some of the images. Students read the poem to find and relate the other images. With the differentiated assignment, the teacher, in a sense, makes some of the responses for the student.

Another way of reducing complexity is to break up the assignment into a series of smaller tasks. The survey/question procedures are modifications of the common and larger task of reading a chapter to answer a set of questions at the end of the chapter or, perhaps, on a test. In the survey step, the student has the smaller task of looking for general ideas. Each question posed by the student is one of several small tasks to be completed while reading. The steps of the survey/question procedure can in turn be broken down into still smaller tasks or steps:

For materials with textbook aids:

1. Survey
   a. Read the title and think about the general idea.
   b. Look at the pictures.
   c. Read the subheadings.
   d. Write down the general idea.
2. Question
   a. Read the first subheading.
   b. Read the first sentence in the paragraph.
   c. Write a question using words in the subheading.

For materials without textbook aids:

1. Survey
   a. Read the title and think about the general idea.
   b. Read the first paragraph as fast as you can.
   c. Look over the rest of the page.
   d. Write down the general idea.
2. Question
   a. Think about the title.
   b. Can you write a *what* question?
   c. Can you write a *who* question?
   d. Can you write a *when* or *where* question?

Amount of Time   Although many students differ in their rate *of learning,* students may also differ in rate of *reading;* that is, the average number of words processed in a particular amount of time. When students must learn by reading a textbook, both factors come into play.

Time limits for tasks are often set on an arbitrary basis without regard for student abilities. For example, one year, a school sets the time for a class period at 50 minutes. A history teacher decides to cover a chapter each week (or in five 50-minute periods). The next year the school reduces the class period to 40 minutes. The teacher tries to cover the same material in the shorter amount of time, even though the previous year many students did not complete their work on time.

If students are responding appropriately to materials and tasks but are not completing tasks on time, an obvious modification is to temporarily increase the amount of time. That is not to say that teachers must always make allowances for slower students. Such students can show major increases in both the learning and reading rates, but they must have the chance to start at a comfortable rate before gradually increasing it. Each successful experience will contribute to a cumulative effect of overall improvement. For example, when students first practice study-skill procedures, they will perform very slowly. But with each succeeding practice, they will make small gains in their rate of surveying, posing more questions more quickly and easily. The overall effect is an increase in rate of both reading and learning new material.

Some teachers make decisions on the amount of practice to provide as arbitrarily as they make decisions about the amount of time for each task. Some teachers provide too much unnecessary practice. Even when students demonstrate success on the first or second set of exercises, they must do additional exercises of the same kind. For example, students who respond successfully to a set of literal-level questions still work through another set instead of moving on to interpretive-level questions. *Amount of Practice*

At the other extreme, many teachers provide no practice. Students have only one opportunity to respond to a particular task. Those who show an average or below-average performance and apparently need further practice have no opportunity to improve. For example, one teacher asks students to read a story and write a description of the plot structure. The next assignment, which calls for them to discuss the roles of characters, is dependent on an understanding of the first assignment. Students who are not entirely successful on the first assignment are apparently unready to do the next. A modification would be to repeat the first assignment but with a new story.

Between the two extremes of no practice and too much are teachers who do provide repeated activities but do not view them as practice intended for gradual improvement. For example, a science teacher asks students to read a chapter a week and answer the comprehension questions in the textbook. The very first week, he expects a complete performance—all pages, all questions. Students who do anything less receive a "0" or "F." The alternative is to 1) use the first assignment for diagnostic purposes and to find out how much students are able or willing to complete, 2) give them credit for what they have accomplished, however small, and then 3) make subsequent assignments that require students to show small, but steady improvement.

When students confront new terminology, concepts, and tasks, they may initially benefit little from abstract explanations. Chapter 6 recommended that teachers also present examples or demonstrations. If students continue exhibiting difficulty, a modification would be to provide additional examples (rather than simply restating the explanations). A chapter in a mathematics, science, or grammar textbook may not have sufficient examples for all students to understand concepts and procedures. The teacher can easily modify the material by doing the first few chapter problems or exercises. An alternative is to have students generate new examples during a discussion of the chapter. In a third procedure, students make a start on the exercises and then stop to compare responses. The teacher can guide the students in contrasting incorrect and correct responses to help them discover the features of desirable responses. In all three of these modifications, the teacher starts the students on a reading assignment, interrupts them to check their understanding and provide any needed instruction and then allows them to proceed. *Number of Examples*

RECOMMENDATIONS FOR SPECIAL STUDENTS

Gifted Students

Activities that come to mind for gifted students usually encourage creative and independent work. The school library is a crucial resource in the development of such activities. The library can provide diverse reading materials that will give the gifted student an opportunity to pursue personal interests and read in depth. Library research procedures will also help with creative projects.[4]

Strang, McCullough, and Traxler,[5] along with Miles Zintz,[6] share the approach that the purpose of schooling for the gifted child should be that of *freeing* the child to learn by providing opportunities to acquire new interests, to study subjects outside of the school curriculum and to develop talents. Such opportunities can include small-group instruction, free time in the library, free time outside the school environment, and extracurricular activities such as special interest clubs and field trips. By working with the student, parents, and other school personnel, teachers can give the student access to several kinds of resources.

Remedial Students

James Kinneavy and William Rutherford make a strong point for developing a balanced program in providing activities to help the reader who needs remedial work.[7] They suggest that teachers should work toward teaching the four aims or basic purposes of discourse: 1) information, 2) persuasion, 3) entertainment, and 4) expression.

Information gathering is one of the prime purposes for reading. Teachers must be careful to select sources that provide information of interest to students. Informative sources should be factual, surprising, and comprehensive.

Much of written communication is persuasive or aimed at influencing opinion. Such materials include advertisements and propaganda. In this area, teachers will have to go beyond traditional textbook sources to find examples for their students.

As discussed in Chapter 20, many educators believe reading for entertainment or pleasure is especially important for less able readers. Teachers should give such students opportunities to select interesting materials and to read on a regular basis. With the development of positive attitudes and the provision for practice, students can overcome major skill deficiencies.

A fourth aim of discourse is self-expression. A student who has reading or other difficulties will find enjoyment and excitement in liter-

---

[4]Burmeister, *Reading Strategies.*
[5]Ruth Strang, Constance M. McCullough, and Arthur E. Traxler, *The Improvement of Reading,* 4th ed. (New York: McGraw-Hill, 1967).
[6]Miles V. Zintz, *The Reading Process—The Teacher and the Learner* (Dubuque, Iowa: William C. Brown, 1975).
[7]James L. Kinneavy and William L. Rutherford, "Junior High School Level: Grades 7–9," in Thomas D. Horn, ed., *Reading for the Disadvantaged—Problems of Linguistically Different Learners.* (New York: Harcourt, Brace & World, 1970), pp. 199–210.

ature which expresses personal feelings and attitudes. Students should also have the opportunity to write for their own self-expression.

The work of Allen Cohen concentrates on the use of materials for the disadvantaged student.[8] He supports the use of self-directing or self-instructional materials, which provide for individualized, self-paced learning and the opportunity for mastery of skills. Characteristics of these materials include:

1. Materials require little or no direct teacher involvement
2. Students receive quick and useful feedback for their performances
3. There is an adequate recordkeeping system
4. Rate of progress is student determined
5. There is allowance for small-group interactions as well as individual study

Linguistically Different Students

Miles Zintz raises two special remedial problems related to linguistic differences: 1) the student who is bilingual in English and another language, whose first language is not English, and 2) the student whose dialect differs from the teacher's.[9] In working with the first group of students, Zintz has developed the following seven-point program:

1. Students have intensive work with speaking and hearing along with reading.
2. A few patterns are presented at one time.
3. Teachers strive for habitual use of important patterns.
4. New patterns should be used with a known vocabulary.
5. Students use vocabulary in contextual situations.
6. Exercises involve authentic speech situations.
7. Instruction aims toward a natural, fluent speech and reading.

Students may differ from one another and from their teacher in their English dialect. *Dialects* are the varieties of a language that speakers of the language who do not share the same dialect can still understand. A dialect has distinctive features that are not found in the same manner or frequency of occurrence in other varieties of English. The most notable dialects are regional; that is, varieties of English spoken in geographic areas of the United States (as well as areas of other English-speaking countries such as Canada and England). Dialects are also spoken by different ethnic, racial, cultural, and economic groups.

Much controversy surrounds dialect because this linguistic phenomena cannot be separated from economic and racial concerns. Many linguists and educators use the term *nonstandard* to refer to the

---

[8]S. Allen Cohen, "Senior High School Level: Grades 10–12," in Thomas D. Horn, ed., *Reading for the Disadvantaged—Problems of Linguistically Different Learners* (New York: Harcourt, Brace & World, 1970), pp. 211–226.
[9]Zintz, *The Reading Process.*

varieties of English spoken by many black Americans, hispanic Americans, as well as white Americans from rural, southern, and economically depressed areas. The choice of the label *nonstandard* suggests a value judgment and also implies the existence of a more common, standard, or desirable dialect. Such a standard dialect seems to be the ideal or at least the preferable style of speech and writing, illustrated by the speech of national news broadcasters or by rules of usage.

A related term to consider is *idiolect,* defined as an individual's personal variety of speech. As voice graphs have demonstrated, no two individuals speak exactly alike. In addition to such matters as voice quality and rate of speaking, individuals also differ in the frequency by which they exhibit certain features of a dialect. Certain pronunciations, syntactic structures, and word choices will identify both an individual's idiolect and the dialect he or she shares with a particular group.

Much research has investigated the relationship between dialect and reading. According to James Laffey and Roger Shuy, research does not support the theory that a particular dialect causes reading difficulties.[10] On the other hand, the subject has not been fully explored.

According to James Ford, nonstandard features are stigmatized; that is, persons react negatively to them.[11] In a number of studies, teachers and prospective teachers responded to lists of nonstandard features and to both oral and videotaped readings which revealed nonstandard features. The subjects, as a group, generally reacted negatively to the features and made negative judgments about the personality, performance, and capability of individuals who exhibited those features.

Those studies imply that students with nonstandard dialects may indeed have problems in learning to read, not because of a linguistic deficit, but because of the attitudes of teachers who speak a different dialect.

Even when teachers are not biased against students, their lack of understanding of the student's speech may result in inaccurate evaluation and diagnosis of the student's performance and ability. This problem is most likely to occur when teachers ask students to read orally for diagnostic purposes. A student may be successful in word recognition and in comprehension, but may make what are to the teacher's ears very different pronunciations and translations of sentence structures. Teachers should not consider such variant responses to be miscues or symptoms of skill deficiencies.

Because of the problems of bias and inaccurate assessment, educators strongly encourage teachers to become knowledgeable about

---

[10]James L. Laffey and Roger W. Shuy, eds., *Language Differences: Do They Interfere?* (Newark, Del.: International Reading Association, 1973).

[11]James F. Ford, "Language Attitude Studies: A Review of Selected Research." *The Florida FL Reporter* 12:1 and 2 (Spring/Fall 1974): 53–54, 100.

the dialects spoken by their students. With this knowledge, teachers will be able to distinguish between responses which are consistent with the students' speech and those that may indeed be symptoms of reading problems and in need of remediation. Teachers can take advantage of research which describes dialects such as the work of William Labov on black dialect or black English.[12] Teachers can also learn about students' speech by providing opportunities for discussion and conversation. Finally, when teachers are in doubt about whether or not an oral-reading response is related to dialect differences, simply asking students to explain the meaning of a word or talk about what they have read will indicate whether or not students understand the vocabulary and syntax.

The preceding discussion also applies to work with students who are bilingual, since their English will exhibit features of any number of dialects. Appendices C and D provide a brief introduction to the study of the relationship between dialect and language differences and reading and provide exercises in identifying commonly occurring phonological features of black English and of the English spoken by many persons who have a Spanish-language background.

Instruction for students of different dialects who have reading problems should follow the same principles of effective remedial instruction for any student. Robert Wilson stresses the idea that students must have successful experiences; these students typically have experienced many years of frustration and discouragement.[13] Successful instruction must be geared to the students' abilities and interests and must start with, then build upon, the strengths the students already possess.

Zintz stresses the importance of a teacher's respect for the student's language experience and competence.[14] He recommends use of the language-experience approach, in which students are given opportunities to talk about their experiences. This "talk" is recorded and used as a text for reading practice and instruction. Such texts will reflect the students' cultural experiences and spoken-language vocabulary. Zintz also recommends that teachers take advantage of commercially published materials written for such students.

According to Strang, McCullough, and Traxler, a final group of readers that deserve special attention are those able readers who for some reason have been retarded in reading development.[15] They suggest: student self-appraisal, group planning by students, attention to interests of the students, intensive practice, use of mechanical teaching devices, good feedback systems, and follow-up instruction. These recommendations apply to any effective remedial situation.

---

[12]William Labov, *Language in the Inner City: Studies in Black English Vernacular* (Philadelphia: University of Pennsylvania Press, 1972).
[13]Robert M. Wilson, *Diagnostic and Remedial Reading for Classroom and Clinic,* 2nd ed. (Columbus, Ohio: Charles E. Merrill, 1972), pp. 146–47.
[14]Zintz, *The Reading Process.*
[15]Strang, McCullough, and Traxler, *The Improvement of Reading.*

SUMMARY   This chapter suggested instructional procedures for the groups of readers who often need special treatment from teachers if they are to develop reading skills. Individual differences have a variety of possible causes and explanations. Teachers should modify instruction to address individual differences.

Suggested Activities

1. Discuss one of the Key Ideas in the Overview of this chapter.
2. Observe a small group of students and identify and categorize their individual differences.
3. Select a set of exercises from a textbook. Describe procedures for modifying the exercises to reduce their difficulty.
4. Identify three students in a class who need remedial help and outline an instructional program for them.
5. Describe ways the library can serve the gifted student.

Recommended Readings

Belloni, Loretta F., and Jongsman, Eugene A. "The Effects of Interest on Reading Comprehension of Low-Achieving Students." *Journal of Reading* 22:2 (November 1978): 106–9.

Chall, Jeanne. "A Decade of Research on Reading and Learning Disability," in S. Jay Samuels, ed., *What Research Has to Say About Reading Instruction.* Newark, Del.: International Reading Association, 1978.

Derra-Piana, Gabriel M. *Reading Diagnosis and Prescription—An Introduction.* New York: Holt, Rinehart, & Winston, 1968, chap. 2.

Dillner, Martha H., and Olson, Joanne P. *Personalizing Reading Instruction in Middle, Junior, and Senior High Schools—Utilizing a Competency-Based Instructional System.* New York: Macmillan, 1977, chaps. 8 and 9.

Hafner, Lawrence E. *Developmental Reading in Middle and Secondary Schools—Foundations, Strategies, and Skills for Teaching.* New York: Macmillan, 1977, chap. 21.

Hittleman, Daniel R. *Developmental Reading: A Psycholinguistic Perspective.* Chicago: Rand McNally, 1978, chap. 12.

Horn, Thomas D., ed. *Reading for the Disadvantaged—Problems of Linguistically Different Learners.* New York: Harcourt, Brace, & World, 1970.

Richards, John P. and Hatcher, Catherine W. "Interspersed Meaningful Learning Questions as Semantic Cues for Poor Comprehenders." *Reading Research Quarterly* 13:4 (1977–78): 538–93.

Roe, Betty D.; Stoodt, Barbara D.; and Burns, Paul C. *Reading Instruction in the Secondary School.* Chicago: Rand McNally, 1978, chaps. 11 and 12.

Smith, Richard J., and Barrett, Thomas C. *Teaching in the Middle Grades,* 2nd ed. Reading, Mass.: Addison-Wesley, 1979, chap. 10.

Spache, George D. *Diagnosing and Correcting Reading Disabilities.* Boston: Allyn & Xacon, 1976, chaps. 10 and 12.

Strang, Ruth; McCullough, Constance M.; and Traxler, Arthur E. *The Improvement of Reading* 4th ed. New York: McGraw-Hill, 1967, part 4.

Wilson, Robert W. *Diagnostic and Remedial Reading for Classroom and Clinic,* 2nd ed. Columbus, Ohio: Charles E. Merrill, 1972.

Zintz, Miles V. *Education Across Cultures.* Dubuque, Iowa: Kendall/Hunt, 1969.

———. *The Reading Process—The Teacher and the Learner,* 2nd ed. Dubuque, Iowa: William C. Brown, 1975, part 4.

5

Appendices

The four appendices that follow are intended to supplement chapter discussions. Appendix A presents a variety of vocabulary games, which are based on the analysis of skills and instructional procedures in Chapter 3 on Vocabulary. Appendix B provides a checklist of levels and types of comprehension responses to aid the teacher in selecting and designing the comprehension questions discussed in Chapter 4. Appendix C and D supplement the discussions of dialect and language differences in Chapter 21 on working with special students. The exercises in the two appendices illustrate the linguistic characteristics some black and hispanic students exhibit when they read orally.

A

Vocabulary Games　　　　**Appendix**

Teachers can use many commercially published games effectively in a program of vocabulary development. Some, like *Phonics Rummy*®, were developed specifically for work on reading skills. Reading and language-arts teachers have also used games like *Scrabble*® in their classrooms. (A selected list of commercially published games appears at the end of this appendix.)

Games have two benefits. First, students enjoy playing them, and, as a result, may develop more positive attitudes toward vocabulary study. Second, all games involve the same kinds of responses as instructional exercises call for. Therefore, the games help develop vocabulary skills and concepts. One disadvantage of commercially published games is that they may not be appropriate for particular students. They may be either too easy or too difficult and may not provide sufficient attention to a needed skill or concept.

Using published games as models, teachers can construct their own games which will meet the needs and interests of their students and relate directly to reading selections being taught. Examples of four types of games and puzzles follow: 1) games requiring students to produce new or changed words, 2) crossword puzzles, 3) other puzzles, and 4) games based on Bingo.

Both students and teachers can construct these games. Involving students has four key benefits:

1. They will find it very enjoyable and rewarding to make games their classmates will use.
2. Differences in interests and ability are addressed.
3. In making games, students are developing skills and concepts at a more sophisticated level than when they are only responding to games.
4. The teacher's burden of finding or producing games is reduced.

The original games that follow are based on examples and suggestions in Edgar Dale and Joseph O'Rourke, *Techniques of Teaching Vocabulary* (Palo Alto: Field Educational Publications, 1971); Lou E. Burmeister, *Reading Strategies for Middle and Secondary School Teachers,* 2nd Ed. (Reading, Mass: Addison-Wesley, 1978); and Harold L. Herber, *Teaching Reading in Content Areas* (Englewood Cliffs, N.J: Prentice-Hall, 1970).

Producing Words In all of the games below students take words or groups of letters and produce new or correct words. The games can be played by individual students, teams, or groups. When teams or groups play, they can compete against each other for the largest number of exercises completed or words produced. If someone makes an incorrect response, the other team or group can challenge it and receive a point.

1. Given a word and a definition of a new word, students form new words by transposing or deleting letters in the original word.

   Word: grub
   Definition: a tiny animal
   New word: bug

   Word: fate
   Definition: when you eat too much
   New word: fat

   Word: spot
   Definition: coming to a halt
   New word: stop

2. Students "find" a word in other words or phrases (which may consist of nonsense words).

al mamm	mammal
dirbs	birds
pile ter	reptile
stlanp	plants
rim pate	primate

3. Students produce new words using some or all of the letters of an original word.

painter	pain pat pin retain
mother	moth rot more the

4. Given words and a definition, students form new words by adding a beginning letter or letters.

ear + the opposite of brave = fear
hop + where you buy something = shop
are + concerned about someone = care
round + not going in a straight direction = around
side + within = inside
view + to look over = review

5. Given words and definitions of new words, students form the new words by adding an ending letter or letters.

far + pay to travel = fare
to + part of a foot = toe
construct + a building = construction
plant + holds plants = planter
stop + keeps water in = stopper

6. Given a riddle sentence, students provide a new word that answers the riddle. The answer must relate to or contain a word in the sentence.

A tiny house that covers a part in a machine. (housing)
The person who sits in this chair is the boss. (chairperson)
You make a sharp looking design with needle and thread. (needlepoint)
This chair moves, but it's not made of stone. (rocking chair)
How is a lawyer like the part of a trumpet? (mouthpiece)

7. Students must provide as many synonyms as they can for a given word. Example: *view: see, look, sight, glance*

8. Students are given a word and must come up with as many different forms as they can. Example: *multiply: multiple, multiplying, multiplicand, multiplier.*

9. Students must come up with as many meanings as they can for a given word.
pink: a color, political persuasion, way of cutting, happy (as in tickled pink).

10. Students must make sentences with different meanings of a word.

The *root* of preview is view.

The square *root* of 4 is 2.

Pigs will *root* for food.

The *root* of the tree cracked the sidewalk.

Your attitude is the *root* of the problem.

11. Students create new words by adding or transposing letters to a small word. Each new word is one letter longer than the one before.

on	not	tone	stone	sonnet
pit	spit	spite	stipen	
an	ant	pant	plant	pliant
on	one	lone	clone	

12. Students must produce the correct word from a scrambled word and a clue.

Directions: Unscramble the letters to produce the word related to the phrase or sentence.

1. stnobo	a. The capital of Massachusetts
2. nepn	b. A colony was named for this famous Quaker
3. sililwam	c. He founded Rhode Island
4. wen kory	d. The colony and its capital have the same name
5. hires pamhwen	e. The colony was named for an area of England
6. nirgavii	f. The first British colony
7. sinolraca	g. Two colonies shared the same name
8. groigea	h. A colony named for a king
9. yandlarm	i. A colony named for a queen
10. ledarawe	j. This colony has an Indian name

Answer Key:

1. Boston	6. Virginia
2. Penn	7. Carolinas
3. Williams	8. Georgia
4. New York	9. Maryland
5. New Hampshire	10. Delaware

13. Given pairs of words which have conceptual relationships, students must complete other pairs.

Sample: A paragraph is to a sentence as a clause is to a noun phrase. The relationship is one of whole to part.

English

1. paragraph: sentence/clause: _____ noun phrase, noun, adverb
2. sentence: noun phrase/noun phrase: _____ verb phrase, noun, clause
3. verb: past tense/noun: _____ adjective, plural, noun phrase
4. coordination: equal/subordination: _____ dependent, complex, clause
5. noun marker: noun/auxiliary: _____ noun phrase, verb, sentence

Mathematics

1. *add: subtract/multiply:* _____
   subtract, divide, compute
2. *triangle: angle/angle:* _____
   ray, line, hypotenuse
3. *linear: quadratic/one:* _____
   two, four, three
4. *part: whole/prime:* _____
   fraction, composite, unit
5. *relation: function/set:* _____
   superset, subset, empty set

14. Several students, after hearing a humorous sentence with a deleted word or phrase, try to match their "guesses." (This use of the cloze technique is the basis of a popular television game show.)
    a. The school librarian said, "If you can't be quiet, then at least stop _____ .
    b. Joe thinks he's so cool that he wore his sunglasses _____ .
    c. Columbus was so dumb that he looked for India in _____ .

Crossword Puzzles
Crossword puzzles develop all vocabulary-related skills: spelling, word-analysis skills, and word relationships. Teachers can use the puzzles in newspapers and books for general development. Teachers and students can construct puzzles to focus on particular skills and concepts and on the vocabulary in particular reading selections:

English Literature
Directions: All the words and names relate to *Billy Budd*.
Across
   1. Provides power to move ship
   2. Billy's job
   4. What Claggart felt for Billy
   6. Billy was commonly called _____
   7. An officer on ship
  10. Famous British admiral
  11. Billy was in the _____ navy
  12. The master-of-arms
Down
   3. Name of ship Billy left
   5. Name of Billy's new ship
   8. The captain
   9. He wrote Billy Budd.

English or foreign language—Antonyms

Directions: Select the word that is the opposite in meaning (antonym) or very different in meaning.

Across

1. exit
4. hit
5. bravery
6. my
7. whole
10. all
11. starve

Down

1. none
2. leave
3. sense
4. ma
8. front (ship)
9. on

			¹E	N	T	²R	A	³N	C	E	
			V			E		O			
⁸A		⁴P	E	T		T		N			
⁵F	E	A	R			U		S			
T			⁶Y	⁹O	U	R		E			
				F		¹⁰N	O	N	E		
		⁷H	A	L	F			S			
								¹¹E	A	T	

Science

Directions: All the words relate to electrical energy.

Down

1. stores electricity
2. conducts electricity
3. a terminal
4. carries electricity

Across

5. produced by friction
6. unit of resistance
7. particle with negative charge
8. produces electricity
9. electrically charged atom
10. unit of pressure

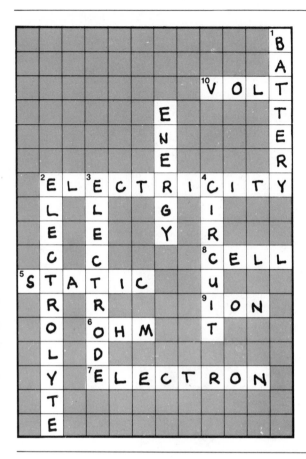

Geometry

Clue: Words for the upper part of the puzzle are names of triangles. Words for the bottom part are parts of triangles.

Across

1. a triangle with a right angle
2. a triangle with at least two congruent sides
3. a triangle with all angles less than 90°
4. triangles with the same size and shape
9. points where two sides intersect
10. part of a triangle

Down

5. a triangle with one angle larger than 90°
6. the side opposite the right angle
7. union of two rays with common end point
8. sides adjacent to the right angle
11. unit of measurement of angle

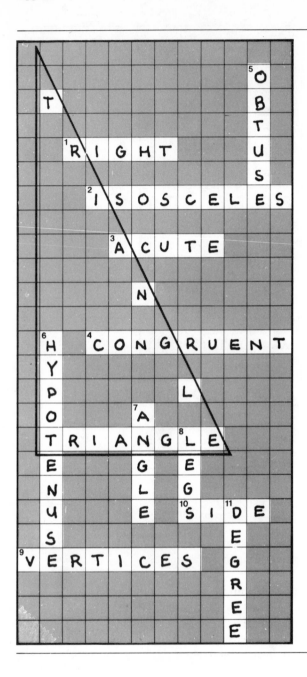

There are a variety of other puzzles whose responses are similar to those for crossword puzzles and develop spelling, word-analysis, and word-relationship skills. The puzzles below have built-in clues which aid the students in finding, matching, or producing the words.

Other Puzzles

Foreign Language

Directions: Write the Latin word for the English word. Then find and circle the word in the puzzle. The first is done for you.

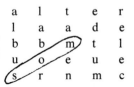

a	l	t	e	r
l	a	a	d	e
b	b	m	t	l
u	o	e	u	e
s	r	n	m	c

English   *Latin*

1. custom   mōs
2. widely
3. nevertheless
4. other
5. white
6. swift
7. both
8. work
9. then
10. down

Answers: a. mōs, 2. lātē, 3. tamen, 4. alter, 5. albus, 6. celer, 7. et, 8. labor, 9. tum, 10. de

Science

Directions: Find and circle names of planets and other words related to "space." Some words are repeated. One is done for you.

v	e	n	v	s	f	e	z	r	p
r	m	e	r	c	u	r	y	m	r
f	z	b	a	t	w	p	s	o	o
c	m	c	n	p	a	n	t	t	l
s	a	t	u	r	n	z	u	n	a
n	r	v	s	s	i	l	r	g	u
g	s	a	i	e	p	g	r	o	r
i	a	z	n	o	t	a	e	z	t
m	u	l	e	s	u	r	o	c	x
i	x	o	a	k	n	l	b	t	n
l	a	e	r	j	e	n	u	s	o
k	p	c	t	i	v	g	a	r	m
y	n	k	h	z	o	s	z	e	h
u	r	a	n	u	s	m	n	c	c

German

Directions: Write the German word for the English word. Then write it in the puzzle. Each German word has an *e*. Check your answers by counting the letters before *e*. The first is done for you.

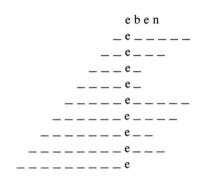

English	German
1. even	eben
2. window	
3. joy	
4. other	
5. garden	
6. interesting	
7. describe	
8. season	
9. actor	
10. story	

Answers:
1. eben, 2. Fenster, 3. Freude, 4. ander, 5. Garten, 6. interessant, 7. beschreiben, 8. Jahreszeit, 9. Schauspieler, 10. Geschichte

Magic Square
Directions:

1. Match the term with the definition.
2. Write in the number of the term in the matching square.
3. The numbers in each row of squares (down and across) should add up to 39. Check your answers by adding the numbers in each row.
4. The first is done for you.
5. There are more terms than definitions.

1. ode
2. metaphor
3. synecdoche
4. lyrical
5. simile
6. theme
7. genre
8. rhyme
9. antagonist
10. image
11. drama
12. personification
13. protagonist
14. short story
15. symbol
16. mood
17. subplot
18. narrative

A implied comparison
B type of literature
C recounts past events
D given human characteristics
E words share sounds
F explicit comparison
G mainly dialogue
H object has abstract meaning
I main character
J secondary "story" paralleling main "story"
K meaning of entire work
L part stands for whole
M atmosphere of work
N word stands for something experienced through senses
O personal, emotional expression
P opposes main character

2 A	B	C	D
E	F	G	H
I	J	K	L
M	N	O	P

Word Bingo or Wordo

Teachers can easily adapt bingo to a vocabulary game. Students work
with words, parts of words, or definitions. Each student has a "board"
(or large card) on which there are words, parts of words, or other
symbols. The teacher calls out items or displays them on flash cards.
Players cover up a matched item with a blank card when they recognize
it. The first player to cover his or her entire board wins.

Words can be used from any content area and can be adapted to
focus on particular skills and concepts: sight-word recognition (of words
and other symbols), word analysis, and word relationships.

Sight words

Flash cards:

then	there	these

those	thin	when

where	who	why

Student's board:

then	who	why	where
there	then	when	why

Mathematics symbols

Flash cards:

x	÷	-	$\sqrt{\ }$

=	·	( )	/

Student's board:

add	multiply	divide
multiply	subtract	multiply

Structural Analysis

Flash cards:

pre-	re-	a-

-ing	-tion	-ed

Student's board:

viewed	prepare	boarded
action	aboard	acting

Word relationships

Teacher's script:

1. the opposite of entrance
2. the opposite of inside
3. the same as inside
4. the opposite of thick

Student's board:

within	entrance	thick
thin	enter	exit

- *African Safari.* Behavioral Research Laboratories.
- *Anagrams.* Behavioral Research Laboratories.
- *Balloon Game.* Visionetics.
- *Blend Bingo.* Behavioral Research Laboratories.
- *Charades for Juniors.* Selchow and Richter.
- *Compound Word Game.* Developmental Learning Materials.
- *Consonant Lotto.* Garrard.
- *Distar and Strategy Games.* Science Research Associates.
- *Easy Crossword Puzzles.* English Language Educational Potluck Services.
- *Educational Password.* Peak Production.
- *Educational Concentration.* Milton Bradley.
- *Fun with Rhymes.* Instructo Products.
- *Games: Phonics–Astro Alley.* Little Brown Bear Learning Associates.
- *Go Fish.* Remedial Education Center.
- *Grab.* Dorothea Alcock.
- *Group Sounding Game.* Garrard.
- *Group Word Teaching Game.* Garrard.
- *Initial Consonant Bingo.* Ideal School Supply.
- *Junior Scrabble.* Selchow and Richter.
- *Motorcycle Motocross.* Bowmer.
- *Object Lotto.* Childcraft.
- *Occupation Word Hunt.* Developmental Learning Materials.
- *Password.* Milton Bradley.
- *Phonetic Quizino.* Milton Bradley.
- *Phonic Rummy.* Kenworthy Educational Service.
- *Rhymming Zig Zag.* Ideal School Supply.
- *Satellite Learning Center.* Childrens Press.
- *Scrabble.* Selchow and Richter.
- *Sentence Builder.* Milton Bradley.
- *Short Vowel Lotto.* Behavioral Research Laboratories.
- *Space Flight.* Ideal School Supply.
- *Spill and Spell.* Childcraft.
- *Sports Close-ups.* EMC.
- *Staro.* Fern Tripp.
- *The Syllable Game.* Garrard.
- *Vocabulary Bingo.* J. Weston Walch.
- *Vowel Dominoes.* Remedial Education Center.
- *Vowel Lotto.* Garrard.
- *Word Games.* Science Research Associates.

B

Checklists for Comprehension   Appendix

This appendix presents a chart illustrating different levels and tasks of comprehension, which teachers can use as a guide 1) for writing comprehension questions and 2) for evaluating and selecting questions in tests, textbooks, and other instructional materials.

The first column presents some common words appearing in questions. The reader will note that some words are used in questions at a variety of levels; therefore, the wording of the question, by itself, will not necessarily determine the level of response. Many of the words are drawn from James A. Banks and Ambrose A. Clegg, Jr., *Teaching Strategies for the Social Studies* (Reading, Mass: Addison-Wesley, 1973), and Francis P. Hunkins, *Involving Students in Questioning* (Boston: Allyn and Bacon, 1976).

The second column lists a variety of tasks for each level of comprehension. Terms used to designate tasks are defined in chapter four.

COMPREHENSION LEVELS AND TASKS	*Question words*	*Common tasks*
	Copy	Confirm, locate, reinspect, or recall
	Define	
Literal comprehension	Describe	
	Distinguish between	details of people, actions,
	Find an example of	places, times, causes,
	How	steps, and stages.
	Identify	
	Indicate	explicit
	List	points: major ideas, main
	List in order	points, rules, classifica-
	Name	tions, or definitions.
	Number	
	Point to	time sequences, actions,
	Tell	steps, stages, or periods
	What	of time.
	What happened	
	When	spatial arrangements.
	(In what time)	
	Where	
	(In what place)	
	Which	
	Who	
	(What is _____'s name, age, . .)	
	Why	

Literal comprehension— translation	*Question words*	*Common tasks*
	Describe	Paraphrase, summarize, out-
	Diagram	line, or illustrate details, ideas,
	Draw	or sequence.
	Give a synonym of	
	Graph	Translate illustrations into
	Illustrate	words, words into illus-
	In your own	trations, words into other
	words. . .	symbols, other symbols into
	List	words.
	Number	
	Outline	
	Paraphrase	
	Rephrase	
	Reorder	
	Reorganize	
	Sketch	
	State	
	Summarize	
	Translate	

Question words
Compare
Compare & Contrast
Conclude
Consider
Contrast
Demonstrate
Differentiate
Distinguish
Estimate
Explain
Extend
Extrapolate
Formulate
Give another
    example of
Give a definition
    of
Hypothesize
Infer
Interpret
Predict
Relate
In your own
    opinion

Common tasks   *Interpretation*
Infer relationships of details
and ideas.

Explain figurative expressions:
metaphors, similes, personification, or synecdoche.

Explain symbolic language.

Arrive at generalizations, conclusions, estimates, predictions, or trends.

Identify purpose, theme or
thesis, motivation, mood, and
tone.

Question words
Apply
Build
Consider how
Construct
Demonstrate
Develop
Design
Determine
How could
Indicate
Plan
Relate
Solve
Show how
Tell how

Common Tasks   *Application*
Apply a principle from one
situation to another situation.

Apply a procedure to solve
new problems.

Apply a definition to find
or create new examples.

Test out the applicability of
a principle, procedure, or
definition.

Analysis	*Question words*	*Common tasks*
	Analyze	Distinguish
	Break down	main points from
	Compare	supporting details;
	Compare & Contrast	conclusions from
	Contrast	supporting statements;
	Classify	stated from unstated
	Describe	assumptions;
	Distinguish	factual from non-factual
	Diagram	statements.
	Explain	
	Find	Identify
	How	cause/effect
	Identify	relationships;
	Relate	parts of a structure;
	Which	comparison-contrast,
		chronological,
		ennumerative,
		extended definition, and
		cause/effect types of structure;
		literary genre.
Synthesis	*Question words*	*Common tasks*
	Create	Present parts of text in new,
	Derive	coherent form.
	Design	
	Determine	Present information from dif-
	Develop	ferent texts in new, coherent
	Discuss	form.
	Elaborate	
	Explain	Present information from
	Formulate	text(s) and other sources in
	Propose	new, coherent form.
	Plan	
	Put together	Compare/contrast two or more
	Synthesize	texts.
	Suggest	
	Show how	Role-play in response to text.
	Think of a way	
		Arrive at an original thesis or
		plan of action.

Questions words | *Common tasks* | *Evaluate*

Questions words
Apply the criteria
Check
Choose
Consider
Criticize
Debate
Decide
Defend
Determine
Evaluate
Give evidence for
Give support for
Formulate criteria for
Judge
Justify
Select
Support

Common tasks
Apply criteria to
judge a text's
accuracy,
validity,
effectiveness,
economy,
interest,
consistency, and
support.

Apply procedures
to judge solution
of a problem.

Apply criteria
in comparing/contrasting
two or more texts.

Generate new criteria.

Evaluate

C

Reading by a Speaker of Black English

Appendix

This appendix is an introduction to a study of the relationship between dialect and reading. It presents a number of recurring features believed characteristic of black dialect.

The characteristics of black English are presented in the following format: 1) a statement of a generalization about the dialect characteristic, 2) examples of how the dialect feature might occur in the oral reading of a sentence and be recorded by a teacher conducting an Informal Reading Inventory, 3) exercises which present further examples in contrast with variant pronunciations which are not the result of dialect differences.[1]

---

[1]William Labov, *Language in the Inner City: Studies in the Black English Vernacular.* (Philadelphia: University of Pennsylvania); and articles in J. L. Laffey and R. W. Shuy, Eds., *Language Differences: Do They Interfere?* (Newark, Del: International Reading Association, 1973).

Phonological features

1. *r*-lessness

Speakers of black English tend not to produce the sound of *r* in the middle or ends of words.

> I know that guard (god).
> My brother (brotha) was in Paris (Pass).

Which would be characteristic of speakers of black English?

    a. They built a fort (for) out of snow.
    b. They built a fort (fot) out of snow.
    a. He wasn't interested (in there).
    b. He wasn't interested (intested).
    a. My dad was sore (saw).
    b. My dad was sore (sure).

2. *l*-lessness

Speakers of black English tend not to produce the sound of *l* in the end of words:

> That's a toll (toe) bridge.
> He was a big help (hep).

Which would be characteristic of speakers of black English?

    a. I don't have the right tool (took).
    b. I don't have the right tool (too).
    a. You can eat all (awe) you want.
    b. You can eat all (alla) you want.

3. Simplification of consonant clusters with *t (st, ft, nt)*.

Speakers of black English tend to simplify consonant clusters by not pronouncing the sound of *t*.

> They drove right past (pass).
> He played a wild rift (riff).

Which would be characteristic of speakers of black English?

    a. He meant (men) you.
    b. He meant (mane) you.
    a. He can run fast (fass).
    b. He can run fast (far).

4. Simplification of consonant clusters with *d* (nd, ld, red, med).

Speakers of black English tend to simplify consonant clusters by not pronouncing the sound of *d*.

> On the lake, there's a cold wind (win).
> You need to hold (hole) on tight.

Which would be characteristic of speakers of black English?

    a. You can bend (ben) that metal.
    b. You can bend (band) that metal.
    a. It was really cold (sold).
    b. It was really cold (cole).

    5. Simplification of the consonant cluster *ts* in contractions.

Speakers of black English tend not to produce the sound of *t* in contractions.

    That's (Tha's) not the right answer.
    It's (I's) in the other room.

Which would be characteristic of speakers of black English?

    a. Let's (Le's) go Friday morning.
    b. Let's (Least) go Friday morning.
    a. What's (That's) in the package?
    b. What's (Wha's) in the package?

    6. Weakening of final *t*.

Speakers of black English tend to exhibit a weakening or loss of the sound of final *t*.

    He lost his boot (boo).
    I see an empty seat (see).

Which would be characteristic of speakers of black English?

    a. That was a neat (nea) show.
    b. That was a neat (near) show.
    a. The light (lit) is too dim.
    b. The light (lie) is too dim.

    7. Weakening of final *d*.

Speakers of black English tend to exhibit a weakening or loss of the sound of final *d*.

    You have to go down a rough road (row).
    He won the deed (dee) to the house.

Which would be characteristic of speakers of black English?

    a. I dread (drea) that exam.
    b. I dread (bread) that exam.
    a. You better avoid (avoi) her.
    b. You better avoid (avid) her.

8. The sound of the letter *f* for the sounds of the letters *th* in final position.

Speakers of black English tend to pronounce the *th* at the end of words with the sound of *f*.

> Ruth (Roof) called you.
> She had a death (deaf) in her family.

Which would be characteristic of speakers of black English?

> a. Will you go with (wif) me?
> b. Will you go with (will) me?
> a. Today is my birthday (birtday).
> b. Today is my birthday (birfday).

Phonological/ grammatical features

1. Loss of *s* in possessives.

Speakers of black English tend not to produce the sound of *s* in possessives.

> John's (John) story is funny.

Which miscue would be characteristic of speakers of black English?

> a. That stereo's (steres) sound is poor.
> b. That stereo's (stereo) sound is poor.
> a. Did you see Ted's (Ted) new car?
> b. Did you see Ted's (Tedes) new car?

2. Loss of the sound of *s* in third person, singular verbs.

Speakers of black English tend not to produce the sound of *s* in third person, singular verbs.

> He runs (run) the mile in 5 minutes.

Which would be characteristic of speakers of black English?

> a. That dog barks (bark) all night.
> b. That dog barks (bars) all night.
> a. He talks (takes) too much.
> b. He talks (talk) too much.

3. Loss of the sound of *l* in the future.

Speakers of black English tend not to produce the sound of *l* in the future tense.

> You'll (You) be sorry.

Which miscue would be characteristic of speakers of black English?

    a. He said he'll (he) be here.
    b. He said he'll (he-ill) be here.
    a. They'll (They) cause trouble.
    b. They'll (There) cause trouble.

    4. Loss of forms of *to be*.

Speakers of black English tend not to "use" a form of *to be* in *some* sentences.

    I'm (I) not going.
    He's (He) a pain, sometimes.

Which miscue would be characteristic of speakers of black English?

    a. We're (We) ready to go.
    b. We're (Were) ready to go.
    a. I don't think you're (you) funny.
    b. I don't think you're (you are) funny.

    5. Loss of *d* or *t* sound in past tense.

Speakers of black English tend not to produce the *d* or *t* sound in past tense forms of verbs.

    He loaned (loan) me some money Monday.

Which miscue would be characteristic of speakers of black English?

    a. I passed (pass) him on the way to school.
    b. I passed (pass-sed) him on the way to school.
    a. They raised (raise) the flag in the morning.
    b. They raised (rised) the flag in the morning.

D

Reading by a Speaker with a Spanish Language Background

This appendix will discuss the relationship between language differences and reading. Certain characteristics frequently occur in the spoken English of many, but not all, persons who have a Spanish language background. Such persons may be bilingual in Spanish and English; Spanish may be their first or second language. The identification of these features is based on research with individuals living in the Southwestern United States.[1]

The speech characteristics of those with a Spanish language background will be presented in the following format: 1) a general statement about the characteristic, 2) examples of how the characteristic might occur in the oral reading of an English sentence and be recorded by a teacher conducting an Informal Reading Inventory, 3) exercises which present further examples in contrast with variant pronunciations which are not the result of a second language and can therefore be considered miscues.

---

[1]D. M. Lance, *A Brief Study of Spanish-English Bilingualism: Final Report.* Research Project-OOR-Liberal Arts—15504 (College Station, Texas: Texas A & M University, 1969); J. H. Matluck and B. J. Mace, "Language Characteristics of Mexican-American Children: Implications for Assessment." *Journal of School Psychology,* 11:4 (1973): 365–86; D. Natalicio and F. Williams, *Repetition as an Oral Language Assessment Technique.* Austin Center for Communication Research, The University of Texas at Austin, 1971.

Phonological features   1. *b* for *v*

When reading English, the speaker with Spanish Language background (SLB) may substitute the sound of the letter *b* for the sound of the letter *v*.

> He was very (bery) happy.
> David (Dabid) saw the dog.

Which pronunciation would be characteristic of some Spanish Language background speakers?

> a. It was a strange-looking vehicle (behicle).
> b. It was a strange-looking vehicle (wehicle).

2. *y* for *j*.

When reading English, the Spanish Language background speaker may substitute the sound of the letter *y* for the sound of the letter *j*.

> My brother flew in a jet (yet).
> I would like that job (yob).
> He rejected (reyected) the gift.

Which pronunciation would be characteristic of some Spanish Language background speakers?

> a. Jim (John) did not like it.
> b. Jim (Yim) did not like it.

3. *j* for *y*

When reading English, the Spanish Language background speaker may substitute the sound of the letter *j* for the sound of the letter *y*.

> He said, "Yes, (Jes,) I want to."
> That car is yours (jours)?

Which would be characteristic of some Spanish Language background speakers?

> a. Yesterday (Yest) was my birthday.
> b. Yesterday (Jesterday) was my birthday.

4. *t* for *th*

When reading English, the Spanish Language background speaker may substitute the sound of the letter *t* for the sound of the letters *th*.

> He thought (taught) he was right.
> He came in fourth (fort).

Which would be characteristic of some Spanish Language background speakers?

    a. What is that thing (ting)?
    b. What is that thing (there)?
    a. Give the dog a bath (bat).
    b. Give the dog a bath (back).

    5. *d* for *th*

When reading English, the Spanish Language background speaker may substitute the sound of the letter *d* for the sound of the letters *th*.

    They (Day) were not at home.
    He called his mother (moder).

Which would be characteristic of some Spanish Language background speakers?

    a. There (They) were too many people.
    b. There (Dere) were too many people.
    a. Her father (fat-hu) was worried about her.
    b. Her father (fader) was worried about her.

    6. *ch* for *sh*

When reading English, the Spanish Language background speaker may substitute the sound of the letters *ch* for the sound of the letters *sh*.

    Ted went shopping (chopping).
    She washes (watches) the clothes.
    He broke the dish (ditch).

Which would be characteristic of some Spanish Language background speakers?

    a. They won't share (chair) the candy.
    b. They won't share (save) the candy.
    a. I heard a loud crash (crack).
    b. I heard a loud crash (cratch).

    7. *sh* for *ch*

When reading English, the Spanish Language background speaker may substitute the sound of *sh* for the sound of the letters *ch*.

    Sit down on that chair (share).
    I don't like those children (shildren).

Which would be characteristic of some Spanish Language background speakers?

    a. He took a big chance (shance).
    b. He took a big chance (change).
    a. They played on the front porch (por).
    b. They played on the front porch (porsh).

    8. *ss* for *s*

When reading English, the Spanish Language background speaker may substitute one sound of the letter *s*, as in hiss, for another sound of the letter *s*, as in his.

    The baby cries (criess) all of the time.
    He is just going through a phase (phace).
    That car is faster than ours (ourss).

Which would be characteristic of some Spanish Language background speakers?

    a. Please (Pleace), stop talking.
    b. Please (Peas), stop talking.
    a. That book is hers (herss).
    b. That book is hers (here).

    9. *s* for *z*

When reading English, the Spanish Language background speaker may substitute the sound of the letter *s* for the sound of the letter *z*.

    The zipper (sipper) is broken.
    He was dozing (dosing).

Which would be characteristic of some Spanish Language background speakers?

    a. The light was buzzing (broken).
    b. The light was buzzing (busing).
    a. We're all going to Zilker (Milker) Park.
    b. We're all going to Zilker (Silker) Park.

    10. *e* for *i*

When reading English, the Spanish Language background speaker may substitute the sound of the letter *e* for the sound of the letter *i*.

    It (Eet) was hot today.
    The ship (sheep) was huge.
    The car ran into a ditch (deesh).

Which would be characteristic of some Spanish Language background speakers?

  a. He got three hits (its).
  b. He got three hits (heets).
  a. He got a bloody lip (lie).
  b. He got a bloody lip (leep).

Glossary

A

Ability grouping — the grouping of students within a class according to estimates of their ability; also called *achievement grouping*.

Abstractions — words that designate qualities, emotions, or ideas rather than concrete or sensory experiences.

Acronym — a short title or name formed with letters from a compound word or from a long title of two or more words.

Advance organizers — a feature in text that gives students a structure or framework for organizing information, e.g. introductions, outlines, etc.

Affective — pertaining to feelings, attitudes, interests, and values.

Affective assessment — collection of information about students' interests, attitudes, feelings or values.

Affective domain — area of learning involving feelings, attitudes, interests, and values and their acquisition and development.

Affix — word structure attached to the beginning (prefix) or end (suffix) of a word to change the meaning or function of the word.

Analysis, reading for — high level comprehension in which student applies a principle learned in one situation to a new situation.

Antonyms — words with opposite meanings.

Application, reading for — high level comprehension in which student applies principle learned in one situation to a new situation.

Appositive — noun or noun phrase occurring next to another noun, which it identifies, clarifies, or defines.

Assessment — systematic collection of information about students' reading abilities, interests, or habits through tests and other procedures for the purpose of diagnosis or evaluation.

Assumptive teaching — an approach to teaching by which the teacher takes for granted that students will be able to perform successfully without direct assistance and guidance from the teacher.

C

Cause/effect — organizational pattern in which cause-and-effect relationships are presented; also designates a type of comprehension, as in *reading for cause/effect*.

Closure — psychological process by which the learner discovers or creates a complete pattern or structure.

Cloze — designates a task or test in which the student supplies words deleted from single sentences or passages.

Cognates — words in two or more languages with the same or similar meanings, spellings, and pronunciations.

Cognitive	of or relating to processes, skills, or operations involved in knowing and understanding.
Cognitive domain	area of learning and intellect having to do with gaining and understanding knowledge.
Comparison/contrast	organizational pattern in which similarities and differences are presented.
Compound words	words consisting of two or more words.
Comprehension	cognitive and linguistic process of deriving or gaining meaning from text.
Concrete words	words that refer to or designate sensory experiences.
Confirmation task	instruction exercise to develop comprehension in which student is given a statement or a question and answer to confirm or reject by reading a text.
Connotation	emotional or qualitative associations of a word.
Consonant blend	single sound produced by the blending of two or more consonant sounds occurring in combination, e.g. *bl, str.*
Context analysis	type of word-analysis skills by which the reader examines words surrounding an unknown word to generate guesses as to the meaning or function of the unknown word.
Context clues	features of text identified through context analysis that aid the reader in making a guess as to the meaning or function of an unknown word.
Continuing assessment	procedures for collecting information about student's ability through a learning experience.
Contracts	a list or schedule of activities to be completed by a student used to facilitate individualized instruction and student independence.
Coordinating committee	committee of teachers, administrators, and others who facilitate the design and implementation of a schoolwide reading program.
Creative reading	high level of reading comprehension involving synthesis or divergent thinking and, commonly, a creative performance in response to the reading.
Criterion-referenced test	test designed to evaluate student's ability by comparing his or her performance to pre-established standards of acceptable performances.
Critical reading	high level of reading comprehension involving evaluation or judgment according to some criteria.

D

Definition by function	clarification of the meaning of a word by considering the function, purpose, or effect of its referent.
Definition by origin	clarification of the meaning of a word by considering its earlier or original meanings or uses.
Denotation	common, literal meanings of a word.
Details, reading for	lowest level of comprehension involving the identification of pieces of information such as names, dates, facts, and times.
Developmental reading	learning experiences, courses, or programs for students making desirable progress in reading.
Diagnosis	collection of information about a student's reading ability using responses to tests or instruction for purposes of determining strengths and weaknesses and making instructional decisions.
Dialect	a variation of a language that has identifiable features of vocabulary, pronunciation, and syntax.

Dictionary analysis	type of word-analysis skills in which the reader uses aids in a dictionary to determine the pronunciation, spelling, meaning, or function of a word.
Differentiated assignment	assignment written in two or more versions that have different levels of difficulty but call for reading the same text for the same purpose.
Digraph	single sound represented by two vowels or two consonants, which is unlike sounds of either member of the pair; e.g., *ch, th*.
Directed Reading Activity	a strategy for designing and conducting instruction that includes preparing students for reading, assigning silent reading, using oral reading and discussion to develop understanding, and providing follow-up and extension activities.
Directed-reading procedure	multistep procedure for guiding student's reading and responses to the reading.
Discourses	multiparagraph text, usually a complete selection.
Discrimination	recognition of an item by its distinctive features.
Distinctive features	characteristics of an item that distinguish it from similar items.

E

Enumeration	organizational pattern in paragraphs and multiparagraph text in which information is presented in a list.
Evaluation	making judgments about or assigning qualities to an individual's reading ability; also a high level of comprehension, as in *reading for evaluation* or *critical reading*.
Exceptional students	those with major differences from average students. Includes both students with unusual abilities and those with severe disabilities or handicaps.
Explanation Pattern	pattern or structure of writing in a textbook whose purpose is to present or explain a concept, principle, process, procedure, or activity.
Expository	type of writing whose purpose is the clear explanation of ideas.
Extensive reading	reading for quantity and variety of experience.
Extrinsic rewards	positive consequences of behavior that are not part of the behavior; also, external rewards, e.g. grades, points, praise.

F

Feedback	knowledge of the results of a performance, or information on a performance that affects subsequent performance.
Feedback systems	instruments with which students can systematically measure their own performances, e.g. graphs, charts, checklists.
Figurative language	a word or words that express one thing in terms normally denoting another with which it may be regarded as analogous, e.g. metaphor.
Fixations	stops in the movement of the eyes while reading during which information is taken in visually.
Flash cards	instructional materials for sight-word recognition and vocabulary.
Flexibility	characteristic of proficient reader who adjusts style and rate of reading to fit purpose and difficulty.
Flow chart	graphic aid that illustrates processes, usually by showing key actions and decisions.
Fluency	speed and ease of reading; also smoothness in silent reading and appropriate intonation and expressiveness in oral reading.
Formal definition	statement that identifies the class or category of an item and the features that distinguish that item from other members of the same class.

Fragmentation	characteristic of a curriculum in which various aspects are taught separately, with a neglect of key meaningful relationships.
Free reading	experience in which a student selects types or subjects of reading or particular reading materials; also called *self-selected, interest,* or *recreational reading.*
Frustrational level	level of material that is too difficult for students to read successfully, with or without help from the teacher.

G

Gifted students	those with unusual ability or talent.
Grade level	used to designate the level of difficulty of text in terms of the grade (or year) in school for which the material is intended.
Grade-level equivalent	the measure of a student's ability in terms of average performance of students in a particular grade (or year) of school.
Graphemes	visual symbols, letters, and letter combinations that represent the sounds of the language.
Graphic aids	textbook aids that present information in graphic form, i.e., maps, illustrations, tables, graphs, and charts.
Group inventory	a modification of the Informal Reading Inventory, given to a whole class to test their ability to read a long passage from the textbook.

H

Hesitation	a pause a student makes during oral reading before reading a word.

I

Identification tasks	activities in which students learn to identify or recognize desirable responses, e.g. multiple choice.
Independent level	level of material that a student can read on his or her own and that presents very few or no vocabulary or comprehension difficulties.
Independent reading	experience in which students read on their own with no guidance or instruction from the teacher.
Individualized instruction	learning experience that is designed or modified in some way to meet individual student differences in ability, interest, or background.
Inference	implied meaning.
Inferential reading	comprehension of meaning which is implied in text, used synonymously with *interpretation.*
Inflectional ending	structure added to end of word that changes its form and meaning as related to gender, tense, possession, or number.
Informal assessment	instruments or procedures designed and used by teachers for diagnosis or evaluation.
Informal Reading Inventory	procedures for assessing oral or silent reading, using instructional materials.
Insertion	during oral reading, the inclusion of a word or phrase that is not in the text.
In-service training	training experiences provided for teachers, commonly through workshops.
Instructional level	level of material students can read successfully but which has a few difficulties.
Instructional unit	organized learning experience one or more weeks in length.
Intensive reading	thorough reading of a single text, usually involving analysis and evaluation.
Interest grouping	organizing students within a class according to their interests.
Interest inventory	list or questionnaire used to collect information about a student's interests, including reading interests.

Interest reading	reading done for pleasure, leisure, or gratification of interests.
Interpretation, reading for	comprehension of meaning that is implied in text.
Interspersed questions	designates questions or exercises inserted throughout a text to facilitate comprehension and learning as opposed to questions presented before or after the text.
Intrinsic rewards	positive consequences of a behavior that are part of the behavior.

L

Linguistics	scientific study of language, including sound systems (or phonetics), syntax (or grammar), and meaning (or semantics).
Linguistic units	structures that are processed in reading, ranging from letters (or phonemes and syllables) to words, phrases, and sentences.
Literal comprehension	low level of understanding gained by deriving meaning from patterns of words, i.e. phrases and clauses.
Locating	comprehension task in which students search through passage to find the answer to a question.

M

Medial	the sound of the middle of a word and the letter representing the sound; usually limited to vowel sounds.
Miscue	a response a student makes to the text that is a departure from the exact words in the text.
Model	the response, or an example of a response, students are to learn.
Modifying instruction	adjusting aspects of instruction to meet individual differences.
Mood	the emotional quality of a text that the reader is to perceive as part of understanding and appreciating the text.
Multiparagraph units	a common structure in secondary-school texts in which major ideas, events, or topics are developed in two or more paragraphs.

N

Needs assessment	the systematic collection of information about the needs of students and teachers, conducted to improve a reading or other school program.
Norm-referenced test	test designed to evaluate a student's ability by comparing his or her performance to a norm or standard performance obtained with a representative group of students.

O

Omission	the failure to read, or say, a word or phrase in the text during oral reading.
Organizational pattern	a logical structure by which information is presented and ideas are developed in paragraphs and multiparagraph text.
Organize	a step in study-reading techniques in which the student writes words to demonstrate his or her understanding of the general idea of a selection.
Orienting procedures	procedures which show a reader the way the reader is to respond to the text, e.g. questions or statements of purpose.

P

Percentile rank	a measure showing a student's relative performance on a test by showing the percentage of scores above and below.
Percent of comprehension	a measure of reading ability obtained by assigning points to questions answered correctly.

Personal dictionary	a notebook kept by a student in which he or she records new words and various responses involved in study of the words.
Persuasive writing	writing for the purpose of changing the opinions of the reader or motivating some action by the reader, as in propaganda.
Phonemes	discrete sounds in a language, represented by letters and letter combinations.
Phonic analysis	type of word-analysis skills by which a word is broken down into letters and letter combinations, the letters are matched with sounds, and the sounds are blended together.
Phonograms	common single-syllable sounds of vowel-consonant combinations and the letters that represent them.
Picture and Text Survey	variation of SQ3R, used to develop comprehension skills.
Picture Survey	variation of SQ3R, used to introduce survey/question procedures using pictures.
Postassessment	the collection of information about a student's ability, knowledge, or interest, conducted at the end of instruction for purposes of evaluation.
Preassessment	the collection of information about a student's ability, knowledge, or interests, conducted prior to instruction for purposes of diagnosis.
Prequestions	questions presented before students read to guide comprehension.
Preventive instruction	teaching procedures that prevent or reduce student problems with vocabulary or comprehension.
Problem pattern	pattern or structure of writing in a textbook whose purpose is to test (or require application of) a student's understanding of principles and procedures; consists of problems, exercises, or other application activities.
Production tasks	activities in which students learn to produce desirable responses.
Proficient reading	performance in which basic skills, e.g. word recognition skills, are mastered to the extent that they occur automatically; the reader is able to attend to and comprehend meanings developed in multiparagraph text.
Propaganda	writing (or communication in other media) intended to persuade the audience, or reader, by using techniques that distort truth or arouse emotion.
Protocol analysis	a comprehension task in which students verbalize as they read.

Q

Question-directed procedures	procedures used by students in which they pose questions to direct or guide their performances in reading, note-taking, and writing.

R

Rate of comprehension	a measure of reading ability obtained by multiplying the percentage of comprehension times the words read per minute.
Readability	the degree of difficulty and level of interest of text.
Readability formula	the quantitative measurement of features of style used to predict the difficulty level of text.
Read-in	regularly scheduled self-selected reading, usually one class period a week or at the beginning of each class period.
Reading rate	measure of reading performance in terms of the amount of text processed in a period of time, usually measured in words read per minute.
Reasoning guides	tasks designed to guide and facilitate comprehension, provided before students read and usually requiring students to make written responses as they are reading.
Recreational reading	reading alone for pleasure or leisure.

Referent	experience referred to, or designated by, a word; more commonly, the word's meaning.
Reinspection	comprehension task in which students look back at or reread a text to answer questions.
Reliability	a quality of tests that give consistent results.
Remedial reading	learning experiences, courses, and programs for students who are not making desirable progress in reading and who have one or more problems; typically for students who test out two or more years below grade level.
Repetition	the repeating of a word in the text during oral reading.
Retrospection	comprehension task in which students talk about a passage after they have read it.

S

Scanning	selective reading at a high rate to gain details.
Schwa	term from phonetics that designates "uh" sound, which can be represented by all the vowel letters, e.g. *o* in *ton*.
Self-assessment	measurement by students of their own performance.
Self-instructional	designates learning experience or material that allows student to perform and learn with little or no teacher direction or supervision.
Self-pacing	feature of learning experience in which a student can learn (or complete work) at his or her own rate or time schedule.
Self-selected reading	reading experience in which a student chooses types or subjects of reading or particular materials.
Self-selection	designates learning experience in which the student chooses objectives, activities, materials, or subjects.
Sentence difficulty	measure used to predict the readability of a text, usually the average number of words in sentences in a passage.
Sequence, reading for	comprehension skill in which a reader is able to understand a time or spatial arrangement.
Sight words	in beginning reading refers to those words that students are taught to read by sight-word recognition.
Sight-word recognition	instantaneous recognition of familiar words.
Sight-word vocabulary	those words a reader can process through sight-word recognition.
Skimming	selective reading at a high rate to gain main ideas.
Speed reading	reading at a rate well above the average of 250 words per minute; includes skimming and scanning.
SQ3R	textbook-reading technique that includes five steps: surveying, posing questions, reading to answer the questions, reciting answers, and reviewing answers.
Standardized reading tests	tests developed, administered, scored, and interpreted following well-established procedures for test design and use.
Stanine	a standard score with equal values from one to nine that shows a student's relative performance on a test.
Structural analysis	type of word-analysis skill in which words are broken down into their large, meaningful parts, i.e., prefixes, roots, suffixes, and inflectional endings.
Study skills	procedures, strategies, or techniques used by students to consciously direct their academic performances.
Substitution	during oral reading, saying one word in place of the actual word in the text.

Suffix	affix or word structure attached to the end of a word to change its meaning or function.
Survey	selective reading at a high rate to gain overview or preview of text.
Survey/question procedures	SQ3R and variations used by students to direct their reading and study of text.
Survey tests	usually standardized tests used to gain an overview of a student's ability and some initial indication of weaknesses.
Synonyms	words with the same or similar meanings.
Syntax	systematic patterns of words in phrases, clauses, sentences.
Synthesis, reading for	high level of comprehension by which the student relates ideas and pieces of information and presents them in a new coherent form.

T

Teaching by demonstration	instruction in which the teacher shows students how to arrive at desired responses, by illustrating a procedure, skill, or performance.
Technical vocabulary	words or usages of words peculiar to a content area or field of study.
Textbook aids	features in a textbook or other material intended to increase interests and reduce the difficulty of reading the text.
Time line	graphic aid that displays the relationships between dates and events.
Tone	the emotional quality of a text that suggests the author's attitude toward his or her subject or audience.
Trace	pattern of discussion in which information is presented in chronological order, often called for in an essay examination.
Translation	comprehension task by which information is presented in some other form to demonstrate a low level of understanding.

V

Validity	a characteristic of a test that gives a good indication of the student's actual ability.
Variant pronunciation	a response by the student that differs from common accepted pronunciations and may indicate a weakness in word-analysis skills.

W

Word-analysis skills	skills a student uses to figure out unfamiliar words; includes phonic, structural, context, and dictionary-analysis skills.
Word difficulty	measure used to predict readability of text, either length of words (number of syllables) or familiarity of words.
Word recognition	responses involved in identifying or discriminating words by their form, sound, or meaning.

Index